The Definitive Guide to Stellent Content Server Development

Brian "Bex" Huff

Apress®

The Definitive Guide to Stellent Content Server Development

Copyright © 2006 by Brian Huff

ISBN-13: 978-1-59059-684-5

ISBN-13 (electronic): 978-1-4302-0178-6

Printed and bound in the United States of America (POD)

Lead Editor: Jonathan Hassell
Technical Reviewer: Samuel White
Editorial Board: Steve Anglin, Ewan Buckingham, Gary Cornell, Jason Gilmore, Jonathan Gennick,
    Jonathan Hassell, James Huddleston, Chris Mills, Matthew Moodie, Dominic Shakeshaft, Jim Sumser,
    Keir Thomas, Matt Wade
Project Manager: Elizabeth Seymour
Copy Edit Manager: Nicole LeClerc
Copy Editor: Nancy Sixsmith
Assistant Production Director: Kari Brooks-Copony
Production Editor: Kelly Gunther
Compositor: Molly Sharp
Proofreader: Dan Shaw
Indexer: Toma Mulligan
Cover Designer: Kurt Krames
Manufacturing Director: Tom Debolski

Distributed to the book trade worldwide by Springer-Verlag New York, Inc., 233 Spring Street, 6th Floor, New York, NY 10013. Phone 1-800-SPRINGER, fax 201-348-4505, e-mail orders-ny@springer-sbm.com, or visit http://www.springeronline.com.

For information on translations e-mail info@apress.com, or visit http://www.apress.com.

The source code for this book is available to readers at http://www.apress.com in the Source Code section.

Contents

About the Author

BRIAN "BEX" HUFF has been programming computers since the age of ten, like many developers these days. He holds several degrees, including Physics, Mathematics, Philosophy, Civil Engineering, and Computer Science. Despite a highly technical background, he has always believed that the greatest skills a technical person can possess are the abilities to communicate and teach.

Brian has worked at Stellent for seven years and has worn many hats in the company. He has been an architect, designer, and developer and has performed training, documentation, and consulting. He is a moderator and frequent contributor to the intradoc_users Yahoo group for Stellent users: http://groups.yahoo.com/group/intradoc_users/. He lives in Minneapolis with his wife, Michelle, and two noisy cockatiels.

About the Technical Reviewer

 **SAMUEL WHITE** grew up in Kampala, Uganda, and Silver Springs and Columbia, MD. After completing a Mathematics Ph.D. at the University of California, Berkeley in 1989, Sam spent four years as a postdoctoral researcher before becoming a full-time software developer. He joined Stellent as a software designer in 1996 and was appointed Vice President of Server Products in 2003. Sam's free time is spent raising a five-year-old daughter with his wife of 16 years, reading books (both nonfiction and fiction), and playing/studying games (particularly bridge).

Acknowledgments

Thanks to Samuel White for designing this product, being the technical reviewer, and motivating me to write this book in the first place. Thanks to everybody who reviewed my book and gave me helpful feedback, in particular Rick Petty, Sebastian Celis, and Jean Wilson. Thanks also to Alec Kloss, with whom I spent many hours discussing the structure and contents of the chapters. Thanks especially to Bruce Silver, who helped me make a few emergency last-minutes changes.

Thanks to all the people who gave me technical writing tips, including Rick Wren and Frank Seidel. Thanks also to the countless authors and bloggers who shared their insights into the secrets of engaging and memorable technical writing.

And finally, thanks to my wonderful wife, Michelle, who more than anybody encouraged me and kept my spirits up when I had writer's block.

Preface

Every business relies on a database of one sort or another to manage important structured information. Everybody needs to keep track of employee records, customer information, and inventory lists—and databases are essential for this. They are an ideal place to put records so they can be secured, searched, updated, and maintained.

As database applications became more commonplace, users realized that they wanted similar functionality for *all* their content. They want simple applications to help them manage and distribute information in all formats, not just rigidly structured database records. Ideally, they can find the information they need without even knowing it exists. Naturally, this presents a huge challenge. Business content is highly unstructured. It includes everything from email messages to policy documents, to scanned contracts, to website graphics. Plus, these items have complex and dynamic relationships with each other that do not cleanly translate into database records.

Solving this problem is the realm of Content Management systems, which have been around for years, but have not yet reached their fullest potential. The Stellent Content Server is the most award-winning Content Management system available. It is considered by many analysts to have the most complete solution to the general problems of Content Management. It is a coherent framework for general Content Management applications, as opposed to the patchwork of single-purpose applications that are offered by most vendors.

I wrote this book to help explain how powerful the Stellent framework is. Developers and customers can use it to write extremely powerful content-centric applications in surprisingly little time. Not only can you create applications quickly, but the applications are also easy to maintain, customize, and upgrade. Doing so requires a bit of discipline, so be sure to follow the best practices outlined in this book.

This is the first book ever to give practical samples of Content Server customizations. It gives a clear overview of Stellent's architecture and how all its pieces fit together. This book covers the basics of writing custom applications: creating custom web forms, modifying the web interface, and running custom Java code inside the Content Server.

This book is designed to be part how-to manual and part reference manual. The first half of the book is designed to give you the information you need to customize the Content Server as quickly as possible. Later chapters in the book cover advanced topics, such as integrating the Content Server with remote applications using Simple Object Access Protocol (SOAP), advanced Java customizing, and customizing the security model. The second half of the book contains appendixes on the inner workings of the Content Server, including its Java API, and the available Content Management services.

This book is intended for people familiar with web application development. You need to know HTML to use this book. You should also have familiarity with at least one programming language.

The Content Server integrates with several web scripting languages, including ASP, JSP, and PHP. It integrates natively with JSP. Using ASP or PHP requires SOAP Web Services, which is covered at the end of this book. The Content Server also natively supports a custom language called IdocScript, which is a straightforward language that you can learn in about an hour. It is similar in form to PHP and ASP. It can be used throughout the Content Server to rapidly customize the interface and the behavior.

It is not necessary for you to have previous knowledge of IdocScript or JSP to use this book. If you know how to set variables and perform loops in JavaScript, you should be able to follow the samples in this book. You can learn IdocScript as you progress from simple changes to advanced customizations. Refer to the appendixes in the back of this book for more information about IdocScript and the JSP integration.

After IdocScript, the most important language for a Stellent developer is Java. The core Content Server engine is written in Java. If you want to modify the behavior of the server in advanced ways, you need familiarity with Java.

The samples are offered as-is, with no warranty. Because they are intended for education and reuse, they can be distributed freely. They are offered under the BSD license, which allows for personal and commercial reuse without attribution.

The examples are available for download at the publisher's website: `http://apress.com/book/download.html`. They are also available from the author's website: `http://bexhuff.com/books/stellent-dev`.

Comments or questions about the book should be directed to the author's website. If you discover a bug, see a typo, or have a suggestion on how to improve the book, please alert the author.

All the samples in this book were written for version 7.5 of the Content Server. Most samples are general, and are applicable for all versions of the Content Server later than version 5.0. Some of the advanced components will work only with version 7.5 (which is explicitly noted when applicable).

Introduction

This chapter is an introduction to Enterprise Content Management (ECM) and the Stellent Content Server (SCS). It gives a brief explanation of what content management is and why people need it. By reading this chapter you'll get an introduction to the Stellent family of products and how they work together to provide ECM. You'll also receive a brief tour of the SCS and learn how it can be customized.

Enterprise Content Management

A complete definition of ECM is difficult because it incorporates so many technologies. In August 2005, the Association for Information and Image Management (AIIM) defined ECM as "the technologies used to Capture, Manage, Store, Preserve, and Deliver content and documents related to organizational processes."

To put it in more concrete terms, an ECM system manages content items throughout phases of its life cycle. The *content* can be anything, but it typically takes the form of digital information, which can be in the form of a scanned invoice, a Microsoft Word document, or a media file.

An ECM system stores and preserves this content in a repository. The content can be submitted to the repository by a user or it can be captured with an automated process. For example, a user might submit a document to the repository from the application that created the item, such as Word. Alternatively, content can be captured by a copier, a scanner, or an email server and then automatically submitted to the repository.

An ECM system also controls how content is delivered. One method is to enable consumers to search the repository with a web browser and download content. Another method is publishing, in which the content is converted to Hypertext Markup Language (HTML) and pushed to a website or portal server. Another method is syndication, in which the content is pushed directly to users or other applications.

Once in the repository, an ECM system manages the items through their entire *life cycle*. This life cycle includes all phases that the item goes through, including creation, modification, and expiration. Additional phases are possible, depending on the type of content and business rules. For example, the following phases and features are supported by the SCS:

- *Revision Control:* Manages how content is submitted to the repository and how it can be modified. Some content might be allowed only one revision, whereas others can be edited multiple times. Revision control typically involves an exclusive check-out process. This means that only one user at a time can make changes to the item. It also ensures that the item found by users is the most recent revision.

- *Metadata:* Additional data about a content item, usually added by a user when the item is submitted to the repository. This data can include a title, the author's name, or the creation date, as well as custom metadata. Metadata is useful for creating a taxonomy for content items or simply to help consumers find the content they need.

- *Conversion and Publishing:* Converts the content into another format, suitable for publishing to other systems. This includes converting the item to HTML for web consumption or to Wireless Markup Language (WML) for wireless consumption.

- *Security:* An essential piece of metadata that controls which content items a consumer is allowed to view. Security also controls what users are allowed to do with the content. For example, a user might be able to view the content, but not make a new revision.

- *Personalization:* Enables users to view the same content in different ways. One example is enabling the user to see a translated version of the content item. Another example entails displaying only the metadata fields relevant for this user.

- *Workflow:* Enables businesses to apply processing rules to items in the repository. One example is that content must be approved by the web master before it can be published to the website. Another example is that after a user submits a purchase request, it is routed to the accounting department for processing.

- *Subscription and Syndication:* Enables users and other applications to receive notifications when new content is available.

- *Searching and Taxonomy:* Helps users find content. Users can search the text of the content or look for specific metadata. Alternatively, the metadata is used to build a directory-based hierarchy.

- *Archiving and Expiring:* Moves content out of the repository at the end of its life cycle.

This is only a small sample of the possible features in an ECM system. Some vendors offer additional rules for processing specific kinds of content.

Benefits of ECM

The list of features in an ECM system is overwhelming. However, these features all have a similar goal: to deliver accurate information from those who have it to where it's needed, in a timely fashion, and in the desired format.

The correct way to implement ECM depends greatly on your needs. A good ECM suite satisfies the information needs of many users for many different kinds of content.

Imagine a system that offers the following benefits:

- Your public website always has up-to-date information.

- Your employees can freely share information between departments. They can find information by browsing your online library or running a search.

- Your business partners and customers can securely access relevant information on your extranet.

- Your engineers always work with the most recent product specifications.

- Your employees always follow the correct procedures for forms and unstructured business content.

- Your employees always conform to laws and regulations about document retention.

- Your employees have one place to find all information about an ongoing project.

- Your call centers always have up-to-date reference information and knowledge about your customers.

After you know your requirements and train your users, a good ECM deployment makes all this possible.

Stellent Content Server (SCS)

The SCS is the foundation of Stellent's ECM suite. Stellent is unique among ECM systems in that it is more than just an application that implements ECM philosophies. It is also a *framework* for creating ECM applications. This framework places content into a universal repository and manages the life cycle of those items with its Service-Oriented Architecture (SOA), which is discussed in greater detail in Chapter 2.

A *universal repository* is a way of storing all types of content in the same location. Web content, compliance documents, records, business forms, video, and customer data are all stored in the same repository. The framework allows all items to be managed differently based on their type. The type is defined by the format of the content or its metadata. Stellent's universal repository contrasts with other ECM products that have a separate repository for each type of content.

An SOA is one way of designing a computer system so it is simple, flexible, robust, and extensible. Like the definition of ECM, SOA is a complex philosophy about how enterprise software should be designed. (SOA is discussed in detail in Chapter 2.) In this case, a *service* is a discrete request to process an item, which includes contributing the item, modifying it, converting it, or downloading it.

An SOA framework is also highly extensible. Stellent uses this framework internally to create new products specific to managing different types of content and their life cycles. Developers can also use this framework to create new applications specific to their needs that add new processing rules to the server.

For example, the Stellent family offers products in several different categories, such as the following:

Document Management: Content Refinery, Content Tracker, Report Parser, XML Converter, Content Categorizer

Web Content Management: Site Studio, Content Publisher, Dynamic Converter

Compliance and Records Management: Records Management, Sarbanes-Oxley Solution

Rich Media Management: Digital Asset Management

Additional Products for Users and Applications: Content Integration Suite (CIS) for J2EE integrations; Stellent Desktop, which includes a Windows Explorer Integration; and Connection Server for syndication

All these products use Stellent's framework to integrate with the universal repository. Some of them, such as Records Management and the Sarbanes-Oxley Solution, add new phases to the life cycle of content items. Specifically, these two products add new rules about how documents must be retained and who needs to approve them.

Other products, such as the Connection Server and the Windows Explorer Integration, use the SOA to present a simplified interface to a user. The Connection Server syndicates important content directly to the user's computer. The Windows Explorer Integration allows users to submit content into the repository with the simplicity of drag and drop on Windows Explorer.

Still other products use a combination of new life cycles and new interfaces to implement fully content-centric applications. For example, Site Studio adds new life cycles and interfaces to allow users to easily manage large websites. A user navigates to the web page that needs updating and clicks a few buttons; the contents are instantly modified. The structure of the site is controlled by administrators, but the content in the site is editable by any contributor.

Stellent's architecture is unique in many aspects and has led the entire industry in innovation for years:

- It was the first commercial server application written in Java.

- It was the first ECM system with a web interface.

- It was the first ECM system to support the Simple Object Access Protocol (SOAP).

- It was the first ECM system to have an SOA.

- It is the only ECM system with an extensible framework and a universal repository.

If imitation is the highest form of flattery, Stellent's competition is extremely flattering. The Content Server was designed from the ground up with the previously listed features. Slowly and grudgingly, the competition has followed. At the time of this writing, most offer a web interface, some have migrated to Java or J2EE, and many have SOAP interfaces for limited SOA compatibility. Most of them also claim to have universal repositories, but none is as complete as Stellent's.

Perhaps the most flattering statistic is this: *six out of the eight leading ECM vendors use Stellent technology in their own products.*

Getting Started with Stellent

Before going further, you need to install the SCS on a test machine. Even if you already have a server in production, it is recommended to set up an additional server for testing. A fresh install defaults to a demo license if a full license is not provided, which limits the functionality of the server. Specifically, the server stops working after a certain number of items are contributed. However, this is sufficient to get a feel for the technology or set up a quick test.

The recommended setup for a test server is to purchase a developer license, which allows you to set up an exact copy of your production server for testing. Developer licenses are available from Stellent at a significantly reduced price.

You can install the Content Server on a test machine in a matter of minutes. The test machine needs a web server and a database. A free sample database is available for test instances installed on the Microsoft Windows operating system. Please refer to the installation documentation for step-by-step instructions.

The next step is to become familiar with the basic functionality of the server, which is best done by diving right in and exploring the features. It is not necessary at this point to learn everything about the server. Instead, focus on the basics of contribution, searching, and the administration applets.

After an install, the URL to access the Content Server looks something like this: `http://hostname.company.com/stellent/`. On this page you see a simplified static home page (see Figure 1-1). The default administrator for the server is the user **sysadmin**, with the password **idc**.

Figure 1-1. *Static home page*

Click Login to log in as this user, which takes you to the dynamic home page (see Figure 1-2). This page contains links to other Content Server pages.

Figure 1-2. *Dynamic home page*

From here, select the User Profile link, which returns the user profile page that contains information about the current user (see Figure 1-3). From here you can customize the interface by changing the Layout or the Skin. These options control how the navigation menus are laid out, and their color schemes. You can also set your email address or preferred email format. The links at the bottom of the page take you to your subscriptions, your workflow inbox, or other personalization pages.

Figure 1-3. *User profile page*

Click the New Check In link, which returns a content check in form for adding new content items to the repository (see Figure 1-4). From here, you can select a file on your computer to add to the repository. You should also fill in the metadata for this item, such as the title and some comments. Some metadata is automatically populated for you, such as the author's name and the date. Other fields might be populated automatically, depending on your server's configuration. You might also need to supply a Content ID, which is a unique identifier for all revisions of this item. Finally, click Check In to add your content to the repository.

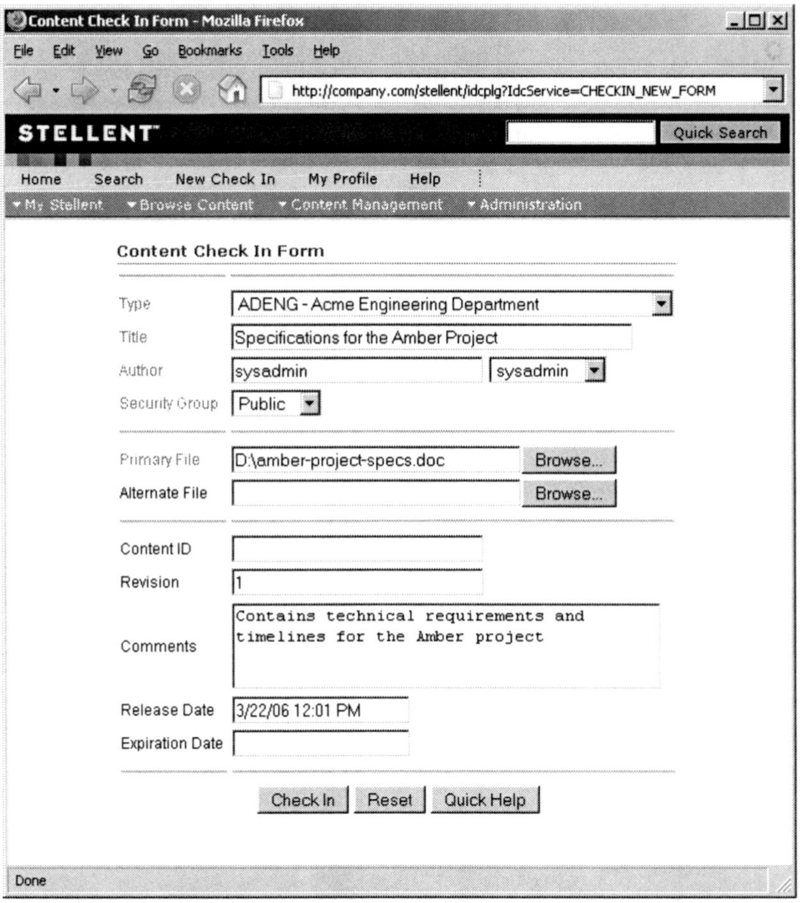

Figure 1-4. *Content check in form page*

You can add items to the repository in other ways. For example, you can use the Batchloader utility that ships with the Content Server to check-in a large number of items simultaneously. Additional Stellent products enable you to check-in directly from Word, an email client, or a remote application server.

After a check-in, the Content Server extracts the text from the content item and places it into the search engine's index, enabling users to quickly search for the item based on its content or its metadata. Items that contain no text, such as images, have only their metadata indexed. Depending on which additional products you have installed, the content server can perform additional processing steps:

- Convert the content to PDF and/or HTML.

- Analyze the item for keywords and set the appropriate metadata values.

- Place the content into a workflow if it needs approval before being made public.

- Replicate the item to other servers.

- Send email notifications to users who have subscribed to this item.

After a few seconds, the item is available in the search index. Click the Search link to go to a search page (see Figure 1-5). From here you can fill in values for specific metadata fields and generate a search query. For example, you can search for all items authored by `sysadmin` or all items with *Stellent* in the title. Leave all fields empty and click Search.

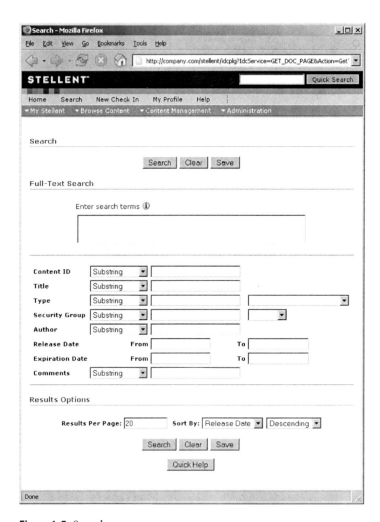

Figure 1-5. *Search page*

This process generates a search results page, which contains all the items that satisfy the search criteria. Because you specified no criteria, all items in the repository are returned. This method is only one of many ways to find content in the repository. Add-on products enable you to also do the following:

- Browse the repository from Windows Explorer.

- Use metadata to create a taxonomy structure for a content library.

- Query the repository from remote applications like J2EE Portal Servers.

- Have items syndicated directly to users' computers.

In the search results page, locate the item you just checked-in. There should be a column containing Actions for this item. Click the Info action, which may appear as an icon with the letter *i* in a circle (see Figure 1-6).

Figure 1-6. *Search results page*

You should now see the content information page for this item, shown in Figure 1-7. From this page, you can view all the metadata for the item and download older revisions. You can also perform actions on it, such as checking-out the item or subscribing to it. By clicking the Check Out action, you are granted exclusive rights to create a new revision of this item. By clicking the Subscribe action, you will be notified by email when a new revision of this item is available. Some add-on products also allow additional actions from this menu, such as the following:

- Check-out and open the item in its native application for immediate editing.

- Generate the list of users who previously downloaded this item.

- Add the item to a *Content Basket,* which is similar to a shopping cart.

- Move the item into a *Folder* so users can more easily browse to find it.

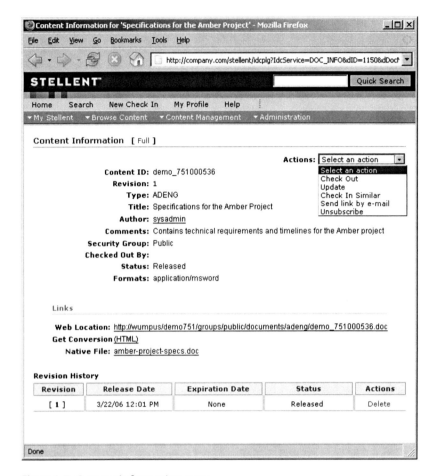

Figure 1-7. *Content information page*

Notice the URLs for these web pages: they all contain at least the parameter `IdcService`. This parameter is the unique name for the service being executed. In the previous page, you executed the service `DOC_INFO` to obtain the content information page. Before that, you executed the `GET_SEARCH_RESULTS` service to run a search. All pages delivered by the Content Server have a similar structure.

Next, click the Administration link or the Admin Applets link in the Administration menu to go to the administration page (see Figure 1-8). From this page, you can run the Administration Applets for the server, view the server logs, or other administrator-specific pages.

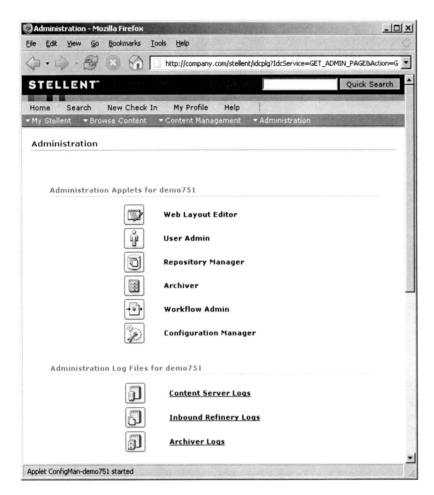

Figure 1-8. *Root administration page*

The Administration Applets enable you to configure the Content Server to suit the needs of your organization. For example, if you need more custom metadata fields, you should run the Configuration Manager applet. You can add fields that store the names of customers, projects, regions, or departments. These fields can be simple text boxes such as the Comments field or a list of values such as the Content Type field. Such lists can be stored in the Content Server as a simple Option List, or you can generate it from database tables you currently have.

After adding a new field and updating the database design, the metadata field is immediately available on the check in and search pages. You also need to rebuild the search index if you want the new metadata field to be searchable.

Because metadata fields can be added so easily, a common problem is that the check in and search pages become too cluttered. You can clean up the clutter by conditionally showing, hiding, and prefilling these metadata fields with the *Content Profiles* functionality in Content Server 7.5, or with a customization in older versions.

This admin page contains additional applets for managing the life cycle of content, users, and portal pages. The Archiver is used to move content out of the repository to other servers, or the file system. The Repository Manager is used to manage the metadata of content items, subscriptions, and the search index. To create users, manage users' metadata, or design your security model, run the User Admin applet. The Web Layout Editor manages built-in library pages that locate content in the repository. Finally, you can use the Workflow Admin applet to design workflows for your specific business rules.

On any web page you can click the Help link to open the online help documentation, which is an extremely useful resource for users, administrators, and developers alike. Users can find help pages on how to check-in an item or run a search. Administrators can find help pages on how to set up custom metadata and design a workflow. Developers can find documentation about the architecture of the Content Server and how to create customizations.

The documentation is also available in Adobe Portable Document Format (PDF) for printing. Most—but not all—documentation is available as HTML pages in the web help. Documents about installing the Content Server are naturally useful only as PDFs.

Customizing the Content Server

After obtaining a feel for the way the Content Server behaves, you might need to modify it to suit your specific needs. This modification might be simple; for example, adding workflows and custom metadata. Or it might be complex; for example, changing the user interface.

Before deploying the server into your enterprise, you need to ask yourself several questions. Some of them are typical for enterprise application deployment: what hardware should you use? What backup schedule works best? What operating system makes the most sense? What are the supported databases and web servers?

Others are more specific to the way your organization needs to manage its content. After answering the following questions, you should have an idea of how much customization will be required:

- How would users like to contribute content to the repository? The standard web interface? A simplified web interface? Directly from your word processor?

- How would users like to locate content in the repository? A rigid library structure? A more ad hoc folder structure? Portal pages for departments? Searching?

- What kinds of content do you want to manage? Microsoft Office documents? Web content? Images and media files? Database reports?

- How should this content be converted to other formats? Is a simple HTML representation sufficient, or should the HTML look exactly like the original content? Do you need additional processing of large media files?

- What should the metadata model be for your repository? Are your users sophisticated enough to fill in the correct metadata?

- Do you need to manage submitted forms for business processes? These forms might include travel requests, purchase requests, or resume submissions.

- What kinds of workflows are needed? Which items require approval, and which do not?

- When should old content be archived out of the repository?

- Should access to the content be monitored? Should you track what search terms and content items are popular?

- Does your content need to comply with certain International Organization for Standardization (ISO) rules or compliance regulations?

- What about security? Which users should be allowed to access which content? Do you need an external user database?

Many of these customizations can be accomplished through the Administrative Applets. You can create new users, set up custom metadata, archive content, configure the security model, and design workflows.

Other customizations require configuration variables. These customizations are specified in the Content Server's primary configuration file. In general, these variables do not significantly change the behavior of the server. Instead, they are used to fine-tune the existing behavior.

In other situations, the administrator might need to install an additional Stellent product. The Content Refinery and Dynamic Converter are used to convert content to other formats. The Content Tracker is used to monitor which items and search terms are the most popular. The Sarbanes-Oxley Solution and Records Management are used to make your content comply with specific rules and regulations.

However, you might not be able to accomplish everything you need with existing products and configuration settings. In such cases, you can use the Content Server's framework to change the behavior of the system. This option should be used as a last resort, but it is common and surprisingly simple.

The purpose of this book is to be a concise reference on how to use the Content Server's framework to make significant customizations to the core. This book contains step-by-step examples and reference material to help you create such customizations.

These customizations take several forms. First, it is possible to create entirely new web pages for running Content Server services. They might include custom contribution pages, custom portal pages to display links to content, and business-processing forms. If you have an understanding of HTML and a working knowledge of IdocScript, these customizations are straightforward.

A customization can also modify the existing interface. Making such a customization requires additional knowledge of the Content Server's architecture because the existing interface is stored in specifically formatted resources. You need to know how to locate these resources, and understand the correct way to modify them, before creating such a customization. This approach is used to make small changes to the default templates, such as custom buttons and input fields on the check-in forms.

It is also possible to alter the behavior of the server at a deeper level. Stellent's SOA enables you to create new services or modify the behavior of existing services. It also has hooks that allow you to execute custom Java code when specific events occur. These customizations are the most difficult because they require extensive knowledge of the server's architecture and familiarity with Java programming.

Summary

Enterprise Content Management (ECM) can be defined in many ways, depending on whom you ask. In general, it is a network application that connects your users with the information they need, when they need it, and in the delivery format they desire. It is vital that your ECM system be robust and scalable so your entire organization can benefit from it. However, it must also be highly flexible and extensible so you can integrate it with your existing applications and support the latest and greatest delivery formats.

The Stellent Content Server (SCS) has been a technology leader in ECM for many years because it builds software that fits these demands. Its core Java engine is robust and scalable, and its Service-Oriented Architecture (SOA) makes it flexible and extensible. This framework is also component-driven, so new enterprise-scalable features can be easily added.

The SCS is highly customizable. An administrator can design workflows, metadata schemas, or the security model with an easy-to-use web interface. If necessary, a developer can design components to modify the existing behavior or add completely new features.

Taken together, the SCS enables you to create highly sophisticated ECM solutions that fit your organization's needs. The remainder of this book covers techniques, samples, and best practices to help you develop your custom solution.

CHAPTER 2

■■■

Architecture

Before customizing your Stellent Content Server, it is important you understand the underlying architecture. This chapter gives an overview of how the pieces of the Content Server fit together, such as services and result templates. Understanding the architecture is necessary to help you customize the Content Server as needed. Customization options include Dynamic Server Pages (DSPs), custom components, and integration with other application servers.

Service-Oriented Architecture

The Content Server is at its core an extensible Java framework. It uses data-driven resources to define *services*, which include the content management features in the server: check-in, checkout, workflow processing, subscriptions, conversion, and search. These services form the core of the Content Server and everything it can do.

These services are typically consumed by a user with a web browser. They can also be consumed by other applications. The Content Server supports several integration protocols and techniques. The most popular ones are the following:

- Hypertext Transfer Protocol (HTTP) for web browsers

- XML-based Simple Object Access Protocol (SOAP) for .NET systems

- XML-based Web Distributed Authoring and Versioning (WebDAV) for Microsoft applications

- Content Integration Suite (CIS) for J2EE Application Servers and Tomcat

- IdcCommandUX ActiveX module for Windows desktop applications

Recently, the Content Server and similar applications have been labeled Service-Oriented Architectures (SOAs). Such applications are popular with enterprise software architects because they integrate well with other applications. They are easier to deploy, maintain, monitor, and upgrade in complex networks.

There is still open debate on what qualifies as an SOA. It is insufficient to merely add a Web Services interface to an existing application. The entire system must be designed from the ground up to be flexible, easy to customize, and easy to deploy. As of this writing, an Oasis Technical Committee is developing a formal set of requirements for an SOA. However, there is general agreement on the following points:

- Service requests must be stateless.

- Services must be coarsely grained.

- There must be a loose coupling between service logic and service data.

- Services must be extensible.

Stateless means that all the data required to execute the service must be present in the request. This data includes information such as who is running the request, their security credentials, what service they are running, and all the data needed to run it. This data is necessary to improve reliability, increase simplicity, and support the stateless nature of the web.

For the vast majority of services, the Content Server obeys this rule. There are situations in which some level of state information is used to enhance services or improve performance. For example, the Content Server stores personalization data so users can customize their web interface. It also supports services that handle large archives of data. Requiring the entire archive in the service request would seriously hinder performance, so the Content Server enables it to be stored elsewhere.

Coarsely grained services mean that services should be as simple as possible for a user to consume. If you want to do *one* thing, you should need to call only *one* service. For example, to check-in a new content item, a user calls the CHECKIN_NEW service. The request contains only as much information as absolutely necessary to process that service. The *consumer* of a service should need to know only *what* they want to do. The consumer shouldn't be bothered with knowing *how* the service works.

This is sometimes called a Descriptive API, which contrasts with the Instructive API model common to object-oriented programming (OOP) interfaces. The OOP model is excellent for creating the business logic for robust services. However, it's a terrible model for the *consumption* of those services over a network. It requires too much effort and knowledge on behalf of the consumer. An SOA must be simpler.

Loose coupling means many things. First, the data in the response should be consumable on any system. Regardless of platform or programming language, the service should be available. By supporting cross-platform XML standards such as SOAP and WebDAV, the Content Server meets this criterion.

However, loose coupling also applies to how the request is processed in the server. There needs to be a flexible relationship between the data used in the service and the logic in the service. In other words, the service should not require the binding of data to rigid structures. Those architectures hinder customizations, upgrades, and reuse of business logic. If done incorrectly, they also significantly degrade performance.

The Content Server achieves loose coupling with a highly flexible request structure. One extra parameter in a check-in request can significantly alter how it is processed. This is important when customizing the service because it allows you to add new features without affecting the old ones.

The Content Server also distinguishes highly structured data from loosely structured data. The line is drawn based on the Content Server's current configuration, such as custom metadata fields. During request processing, highly structured data is stored in customizable database tables, whereas loosely structured data either affects how the process runs or it is stored in loosely structured data files. Such files are formatted either in XML or HyperData (HDA) format. The HDA format is covered in Appendix J.

This kind of loose coupling allows the best of all worlds: fast database access, flexible data storage, and dynamic modification of service processing. It does come with a modest cost. Developers writing new customizations don't immediately know how structured the request data is. However, by following certain naming conventions for the data, structured and unstructured data can be distinguished.

Finally, and most important, an SOA must be *extensible*. Business needs change frequently. To support future needs, the services must be customizable. No matter how advanced an application, there is no way to satisfy all business needs with mere configuration. An administrator must be able to modify the core application without significant effort.

Because the Content Server's framework is mostly data-driven, it can be easily extended. You can create a new interface with *Dynamic Server Pages (DSPs)* or a separate application. You can modify the existing web interface with a *component*. These components can also be used to modify how services behave or add new services. As a result, the Content Server is highly extensible.

Core Content Server Architecture

The Content Server has an internal architecture similar to a middleware application. It stores data about content items on a file system and in a database. It stores user information in a database or an external repository such as a Lightweight Directory Access Protocol (LDAP) repository. A plug-in to a web server authenticates the users and forwards service requests to the Content Server. A J2EE application server can replace the web server. In this case, authentication is performed on the application server, and service requests are made directly to the Content Server. Starting with CIS version 7.6.1, you can also configure the J2EE connections to be authenticated at the web server.

Figure 2-1 illustrates one architecture for a Content Server solution. It is possible, however uncommon, for all the applications listed in this figure to run on the same computer. In practice, the web server and the Content Server are on the same machine. Most other applications—the database, file server, user repository, and J2EE application server—run on separate machines, so you can cluster each application and the Content Server for better performance and reliability.

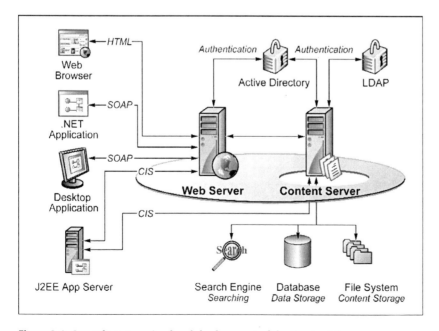

Figure 2-1. *Sample enterprise-level deployment of the Content Server*

Services which are the foundation of the Content Server are defined in HTML configuration resources. They are described later in this chapter.

A service request initiates a series of events. Briefly, the steps are as follows:

1. The user makes a web request.

2. The web server authenticates the user.

3. If the request is a service call, the web server forwards it to the Content Server.

4. The Content Server parses the data in the request (this data includes user information, the service to run, and all service parameters). It places this data in an HDA-based `DataBinder` object (discussed in Appendix J).

5. The server loads the definition for the service, including security information, a template page, and a list of actions to perform for this service.

6. The server validates that this user can run the service.

7. The server executes the service actions, which can be SQL queries or Java code.

8. Each action pulls request parameters from the `DataBinder` and pushes the results back into it.

9. After all actions are complete, and no error occurred, the server loads the response template.

10. The server renders the template into HTML with the data in the `DataBinder`.

11. The server sends the response HTML to the web server.

12. The web server sends the HTML to the user.

The Content Server separates the logic in the services from the page display in step 10. The *templates* render an HTML web page based on the response data. This separation allows for easier customization of the interface and consumption of the services and is sometimes referred to as a Model View Controller (MVC) architecture. Templates are a combination of HTML and a custom scripting language called IdocScript.

This process is not the only way that service requests are executed. For example, a J2EE application server can connect directly to the Content Server and run services directly, which optionally bypasses the web server layer in steps 1–3. The Content Server's response is XML- or HDA-formatted data. The application server then displays this data inside its own MVC framework.

The service also runs differently if an external user database is present—for example, LDAP or Active Directory. In these cases, the web server plug-in connects to them for authentication and authorization, or the web server plug-in requests that the Content Server authenticate the user with a *User Provider*.

Also, the web server does not always forward the request to the Content Server because of the way the Content Server separates content items into two renditions. One rendition is the original file stored in the vault, which is accessible only with a service request. The other rendition is a conversion of the original file, suitable for consumption with a web browser, which is placed in the `weblayout` directory.

For example, when a Microsoft Word document is checked-in, the Content Server might process it into a Portable Document Format (PDF) document. It might also generate a thumbnail image representing the item. This processing is done with the Content Refinery application. The original Word Document is placed into the *vault*, and the web files are placed into the weblayout directory when conversion is complete.

The web server can authenticate the user and return the web-viewable file without making a service request because the URLs to items in the Content Server contain the required security information: http://localhost/stellent/groups/public/documents/adacct/file.pdf.

Notice that the word public is in the URL, right after the directory groups: it tells the web server that the content item is in the public security group. Although it might seem verbose, it brings significant performance advantages. If a user requests this file, the web server can do the authentication based on the URL and the user's credentials. The Content Server never has to deliver content dynamically unless the vault file is requested.

An additional advantage is that the preceding URL always points to the most recent revision of a content item. For example, assume there was a typo in the original Word document. You would check-out the content item, modify it, and check it back in, which places the new revisions in the vault and weblayout.

The older item in the vault remains unchanged. However, the older item in the weblayout must be moved. Because the latest content item must have the previous URL, the older revision is renamed: http://localhost/stellent/groups/public/documents/adacct/*file~1.pdf*

In this manner, all revisions of all content items are stored in both the weblayout and the vault until deleted.

Modifying the Content Server

The Content Server is designed to be flexible, and you can modify it by setting any one of the hundreds of configuration flags. You can also modify it with the administrative applets. You can create workflows, content profiles, or custom metadata to alter how it works. However, you cannot change everything in the Content Server with simple configuration.

When configuration is not enough, you have three other options: create a new HTML interface with Dynamic Server Pages, create a custom component to alter how the services work, or create a completely separate application and connect to the Content Server through its SOA.

The first method entails custom HTML pages, DSPs, which are checked-into the Content Server. These forms can be used to process data or make simplified template pages. Any contributor can create DSPs: administrator privilege is not required. Use these pages to process HTML-based business forms or to make simplified versions of Content Server templates. This method is useful because you do not need to be an administrator to create and use them. However, DSPs are limited in that they cannot modify the standard pages. They can only be used to completely replace the current template. For small changes to the interface, using DSPs is not the best approach. Samples of DSPs are included in Chapters 3–6.

The second method is to create a component to customize the Content Server. For small user interface (UI) changes, this approach always requires the least amount of code. Components can be created and deployed only by administrators, however. Creating components requires more knowledge of the Content Server: an administrator must know how to find the correct resource to change, the correct way to modify it, and how to create a component to contain it. Components are also useful when altering existing functionality. Because the

Content Server is a data-driven Java framework, it is easy to plug in custom code. This code can alter how the standard services work and can also be used to add completely new services to the Content Server. Samples of components are included in Chapters 7–11.

The third method is to create a web application from scratch that connects to the Content Server with the web services. Stellent supports several connection techniques and protocols, including J2EE, ActiveX, and SOAP. This method is useful if you have a sophisticated application that makes limited use of the Content Server. The main drawback of this method is the complexity, so this approach is not recommended for small modifications of the web interface. Instead, use one of the first two methods. (A discussion of all three methods is included in Chapter 12.)

Dynamic Server Page Architecture

Dynamic Server Pages, which are files that are a combination of HTML and a scripting language, are checked-into the Content Server and rendered dynamically by the server. They can execute Content Server services, and display the results. The scripting languages supported in DSPs are IdocScript, XML IdocScript, and Java Server Pages (JSPs).

Because DSPs are checked-into the Content Server, they are revision controlled like all other content.

Purpose

DSPs have several uses. The most common is to be a wrapper for content that has been converted to HTML. For example, Dynamic Converter, Publisher, and Site Studio can all convert Word documents into HTML. DSP technology is used as a wrapper to mix the static converted content with dynamic content to give it the look and feel of the rest of the website.

Another common use is HTML-based forms for data entry and storage. Examples include forms for processing purchase requests, travel requests, or lists of comments about an item in workflow. Once submitted, these forms encapsulate the data in an XML-formatted file, which enables arbitrarily complex web forms without needing to create new tables in a database. The XML files are full-text indexed, so the data in them can be queried with the standard search page.

The third use of DSPs is to change the Content Server's look and feel. For example, if you want a simplified search page, you can use DSPs to create one. You can also use DSPs to create a simplified page for the results of the service, which is useful for quick customizations of the core pages that any contributor can create.

Format of Dynamic Server Pages

A DSP must be checked-into the Content Server with a file extension identical to its format. The five supported formats are the following:

Hypertext Content Server Template (HCST): Contains HTML and IdocScript code for running services.

Java Server Page (JSP): Contains JSP code for running services.

Hypertext Content Server Page (HCSP): Contains HTML and XML IdocScript for running services or processing forms. When the HCSP form is submitted, a new revision of the HCSP is checked-into the Content Server. The new revision stores the submitted form data in XML.

Hypertext Content Server Form (HCSF): Contains HTML and XML IdocScript for running services or processing forms. These forms are similar to HCSPs except when a new HCSP content item is generated. The original HCSF remains unchanged.

IdocScript Resource Files (IDOC): Contains resources that can be loaded and displayed on the previous pages.

HCSTs are identical in format to Content Server templates: they contain HTML and IdocScript and are used mainly to create custom search and check-in pages. They can also be used to generate custom portal pages. HCSTs are covered in detail in Chapter 3.

JSPs are similar to HCSTs and are rendered inside the Content Server using an embedded Tomcat engine. They support Java-based JSP syntax. In addition, a small API is available to render IdocScript and execute services.

The Tomcat integration can also run servlets, if they are packaged as a Web Archive (WAR) file. After checking-in the WAR file, the web applications can be started and stopped from the JSP Web App Administration page. Frameworks such as JSP tag libraries, Jakarta Struts, and Java Server Faces are supported, but they must be manually deployed. JSPs are covered in Chapter 4.

HCSPs and HCSFs are similar to HCSTs. Both are a combination of HTML and IdocScript. In fact, both can do anything an HCST can do. The differences are as follows:

- HCSP and HCSF pages use a special version of IdocScript called XML IdocScript, which is XML-compliant. Specifically, the code is placed inside specially formatted HTML comments.

- Because HCSP and HCSF pages are XML-compliant, the content in them can be found with a full-text search. In contrast, the content inside an HCST cannot be indexed.

- HCSP and HCSF pages can be used to store and display XML content from submitted forms.

HCSPs are used as wrappers for content converted with Publisher, Dynamic Converter, or Site Studio. They are also used extensively for HTML forms. Because they are more flexible than HCSTs, they are used more often.

HCSFs are identical to HCSPs—with one subtle difference. When an HCSP is submitted as a form, a new revision of that same HCSP item is created. This new HCSP either overwrites the existing HCSP form data or appends to it, depending on how the form is designed. This process continues until the `isFormFinished` flag is passed in the request.

In contrast, when an HCSF is submitted as a form, it does not create a new revision of itself. Instead, it creates a new HCSP with the appropriate form data. The original HSCF is not altered at all. The new HCSP can be submitted multiple times until the `isFormFinished` flag is set.

Therefore, a form that enables you to append your comments to it is an HCSP, and a form that enables you to make new discussion topics is an HCSF. HCSPs and HCSFs are covered in Chapter 5. The differences between IdocScript and XML IdocScript are covered in Appendix A.

In contrast with the other DSPs, IDOC pages are not used to display HTML. They are designed to contain HTML and IdocScript resources which enable code reuse and maintenance of pages. These resources can be included on any DSP, but they must always be coded in standard IdocScript; they cannot contain JSP or XML IdocScript. Using IDOC pages is the recommended practice for all DSPs. They are covered in detail in Chapter 6.

HCSPs are the most common of the previous options. They are the most flexible, they have the most features, and they can be full-text indexed. The only difficulty with them is the fact that they use XML IdocScript, which makes the pages more verbose and adds new problems when it comes to properly encoding variable names. Using IDOC resources or components bypasses this problem.

A DSP is rendered whenever a user navigates to its URL: `http://localhost/stellent/groups/public/documents/adacct/form.hcsp`.

When this happens, the web server forwards the request to the Content Server for rendering with the `GET_DYNAMIC_URL` service, which loads up information about the DSP and then renders it with the appropriate engine. More information about this service is covered in Appendix E.

Component Architecture

Component Architecture is the extensible framework at the core of the Content Server. It is a data-driven framework that is based on dozens of resource types. Its goal is to expose the inner working of the Content Server's core. By doing so, it enables developers to create advanced customizations that are not possible with simple configuration. You can override these resources with a custom component in which you can alter both the look and feel of the Content Server and its behavior.

For example, you can do any of the following:

- Modify the HTML that is displayed after a service request.

- Modify the SQL statements executed during a service.

- Add new SQL statements to a service.

- Modify the Java methods executed during a service.

- Add new Java methods to be executed during a service.

- Add a completely new service with custom SQL, custom Java, and custom templates.

As you can see, custom components give you more power than Dynamic Server Pages. Instead of simply consuming services, you can modify them.

There are several different resources used in Component Architecture, which can be in any of the following formats:

- Structured data tables for generic configuration

- Service definitions

- Templates written in HTML and IdocScript

- Dynamic HTML includes written in HTML and IdocScript

- Parameterized SQL statements

- Localization strings

- Environment configuration files

- Java code

- Native C/C++ code

All the core resources that describe the out-of-the-box behavior are in the `shared` directory. Some of the more interesting files and subdirectories are as follows:

`stellent/shared/classes/`: Contains the Java class files for the Content Server and dependent libraries

`stellent/shared/config/resources/`: Contains the core web resources and configuration tables

`stellent/shared/config/resources/std_page.htm`: Contains most of the HTML and IdocScript resources used on template pages

`stellent/shared/config/resources/std_services.htm`: Contains the definition of most core services

`stellent/shared/config/resources/workflow.htm`: Contains workflow-related services and data tables

`stellent/shared/config/resources/std_resources.htm`: Commonly used configuration in data tables

`stellent/shared/config/resources/lang/`: Localization strings for translating the interface into different languages

`stellent/shared/config/templates/`: Contains the HTML templates returned after service requests

Components generally take two forms: basic and advanced. *Basic components* modify only the Content Server's display. They always contain HTML and IdocScript resources. They occasionally contain localized string resources if the interface supports multiple languages.

Advanced components enhance or alter the Content Server's behavior. They usually contain Java and SQL resources. Although rare, native C or C++ code can also be included in a component. Native code is mainly used to modify how the web server authenticates the user.

A component is typically created with the Component Wizard utility, which helps create and manage custom resources. It is also used to enable and disable components, or package a component into a portable ZIP archive.

The next section covers the specifics of these resources, including how they are formatted. It then covers the format of a custom component. Step-by-step examples are included in Chapter 7.

Component Definition File

This is the file that ties together all the resources in a custom component. The Content Server automatically loads all the resources listed in the previous section. However, to make it load custom resources, you need a component definition file, which describes what resources are in a component and how the Content Server should load them.

This file is created automatically with the Component Wizard when you add a new component. Although you usually never need to make this file from scratch, if you create a Java customization, you might need to manually edit it.

For a component with no resources, the file would look like this:

```
<?hda version="7.5.1 (050317)" jcharset=Cp1252 encoding=iso-8859-1?>
@Properties LocalData
blFieldTypes=
blDateFormat=M/d/yy {h:mm[:ss] {aa}[zzz]}!mAM,PM!tAmerica/Chicago
@end
@ResultSet ResourceDefinition
4
type
filename
tables
loadOrder
@end
@ResultSet MergeRules
4
fromTable
toTable
column
loadOrder
@end
@ResultSet Filters
4
type
location
parameter
loadOrder
@end
@ResultSet ClassAliases
2
classname
location
@end
```

This file contains four tables of data in HDA ResultSet format. It also contains several name-value pairs in the LocalData section. The important data in the component is contained in the tables.

The ResourceDefinition table contains references to component resource files, which comprise the majority of the data in a customization. These files can contain several resources, such as services, queries, a list of templates, or generic HTML resource includes. For simplicity, it is typical to place only one type of resource in a given file. This type is reflected in the type field, which can be resource, service, template, query, or environment. The type of resource causes the Content Server to process the resource in different ways. The filename field is a relative path to where the resource file is located. The tables field is deprecated, but in the past it was used to explicitly load custom tables into the Content Server. The loadOrder field dictates when this resource should be loaded.

The loadOrder is an important concept for resolving resource name conflicts. It's common for two components to have tables or services with the same name, which typically happens when one component needs to override the behavior of another component. Component resources are loaded in increasing order, based on their loadOrder. The resource with the highest loadOrder is loaded last and is therefore the one used in the Content Server. The default loadOrder is 1. Increase or decrease it to control which component's resources are loaded first.

The MergeRules table is used to merge table data from this component into the core Content Server tables. For example, the list of templates is stored in the Content Server as a data table. If this component added a new template, its data would need to be merged into the core table. The fromTable field is set to the name of a custom table resource. The toTable field is the name of the core Content Server table to merge the data into. The column field is the primary key of the table. In other words, that value for this field is unique for all rows. The loadOrder field is the same as described previously.

The Filters table is used only for custom Java components. The code in a Filter is executed when specific events occur inside the Content Server. For example, when checking a new item into the Content Server, the validateStandard filter is called, among others. The type field is the unique name of the filter event. The location field is the classpath to the custom Java object to use for this filter. The parameter field is not often used; it contains arguments that you want to pass to your filter code. The loadOrder field is the same as described previously. Filters are covered in greater detail in Chapter 10.

The ClassAliases table is also used only for advanced Java components. Some—but not all—Java objects in the Content Server can be replaced with custom objects. Although this practice is not typical, even for Java components, it's available as a last resort for customizations. The classname is a unique name for the class in the core. This name is sometimes—but not always—the name of the class itself. The location field is the fully qualified classpath of the custom object. Also notice that it is the only ResultSet that does not have a loadOrder because only one component is allowed to create an alias for a specific class. This changed in version 8.0 to help support conflicts between complex Java components. Class aliases are covered in greater detail in Chapter 10.

Structured Data Tables

This is a generic resource that is used to store structured configuration information. Services, templates, and queries are also structured data tables, but they are processed in special ways after being loaded. Other data tables, such as the list of supported locales and the list of known document formats, are loaded in a generic fashion.

Most standard tables are defined in the file stellent/shared/config/std_resources.htm. Other standard table resources are located in the same directory. These resources are mainly useful for advanced components that alter Content Server behavior; they are not needed for general user interface modifications.

Structured data tables are available in two formats: HTML and HDA. The former is usually referred to as a *static table*, and the latter is a *dynamic table*. There is not much difference between the two, other than their formatting. However, if a component needs to dynamically modify its own data table, the HDA format is recommended. Hence the name Dynamic Table.

An HTML-formatted table resource looks like the following:

```
<html>
<body>
<@table MyDataTable@>
<table border=1><caption>MyDataTable</caption>
<tr>
  <td>Name</td><td>Caption</td><td>Data</td>
</tr>
<tr>
  <td>name1</td><td>caption1</td><td>data1</td>
</tr>
<tr>
  <td>name2</td><td>caption2</td><td>data2</td>
</tr>
</table>
<@end@>
</body>
</html>
```

Notice that the resource is encapsulated with the tags `<@table MyDataTable@>` and `<@end@>`. The first row in the table represents the names of the columns, and subsequent rows are for the values.

The same resource in HDA format looks like this:

```
<?hda version="7.5.1 (050317)" jcharset=Cp1252 encoding=iso-8859-1?>
@Properties LocalData
@end
@ResultSet MyDataTable
3
Name
Caption
Data
name1
caption1
data1
name2
caption2
data2
@end
```

In this case, the data is HDA-formatted, and the table is defined in a ResultSet.

In practice, these data tables must be explicitly merged into the Content Server, which requires the MergeRules table in the Component Definition File, mentioned earlier.

Service Definitions

Services are at the core of what the Content Server does and are defined in specially formatted data tables. They reference other resources, including templates, Java methods, and SQL statements. They are complex, but very important, so they need to be covered in detail.

One of the most commonly used services is GET_SEARCH_RESULTS, which queries the search engine for content matching specific criteria. It then renders the results of the query in a HTML page.

Using the Component Wizard, you can create a new service based on this service. The generated resource file looks like this:

```
<html>
<body>
<@table MyCustomServices@>
<table border=1><caption><strong>Scripts For Standard Services
    </strong></caption>
<tr>
    <td>Name</td><td>Attributes</td><td>Actions</td>
</tr>
<tr>
    <td>GET_SEARCH_RESULTS</td>
    <td>SearchService
        33
        StandardResults
        null
        null<br>
        !csUnableToRetrieveSearchResults</td>
    <td>3:getSearchResults::0:null</td>
</tr>
</table>
<@end@>
</body>
</html>
```

The Component Wizard also modifies the Component Definition File for this component. A reference to the new services is added as a new resource to the ResultSet ResourceDefinition:

```
@ResultSet ResourceDefinition
4
type
filename
tables
loadOrder
service
resources/custom_service.htm
MyCustomServices
1
@end
```

In this case, the resource type is set to service. The value for table is set to MyCustomServices, which is the name of the table resource.

The definition of the service is difficult to understand when viewed in the HTML format. It is best to view and edit service definitions with the Component Wizard, which parses the definitions and presents you with easy-to-understand descriptions. In this case, the previous HTML defines a service with the following attributes:

```
Name:               GET_SEARCH_RESULTS
Service Class:      SearchService
Access Level:       33 (Read, Scriptable)
Template:           StandardResults
Service Type:       null
Subjects Notified:  null
Error Message:      !csUnableToRetrieveSearchResults
Action 1:
        Type:            Java Method
        Action:          getSearchResults
        Parameters:      none
        Control Mask:    0
        Error Message:   null
```

Name

Name is the unique name for the service. To run this service, the value for IdcService in the request must correspond to it. For standard web requests, this parameter is almost always in the URL to the Content Server web page.

Service Class

The *Service Class* is the name of the Java class object that this service call instantiates. The classpath prefix intradoc.service is assumed unless a full path is given. This object contains Java methods that can be run in this service. See Chapter 10 for more information on Service Classes.

Access Level

Access level contains flags used to secure access to this service. The service security model is tightly coupled to the document security model used throughout the Content Server. For example, a user has roles, such as contributor. This role has access to different security groups. Out of the box, the contributor role has Read and Write access to the Public security group.

This same model is used to add security to services. A service defines in its access level if it is a Read or Write service, among other flags. This is used, along with the security group information, to secure the service. For example, the guest user has Read access to the Public group, but no access to the Secure group. Therefore, a Read service such as GET_FILE works fine for the guest for any items in the Public security group. However, that same service fails if the item were instead in the Secure security group.

The security access is stored as bit-flags in the Content Server. This means the flag is stored as the sum of all the bit-flags that apply. The integer values for these flags are as follows:

1—Read: The user must be able to read the security group referenced in this service.

2—Write: The user must be able to write the security group referenced in this service.

4—Delete: The user must be able to delete the security group referenced in this service.

8—Admin: The user must be able to administer the security group referenced in this service.

16—Global: Used for services that do not apply to a specific content item, or do not have a specific security group set in the request. For example, when used in combination with the Write flag, a user must have Write privileges to at least one security group to run this service. This is typically used with the Admin flag to secure administrative services.

32—Scriptable: This service can be executed with the executeService IdocScript function. This is restricted to safe services that read data only from the Content Server, such as GET_SEARCH_RESULTS and DOC_INFO.

The value stored in the definition is the integer sum of the flags. For example, the access level for GET_SEARCH_RESULTS is 33. That means its security flags are 1 and 32 for the Read and Scriptable flags. To run a search, the user thus must have at least Read access to the documents in the group.

The GET_FILE service has identical access level flags to GET_SEARCH_RESULTS. To run it on a document in the Secure security group, you need Read access to the Secure group. The CHECKOUT service has an access level of 34, meaning that you need Write access to the Secure group to check-out that item.

All these flags depend on the value for the security group. But how is that value determined?

The security group is sometimes determined from the data in the request. For example, a CHECKIN_NEW request would contain the security group information for the new item. If the user does not have Write access to that group, the check-in fails immediately.

However, this data is not always available in the request, or it is unwise to trust it. For example, in a GET_FILE request, the item's security group is unknown prior to a database query. Therefore, the first action in this service is to check the database for security information. The next action is the checkSecurity method, which will fail if the user does not have Read access to the item. If a service fails for security reasons, any compromising data is removed from the response.

Some services, such as administrative services, are not directly tied to documents at all. These usually specify the Admin flag, and the Global flag. This will limit the service to users that have administrator access to at least one security group. This is the primary use of the Global flag. Another use is for services such as CHECKIN_NEW_FORM, in which case the user must have Write access to at least one security group to access the check-in page.

Template

This is the name of the template resource used to render the result. In the GET_SEARCH_RESULTS service, the name of the template is StandardResults. Other common template names include HOME_PAGE and CHECKIN_NEW_FORM.

Templates are a combination of HTML and IdocScript. The IdocScript is used to format the HTML and display the data in the response. Templates are described later in this chapter.

Service Type

This is used to specify the type of service. At present, the only supported types are null or SubService. A SubService is unique in that it can be called from another service. For example, you can check-out a piece of content with the service CHECKOUT or the service CHECKOUT_BY_NAME. Most of the code used in these services is identical. Therefore, it makes sense to put all common code in the SubService named CHECKOUT_SUB. The SubService is executed from other services with the doSubService action. Please note that SubServices cannot be called directly.

Subjects Notified

Subjects are used in the Content Server to signify that special remote data has been updated. For performance reasons, data in remote sources—such as database tables—is cached by the Content Server. When a service modifies the remote data, it must notify a subject. The notification signifies that the cache is invalid and needs to be refreshed. For example, when checking-in a new item, the documents subject is notified. Subjects Notified is typically null.

Error Message

This is a formatted string representing the message to return in the event of an error. For example, if a check-in fails, the error message is the following:

```
!csUnableToCheckIn(dDocName)
```

This is an encoded string that represents a String resource and tokens to place in the localized string. If an English user could not check-in a content item with a Content Name of test, they would see this error:

```
Content item "test" was not successfully checked-in.
```

The Error Message does not need to use a String resource. It can also be hard-coded to a specific language. However, String resources are recommended to support multiple languages.

List of Service Actions

The list of *service actions* is a sequence of zero or more steps to take to process the service. Each action pulls data from the request and also sets data in the request. In this manner, the data returned by one service action can alter the behavior of later service actions.

An action's attributes are formatted as a colon-separated string:

```
Action Type:Action:Parameters:Control Mask:Error Message
```

In the case of GET_SEARCH_RESULTS, the action string is this:

```
3:getSearchResults::0:null
```

This string denotes an action type of 3, an action of getSearchResults, an empty control mask, and null for an error message. These are covered in the following sections.

Action Type

There are five possible types of actions. Each type either performs a predefined SQL statement or executes Java code. The supported action types are the following:

- *Select Query*: Runs a predefined SQL query and then discards the results. This type is almost never used, except to check the database for integrity before running a service. Because this query discards the results, most actions use a select cache query instead (described at the end of this list).

- *Execute Query*: Runs a predefined SQL statement that can alter database values with UPDATE, INSERT, or DELETE methods. The results are discarded.

- *Java Method*: Executes a Java method for this Service Class.

- *Load Option List*: Deprecated.

- *Select Cache Query*: Runs an SQL query and caches the results in a ResultSet object. This ResultSet can then be used by later actions or displayed with IdocScript.

Action

The *action* itself is the name of the Java method or the predefined SQL statement. A Java method could be defined in the Service Class object. It might also be defined in a Service Handler for this Service Class, which is described in Chapter 10. A predefined SQL statement is configured in a separate resource file, which is described later in this chapter.

Action Parameters

This is a list of zero or more parameters for the action. For example, in a select cache query, the first parameter is the name of a ResultSet. The result of the query is saved to a ResultSet object with this name. For a Java method, these parameters are typically used for anything that you do not want to hard-code into the Java. This may be the names of queries to run in the Java method, or the names of ResultSets.

Action Control Mask

The *action control mask* is an optional bit-flag, similar to the access level, which controls how errors are processed in an action. It is also used to control database transactions. The integer values and short names for this flag are as follows:

1—*Ignore Error* (ignoreError): If an error occurs during this action, do not stop the service. This option is rarely used. If an error occurs, you usually want to log it unless it occurs during logging.

2—*Check Result Non Empty* (mustExist): If the action is a select query or a select cache query, and the database returned an empty result, the action throws an error. This option is used to verify that the proper data exists before trying to process it. For example, verifying that an item exists before executing a check-out.

4—Begin Transaction (beginTran): This option begins a database transaction at the beginning of this action. All modifications to the database afterward are temporary; they are not stored until the transaction is committed. In the event of an error in a later action, the transaction will be rolled back. This option is used on all services that modify data in the database, such as a check-in. It is usually set on an action near the beginning of a service.

8—Commit Transaction (commitTran): This option commits the data in the current transaction after the action is completed. As a general rule, one service should have only one transaction that ensures the robustness of the service and the integrity of the database.

16—Check Result Empty (mustNotExist): If the action is a select query or a select cache query, and the database returned non-empty results, the action will throw an error. This option is used to verify that data does not exist before trying to add new data. For example, verify that a Content ID is not currently in use before processing a check-in.

32—Retry Query (retryQuery): If the action is an execute query, this flag can be used to retry the action in the event of an error. It retries twice: first after waiting three seconds and then again after waiting another six seconds. This option is rarely used, but is useful if the service makes heavy use of the database. It is mainly a workaround for synchronization bugs in some JDBC drivers.

64—Do Not Log (doNotLog): This flag is no longer used in the Content Server.

Similar to the access level flag, the action control mask is stored as the integer sum of all flag values. Alternatively, it can also be a list of the short names of the flags. For example, the CHECK_IN_NEW service has the following action:

```
3:doSubService:CHECKIN_NEW_SUB:12:null
```

The 12 is the sum of flags with integer values 4 and 8, which means that this action begins a transaction, runs the subservice, and then commits the transaction. In a component, you can also format the action control mask in this way:

```
3:doSubService:CHECKIN_NEW_SUB:beginTran,commitTran:null
```

Action Error Message

This message displays if an error occurred while running this action. It is appended to the error message for the service. Although not required, this option is useful to help track down exactly where an error occurred.

Templates

After running a service, the results of the request are displayed on a HTML page. This final step is optional. For example, remote applications typically want raw response data, not rendered HTML. However, most users will see their results rendered with a template.

These templates are comprised of HTML and IdocScript. IdocScript is a very simple language geared toward HTML display. In this way, it encourages the separation of business logic and display logic. Please see Appendices A through D for more information on IdocScript.

Not all the display logic is on the template; most of it is defined in dynamic HTML resources, which are described later. These resources also contain IdocScript and HTML, and are contained in separate files, which enables multiple templates to reuse the code in the dynamic HTML resources.

For example, a simple template used in the Content Server is MSG_PAGE, which is used to display a basic status message to the user. It is located here:

```
stellent/shared/config/templates/msg_page.htm
```

and contains the following code:

```
<!DOCTYPE HTML PUBLIC "-//IETF//DTD HTML//EN">
<html>
<head>
  <$msgPageTitle=lc("wwContentServerMessage")$>
  <$defaultPageTitle=msgPageTitle$>
  <$include std_html_head_declarations$>
</head>

<$include body_def$>
<$include std_page_begin$>
<$include std_header$>

<!--Message--->
<table border="0" cellpadding="0" cellspacing="0">
<tr>
  <td width="465" align="center">
    <table border = "0">
      <caption><h3><$msgPageTitle$></h3></caption>
      <tr>
        <td width=100%><span class=title>
          <$if msgResourceInclude$><$inc(msgResourceInclude)$>
          <$else$><$StatusMessage$>
          <$endif$>
        </span></td>
      </tr>
    </table>
  </td>
</tr>
</table>

<$include std_page_end$>

</body>
</html>
```

This page is a good example of the bare minimum needed to display the standard Content Server look and feel. It contains some IdocScript and HTML, but the majority of the page is in the following Dynamic HTML includes:

- std_html_head_declarations

- body_def

- std_page_begin

- std_header

- std_page_end

Besides the standard look and feel, there is very little on the page itself. The following line sets the variable msgPageTitle to a localized string:

```
<$msgPageTitle=lc("wwContentServerMessage")$>
```

In English, it is translated into Content Server Message. It displays this title with a combination of HTML and IdocScript:

```
<caption><h3><$msgPageTitle$></h3></caption>
```

Then the message itself displays:

```
<$if msgResourceInclude$><$inc(msgResourceInclude)$>
<$else$><$StatusMessage$>
<$endif$>
```

The message can be in one of two forms: as a simple variable (StatusMessage) or a variable that references a Dynamic HTML resource (msgResourceInclude). If the latter was set during the service, the inc function displays the include. Otherwise, the value of StatusMessage displays.

In addition to the template file itself, a component must also have a resource file listing all custom templates defined by the component. This resource file is HDA-formatted, and contains the following:

```
<?hda version="7.5.1 (050317)" jcharset=Cp1252 encoding=iso-8859-1?>
@Properties LocalData
@end
@ResultSet MyTemplates
5
name
class
formtype
filename
description
MSG_PAGE
Message
MessagePage
custom_msg_page.htm
My custom msg page
@end
```

The name field corresponds to the name of the template. The filename field is the path to the template relative to the template definition file. The other fields are not used by the Content Server and are there for organizational purposes.

This template definition file is referenced in the Component Definition File in this way:

```
@ResultSet ResourceDefinition
4
type
filename
tables
loadOrder
template
templates/mytemplates_template.hda
null
1
@end
@ResultSet MergeRules
4
fromTable
toTable
column
loadOrder
MyTemplates
IntradocTemplates
name
1
@end
```

The ResourceDefinition ResultSet is configured to point to the template resource file. The type field is template, and the filename field is the relative path to the resource file. The table does not need to be explicitly named in this ResultSet.

The MergeRules ResultSet is used to merge the custom template table definitions into a core table. In this case, the fromTable is MyTemplates. This is the name of the ResultSet in the preceding template definition file. The toTable is IntradocTemplates, which is the name of the table that contains the definitions for all the core templates. The column, describing the primary key for this table, is name. The loadOrder, as usual, is 1.

A component can override an existing template or create a new one. For example, you might want to modify the template HOME_PAGE with a component. Alternatively, you can create a unique template for a new service. Overriding templates is sometimes required, but you should avoid doing it whenever possible. In the next section, you will see that there are better ways to override the display of a result page.

In addition to customizing a template, a developer can put additional parameters in a service request to change the result page. For example, to change how GET_SEARCH_RESULTS is rendered, you could modify the SearchResults template, or pass one of these parameters in the request. The latter method is a very useful way to dynamically change how response pages are displayed.

The parameters that control result templates are as follows:

urlTemplate: This parameter is set to the URL for a Dynamic Server Page. This page is rendered with the response data after a successful request. It is a full-relative URL, such as /stellent/groups/public/documents/adacct/my_result.hcst.

docTemplateName: Similar to urlTemplate. However, instead of supplying the entire URL, you can supply just the Content Name (dDocName) of the template.

docTemplateID: Same as docTemplateName; is set to the Content ID (dID) of the template.

RedirectUrl: After executing a service that requires a POST, such as a check-in, the Content Server redirects to a confirmation page. In this way, the result page can be refreshed without resubmitting the POST. To change the confirmation page for such a service, set the RedirectUrl parameter to the URL of a Content Server service, such as <$HttpCgiPath$>?IdcService=DOC_INFO&dID=<dID>.

RedirectParams: Similar to RedirectUrl, but the prefix <$HttpCgiPath$>? is assumed.

Please refer to Appendix C for more information on these parameters.

Dynamic HTML

These resources are the most commonly used resources in components. The majority of the code for rendering templates does not exist in those templates. Instead, it is in Dynamic HTML resources that are included on those templates. As shown in the previous section, these resources are included on the page with IdocScript in one of two ways:

```
<$include my_dynamic_html_resource$>
<$inc("my_dynamic_html_resource")$>
```

Most of the Dynamic HTML resources used in the core are defined in this file: stellent/shared/config/resources/std_page.htm.

One simple resource, which is used on almost every page, is named body_def. It looks like this:

```
<@dynamichtml body_def@>
<!--Background image defined as part of body tag--->
<body <$include body_def_internal$> >
<@end@>

<@dynamichtml body_def_internal@>
<$if background_image$>
  background="<$HttpImagesRoot$><$background_image$>"
<$elseif colorBackground$>
  bgcolor="<$colorBackground$>"
<$endif$>
  link="#000000" vlink="#CE9A63" alink="#9C3000"
  marginwidth="0" marginheight="0" topmargin="0" leftmargin="0"
<@end@>
```

The resource body_def includes the resource body_def_internal and is used to set some standard attributes for the HTML BODY element. Most of these flags are overridden with Cascading Style Sheets (CSS) in recent versions of the Content Server. However, this is still a useful include to override when adding onLoad event handlers or page headers.

Most modifications of the web interface require a customization of a core include. It is generally not necessary to override a core service or even a core template to modify the interface. The majority of customizations involve simple modifications to small resource includes.

For example, to add a custom header to every HTML page, you could modify the body_def resource. Using the Component Wizard, you can create a new resource file and add the following definition:

```
<@dynamichtml body_def@>
<!--Background image defined as part of body tag--->
<body <$include body_def_internal$> >
<h1>My Header</h1>
<@end@>
```

The following updates the Component Definition File as well:

```
@ResultSet ResourceDefinition
4
type
filename
tables
loadOrder
resource
resources/myresource_resource.htm
null
1
@end
```

Adding this resource modifies the ResultSet ResourceDefinition. In this case, the type is resource. As usual, the filename is the relative path to the resource file, and loadOrder is 1. The table field is blank unless this page also contains a data table resource.

The previous modification to body_def has one significant problem, and it is the same problem that occurs when overriding any resource: only one component can override a named resource. For example, after one component overrides the service GET_SEARCH_RESULTS, no other component can do so. The same is true if a component overrode the HOME_PAGE template.

For Dynamic HTML there is an alternative. It is the super keyword, which allows multiple components to override the same include. The super keyword is used to include the previously defined value for this include. The first time it is used, it is the resource defined in the core; the second time it is used, it is the definition of this resource from another component.

It allows multiple components to override the same include, provided that they are only appending or prepending code. For example, to add one line at the bottom of body_def, there is no need to override the entire component. The following code yields equivalent HTML to the previous one:

```
<@dynamichtml body_def@>
<$include super.body_def$>
```

```
<h1>My Header</h1>
<@end@>
```

This code allows other component to also override this resource. For example, define the following resource in a separate component:

```
<@dynamichtml body_def@>
<$include super.body_def$>
<h1>My Other Header</h1>
<@end@>
```

When the resource is rendered, both modifications are present:

```
<!--Background image defined as part of body tag--->
<body link="#000000" vlink="#CE9A63" alink="#9C3000"
    marginwidth="0" marginheight="0" topmargin="0" leftmargin="0">
<h1>My Header</h1>
<h1>My Other Header</h1>
```

More examples of using the super keyword are available in Chapter 7.

SQL Statements

Predefined SQL statements serve three purposes. The first is to put commonly used SQL statements in a resource so they are reusable. The second is to help generate SQL statements dynamically, based on data in the service. The third is to help us abstract the database connection, so the Content Server can support multiple databases.

The predefined SQL resources are located in these files:

```
stellent/shared/config/query.htm
stellent/shared/config/workflow.htm
stellent/shared/config/indexer.htm
```

These files contain the commonly used queries for standard services, workflow services, and the indexer. For example, many services call the QdocInfo query, which obtains metadata information about a specific revision of a content item. It is defined in the table QueryTable in query.htm like this:

```
<@table QueryTable@>
<table border=1><caption><strong>Query Definition Table</strong></caption>
<tr>
    <td>name</td><td>queryStr</td><td>parameters</td>
</tr>
...
<tr>
    <td>QdocInfo</td>
    <td>SELECT Revisions.*, Documents.*, DocMeta.*
        FROM Revisions, Documents, DocMeta
        WHERE Revisions.dID=?
        AND Revisions.dID=Documents.dID
```

```
      AND DocMeta.dID = Documents.dID
      AND Revisions.dStatus<>'DELETED'
      AND Documents.dIsPrimary<>0
   </td>
   <td>dID int</td>
</tr>
```

Similar to a service definition, the query definition is specially formatted HTML table. The name column is the unique identifier for the query. It follows a general naming convention. If the SQL is a SELECT query, it starts with a Q. If it's an INSERT statement, it begins with an I. If it's a DELETE, it begins with a D. If it's an UPDATE, it begins with a U.

The queryStr column is the SQL statement itself. It is not always a complete statement. In most cases it contains a ? character so that the query can be assembled dynamically. For example, in the following line, the ? character will be replaced with data in the request to fully assemble the query:

```
WHERE Revisions.dID=?
```

It is assembled based on the data in the parameters column, which is an ordered list of variable names and types. In this case, the parameters column contains one item:

```
dID int
```

This item causes the value for dID in the request to be inserted into the SQL statement, replacing the ? character. This data is validated before being inserted, based on its type. It is a security feature that prevents badly formatted data from being inserted into the database. It also prevents malicious users from trying to alter the query with cleverly formatted request data.

The supported types match standard SQL data types:

- Boolean: True or false flag

- date: JDBC-formatted date field

- int: Integer field

- varchar: Variable length character string; Unicode is automatically used if supported

When validating, the value is converted into the proper format. For example, if the data type is a date, it is converted into the JDBC date format. If it is an int, the parameter is converted to an integer. If it is a varchar, all special SQL characters are escaped, and the value is inserted inside quotes.

To support multiple databases, aliases for column names are also needed. Recall that Oracle returns data with uppercase column names. To treat all databases equally, the column names must be converted back into mixed case.

This conversion is done with the table ColumnTranslation, which is located in the file stellent/shared/config/resources/upper_clmns_map.htm.

If you create a new database table and run custom queries, you need to add your column aliases to this table. You can do this with the Component Wizard by creating a custom HTML data table and merging it into the ColumnTranslation table.

Additionally, there is another kind of predefined SQL query called a Data Source, which is different from a predefined query in that it is only half of an SQL query. The entire WHERE clause can be appended dynamically. These are defined in the table `DataSources` in `std_resources.htm`:

```
<@table DataSources@>
<table border=1>
<caption><strong>Scripts For Standard IDC Services</strong></caption>
<tr>
    <td>name</td>
    <td>dataSource</td>
    <td>useMaxRows</td>
</tr>
<tr>
    <td>Documents</td>
    <td>SELECT Revisions.*, DocMeta.*, Documents.*
        FROM Revisions, DocMeta, Documents
        WHERE Revisions.dID = Documents.dID
        AND Revisions.dID = DocMeta.dID
        AND Documents.dIsPrimary <> 0
    </td>
    <td>Yes</td>
</tr>
...
</table>
<@end@>
```

The field `name` is the unique name for the Data Source. The field `dataSource` contains the SQL for the Data Source. The field `useMaxRows` is used to limit the number of result to the value of `MaxQueryRows`, which defaults to 200.

Data Sources are most commonly used by the Web Layout Editor, which enables you to generate reports with the data in the Content Server's database. They are also used by some core services. For example, to obtain the list of content items that have expired, the `GET_EXPIRED` service uses the `WorkingDocs` Data Source. The action `createResultSetSQL` runs the Data Source to obtain the list:

```
<tr>
  <td>GET_EXPIRED</td>
  <td>DocService
      18
      EXPIRED_PAGE
      null
      null<br>
      Unable to retrieve expired list.</td>
  <td>3:setLocalValues:resultName,EXPIRED_LIST,dataSource,WorkingDocs::null
      3:buildExpiredContentQuery:::null
      3:createResultSetSQL:::null
      3:computeDocInfoInHtmlPage:EXPIRED_LIST::null</td>
</tr>
```

The createResultSetSQL action uses the following parameters:

- resultName: The results of the query are stored in a result set with this name

- dataSource: The name of the Data Source

- orderClause: The SQL to place after a SORT BY clause in the Data Source

- whereClause: The SQL to place after the WHERE clause in the Data Source

Similar to queries, the orderClause and whereClause are inspected before being processed. If the Content Server detects malicious data, the request fails.

Additionally, if these queries are executed on a database table that contains content items, the Content Server appends an additional WHERE clause to the SQL. The clause restricts the query to return only items from a security group that the user has Read access to.

Localization Strings

Localization strings, which are found throughout the Content Server, are used for labels in the Administration Applets, error messages, logging, and display strings on the web page. Some examples are the following:

```
<@wwMyString=My String@>
<@wwHelloUser=Hello {1}!@>
<@ja.wwMyString=My String in Japanese@>
<@fr.wwMyString=My String in French@>
```

In these resources, the unique identifier of the string is on the left of the equals sign. These identifiers, which usually contain all or most of the text of the string as well as a prefix, follow a string naming convention:

- ww: This string can be displayed on a web page with the lc IdocScript function.

- ap: This string is a label in an Administrative Applet.

- sy: This string is an error that only occurs deep in the core Content Server.

- cs: This is a message or error string returned in a service's response.

- es. / ja. / fr.: These are two-letter codes that signify which language the string is in. This code corresponds to the ISO-639 standard. If no language prefix is used, it is assumed to be the same language as the default system language.

On the right side of the resource is the localized value of the string, which sometimes contains tokens, such as {1}. These tokens signify that this string requires a parameter to be properly localized. In the case of wwHelloUser, the localization requires one parameter, which replaces the {1} token when drawn to the page.

For example, the preceding strings can be displayed with IdocScript in the following way:

```
<$lc("wwMyString")$>
<$lc("wwHelloUser", "nobody")$>
<$lc("wwHelloUser", UserName)$>
```

When viewed by the user `sysadmin`, the output is this:

```
My String
Hello nobody!
Hello sysadmin!
```

If the `sysadmin`'s default locale is Japanese, the first string is localized to this:

```
My String in Japanese
```

For locales other than French or Japanese, the default value for `wwMyString` is displayed.

Environment Configuration Files

Environment files are similar to the default configuration file, located here: `stellent/config/config.cfg`

It is a simple text file with name-value pairs. It can be used to set any Content Server configuration variable:

```
<?cfg jcharset="Cp1252"?>
IsAutoNumber=true
AutoNumberPrefix=stel_
```

The advantage of these files is that you can enable component configuration flags when you enable a component. The disadvantage is that if you make extensive use of them, it is difficult to know where a flag has been set. It can be set in the `config.cfg` or in one of the dozen components you have.

Additional Component Resources

A component can contain resources that do not get directly loaded into the Content Server. For example, a custom web page can reference CSS or JavaScript files that need to be in the `weblayout` directory.

Some of these additional resources include the following:

- Java classes and JAR files

- Native C/C++ libraries

- Images

- JavaScript and CSS files

- Web help files

- Applets and ActiveX controls for web browsers

- Additional component documentation and samples

The filenames of these resources are not referenced directly in the Component Definition File. Java class paths can be referenced indirectly in this file, as well as in a Service definition. The other ones can be referenced in Java code or in a URL.

These resources can still be packed with a component by using the *Build Settings* option in the Component Wizard.

There are few restrictions to the format of these additional resources. The images and help files can be in any format you require. The JavaScript and CSS files can also be anything you need, although their location should be restricted to the `weblayout` directory.

There are additional restrictions in how custom Java code is written. It is possible to have the Content Server run custom Java code, which allows you to modify services or create new ones. See Chapter 10 for an in-depth discussion on creating custom Java components.

Custom C++ code can also be plugged-in to the Content Server with a component. The most common use is a customization to how the web server plug-in works. For example, adding a custom authentication filter. A brief discussion of such security customizations is covered in Chapter 12.

■ ■ ■

CHAPTER 3

Using HCSTs

Hypertext Content Server Template (HCST) pages are a quick and easy way to create custom dynamic web pages in the Content Server. A developer can execute any service with a properly constructed HCST. Any of the hundreds of standard services can be executed from a form post, including check-in, workflow processing, subscriptions, or searches. A small subset of read-only services, such as search and content info, can be executed directly on the page with IdocScript.

The most common use of HCSTs is to create check-in screens, search pages, and portal pages. Pages that execute custom services or database queries are also possible, but they require a bit more work. This chapter covers the most common uses of HCST pages.

Simple HCSTs

Any IdocScript function or variable can be rendered on an HCST. For example, a simple page to say hello to the current user looks like this:

```
<html>
<head></head>
<body>
<h1>Hello <$UserName$></h1>
</body>
</html>
```

To render this page, simply save the preceding text into a file named `hcst-hello.hcst` and then check that file into the Content Server. Run a search to find it and then click on the `weblayout` URL for that file. You will see a page similar to Figure 3-1.

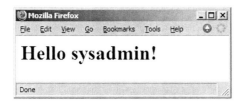

Figure 3-1. *Simple Hello User HCST*

In addition, any standard `dynamichtml` include can be referenced on this page. These includes are used throughout the core templates to establish a standard look and feel for all Content Server templates. To give the HCST the standard look and feel, four core includes are needed:

```
<html>
<head>
<title>Hello</title>
<$include std_html_head_declarations$>
</head>
<$include body_def$>
<$include std_page_begin$>

<h1>Hello <$UserName$></h1>

<$include std_page_end$>
</body>
</html>
```

When viewed in the web browser, the page looks like any other page in the Content Server (see Figure 3-2):

Figure 3-2. *Hello User HCST with standard layout*

This HCST is a good starting point for any page that a developer wants to present to the user. The `std_page_begin` and `std_page_end` includes are on almost all HTML templates used by the Content Server. The `body_def` include is found on most pages; if not, `body_def_internal` is used:

```
<html>
<head>
<title>Hello</title>
<$include std_html_head_declarations$>
</head>
<body <$include body_def_internal$> >
```

```
<$include std_page_begin$>

<h1>Hello <$UserName$></h1>

<$include std_page_end$>
</body>
</html>
```

The `std_html_head_declarations` include is almost always present, but it does not contain enough information for some pages. Search and contribution pages need additional JavaScript code to be defined in the HEAD of the HTML page. On these pages, specialized versions of these includes are used. They will be covered in the next few examples, which demonstrate how to run services from an HCST and how to make custom search and check-in pages.

For a list of the commonly used includes, see Appendix D.

Search Results Portal

There are several ways to execute the core Content Server features in an HCST. One simple and common method is to use the `executeService` IdocScript function. This function enables you to run a small subset of core Content Server services directly in IdocScript (for example, obtaining the content info for an item or running a search).

This example is a page that displays a list of search results. It can be used to obtain a list of the most recent items, all items by a specific author, or items that are from a specific department. To obtain a list of all items that have the word `test` in their titles, create a file with the following code:

```
<html>
<head>
<title>Search</title>
</head>
<body>

<h3>Test Documents</h3>

<$if not QueryText$>
<$QueryText="dDocTitle <substring> `test`"$>
<$endif$>

<$executeService("GET_SEARCH_RESULTS")$>
<ul>
<$loop SearchResults$>
<li><a href="<$URL$>"><$dDocTitle$></a></li>
<$endloop$>
</ul>

</body>
</html>
```

As in the previous example, this text needs to be saved to a file named hcst-search.hcst and checked-in to the Content Server. Be sure to give this HCST the content ID value of hcst-search. When viewed from the web, it looks like Figure 3-3.

Figure 3-3. *Simple HCST search portal*

The content ID is important in this case because it is used in the URL to the item. Notice the URL shown in Figure 3-3:

```
http://localhost/stellent/groups/public/documents/adacct/hcst-search.hcst
```

This URL contains several pieces of metadata that you filled in on the check-in page. The first piece is public, which denotes that this content item is in the *Public* security group. The next piece is adacct, which means that this item has a content type of *ADACCT*. The final piece is the web filename, which corresponds to the content ID of the item, followed by a dot, and then the extension for this file's format. In this case, the web filename equals hcst-search.hcst because the content ID is hcst-search and the file extension is hcst. It is pure coincidence that this web filename is equal to the title of the checked-in file.

These URLs seem verbose, but they are useful for many purposes. One of them is fast security checks, as mentioned in Chapter 2. Another is to make easy references from one file to another. If two items have the same security group and content type, they reside in the same web folder, and links between them are simple (this becomes important later).

This page runs the service GET_SEARCH_RESULTS with all the variables currently defined on the page, including any variable explicitly set in IdocScript and any parameter from the URL of the request. For example, if the URL looks like this, the results from the search are sorted according to their titles:

```
http://localhost/stellent/.../hcst-search.hcst?SortField=dDocTitle
```

Likewise, the value for SortField can be set on the page itself, just as QueryText is. The following change in the code yields a similar result:

```
<$if not QueryText$>
<$QueryText="dDocTitle <substring> `test`"$>
```

```
<$endif$>
<$SortField="dDocTitle"$>
```

After executing this search, the response data is available on the page as IdocScript variables. For example, the variable `TotalRows` is now available, telling us how many results are present. Tables of data in IdocScript are called `ResultSets`. In this case, the `ResultSet` named `SearchResults` contains all the needed data. To display the results, use the following code:

```
<$loop SearchResults$>
<li><a href="<$URL$>"><$dDocTitle$></a></li>
<$endloop$>
```

For each row in the results, one HTML bulleted list item is output to the page. Each row in the `ResultSet` has multiple columns, or fields. There exists one field for each piece of custom metadata for this item, as well as standard document metadata. In the preceding example, you extracted the values for `URL` and `dDocTitle` and output them to the page as HTML. Other values are present, such as `dDocAuthor`, `dDocType`, and `xComments`.

More information about IdocScript syntax and looping is available in Appendix A. More information about the `GET_SEARCH_RESULTS` service is in Appendix E.

As mentioned, this search is run based on the variables currently in the local data, including any parameter in the URL to the `hcst-search.hcst` page itself. This line is used to set a default value for `QueryText` if one is not present in the URL:

```
<$if not QueryText$>
<$QueryText="dDocTitle <substring> `test`"$>
<$endif$>
```

This page can also be used as the result page for a search form. For example, the following HTML page can be used as a simple search form:

```
<html>
<head>
<title>Search</title>
</head>
<body>

<form action="hcst-search.hcst">
<input name="QueryText" value="dDocTitle <substring> `test`">
<input type="submit">
</form>

</body>
</html>
```

Save this HTML to a file named `hcst-search-simple.hcst`. Next, check it into the Content Server with the same security group and content type as `hcst-search.hcst`, after which the `action` parameter in the HTML form points to the URL of the previously created search portal. When the user clicks Submit, the form data is sent to the search portal. Because the value for `QueryText` is submitted as well, the search portal uses the submitted value to run the search.

Congratulations! You have just created your first web application with the Content Server!

The default search on the portal page uses the Verity Full Text search engine to find all content with test in their titles. Using this engine, you can query the metadata in the document along with the text in the document. This is extremely powerful, especially if you have XML or keywords embedded in your documents that are not present in the metadata.

However, this example does not need to query the contents of the documents, just the title metadata. If you have version 7.0 or later of the Content Server, you can bypass the search engine and query the database directly. This procedure is faster when it comes to metadata queries that do exact matches, but is sometimes slower when doing wildcard searches. Querying the database directly requires slightly different parameters:

```
<html>
<head>
<title>Search</title>
</head>
<body>

<h3>Test Documents</h3>

<$if not QueryText$>
<$QueryText="dDocTitle LIKE '%test%'"$>
<$endif$>
<$SearchEngineName="DATABASE"$>
<$executeService("GET_SEARCH_RESULTS")$>
<$loop SearchResults$>
<li><a href="<$URL$>"><$dDocTitle$></a>
<$endloop$>

</body>
</html>
```

Notice that the value of SearchEngineName is DATABASE, which instructs the Content Server to execute the query using the database. It requires slightly different query syntax than the previous example. In version 7.0, the QueryText must be pure SQL. In version 7.5, this is not required, but still recommended. In either case, the result page will still look like Figure 3-3.

Not all Content Server services can be executed with the executeService IdocScript function. The Content Server supports hundreds of different service requests, but most are used by the administrative applets and are not generally useful on an HCST. Only a small handful of service requests are relevant to developers. See Appendix E for a list of these services.

Advanced Search Page

As mentioned in the previous example, it is fairly simple to create an HTML form that can submit to an HCST and run a search. However, doing so requires the HCST developer to write some custom code to properly assemble the QueryText. This is not complicated; executing a substring search on a metadata field requires fairly simple syntax. However, it becomes more complicated when you add more fields and more options. Integer field, date field, and precise matches all add complexity to assembling the QueryText.

For complex search pages with multiple fields, it makes sense to take advantage of the resources that the Content Server uses. In particular, it makes sense to use the same JavaScript functions and create forms with similar fields. This example presents one possible way to create an advanced search page similar to the Content Server's search pages.

This example uses these Content Server resources to create an advanced search page. It also demonstrates how to use the urlTemplate parameter to redirect a service to a custom template. It finally displays the service response in a way that handles multiple result pages.

To begin, create the file hcst-advanced-search.hcst with the following code:

```
<html>
<head>
<$PageTitle="Guest Search Page"$>
<$if isTrue(IsLoggedIn)$>
    <$PageTitle="Search Page For " & UserName$>
<$endif$>
<$include std_query_html_head_declarations$>
<script language="JavaScript">
<$include query_form_submit_script$>
</script>
</head>

<$include body_def$>
<$include std_page_begin$>

<h3 class=pageTitle>HCST Search Page</h3>
<form name="QUERYTEXTCOMPONENTS">
<input type=hidden name="QueryText" value="">
<table>
<tr>
    <td align=right><span class=searchLabel>Title</span></td>
    <td>
        <input type="hidden" name="opSelected"
            value="hasAsSubstring">
        <input type="text" size=30 name="dDocTitle"
            value="">
    </td>
</tr>
<tr>
    <td align=right><span class=searchLabel>Content ID</span></td>
    <td>
        <input type="hidden" name="opSelected"
            value="hasAsSubstring">
        <input type="text" size=30 name="dDocName" value="">
    </td>
</tr>
<tr>
    <td align=right><span class=searchLabel>
        Release Date From</span></td>
```

```
        <td align=left>
            <input type="hidden" name="opSelected" Value="dateGE">
            <input type="text" size=12 maxlength=20
                name="dInDate" value="">
            <span class=searchLabel>To</span>
            <input type="hidden" name="opSelected" Value="dateLess">
            <input type="text" size=12 maxlength=20
                name="dInDate" value="">
        </td>
</tr>
<tr>
        <td align=right><span class=searchLabel>Full Text</span></td>
        <td><input type="text" name="FullTextSearch" size=30></td>
</tr>
</table>
</form>
<$c="This page is hcst-advanced-search.hcst, and we wish to render the results
with the template hcst-advanced-search-results.hcst"$>
<$urlTemplate = strSubstring(fileUrl, 0, strLength(fileUrl)-5)
    & "-results.hcst"$>
<form name="SEARCHFORM" method="GET"  action="<$HttpCgiPath$>">
<input type=hidden name="IdcService" value="GET_SEARCH_RESULTS">
<input type=hidden name="urlTemplate" value="<$urlTemplate$>">
<input type=hidden name="QueryText" value="">
<input type=hidden name="ResultCount" value="5">
<table>
<tr>
    <td><span class=searchLabel>Sort By:</span></td>
    <td><select name="SortField">
        <option selected  value="dInDate">Release Date
        <option  value="dDocTitle">Title
        <option  value="Score">Score
        </select>
    </td>
    <td><select name="SortOrder">
        <option value="Asc">Ascending
        <option selected value="Desc">Descending
        </select>
    </td>
    <td>
    <input type=submit value ="Search" onClick="submitFrm(false)">
    </td>
</tr>
</table>
</form>


<$include std_page_end$>
```

```
</body>
</html>
```

Next, check this file into the Content Server with the same security group and content type as the previous two HCSTs. Be sure to give the file the content ID hcst-advanced-search. When viewed from the web, this page looks like Figure 3-4.

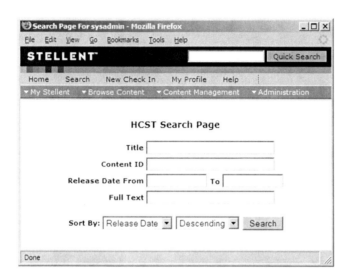

Figure 3-4. *Advanced HCST search form*

The first thing to notice about this page is that there are two HTML forms. The primary purpose in using two forms is to simplify the URL to the search results page. It is only necessary to pass in the value for QueryText in the request. Passing any other data only clutters the URL to the results page, making it less portable and harder to reuse. To this end, the page is split into two forms: one with the search terms and another to help create the search terms.

The first form, named QUERYTEXTCOMPONENTS, contains metadata fields such as title (dDocTitle) and release date (dInDate). This data is used in JavaScript functions to generate the QueryText parameter for the search. This form is simply a placeholder for these fields, so it does not have a Submit button.

The second form (named SEARCHFORM) is the actual form submitted to run the search, which contains optional search terms such as SortOrder and SortField. When the Search button is clicked, it executes the JavaScript function submitFrm. This function takes one parameter. If true is passed, the search terms will be saved after the search is submitted. This is not necessary at this point, so false is passed.

The submitFrm function is defined in the resource query_form_submit_script or query_form_submit_form_function, depending on the Content Server version. Both resources are defined in the std_page.htm resource file mentioned in Chapter 2.

The submitFrm function builds the value for QueryText by analyzing the fields in the QUERYTEXTCOMPONENTS form. If a field in that form contains a value, it is appended as a token in the QueryText string.

This process works automatically because of the special structure of the fields in the form. For example, to allow a user to search the title field (dDocTitle), place this code in the form:

```
<td align=right><span class=searchLabel>Title</span></td>
<td>
    <input type="hidden" name="opSelected"
        value="hasAsSubstring">
    <input type="text" size=30 name="dDocTitle"
        value="">
</td>
```

Notice that the preceding code contains two input fields. The hidden one is named opSelected; the other is the name of the metadata field to query.

The value for opSelected determines how this metadata field is queried. In the preceding case, it is set to hasAsSubstring, which is used in version 7.0 to do a substring query of a text field. In older versions, it is simply Substring. Other useful values for opSelected for strings include beginsWith, hasAsWord, equals, and endsWith. For systems older than version 7.0, they correspond to Starts, Contains, Matches, and Ends, respectively.

On this form the content ID field is nearly the same as the title field, which is possible because submitFrm automatically configured itself based on the names of the fields. The only two differences are the name of the field and the label.

Date fields, such as the release date (dInDate) and the expiration date (dOutDate), are more complex. Typically, a user is more interested in a range instead of equality or substring tests. Therefore, the submitFrm function uses different values for opSelected for date fields. The release date field is formatted in this way:

```
<tr>
    <td align=right><span class=searchLabel>
        Release Date From</span></td>
    <td align=left>
        <input type="hidden" name="opSelected" Value="dateGE">
        <input type="text" size=12 maxlength=20
            name="dInDate" value="">
        <span class=searchLabel>To</span>
        <input type="hidden" name="opSelected" Value="dateLess">
        <input type="text" size=12 maxlength=20
            name="dInDate" value="">
    </td>
</tr>
```

In this case, the user has two form fields. These fields are labeled From and To, but both have the field name dInDate. If a value for the From field is specified, the generated query finds all items with a release date after the specified date. If the To field is specified, the query finds all items released before the specified date. If they are both specified, the query returns all items in a specific date range.

Number fields are used in a similar fashion to date fields. Useful values for opSelected for numbers include numberEquals, numberGE, numberGreater, numberLE, and numberLess. For systems older than version 7.0, they correspond to Equal, GreaterEqual, Before, LessEqual, and After, respectively.

The third thing to notice is the structure of the form SEARCHFORM. Unlike the previous example, the action parameter does not point to an HCST page. Instead, it points directly to the content server. It sets the parameter IdcService to GET_SEARCH_RESULTS and a specific value for urlTemplate, as shown following:

```
<$urlTemplate = strSubstring(fileUrl, 0, strLength(fileUrl)-5)
    & "-results.hcst"$>
<form name="SEARCHFORM" method="GET"  action="<$HttpCgiPath$>">
<input type=hidden name="IdcService" value="GET_SEARCH_RESULTS">
<input type=hidden name="urlTemplate" value="<$urlTemplate$>">
```

As mentioned in Chapter 2, when you execute a service request it formats the response with the standard template for the service. Parameters such as urlTemplate and docTemplateName can be used to redirect the service to a different template. This example redirects the response to the page hcst-advanced-search-results.hcst, which is shown later.

The URL to the result page is determined from the URL of the current page. As in the previous examples, the result page is checked-in with the same security group and content type so they appear in the same folder in the weblayout directory. This is important for determining the path to the result template.

To generate the path to the result template, you also need the fileUrl parameter. This parameter is set for all Dynamic Service Pages (DSPs) and contains the URL to the current file. The result template is in the same directory as the current page and it has a similar name. Therefore, it is a simple matter to determine the result URL: strip off the last five letters of the URL and append the letters -result.hcst. The first line in the previous code does precisely this.

When the Search button is clicked, the function submitFrm generates a value for QueryText. This value is then inserted into the form SEARCHFORM. Finally, the form SEARCHFORM is submitted. The Content Server runs the query and generates the response based on the template hcst-advanced-search-results.hcst.

Before testing, you need to create the result page, which is similar to the previous simple portal pages, with a handful of differences. First, because it is purely a result template, it does not run the executeService IdocScript function. Second, it can display multiple pages of results.

Now create the file hcst-advanced-search-results.hcst with the following code:

```
<html>
<head>
<$PageTitle="Guest Search Page"$>
<$if isTrue(IsLoggedIn)$>
    <$PageTitle="Search Page For " & UserName$>
<$endif$>
<$include searchapi_result_html_head_declarations$>
</head>

<$include body_def$>
<$include std_page_begin$>
```

```
<h3 class=pageTitle>HCST Search Results Page</h3>

<p>Found <$TotalRows$> results.</p>

<$c="You can also use the include searchapi_navigation_list"$>
<p align="center">
<$if PreviousPage$>
[ <a href="<$strRemoveWs(inc("searchapi_navigation_previous"))$>">
        PREV</a> ]
<$endif$>
<$if NextPage$>
[ <a href="<$strRemoveWs(inc("searchapi_navigation_next_page"))$>">
        NEXT</a> ]
<$endif$>
</p>

<br><br>

<table border='1' cellpadding='0' cellspacing='3' width='540'>
<$loop SearchResults$>
    <tr>
    <td align='left'>
        <a href='<$URL$>'><$dDocName$></a>
    </td>
    <td>
        <b><$dDocTitle$></b><br>
        Release Date: <$dInDate$><br>
        Author: <$dDocAuthor$>
    </td>
    <td align='center' width='50'>
        <a href='<$HttpCgiPath$>?IdcService=DOC_INFO&dID=<$dID$>'>
        <img src='<$HttpWebRoot$>/images/stellent/InfoIcon_sm.gif'
            border='0'>
        </a>
    </td>
    </tr>
<$endloop$>
</table>

<$include std_page_end$>

</body>
</html>
```

   Check-in the file with the same security group and content type as the previous HCST and give it the content name hcst-advanced-search-results. Now if you execute a search, the results look like Figure 3-5.

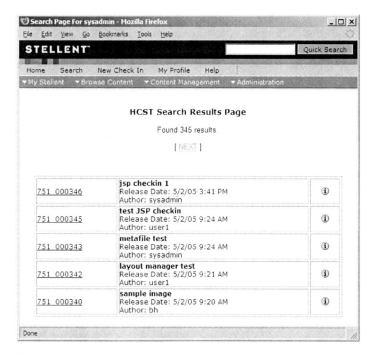

Figure 3-5. *Advanced HCST search results*

This page is slightly more complex than the previous search results page. It outputs the title of the item inside a link to the web-viewable rendition of it. It also has an additional link that takes the user to the Content Information page for this item. From that page, the user can check-out the item or subscribe to it.

In addition, if the flags PreviousPage or NextPage are present, some simple navigation also appears. The parameter ResultCount is hard-coded to 5 on the search page, which means that only five results will appear at a time. If more than five are present, the NEXT link is visible.

Clicking the NEXT link takes the user to the next five results, which display the PREV link. That link takes the user to the previous five results. If more than 10 results exist, another NEXT link is present.

These links to other pages are generated with core resource includes. The include searchapi_navigation_next_page creates the URL to the next page, whereas the include searchapi_navigation_previous creates the URL for the previous page. These resources are included with the inc function and then post-processed with the strRemoveWs function. Together they extract all the white space from the includes, which ensures a URL on a single line. See Appendixes A and B for more information on these functions.

The value for urlTemplate is automatically placed in these URLs to make sure that the pages are all generated in the same manner.

In conclusion, the search functionality is easy to implement on an HCST. A search can be run from IdocScript or by using the urlTemplate parameter. Most service requests can be altered in a similar manner (one important exception is the check-in service).

Custom check-in pages are more complex because they require special HTML to support a file upload and a larger list of metadata fields. The next example covers this very subject.

Custom Check-In Pages

The contribution and update pages display metadata based on complex rules. These rules are based on internal metadata definitions for proper HTML display. Simple core includes were covered earlier, such as std_page_begin and std_page_end. To display a check-in page, you need std_checkin_html_head_declarations and std_meta_field_display as well. The first loads up the metadata definitions, whereas the second renders them as HTML. The std_meta_field_display include also contains the logic needed to display option lists and render content profiles.

To create a custom check-in page, create the file hcst-checkin.hcst with the following code:

```
<html>
<head>
    <$PageTitle="Check In", isNew=1$>
    <$include std_checkin_html_head_declarations$>
</head>

<$include body_def$>
<$include std_page_begin$>

<h3>HCST Check In</h3>

<p>This check-in page gives the HCST developer total control over which
metadata fields to display, and how to format the HTML.</p>

<form name="Checkin" method="post" enctype="multipart/form-data"
    action="<$HttpCgiPath$>">

<!-- prefilled default values... you can place other default
     values here for metadata such as 'dDocType' and 'dSecurityGroup'
     to make specialized contribution paes -->
<input type=hidden name="IdcService" value="CHECKIN_NEW">
<input type=hidden name="dDocAuthor" value="<$UserName$>">
<input type=hidden name="dRevLabel" value="1">

<$c="This page is hcst-checkin.hcst, redirect to the page
    hcst-checkin-results.hcst after the checkin"$>
<$redirectUrl = strSubstring(fileUrl, 0, strLength(fileUrl)-5) &
    "-confirm.hcst?dDocName=<$dDocName$>&dID=<$dID$>"$>
<input type=hidden name="RedirectUrl" value="<$redirectUrl$>">

<table>

<!-- This field is optional if auto numbering is turned on for the
     Stellent Content Server.  -->
<tr>
    <td>Content ID</td>
```

```
    <td><input type="text" name="dDocName" size=35 maxlength=30
        value="">
    </td>
</tr>
<tr>
    <td>Type</td>
    <td>
        <select name="dDocType">
        <$loop DocTypes$>
            <option value="<$dDocType$>"><$dDescription$>
        <$endloop$>
        </select>
    </td>
</tr>
<tr>
    <td>Title</td>
    <td><input type="text" name="dDocTitle" size=35     maxlength=30>
    </td>
</tr>
<tr>
    <td>Security Group</td>
    <td>
        <$rsMakeFromList("SecurityGroupSet", "securityGroups")$>
        <select name="dSecurityGroup">
        <$loop SecurityGroupSet$>
            <option><$row$>
        <$endloop$>
        </select>
    </td>
</tr>
<tr>
    <td><hr></td><td><hr></td>
</tr>
<tr>
    <td>File</td>
    <td><input type="file" name="primaryFile" maxlength=250>
    </td>
</tr>

<!-- custom metadata section -->
<$loop DocMetaDefinition$>
    <$showSimple=""$>
    <$if showSimple$>
        <tr>
            <td><$lc(dCaption)$></td>
            <td><input name="<$dName$>"></td>
        </tr>
    <$else$>
```

```
        <$strTrimWs(inc("std_meta_field_display"))$>
    <$endif$>
<$endloop$>

<tr>
    <td><hr></td><td><hr></td>
</tr>
<tr>
    <td align=center colspan=2>
    <input type=button name=javaSubmit value=" Check In "
        onClick="postCheckInStandard(this.form)">
    <input type=reset name=reset value=" Reset ">
    </td>
</tr>
</table>
</form>

<$include std_page_end$>
</body>
</html>
```

Check this file into the Content Server with a Content ID of hcst-checkin. It looks like Figure 3-6.

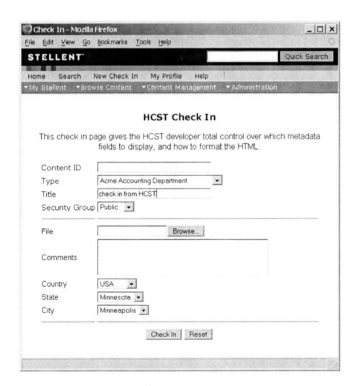

Figure 3-6. *HCST check-in form*

The core includes do most of the work to render this page. This page has a form with the value of IdcService set to CHECKIN_NEW. This service requires several mandatory parameters, which are also input fields: dDocTitle, dDocType, dSecurityGroup, dDocAuthor, dRevisionLabel, and primaryFile.

Beneath the standard fields are the custom metadata fields. These fields are displayed by looping over the ResultSet named DocMetaDefinition, which contains information about the custom metadata fields. There are two options on the page to display the field. One is simple, which displays only the field name with a text input field. The other way uses the resource std_meta_field_display, which renders the field exactly as it would appear on the default check-in page. The former is useful when you need total control over the HTML; the latter is useful when the field contains option lists.

Notice that the HTML form on this page has an encoding type of multipart/form-data, which is required to tell the browser to upload a file. Without it, it is impossible to upload a file from a client's browser.

Another important thing to note is the value for RedirectUrl in the form. This parameter is used by many services to redirect a POST request to a GET request after the POST request is successful. This URL typically contains IdocScript to generate a URL based on the response data from the POST service. After a check-in, we want to redirect to the page hcst-checkin-confirm.hcst, but the RedirectUrl needs the full URL, which includes the content type and group. We know that the fileUrl for the current page contains the security group and content type, and ends with hcst-checkin.hcst. So, instead of hard-coding the group and type information, we can parse out the last five characters of fileUrl, and append -confirm.hcst to make a full URL to the confirmation page:

```
<$redirectUrl = strSubstring(fileUrl, 0, strLength(fileUrl)-5) &
    "-confirm.hcst?dDocName=<$dDocName$>&dID=<$dID$>"$>
<input type=hidden name="RedirectUrl" value="<$redirectUrl$>">
```

Notice that the parameters dID and dDocName are appended to this URL, which is needed because unlike when urlTemplate is used, the response data is not forwarded to the redirected page. The IdocScript inside RedirectUrl is evaluated with the response data, but other than that no response data is available. So if you want the results of the service to be present on the confirmation page, each piece of data must be explicitly mentioned in the RedirectUrl parameter and encoded as IdocScript.

In addition, this page uses the IdocScript functions lc, strTrimWs, and rsMakeFromList. The lc function localizes a string into the user's language. The strTrimWs function is similar to strRemoveWs, except it only removes white space at the beginning or end of a string. The function rsMakeFromList turns an OptionList object into a ResultSet object so it can be more easily rendered on the page. See Appendix B for more information about these functions.

Finally, this example needs a custom confirmation page. This page does not need to be complicated; it need only display some information about the item and mention that it was successfully processed. To do this, create the file hcst-checkin-confirm.hcst with the following contents:

```
<html>
<head>
    <$PageTitle = "Check In Confirmation"$>
    <$include std_html_head_declarations$>
</head>
```

```
<$include body_def$>
<$include std_page_begin$>

<h3>Check In Confirmation</h3>

<p>Successfully checked-in content item:
<a href="<$HttpCgiPath$>?IdcService=DOC_INFO&dID=<$dID$>">
    <$dDocName$></a></p>

<$include std_page_end$>

</body>
</html>
```

This page should be checked-in with the same security group and content type as the hcst-checkin.hcst page.

After a successful check-in with the custom page, the result page looks like Figure 3-7.

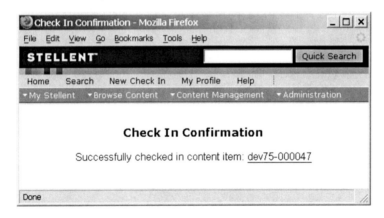

Figure 3-7. *HCST check-in confirmation page*

The check-in page for this example looks very similar to the default check-in page. The HTML has a two-column presentation style, with the label in one column and the field in another. But what if you want the display to be different? What if you want a four-column display or a check-in form that isn't in a table at all? The std_meta_field_display include uses flags to display a field differently, but it cannot do everything you might want. These flags are discussed in Appendix D.

One option is to set the showSimple flag in the HCST, which gives the developer complete control over how the metadata fields are displayed. This option has its limitations because it's more difficult to maintain. Option lists need to be hard-coded in HTML, and neither dependent choice lists nor content profiles will work.

The other option is to modify the includes that are referenced by std_meta_field_display. In this way, a developer can override the include that forces a user into the two-column display and make it display different HTML. This is the preferred approach, but it requires IDOC files or a component. This method is discussed further in Chapter 6 and Chapter 9.

Summary

For version 7.0 and older systems, HCSTs are commonly used to customize search, content info, and check-in pages. However, in version 7.5, the Content Profiles functionality eliminates the need for many of these custom pages because it is possible to customize the look and feel of metadata pages with the Configuration Manager applet. However, HCSTs are still used for custom portal pages, custom workflow pages, or other pages that are too complex to be created with profiles. But most developers generally move away from HCSTs in favor of custom components, content profiles, or HCSPs.

CHAPTER 4

■ ■ ■

Using JSPs and Servlets in Stellent

In addition to IdocScript, the Content Server supports Java Server Page (JSP) syntax on Dynamic Server Pages, which enables web designers to create dynamic Content Server pages without much knowledge of IdocScript. This JSP integration is also helpful when adding content management functionality to existing JSP- and Servlet-based applications. For example, the Site Studio product enables you to create your applications with fragments of JSP code, if you prefer that over IdocScript.

A JSP/Servlet-based web application can be integrated with the Content Server in two ways. One way is to develop it in a remote Servlet container, such as Weblogic, WebSphere, or Tomcat. You can then execute Content Server services with Simple Object Access Protocol (SOAP) or the Stellent Content Integration Suite (CIS) for J2EE applications

The second method is to check-in JSPs to the Content Server and then run them with the embedded Tomcat server. Such applications use the `idcserver.ServerBean` object to execute Content Server services. The methods in this object can be used to perform requests, loop over or display the results, or execute arbitrary IdocScript. You can also bundle several JSPs and Servlets into a standard Web Archive (WAR) file, and deploy that to the Content Server.

Which way is correct for your application? That usually depends on how complex the web application is and how tightly integrated it needs to be with the Content Server.

If your web application requires any J2EE features not available in Tomcat 5, you should not use the Content Server to run your web application. Likewise, if it is a highly complex web application that rarely executes Content Server services, it is not recommended to run the web application inside the Content Server. It is best to deploy it to a separate application and connect to the Content Server when needed.

However, if your web application is fairly simple or if it is just a few dozen Servlets and JSPs, it is generally better to run it from the Content Server's core engine. It makes even more sense if the web application needs to frequently run Content Server services because the JSPs are executed in the same memory and processor as the Content Server. The network is not involved in transferring data from the Content Server to the Servlet container, which yields an obvious performance advantage. In addition, it is much easier to execute IdocScript and include resources on a JSP if it is rendered in the integrated Tomcat engine.

Executing services from a remote J2EE application server is an advanced topic beyond the scope of this book (it is covered briefly in Chapter 12). The other option, rendering JSP and Servlets from inside the Content Server, is presented in this chapter.

Initial Steps

When creating a JSP to connect to the Content Server, the first thing to do is upgrade your version of Tomcat. Unless you are running version 7.5, you should download Tomcat 5 from the Stellent support site. It's available for versions 6.2 and 7.1 and is compatible with the latest versions of Site Studio.

Second, you should create a new security group called JSP. Only administrators and developers should be given write access to this group, but allow read access for everyone.

Third, open the System Properties Editor. In the Server tab enable JSP execution for the JSP security group you just created. Click OK and then restart the Content Server.

To test that the Tomcat engine is working properly, check-in a sample WAR file, such as the one that ships with Tomcat. To deploy this WAR file, simply check it into the JSP security group. To enable it, you must navigate to the JSP web application administration page from the standard administration page. It should look like Figure 4-1.

Figure 4-1. *JSP web application administration page*

Click the arrow icon to start the web application; then click on the link to go to the deployed web application. When the web application is started, the contents of the WAR file are extracted to the weblayout directory.

The Tomcat engine is launched internally by the Content Server. To alter its configuration, modify the server.xml or web.xml files located in this directory:

```
stellent/shared/jspserver/conf/
```

If you are using Content Server version 7.5 or later, or an older version with the Tomcat 5 component, these configuration files are located here instead:

```
stellent/data/jspserver/conf/
```

The Tomcat 5 component is highly recommended because it fixes a lot of bugs and adds newer features. It also has more robust logging and output of generated Java files in the following directories:

```
stellent/data/jspserver/logs/
stellent/data/jspserver/webapps/
stellent/data/jspserver/work/
```

Each deployed WAR file can have the standard `WEB-INF` directory for Java classes, packaged Java libraries, and XML configuration files. In addition, each JSP-enabled security group will have its own `WEB-INF` directory. To use a JSP tag library system-wide, it needs to be manually deployed to this directory. In the current example, this folder is located here:

```
stellent/weblayout/groups/jsp/WEB-INF/
```

For example, to deploy the Apache Struts framework globally, simply copy the contents of a `WEB-INF` directory of a Struts web application and place it in this folder. This content includes all libraries, class files, TLDs, and XML files. It is also necessary to restart the Content Server. Now any JSP checked-in to the `JSP` security group can use features from the Struts framework.

The key to integrating a JSP with the Content Server is the very small `idcserver` package. This package contains only four classes, the most useful being `ServerBean` and `ServerResultSet`. The former contains all the methods needed to run service requests and handle response data. The latter can be used to loop over any result set returned. See Appendix F for more information about these objects.

Simple JSPs

A hello page in JSP can be done in the same straightforward manner as a Hypertext Content Server Template (HCST). The `ServerBean` object must first be initialized and then it can be used to evaluate IdocScript code. The source for the JSP Hello Page looks like this:

```
<%@ page import = "idcserver.*" %>
<jsp:useBean id="sb" class="idcserver.ServerBean" />
<%
    sb.init(request);
    String user = sb.evalIdcScp("UserName");
%>
<html>
<head></head>
<body>
<h1>Hello <%=user%>!</h1>
</body>
</html>
```

Save this text to a file named `hello.jsp`. Next, check it into the Content Server with a security group of `JSP`. When you navigate to the `weblayout` URL for this JSP, the results look like Figure 4-2.

Figure 4-2. *Simple Hello User JSP*

For a more complex hello page that includes the standard look and feel, a bit more code is needed. The standard resource includes std_page_begin, std_page_end, body_def, and std_html_head_declarations can be referenced from a JSP like so:

```
<%@ page import = "idcserver.*" %>
<jsp:useBean id="sb" class="idcserver.ServerBean" />
<%
    sb.init(request);
    String user = sb.evalIdcScp("UserName");
%>
<html>
<head>
<title>Hello</title>
<%= sb.evalResInc("std_html_head_declarations")%>
</head>
<%= sb.evalResInc("body_def")%>
<%= sb.evalResInc("std_page_begin")%>

<h1>Hello <%=user%></h1>

<%=sb.evalResInc("std_page_end") %>
</body>
</html>
```

This code yields a hello page with the standard look and feel (see Figure 4-3):

Figure 4-3. *Hello User JSP with standard layout*

It is important to mention that dynamichtml resource includes cannot contain JSP code; only IdocScript is rendered inside an include. If you want to use a framework of JSP fragments, you should use one specific to JSPs. Both Apache Struts and Java Server Faces can be used as a framework using the latest Tomcat Integration.

Search Results Portal

As mentioned earlier, it is possible to execute a Content Server service from a JSP. One way to do this is to use the method ServerBean.evalIdcScp, which executes any IdocScript code that you need. To run a scriptable service, simply pass in code containing the executeService function.

However, the ServerBean can be used to create much more powerful integrations. Because a JSP execution is restricted by security group, the Content Server allows JSP to do things not possible with IdocScript. For example, the method ServerBean.parseExecuteService can be used to execute any service whatsoever. Check-in, update, delete—anything that is required. Later samples cover the check-in process. This example covers the more basic requirements for running a search.

The parseExecuteService method takes a URL encoded string that contains the parameters required to execute the service. When run, the service parameters are extracted from the string, and the service is executed. The results are stored in the ServerBean object. Values can be pulled from it by using the getLocal or getResultSet methods. The evalIdcScp method can also be used to generate HTML from IdocScript passed in the method.

A simple JSP portal page that executes a search looks like this:

```
<%@ page import="idcserver.*" %>
<jsp:useBean id="sb" scope="page" class="idcserver.ServerBean" />
<%
    sb.init(request);
    String str = "IdcService=GET_SEARCH_RESULTS" +
        "&SearchEngineName=DATABASE";
    String queryText = sb.getLocal("QueryText");
    if (queryText == null)
        queryText = "dDocTitle LIKE '%test%'";
    str = str + "&QueryText=" + queryText;
    sb.parseExecuteService(str);
    ServerResultSet results = sb.getResultSet("SearchResults");
%>
<html>
<head>
<title>Search</title>
</head>
<body>

<h3>Test Documents</h3>

<%
    for (results.first(); results.isRowPresent(); results.next())
```

```
        {
            String url = results.getStringValue("URL");
            String title = results.getStringValue("dDocTitle");
            out.println("<li><a href='" + url + "'>" + title + "</a>");
        }
%>

</body>
</html>
```

This is very similar to the search portal for an HCST, which was presented in the previous chapter. However, the service is executed with parseExecuteService. The results are extracted from the bean as a ServerResultSet object. We iterate over the results with the next and isRowPresent methods. We can extract values from the current row with the method getStringValue. There are other ways to iterate over the results and extract values. See Appendix F for more details.

The resulting HTML looks exactly the same as the HCST search portal (see Figure 4-4).

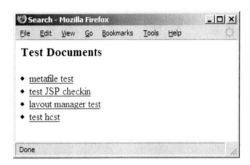

Figure 4-4. *Simple JSP search portal*

Like the HCST, if a value for QueryText is passed in the URL to this JSP, it automatically becomes available in the local data. The value is extracted with the getLocal method; if it exists, it is used.

Advanced Search Page

It is also possible to create a more complex search page with JSPs. For example, you can enable the user to execute a search based on specific metadata fields and give the page the standard look and feel.

Following is the code needed to display an advanced search page in JSP:

```
<%@ page import = "idcserver.*" %>
<jsp:useBean id="sb" class="idcserver.ServerBean" />

<html>
<head>
```

```
<%
    sb.init(request);
    // create a title for the page based on if the user is logged in
    String pageTitle = "Guest Search Page";
    if (sb.evalIdcScp("IsLoggedIn").equals("1"))
        pageTitle = "Search Page For " + sb.evalIdcScp("UserName");
    sb.putLocal("PageTitle", pageTitle);
%>
<%=sb.evalResInc("std_query_html_head_declarations")%>
<script language="JavaScript">
<%=sb.evalResInc("query_form_submit_script") %>
</script>
</head>

<%= sb.evalResInc("body_def")%>
<%= sb.evalResInc("std_page_begin")%>

<h3 class=pageTitle>JSP Search Page</h3>

<form name="QUERYTEXTCOMPONENTS">
<input type=hidden name="QueryText" value="">
<table>
<tr>
    <td align=right><span class=searchLabel>Title</span></td>
    <td>
        <input type="hidden" name="opSelected"
            value="hasAsSubstring">
        <input type="text" size=30 name="dDocTitle" value="">
    </td>
</tr>
<tr>
    <td align=right><span class=searchLabel>Content ID</span></td>
    <td>
        <input type="hidden" name="opSelected"
            value="hasAsSubstring">
        <input type="text" size=30 name="dDocName" value="">
    </td>
</tr>
<tr>
    <td align=right><span class=searchLabel>
        Release Date From</span></td>
    <td align=left>
        <input type="hidden" name="opSelected" Value="dateGE">
        <input type="text" size=12 name="dInDate" value="">
        <span class=searchLabel>To</span>
        <input type="hidden" name="opSelected" Value="dateLess">
        <input type="text" size=12 name="dInDate" value="">
```

```
        </td>
    </tr>
    <tr>
        <td align=right><span class=searchLabel>Full Text</span></td>
        <td><input type="text" name="FullTextSearch" size=30></td>
    </tr>
    </table>
</form>

<form name="SEARCHFORM" method="GET"  action="jsp-search-results.jsp">
<input type=hidden name="QueryText" value="">
<input type=hidden name="ResultCount" value="5">
<input type=hidden name="ftx" value="">
<table>
<tr>
    <td><span class=searchLabel>Sort By:</span></td>
    <td><select name="SortField">
        <option selected  value="dInDate">Release Date
        <option  value="dDocTitle">Title
        <option  value="Score">Score
        </select>
    </td>
    <td><select name="SortOrder">
        <option value="Asc">Ascending
        <option selected value="Desc">Descending
        </select>
    </td>
    <td>
    <input type=submit value ="Search" onClick="submitFrm(false)">
    </td>
</tr>
</table>
</form>

<%=sb.evalResInc("std_page_end") %>

</body>
</html>
```

Save this code into a file named jsp-search.jsp and check it into the JSP security group. Make sure to set Content ID to jsp-search during the check-in.

The rendered page looks like Figure 4-5, which is similar to the Advanced Search HCST from Chapter 3. This JSP uses the same core includes, but references them with evalIdcScp instead of include.

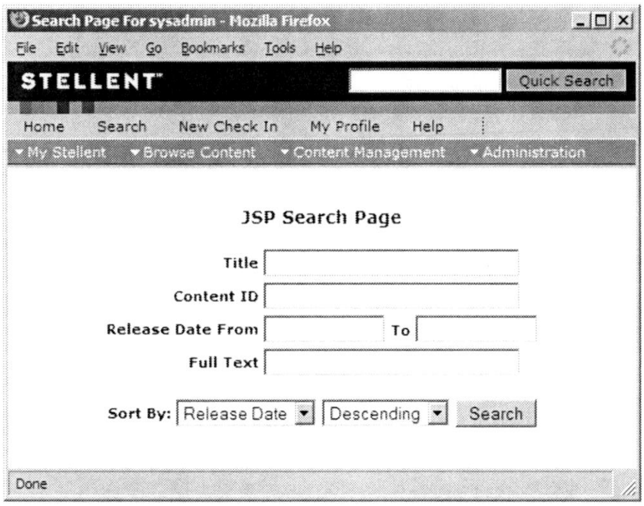

Figure 4-5. *Advanced JSP search form*

This page has two forms: QUERYTEXTCOMPONENTS and SEARCHFORM. The first form contains all the parameters used to build up the QueryText parameter; the second one contains all the parameters used in the search itself. When you click Search, the JavaScript function submitFrm is executed, which generates the QueryText based on the fields in QUERYTEXTCOMPONENTS. This functions is defined in the include query_form_submit_form_function, which is referenced deep inside the include std_query_html_head_declarations. Refer to the Advanced Search example in Chapter 3 for more information about these resources.

One difference between the HCST and the JSP is the action attribute for the SEARCHFORM, which is set to jsp-search-results.jsp. In the Advanced Search HCST, the action is set to the Content Server's HttpCgiPath. In that case, the search is executed by the Content Server, and the results are rendered with the template corresponding to the parameter urlTemplate. Unfortunately, the urlTemplate parameter does not work with JSPs.

Instead, this action attribute is set to the URL jsp-search-results.jsp. When the form is posted, this result page must execute the service and display the results.

To create the result page, first save the following code to the file jsp-search-results.jsp. Check it into the Content Server with the same security group and content type as the previous page. Make sure that it has the content ID jsp-search-results so the action attribute points to the correct URL.

```
<%@ page errorPage="error.jsp" session="true" %>
<%@ page import="java.util.*" %>
<%@ page import="idcserver.*" %>
<jsp:useBean id = "sb" scope="page" class="idcserver.ServerBean" />
<%
    sb.init(request);
    sb.parseExecuteService("IdcService=GET_SEARCH_RESULTS");
    ServerResultSet results = sb.getResultSet("SearchResults");
%>
```

```
<html>
<head>
<%
    // create a title for the page based on if the user is logged in
    String pageTitle = "Guest Search Results Page";
    if (sb.evalIdcScp("IsLoggedIn").equals("1"))
    {
        pageTitle = "Search Results For " +
        sb.evalIdcScp("UserName");
    }
    sb.putLocal("PageTitle", pageTitle);
%>
<%= sb.evalResInc("searchapi_result_html_head_declarations")%>
</head>

<%= sb.evalResInc("searchapi_result_body_def")%>
<%= sb.evalResInc("std_page_begin") %>

<h3 class=pageTitle>JSP Search Results Page</h3>

<p>Found <%=sb.getLocal("TotalRows")%> results.</p>

<%
    // determine if there are more search results, if so, show back
    // and forward buttons
    int resultCount = Integer.parseInt(sb.getLocal("ResultCount"));
    int total = Integer.parseInt(sb.getLocal("TotalRows"));

    if (resultCount < total)
    {
        // the base URL for a query
        String urlBase = "search-results.jsp?" +
            "SortOrder=" + sb.getLocal("SortOrder") +
            "&SortField=" + sb.getLocal("SortField") +
            "&ResultCount=" + sb.getLocal("ResultCount") +
            "&QueryText=" + sb.getLocal("QueryText");

        int startRow = Integer.parseInt(sb.getLocal("StartRow"));
        int endRow = Integer.parseInt(sb.getLocal("EndRow"));
        int pageNumber =
            Integer.parseInt(sb.getLocal("PageNumber"));
        int numPages = Integer.parseInt(sb.getLocal("NumPages"));
        if (numPages > 1)
        {
            if (pageNumber > 1)
            {
                String prevUrlSuffix = "&StartRow=" +
```

```
                    (startRow-resultCount) +
                    "&EndRow=" + (endRow-resultCount) +
                    "&PageNumber=" + (pageNumber-1);

                out.print("[<a href=\"" + urlBase +
                    prevUrlSuffix + "\">PREV</a>]");
            }
            if (pageNumber < numPages)
            {
                String nextUrlSuffix = "&StartRow=" +
                    (startRow+resultCount) +
                    "&EndRow=" + (endRow+resultCount) +
                    "&PageNumber=" + (pageNumber+1);
                out.print("[<a href=\"" + urlBase +
                    nextUrlSuffix + "\">NEXT</a>]");
            }
        }
    }

    String httpCgiPath = sb.evalIdcScp("HttpCgiPath");
    String httpWebRoot = sb.evalIdcScp("HttpWebRoot");
%>


<br><br>

<table border='1' cellpadding='0' cellspacing='3' width='540'>
<%
    for (results.first(); results.isRowPresent(); results.next())
    {
%>
    <tr>

    <td align='left'>
        <a href='<%=results.getStringValue("URL")%>'>
        <%=results.getStringValue("dDocName")%></a>
    </td>

    <td>
        <b><%=results.getStringValue("dDocTitle")%></b><br>
        Release Date: <%=results.getStringValue("dInDate")%><br>
        Author: <%=results.getStringValue("dDocAuthor")%>
    </td>

    <td align='center' width='50'>
        <a href='<%=httpCgiPath%>?IdcService=DOC_INFO&dID=<%=
            results.getStringValue("dID")%>'>
        <img src='<%=httpWebRoot%>/images/stellent/InfoIcon_sm.gif'
            border='0'>
```

```
        </a>
    </td>

    </tr>
<%
    } // end for loop
%>
</table>

<%= sb.evalResInc("std_page_end") %>

</body>
</html>
```

At the top of this page, we `init` the `ServerBean` object and then immediately call `parseExecuteservice`. Notice that we only need to pass in the `IdcService` into `parseSearchResults` because the `init` call places any data in the URL into the `ServerBean` object as local data. This local data is automatically used when the service is executed.

Next, we extract the `SearchResults` into a `ServerResultSet` object. We also extract the flags `ResultCount` and `TotalRows`. If more total rows exist than we can display on one page, we need to generate navigation links. Similar to the HCST, we generate simple `NEXT` and `PREV` links to go to the next or previous search results page. The URLs to these pages is similar to the URL to the current page. The only parameter that needs to be different is `StartRow`. The parameters `EndRow` and `PageNumber` are passed along for convenience.

Finally, we loop over the `SearchResults` and extract values for display. This is done in a fashion similar to the previous example.

Running a search from the JSP search page yields a result page like Figure 4-6.

Figure 4-6. *Advanced search results JSP*

Additional JSPs of use are Content Information JSPs or ones to display Workflow information. You can also use JSPs to display content directly in a web page. For more advanced pages, such as check-in and update, we need to execute service calls in a different way.

Custom Check-In Pages

A custom contribution page in JSP is very similar to the custom page in an HCST. Just like a search page, the check-in form can be very simple or very complex. It can be just a title field and a file upload field, or it can contain custom metadata fields and option lists.

For this example, we create a check-in page that looks very similar to the standard check-in page and then discuss ways to modify it. To begin, create the page jsp-checkin.jsp with the following code. Check it into the Content Server in the JSP security group with the Content ID jsp-checkin:

```jsp
<%@ page import="idcserver.*" %>
<%@ page import="java.util.*" %>
<jsp:useBean id = "sb" scope="page" class="idcserver.ServerBean" />
<%
    // initialize the server bean object
    sb.init(request);
    sb.putLocal("PageTitle", "Check In");
    sb.putLocal("isNew", "1");
%>
<html>
<head>
    <%= sb.evalResInc("std_checkin_html_head_declarations")%>
</head>

<%= sb.evalResInc("body_def")%>
<%= sb.evalResInc("std_page_begin") %>

<%
    // execute a service call to load the custom metadata info,
    // and content types
    sb.parseExecuteService("IdcService=GET_DOC_CONFIG_INFO");

    // this is the location of the current JSP
    String fileUrl = sb.getLocal("fileUrl");

    // this is the location of the confirm page to redirect to,
    // after the checkin is complete. Note that we have to pass the
    // 'dDocName' in the redirect URL so that we can access its value
    // on the redirected page
    String redirectUrl = fileUrl.substring(0,
        fileUrl.lastIndexOf("/")) + "/jsp-checkin-confirm.jsp?" +
        "dDocName=<$dDocName$>&dID=<$dID$>&" +
        "dDocTitle=<$dDocTitle$>";
%>
```

```html
<h3>JSP Check In</h3>

<p>This check-in page gives the JSP developer total control over which
metadata fields to display, and how to format the HTML.</p>

<form name="Checkin" method="post" enctype="multipart/form-data"
    action="<%=sb.evalIdcScp("HttpCgiPath")%>">

<!-- prefilled default values... you can place other default
    values here for metadata such as 'dDocType' and 'dSecurityGroup'
    to make specialized contribution pages -->
<input type=hidden name="IdcService" value="CHECKIN_NEW">
<input type=hidden name="dDocAuthor" value="<%=sb.evalIdcScp("UserName")%>">
<input type=hidden name="dRevLabel" value="1">
<input type=hidden name="RedirectUrl" value="<%=redirectUrl%>">

<table>

<!-- This field is optional if auto numbering is turned on for
    the Stellent Content Server.  -->
<tr>
    <td>Content ID</td>
    <td><input type="text" name="dDocName" size=35 maxlength=30
        value="">
    </td>
</tr>
<tr>
    <td>Type</td>
    <td>
        <select name="dDocType">
<%
    ServerResultSet types = sb.getResultSet("DocTypes");
    for (types.first(); types.isRowPresent(); types.next())
    {
        out.println("<option value='" +
            types.getStringValue("dDocType") + "'>" +
            types.getStringValue("dDescription"));
    }
%>
        </select>
    </td>
</tr>
<tr>
    <td>Title</td>
    <td><input type="text" name="dDocTitle" size=35    maxlength=30>
    </td>
</tr>
```

```
<tr>
    <td>Security Group</td>
    <td>
        <select name="dSecurityGroup">
<%
    Vector v = sb.getOptionList("securityGroups");
    if (v != null)
    {
        Enumeration en = v.elements();
        while (en.hasMoreElements())
            out.println("<option>" + (String)en.nextElement());
    }
%>
        </select>
    </td>
</tr>
<tr>
    <td><hr></td><td><hr></td>
</tr>
<tr>
    <td>File</td>
    <td><input type="file" name="primaryFile" maxlength=250>
    </td>
</tr>

<!-- custom metadata section -->
<%
    ServerResultSet metaDefs = sb.getResultSet("DocMetaDefinition");
    for (metaDefs.first(); metaDefs.isRowPresent(); metaDefs.next())
    {
        String name = metaDefs.getStringValue("dName");
        String caption = sb.evalIdcScp("lc(dCaption)");

        // this simple string will only show the metadata field and
        // its caption, giving the developer total control over HTML
        //String simple = "<tr>\n<td>" + caption + "</td>\n" +
        //    "<td><input name='" + name + "'></td>\n</tr>";
        //out.println(simple);

        // this string will leverage internal includes to display
        // option lists, as well as hide fields that are configured
        // to be hidden
        String advanced =
            sb.evalIdcScp("inc('std_meta_field_display')");
        out.println(advanced);
    }
%>
```

```
<tr>
    <td><hr></td><td><hr></td>
</tr>
<tr>
    <td align=center colspan=2>
    <input type=submit name=submit value=" Check In ">
    <input type=reset name=reset value=" Reset ">
    </td>
</tr>
</table>
</form>

<%= sb.evalResInc("std_page_end") %>

</body>
</html>
```

This page is very similar to the check-in HCST from Chapter 3. It uses the same includes and a generally similar structure. When rendered, it looks like Figure 4-7.

First, notice how the Checkin HTML form is structured. The action is set to the standard HttpCgiPath, which means that the request is processed by the core Content Server. The enctype must be multipart/form-data to signify a file upload.

Figure 4-7. *JSP check-in form*

The required parameters for a check-in are dDocAuthor, dRevLabel, dDocType, dDocTitle, dSecurityGroup, and primaryFile. The parameters dDocName and dDocAccount might be required, depending on your server's settings. All other parameters are optional.

One parameter of interest is the RedirectUrl parameter. After a successful check-in, the service redirects to the URL in that parameter. In our case, we want to redirect to the page jsp-checkin-confirm.jsp. To display this page properly, we need to pass in the value for dID and dDocName, which are generated based on the data in the response. Any data not explicitly passed in this URL is not available.

Other interesting parameters are the custom metadata fields, which are present in the result set DocMetaDefinition. This result set is loaded onto the page with the include std_doc_page_definitions, which is referenced in the include std_checkin_html_head_declarations.

Similar to the check-in HCST, there are two ways to render metadata form fields on the page. The simple way is to create a basic row with the caption and an input field. This method works fine for text fields, but becomes difficult when using option lists.

The better way to render metadata form fields on the page is to include the resource std_meta_field_display, which allows you to use the standard Content Server logic for displaying metadata fields. This includes the complex logic needed to display Schema-based dependent choice lists, content profiles, and other features.

If you want to display option lists with custom code, you need to extract an option list manually and iterate over it. For example, for the field Country, you can obtain the option list with the following code:

```
<%
    Vector v = sb.getOptionList("xCountry.options");
%>
```

The Vector contains String objects containing the values in the option list. However, doing it in the previous fashion does not allow you to use the 7.0 Schema architecture for option lists or dependent choice lists. So its use is discouraged.

It is possible, if not complicated, to use the Schema API directly on a JSP to render an option list. You can do this with pure JavaScript, not the complicated IdocScript of JSP code. This topic is covered in more detail in Chapter 9.

After the user clicks Check In on the form, the data is submitted to the Content Server for processing with the CHECKIN_NEW service. This service redirects to a confirmation page if successful. Instead of using the default confirmation page, this form sets the parameter RedirectUrl, which causes the service to redirect to a custom confirmation page.

Because this page displays only a confirmation message, the source code is fairly simple:

```
<%@ page import="idcserver.*" %>
<jsp:useBean id = "sb" scope="page" class="idcserver.ServerBean" />
<%
    sb.init(request);
    sb.putLocal("PageTitle", "Check In Confirmation");
%>
<html>
<head>
    <%= sb.evalResInc("std_html_head_declarations")%>
</head>
<%= sb.evalResInc("body_def")%>
```

```
<%= sb.evalResInc("std_page_begin") %>

<h3>Check In Confirmation</h3>

<p>Successfully checked-in content item:
<a href="<%=sb.evalIdcScp("HttpCgiPath")
    %>?IdcService=DOC_INFO&dID=<%=sb.getLocal("dID")%>">
<%=sb.getLocal("dDocName")%></a></p>

<%= sb.evalResInc("std_page_end") %>

</body>
</html>
```

This redirect page, like `jsp-search-results.jsp`, must be checked-in to the Content Server with the same security group and content type as `jsp-checkin.jsp`. It must also have a content ID of `jsp-checkin-confirm`. The value for `RedirectUrl` on the check-in page must be the full URL to this JSP, plus some IdocScript containing any parameters you want to pass to the page. In this case, the values for `dDocName` and `dID` must be set in the URL as well.

This page looks like Figure 4-8, which is very similar to the HCST check-in confirmation page.

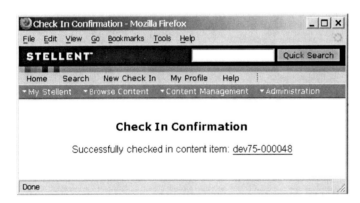

Figure 4-8. *JSP check-in confirmation page*

This same structure can be applied to any service that supports the `RedirectUrl` parameter, such as `SUBSCRIBE`, `UPDATE_DOCINFO_BYFORM`, and `WORKFLOW_APPROVE`. For more information about which services support the `RedirectUrl` parameter, see Appendix E.

Best Practices

Security is the most important issue with JSPs. Because IdocScript is a language specific to HTML rendering and delivery, there are very few security problems exposed by allowing all contributors to check-in Dynamic Server Pages. However, because a poorly designed or malicious JSP can crash even the most robust server, it is absolutely vital to allow only JSP developers to have write access to JSP-enabled security groups.

It is also important to remember that the content info page exposes a link to download the native file for any content item. By using this link, a user can download the raw source code of a JSP, which might not be a problem unless secure information such as JDBC passwords for external databases are hard coded in the JSPs. This is not standard practice on JSPs and is strongly discouraged, but it sometimes happens.

There are two solutions to this problem. One is to configure the Content Server to restrict native file download to only those who have write access to that security group. This is a system-wide setting and it restricts users to just the file that is rendered or converted into the weblayout directory. For JSPs, this means that they will only be able to access the rendered HTML, not the source code. This is the recommended solution.

If that is not feasible, all JSPs must be sanitized. All passwords should be offloaded into XML files. Any special business logic that you want to protect should be compiled into a JAR file and the source code should be obfuscated. This JAR file can be deployed along with the JSPs in a WAR file, or it can be manually placed in the WEB-INF directory for the specific security group.

Debugging a JSP can also be tricky. If you have access to the console output of the server, and you are running version 7.5, the following JSP code dumps the context of the request and the response to the console:

```
<%
    sb.evalIdcScp("trace('#all', 'debugTrace')");
    out.println(sb.getLocal("debugTrace"));
%>
```

If you are instead running version 7.1 or older, the context needs to be manually read and output to the console. All result sets need to be explicitly looped over as well:

```
<%
    out.print(sb.getEnvironment().toString());
    out.print(sb.getLocalData().toString());

    Enumeration e = serverbean.getResultSetList();
    while(e.hasMoreElements())
    {
        String name = (String)e.nextElement();
        ServerResultSet srs = sb.getResultSet(name);
        out.print("\n\n" + name + ":\n");

        int numFields = srs.getNumFields();
        for (srs.first(); srs.isRowPresent(); srs.next())
        {
            out.print("------\n");
            for (int i=0; i<numFields; i++)
            {
                out.print(srs.getFieldName(i) + ": " +
                    srs.getStringValue(i) + "\n");
            }
        }
    }
%>
```

When making repeated small changes to the JSP in an attempt to fine-tune the look and feel of a page, the web-based check-in–check-out cycle might become tedious. In this situation, the Stellent WebDAV integration might be preferable. Then the entire check-in–check-out cycle can be done from Windows Explorer. See Chapter 12 for a discussion of this product.

You need not put Java code into a JSP to integrate it with the Content Server. A Servlet can also use the methods in the ServerBean object. It simply needs to be created and initialized with the HttpServletRequest object that is present in all Servlets.

Summary

JSPs are the primary choice for Content Server developers who want to write custom pages, but do not want to use IdocScript. Using JSPs gives you more control because Java allows a web developer to do more than standard IdocScript. You can even extend the JSP support with custom Servlets, tag libraries, or third-party JSP frameworks.

Using JSPs does not limit your abilities to use Content Server resources. You can still execute service requests, run IdocScript functions, and include Content Server resources from your JSP. This is mostly important when you want to create check-in or search pages with JSPs, but you still want them to be configurable with the Content Server administration applets.

Whichever you choose, IdocScript or JSP, the Content Server gives you a powerful framework for running custom applications.

CHAPTER 5

■ ■ ■

Using HCSPs and HCSFs

As mentioned in Chapter 2, Hypertext Content Server Pages (HCSPs) and Hypertext Content Server Forms (HCSFs) are very similar to Hypertext Content Server Templates (HCSTs). The differences are subtle but important:

- An HCSP/F contains XML-formatted IdocScript instead of standard IdocScript.

- An HCSP/F is used to process business forms and encapsulate the submitted data as XML.

XML IdocScript syntax looks different from the syntax used on HCSTs and in resources. For example, the Hello User sample looks like this:

```
<h1>Hello <!--$UserName--></h1>
```

The preceding code is fully valid XML because the IdocScript tags are embedded in HTML comments. This makes the code more portable, but has its drawbacks. In an HTML editor, such as Dreamweaver or FrontPage, the code is invisible in WYSIWYG mode. Alternatively, you can use square brackets to contain the code:

```
<h1>Hello [!--$UserName--]</h1>
```

This change enables XML IdocScript to appear in WYSIWYG mode so it can be edited more easily. See Appendix A for more information on XML IdocScript.

The most powerful feature of HCSPs and HCSFs is their capability to be used as simple data entry forms. These forms, which are known as *HTML forms*, enable contributors to create data processing forms without any knowledge of scripting languages or databases.

For example, assume that your accounting department wants to reduce paper and make greater use of web-based forms. Specifically, it wants all employees to fill out a special purchase request for all items costing more than $1000.

To accomplish this, the accountant could create an HCSF with the relevant fields and check it into the Content Server. When a user views this HCSF in a web browser, she sees an HTML form with several fields and a Submit button. This user then fills out the form and clicks Submit. As mentioned in Chapter 2, once an HCSF is submitted, the Content Server generates a new HCSP content item based on that HCSF. The server saves the submitted data as XML, embedded at the top of the HCSP.

The accountant needs only a basic understanding of IdocScript to create this form. Even if the accountant knows nothing about IdocScript, he can use the Contribution Template Editor to create the HCSF.

Table 5-1 lists all IdocScript-based Dynamic Server Pages (DSPs).

Table 5-1. *Hypertext Content Server Page Types*

Type	Description
HCST	A basic template. Similar to an HTML page, but can also execute IdocScript code.
HCSF	Similar to HCST, but uses XML IdocScript. When the SUBMIT_HTML_FORM service is executed with an HCSF, it creates a copy of itself and checks in the copy as a new HCSP content item. This HCSP contains the submitted data embedded in XML.
HCSP	The most common type, it uses XML IdocScript, similar to HCSF. When the SUBMIT_HTML_FORM service is executed with an HCSP, it creates a new revision of this HCSP and updates the data in it.
HCSW	An XML-formatted file used exclusively by the Web Forms Editor, discussed later. The Content Server processes this file into an HCSF.

Using an HTML form is superior to simple database entry because the submitted XML file is processed exactly as if it were a check-in of a new item. The item can be routed through business rules with workflows or subscriptions. You can even specify rules about how long the form must be stored if you have the Records Management application installed.

Placing your form data into an HCSP enables you to manage the life cycle of the form. For example, you can create a special workflow for all purchase requests, which can route to different people based on the purchase amount. Perhaps the purchase requires only the approval of the user's boss, or perhaps the order is large enough that it needs CFO approval as well.

The XML content is indexed into the search engine. Users can search for phrases and do not need to know which fields the phrase was entered into. For example, you might have several forms for managing customer information (for example, purchase requests, customer support requests, and contact information). To find all forms that explicitly or implicitly mention that customer, all you need to do is run a full-text search for that customer's unique identifier.

And finally, the form data is revision-controlled, as are all items in the server. If you update the form data, you do not delete the existing data. Instead, you create a new revision of the form with the new data.

The primary disadvantage of placing data in XML format is performance. It is much faster to run reports on content if they are in a well-formatted database table. To obtain the best of both worlds, you could create a customization to how the form data is saved. For example, you could customize the service request to store specific data in the database in addition to processing the form. See Chapter 11 for more information on Java customizations and database connections.

In a typical request, an HTML form is processed in the following way:

1. The SUBMIT_HTML_FORM service is called with the parameter SourceID.

2. The Content Server loads up the content item with a dID equal to SourceID from the vault.

3. The XML data in this form is modified, and a new content item is created.

4. If the form is an HCSF, this new item will become a completely new content item with a new content ID.

5. If the form is an HCSP, this new item will be checked-in as a new revision of the current item using the same content ID.

There are many ways to design these data entry forms. The standard practice is to place as little logic as possible in the HCSP. Use them as just the wrapper for the XML data and place all logic in Components or IDOC files, which ensures that the data for the form is stored separately from the display logic. This is a general best practice that makes forms more forward compatible.

The best practices for creating forms will be covered in Chapter 6. In this chapter, we will be covering only the basics.

HTML Form Designer Tools

What if your users are completely unfamiliar with IdocScript and HTML, and you do not have time to train them? In this case, you need a tool that helps your users draw a form as easily as drawing an HTML page. Stellent offers two such tools, and others are available from third-party vendors.

The first form designer tool from Stellent was the Contribution Template Editor, or CTE. It is useful for creating basic forms, but lacks advanced features. It is available as a free download from Stellent.

At the time of this writing, Stellent is about to release a more powerful tool, tentatively called the Web Forms Editor. This editor is a web-based tool that allows a designer to create a business form by drawing it on an HTML page. It is more powerful than the CTE and it works on most platforms because it is written in JavaScript and HTML.

If you choose to use a form designer to create simple HCSPs, you can skip this chapter. However, if you want to understand the underlying technology so you can create advanced forms, continue reading for some tips, tricks, and step-by-step examples (Chapter 6 covers additional tricks and best-practices for advanced forms).

Useful Variables on HCSPs and HCSFs

Similar to an HCST and a Java Server Page (JSP), an HCSP is rendered with a call to the GET_DYNAMIC_URL service, which returns some information about the metadata for the item, as well as global configuration data and option lists. This information includes the result sets DocTypes, DocFormats, as well as custom metadata option lists. See Appendix E for more information about this service.

In addition to the standard response data, HCSFs and HCSPs have the following parameters returned by the GET_DYNAMIC_URL service:

ref:dDocType: The content type for this document.

ref:dDocName: The content name for this document.

ref:dExtension: The web extension (HCSF or HCSP) of this document.

ref:dSecurityGroup: The security group for this document.

ref:hasDocInfo: True if some content information is available on the page.

ref:isLatestRevision: True if the current item is the most recently released revision.

idcformrules:isFormFinished: Set to true if no more revisions of an HCSP should be allowed. An HCSP can be continually resubmitted until this flag is set.

idcformrules:resultsets: A comma-separated list of result sets in the form. Generally there is only one, as in the case of the comments forms.

SourceID: The dID of this content item.

fileUrl: A URL to this item relative to the root of the web server, such as /groups/public/adacct/sample.hcsp.

The ref: prefix is used to signify a parameter relating to the document being referenced. Some of these parameters should be submitted in the SUBMIT_HTML_FORM service. Others are needed only when designing complex HTML forms.

Designing Simple HTML Forms

Even the simplest HCSF must contain modest amounts of XML IdocScript to properly display the values of the form fields. Following is an example of a very basic HCSF to allow a user to submit a form that contains only a title and some data. The code will be explained in detail later:

```
<html>
<head>

<!--$include std_html_head_declarations-->

<!--$idcbegindata-->
<idcformrules />
<formTitle></formTitle>
<formData></formData>
<!--$idcenddata-->
</head>

<!--$include body_def-->
<!--$include std_page_begin-->

<!--$c="Determine if this is the original HCSF or the HCSP, and if so
    make every field read only. Otherwise, if it's the original HCSF,
    only make the date and author fields read only."-->
<!--$if ref:dExtension like "hcsp" -->
    <!--$isHcsp = 1-->
    <h3>Submitted Data From Simple Form</h3>
<!--$else-->
    <h3>Simple Form</h3>
```

```
    <p>This page will allow a user to fill out a form, and check the
    data into the Content Server.</p>
<!--$endif-->

<form name="SimpleForm" method="POST" action="<!--$HttpCgiPath-->">
<input type=hidden name="IdcService" value="SUBMIT_HTML_FORM">
<input type=hidden name="dID" value="<!--$SourceID-->">
<input type=hidden name="isFormFinished" value="1">
<input type=hidden name="FormDocTitleScript"
value="&lt;$UserName &amp; '-' &amp; formTitle$&gt;">
<table>

<!--$c="If this is the original HCSF, show a form, otherwise it is
        a HCSP, so just show the data."-->
<!--$if isHcsp-->
    <tr>
        <td>Title:</td>
        <td><!--$formTitle--></td>
    </tr>
    <tr>
        <td>Data:</td>
        <td><!--$formData--></td>
    </tr>
<!--$else-->
    <tr>
        <td>Title:</td>
        <td><input name="formTitle" size="50"></td>
    </tr>
    <tr>
        <td>Data:</td>
        <td><textarea name="formData" rows="8"
            cols="40"></textarea></td>
    </tr>
    <tr>
        <td colspan=2 align=center>
            <input type=submit>  
            <input type=reset>
        </td>
    </tr>
<!--$endif-->
</table>
</form>

<!--$include std_page_end-->

</body>
</html>
```

This form contains all the code for the HCSF and for the HCSP item that is generated when the HCSF is submitted. It looks different depending on whether it is a form or a content item. When viewed from a web browser, it looks like Figure 5-1.

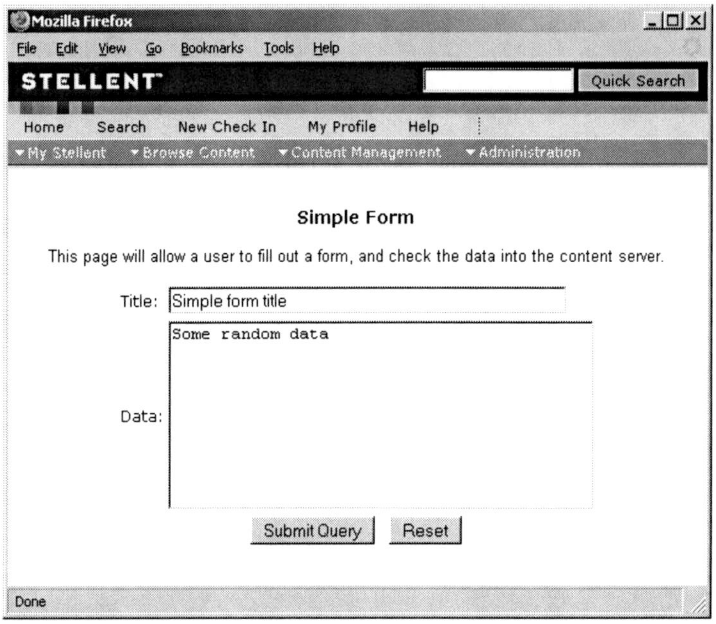

Figure 5-1. *Simple HCSF*

Notice the XML nodes at the beginning of the page, between the flags idcbegindata and idcendata:

```
<!--$idcbegindata-->
<idcformrules />
<formTitle></formTitle>
<formData></formData>
<!--$idcenddata-->
```

These nodes represent the XML *data island* on an HCSF/P. For HCSFs, it contains empty XML nodes; in this case, they are nodes named formTitle and formData. When you submit this HCSF, the Content Server generates a new HCSP content item and fills form data into these nodes.

So how does the Content Server fill data into these nodes? To fill these nodes with data, it must be submitted in the SUBMIT_HTML_FORM request. For example, you must pass in the parameters formTitle and formData to properly submit this form. Note that the names of the nodes in the XML data island coincide exactly with the names of INPUT fields in the form SimpleForm. On an HCSF, the form code looks like this:

```
<form name="SimpleForm" method="POST" action="<!--$HttpCgiPath-->">
<input type=hidden name="IdcService" value="SUBMIT_HTML_FORM">
<input type=hidden name="dID" value="<!--$SourceID-->">
<input type=hidden name="isFormFinished" value="1">
<input type=hidden name="FormDocTitleScript"
value="&lt;$UserName &amp; '-' &amp; formTitle$&gt;">
<table>

...

    <tr>
        <td>Title:</td>
        <td><input name="formTitle" size="50"></td>
    </tr>
    <tr>
        <td>Data:</td>
        <td><textarea name="formData" rows="8"
            cols="40"></textarea></td>
    </tr>
    <tr>
        <td colspan=2 align=center>
            <input type=submit>  
            <input type=reset>
        </td>
    </tr>
```

Most of the parameters on this form are used to control how the form is processed in the SUBMIT_HTML_FORM service. The dID parameter is the only required parameter for this service; it is needed to locate the HCSF content item that originated the request. The rest of the hidden form fields are optional and discussed later.

However, the visible form fields, named formTitle and formData, are special. Notice that they coincide with the names of the empty XML nodes in the original HCSF.

When this HCSF is submitted, the content server loads the original HCSF from the vault. It uses the values for formTitle and formData in the request to generate a new XML data island and saves the result to an HCSP. Finally, it checks in the generated HCSP as a new content item.

Most of the metadata for the new HCSP is the same as the original HCSF. Naturally, the Content Name and Content ID must be different. In addition, the values for dDocAuthor, dDocTitle, and dInDate are typically different. The date field is set to the date when the HCSF was submitted, and the author field is whoever submitted the form.

By default, the title field is autogenerated with the following script:

```
<$dDocAuthor$> - <$dDocType$> - <$dateCurrent()$>
```

If you do not explicitly set dDocTitle in a form field, the generated HCSP has a title in that format.

There are several methods to change the way the title is generated. The first way is to change the name of the field formTitle to simply dDocTitle. That way, the title is based on user input on the form.

The second alternative is to set a value for FormDocTitleScript in the form. This is used in HCSF processing to generate a title for the new HCSP. The previous example does precisely this: it assembles the title based on the user name and the user input value for formTitle, which is equivalent to the following script:

```
<$UserName$> - <$formTitle$>
```

So on the HTML form, we have the following input field:

```
<input type=hidden name="FormDocTitleScript"
    value="&lt;$UserName &amp; '-' &amp; formTitle$&gt;">
```

Note that on an HCSF, the IdocScript needs to be XML-encoded so that it will not be processed immediately on the HCSF. It will be decoded and executed once the form is submitted.

A third alternative is to use the DataScript parameter, which is a convenience field used to execute any IdocScript you wish. It can be used to set metadata fields or to alter data in the HTML form. For example, you can use the following input field instead of the FormDocTitleScript field:

```
<input type=hidden name="DataScript" value="&lt;$dDocTitle=
    UserName &amp; '-' &amp; formTitle $&gt;">
```

After the new HCSP is created, the server redirects to a confirmation page like Figure 5-2. Similar to HCST and JSP, the parameter RedirectUrl can be used to redirect to a custom confirmation page.

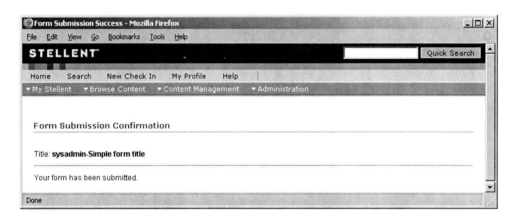

Figure 5-2. *Simple HCSF submit confirmation page*

The form is displayed differently, depending on the value for ref:dExtension. In the preceding case, the extension is hcsf, so the form fields are displayed. After being submitted, the new extension is hcsp, so only the values for the metadata are displayed. When viewed from the web, it looks like Figure 5-3.

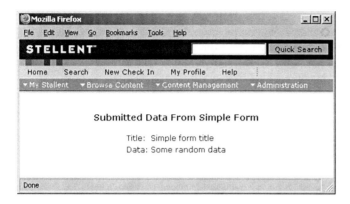

Figure 5-3. *HCSP created by the simple HCSF*

The submitted HCSP is based on the contents of the original HCSF. If you view the native document, they look almost identical. The only difference is the XML data island between idcbegindata and idcenddata. In the original HCSF, the data is mostly blank:

```
<!--$idcbegindata-->
<idcformrules />
<formTitle></formTitle>
<formData></formData>
<!--$idcenddata-->
```

If you view the vault file for the submitted HCSP, you see the form data encoded in XML:

```
<!--$idcbegindata-->
    <idcformrules jcharset="Cp1252" isFormFinished="true" encoding="iso-8859-1"/>
    <formTitle>Simple form title</formTitle>
    <formData>Some random data</formData>
<!--$idcenddata-->
```

These node values were pulled from the parameters in the request. Likewise, when the HCSP is rendered in a web browser, the XML data is extracted and put into the local data, which enables us to use the following code to display it:

```
<!--$if isHcsp-->
    <tr>
        <td>Title:</td>
        <td><!--$formTitle--></td>
    </tr>
    <tr>
        <td>Data:</td>
        <td><!--$formData--></td>
    </tr>
<!--$else-->
...
<!--$endif-->
```

Because the HCSP is valid XML, all data in the submitted form will be available in the full text search index. In other words, this HCSP would appear in the results of a full text search for *simple form title*. This feature is extremely useful to find unstructured data in submitted forms, such as information in large text fields or comments threads.

The XML data can be easily extracted from the HTML form with the `IsXml` parameter. A URL similar to the following:

```
http://localhost/stellent/groups/public/documents/adacct/000021.hcsp?IsXml=1
http://localhost/stellent/idcplg?IdcService=GET_FILE&dID=25&Rendition=Web&IsXml=1
http://localhost/stellent/idcplg?IdcService=GET_DYNAMIC_URL&IsXml=1&➥
    fileUrl=%2Fstellent%2Fgroups%2Fpublic%2Fdocuments%2Fadacct%2F000021.hcsp
```

returns an XML page with the following contents:

```
<?xml version="1.0" encoding="iso-8859-1"?>
<idcformwrapper>
<SourceID>25</SourceID>
<TemplateClass>IdcDynamicFile</TemplateClass>
<TemplateType>hcsp</TemplateType>

    <idcformrules jcharset="Cp1252" isFormFinished="true" encoding="iso-8859-1"/>
    <formTitle>Simple form title</formTitle>
    <formData>Some random data</formData>

</idcformwrapper>
```

By using an XML parser, it is possible to extract the submitted form data to display HCSP data on any remote application server. It is also possible to execute the `SUBMIT_HTML_FORM` service from a remote application server to submit the form.

Likewise, because you can submit the form from any HTML page, it is relatively easy to add form processing capabilities to any Active Server Page (ASP), JSP, or Site Studio fragment. All that is needed is the `SourceID` of the HTML form. Setting the `RedirectURL` parameter helps redirect back to another page after the post is complete.

The node `idcformrules` contains information about how this form should be processed by the Content Server. It contains encoding information, and the flag `isFormFinished` set to `true`, which ensures that the form cannot be processed again. It is a one-time process, in which the HCSF creates one HCSP.

It is also possible to have an HCSP in which the values are updated numerous times, such as a discussion thread. To do this, we need to always set `isFormFinished` to `false` and always show a form field (this is discussed in the next example).

Designing Comments Forms

A common form used on the web is one that allows a user to add comments to a piece of content. This is trickier than the previous example because not only are you storing name-value pairs of content but also a list of items that are repeatedly updated. Although this data can be stored in XML, translating from XML to parameters in a request requires a bit more effort.

```
<html>
<head>
<!--$PageTitle="sample discussion thread", isNew=1-->
<!--$include std_checkin_html_head_declarations-->
<!--$idcbegindata-->
    <idcformrules resultsets="comment" />
<!--$idcenddata-->
</head>

<!--$include body_def-->
<!--$include std_page_begin-->

<form name="SubmitThread" method="POST" action="<!--$HttpCgiPath-->">
<input type=hidden name="IdcService" value="SUBMIT_HTML_FORM">
<input type=hidden name="dID" value="<!--$SourceID-->">
<input type=hidden name="RedirectUrl" value="<!--$fileUrl-->">
<table>
<!--$ isInfoOnly=1 -->
<!--$loop comment-->
    <tr>
        <td colspan=2><b><!--$comment!author--></b>
            [<!--$comment!date-->]</td>
    </tr>
    <tr>
        <td colspan=2><b><!--$comment!title--></b></td>
    </tr>
    <tr>
        <td colspan=2><!--$comment--></td>
    </tr>
    <tr>
        <td colspan=2><hr></td>
    </tr>
<!--$endloop-->

<!--$isInfoOnly="", isEditMode=1-->
<!--$fieldName="comment!author", fieldCaption="<b>Author:</b>",
    fieldValue=UserName, isInfoOnly=1 -->
<!--$include std_display_field-->

<!--$fieldName="comment!title", fieldCaption="<b>Title:</b>"-->
<!--$include std_display_field-->

<!--$fieldName="comment", fieldCaption="<b>Comment:</b>", fieldType="Memo"-->
<!--$include std_display_field-->

<!--$fieldName="comment!date", isHidden=1, fieldValue=dateCurrent()-->
<!--$include std_display_field-->
```

```
    <tr>
        <td colspan=2 align=center><input type=submit>  
        <input type=reset></td>
    </tr>

</table>
</form>
</body>
</html>
```

Similar to the previous form, this code contains XML data in the `idcbegindata`/`idcenddata` section. It contains one single node: `idcformrules`. This node contains information about how the form should be processed by the Content Server. It can contain encoding information, the `isFormFinished` flag, or the `resultset` attribute. That attribute tells the Content Server that some data in this form will be appended to a new row in the `comment` result set and saved as XML on this page.

Because the flag `isFormFinished` is never set in the request, this HCSP can be submitted multiple times. Each submission creates a new revision of this HCSP and checks it into the Content Server. After a few submissions, the page looks like Figure 5-4.

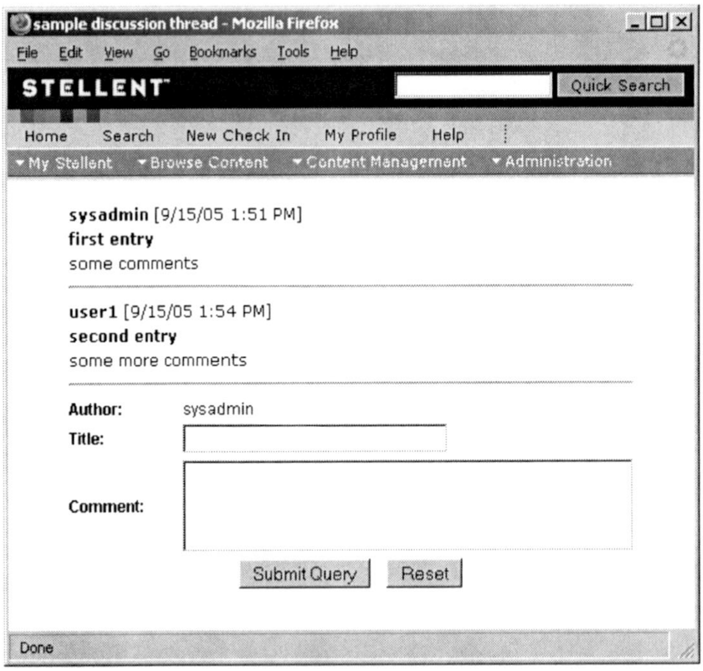

Figure 5-4. *Discussion thread HCSP*

The embedded XML in this HCSP is this:

```
<!--$idcbegindata-->
    <idcformrules jcharset="Cp1252" resultsets="comment"
        isFormFinished="false" encoding="iso-8859-1"/>
    <comment>some comments
        <date>9/15/05 1:51 PM</date>
        <author>sysadmin</author>
        <title>first entry</title></comment>
    <comment>some more comments
        <date>9/15/05 1:54 PM</date>
        <author>user1</author>
        <title>second entry</title></comment>
<!--$idcenddata-->
```

In most situations in which an HCSP is resubmitted, the form data is overwritten with the new data. This rule does not apply to parameters in a result set: the new parameters are appended as new rows instead of overwriting existing fields.

The result set parameters need to be have a very specific format. Because XML is a hierarchical structure, we need to encode the parameter names to represent the depth. To do this, we encode the node depth with the exclamation point character (!) and an attribute with the colon character (:).

For example, to have author and title fields inserted into the comment result set, the input fields names need to be named comment!author and comment!title.

To extract attributes from the idcformrules node, we need to use the colon:

```
<!--$getValue("#active", "idcformrules:isFormFinished")-->
```

After a submit, the XML in the page is full text indexed by the Verity search engine. On a busy system, this process might take several seconds—or even several minutes. The data is already processed and checked-in, but it will not become the latest revision until the indexer is complete. This delay is usually not a problem with most HTML forms, but when you have a discussion thread it becomes noticeable.

One way around this problem is to use the RedirectURL parameter to forward the user to a different page after posting a discussion thread. For example, the GET_FILE service can be used to redirect to the most recent web rendition of a piece of content, regardless of whether it's been fully indexed:

```
<input type="hidden" name="RedirectURL"
    value="<!--$HttpCgiPath-->?IdcService=GET_FILE&dDocName=<!--$
    ref:dDocName-->&Rendition=Web&RevisionSelectionMethod=Latest"
```

Using this input field ensures that the most recent file is displayed after a new comment has been added, which makes the correct form data appear. There are limitations, however. Because we used the GET_FILE service to obtain this HCSP, the ref: flags are not available. Instead, we can use dDocName and dID on these pages if absolutely necessary.

Localized Date Formats in HTML Forms

One other thing to notice about the XML data is that all fields, including the date field, are stored as strings. Although this is fine if all users are in the same country and locale, it can become complicated if you need to support multiple date format.

You can use the parseDate IdocScript function to parse a date string into a date object and then localize it as needed. However, even this procedure has complications. What if you create this file with a German date format and then archived it to another server that doesn't support German? What if you want to download the raw XML from this form and import it into a different application? In both cases, it is likely that the date strings will be unreadable and you will lose an important piece of information.

The best option when storing dates in multilingual environments is to use the Java Database Connectivity (JDBC) date format, which is an open standard supported by all Java applications and most web-based applications. On an HCSP, you can use the formatDateDatabase function to convert a date string into a JDBC date string. In this case, change the lines that output the date field to this:

```
<!--$fieldName="comment!date", isHidden=1,
    fieldValue=formatDateDatabase(dateCurrent())-->
<!--$include std_display_field-->
```

When displayed on a page, the JDBC date string looks something like this:

```
{ts &#39;2005-09-15 11:05:40.181&#39;}
```

Naturally, this date format looks terrible. It should be placed in a hidden input field, so the user need not see it. To display this string into a human-readable format, use the parseDate function. In this case, change the lines that output the author and date field to this:

```
<tr>
    <td colspan=2><b><!--$comment!author--></b>
        [<!--$parseDate(comment!date)-->]</td>
</tr>
```

Because the value for the date field is JDBC-formatted, the parseDate function always works, which ensures that people in multiple countries with multiple date formats can all view the same form, and the dates will always be legible.

Forms to Generate Comment Forms

By itself, a form that allows comments is not particularly useful. Every user who wants to open a discussion on a topic needs to create an individual HCSP and check it into the Content Server. What is more useful is an HCSF that creates these HCSPs for the purposes of creating a discussion on a particular topic.

For example, many times users need to fill out forms that require some kind of feedback, such as a travel request, an IT help request, or a purchase request. When one of these forms is filled out, it can trigger a workflow or subscription, notifying the person who needs to respond. The feedback to the form is kept with the form as a series of comments. After the issue is resolved, the form can be closed.

For this example, we will make a form that contains information about a specific customer and a product by combining elements from the first two pages to create a hybrid. The
finished form looks like this:

```
<html>
<head>
<!--$if title-->
    <!--$PageTitle=title-->
<!--$else-->
    <!--$PageTitle="Comments Maker Form"-->
<!--$endif-->

<!--$isCheckin=1-->
<!--$include std_doc_page_definitions-->
<!--$include std_html_head_declarations-->

<!--$idcbegindata-->
<idcformrules resultsets="comment" />
<title></title>
<originalAuthor></originalAuthor>
<creationDate></creationDate>
<customerName></customerName>
<productName></productName>
<details></details>
<!--$idcenddata-->
</head>

<!--$include body_def-->
<!--$include std_page_begin-->

<!--$c="Determine if this is the original HCSF or the HCSP, and if so
    make every field read only. Otherwise, if it's the original HCSF,
    only make the date and author fields read only."-->
<!--$if ref:dExtension like "hcsp" -->
    <!--$isHcsp = 1-->
<!--$endif-->
<!--$if isTrue(getValue("#active", "idcformrules:isFormFinished"))-->
    <!--$isFormFinished=1-->
<!--$endif-->

<!--$if isHcsp -->
    <h3>Comments Page</h3>
<!--$else-->
    <h3>Comments Page Creator</h3>

    <p>This page will create a new discussion thread page based
on some information about a specific customer and product.</p>
<!--$endif-->
```

```
<form name="CommentsPageForm" method="POST"
action="<!--$HttpCgiPath-->">
<input type=hidden name="IdcService" value="SUBMIT_HTML_FORM">
<input type=hidden name="dID" value="<!--$SourceID-->">
<table>

<!--$fieldName="originalAuthor",
    fieldCaption="<b>Original Author:</b>",
    fieldValue=UserName, isInfoOnly=1 -->
<!--$include std_display_field-->

<!--$fieldName="title", fieldCaption="<b>Discussion Title:</b>",
    isInfoOnly=#active.isHcsp-->
<!--$include std_display_field-->

<!--$fieldName="creationDate", fieldCaption="<b>Creation Date:</b>",
    isInfoOnly=1, fieldValue=dateCurrent()-->
<!--$include std_display_field-->

<!--$fieldName="customerName", fieldCaption="<b>Customer Name:</b>",
    isInfoOnly=#active.isHcsp -->
<!--$include std_display_field-->

<!--$fieldName="productName", fieldCaption="<b>Product Name:</b>",
    isInfoOnly=#active.isHcsp -->
<!--$include std_display_field-->

<!--$fieldName="details", fieldCaption="<b>Details:</b>",
    fieldType="Memo", isInfoOnly=#active.isHcsp -->
<!--$include std_display_field-->

<!--$c="If this is the original HCSF, no comments exist yet,
        so don't show the comments section"-->
<!--$if isHcsp-->

    <tr>
        <td colspan=2><hr></td>
    </tr>
    <tr>
        <td colspan=2><h3>Comments:</h3></td>
    </tr>
    <tr>
        <td colspan=2><hr></td>
    </tr>

<!--$isInfoOnly=1 -->
<!--$loop comment-->
```

```
        <tr>
            <td colspan=2><b><!--$comment!author--></b>
                [<!--$comment!date-->]</td>
        </tr>
        <tr>
            <td colspan=2><b><!--$comment!title--></b></td>
        </tr>
        <tr>
            <td colspan=2><!--$comment--></td>
        </tr>
        <tr>
            <td colspan=2><hr></td>
        </tr>
<!--$endloop-->

    <!--$if not isFormFinished-->
        <!--$isInfoOnly="", isEditMode=1-->
        <!--$fieldName="comment!author", fieldCaption="<b>Author:</b>",
            fieldValue=UserName, isInfoOnly=1 -->
        <!--$include std_display_field-->

        <!--$fieldName="comment!title", fieldCaption="<b>Title:</b>"-->
        <!--$include std_display_field-->

        <!--$fieldName="comment", fieldCaption="<b>Comment:</b>",
         fieldType="Memo"-->
        <!--$include std_display_field-->

        <!--$fieldName="comment!date", isHidden=1,
         fieldValue=dateCurrent()-->
        <!--$include std_display_field-->

        <!--$fieldName="isFormFinished", isHidden=1, fieldValue=0-->
        <!--$include std_display_field-->
    <!--$endif -->

<!--$endif -->

<!--$if isFormFinished-->
        <tr>
            <td colspan=2>Discussion on this topic is now closed.</td>
        </tr>
<!--$else-->
        <tr>
            <td colspan=2 align=center>
                <input type=submit value="Submit">  
                <input type=reset>  
```

```
        <!--$c="If this is a HCSP, show a button to allow
        the discussion to be ended"-->
        <!--$if isHcsp-->
            <input type=button value="Close Discussion"
            onClick="this.form.isFormFinished.value=1;
                    this.form.submit();">
        <!--$endif -->

        </td>
    </tr>
<!--$endif-->

</table>
</form>

<!--$include std_page_end-->

</body>
</html>
```

This form is very similar to the previous HCSP. It contains an XML data island with a result set, along with several global parameters. If the form is the original HCSF, we display input fields for those global values. If not, we just show the data for those fields, along with a comments form. The original HCSF looks like Figure 5-5, and the subsequent HCSP looks like Figure 5-6.

Figure 5-5. *Comments Maker HCSF*

Figure 5-6. *HCSP generated by Comments Maker HCSF*

The text of this page is a copy of the original HCSF, but with the data encapsulated in the XML data island. The top of the page looks like this:

```
<!--$idcbegindata-->
    <idcformrules jcharset="Cp1252" isFormFinished="false"
        resultsets="comment" encoding="iso-8859-1"/>
    <title>sample discussion thread</title>
    <originalAuthor>user1</originalAuthor>
    <creationDate>9/19/05 5:08 PM</creationDate>
    <customerName>test customer</customerName>
    <productName>test product</productName>
    <details>This will be a discussion thread about a customer and product</details>
    <comment>comment 1
        <date>9/19/05 5:07 PM</date>
        <author>sysadmin</author>
        <title>title 1</title></comment>
```

```
    <comment>comment 2
        <date>9/19/05 5:08 PM</date>
        <author>user1</author>
        <title>title 2</title></comment>
<!--$idcenddata-->
```

This discussion continues until the Close Discussion button is clicked. At this point the flag isFormFinished is set, and no new revisions of this HCSP can be submitted. If at a later date you want to reopen this discussion, you need to check-out the HCSP and manually remove that flag.

Instead of using the variable isFormFinished, some people use a custom flag, such as isFormCompleted. This flag can be stored in the XML data island like any other form field. The difference is that a discussion can be reopened at a later date without requiring the user to manually edit the XML data.

On this form we also switched from using simple HTML form input fields to the std_display_field include, mentioned in the previous two chapters. By setting the flags fieldName, fieldCaption, and fieldType, we can easily get a standard look and feel for the input fields. This becomes even more important when we want to put option lists on HTML forms.

Option Lists on Forms

In the first example, the form data for the HCSF was mostly done with HTML. No core Content Server includes were needed to draw the form. This method is the easiest way to completely control how the HTML looks, but it is not forward compatible. If you want to alter the display of the formTitle field, dozens of HCSFs and HCSPs need to be modified.

In the last two examples, we instead used the include std_display_field. The field display was entirely controlled by this include: on an HCSF, it displayed a form field to fill out, whereas on an HCSP the current data was presented in a read-only manner. This include enables a uniform look and feel on the form, but restricts each form field to a single table row.

At first glance, using the std_display_field include may appear to be too restrictive. What if you do not want the standard two-column look and feel? What if, for example, you want to put two input fields in the same table row? You can do this by using std_display_field, but it requires a slightly different approach (covered in more detail in Chapter 6).

But why go through all the extra work? Why not just always hard-code the HTML? One additional reason to always use std_display_field is to automatically leverage the existing Content Server logic to display metadata fields. For example, if you wanted to display an option list for a custom metadata field, it is much easier to do so with the std_display_field include. You also gain the benefits of the schema architecture for dependent choice lists and Content Profiles with this include. Therefore, it is in your best interests to use std_display_field as much as possible.

For example, to display the content type and security group metadata fields on an HCSF, all that we need is the following code:

```
<!--$fieldName="dSecurityGroup", fieldCaption="<b>Security Group:</b>",
    fieldIsOptionList=1, optionListName="securityGroups",
    noSchema=1, isInfoOnly=#active.isHcsp -->
```

```
<!--$include std_display_field-->

<!--$fieldName="dDocType", fieldCaption="<b>Content Type:</b>",
    fieldIsOptionList=1, optionListResultSet="DocTypes",
    isInfoOnly=#active.isHcsp -->
<!--$include std_display_field-->
```

You can place the preceding code anywhere on an HCSF to allow the user to set the Content Type and Security Group for the submitted HCSP.

The list for dSecurityGroup is in an option list named securityGroups. To display this list, we set the flag optionListName. We also need to set the flag fieldIsOptionList=1, as well as noShema=1. Doing so ensures that the code is displayed based on the option list data alone.

The list for dDocType is not in an optionList object; it is in a result set named DocTypes. So we have to set the flag optionListResultSet instead of noSchema=1.

This code must be slightly altered if using a custom metadata field. In that case, the option list name will be xFieldName.options. For example, if we had a custom metadata field named Country that was an option list, we could place it on the form with this code:

```
<!--$fieldName="xCountry", fieldCaption="<b>Country:</b>",
    fieldIsOptionList=1, optionListName = "xCountry.options",
    noSchema=1,    isInfoOnly=#active.isHcsp -->
<!--$include std_display_field-->
```

The previous code works only if the field is based on a simple option list. If your field is based on a database table and a schema view, your code must be slightly different. As long as we use the std_display_field include, it is still easy to display a schema-based option list or a dependent choice list. We need a handful of other includes at the top and bottom of the page to define the correct schema support functions and link to the correct JavaScript resources:

```
<!--$include std_doc_page_definitions-->
<!--$include std_html_head_declarations-->

...

<!--$fieldName="xCountry", fieldCaption="<b>Country:</b>",
    fieldIsOptionList=1, isInfoOnly=#active.isHcsp -->
<!--$include std_display_field-->

<!--$fieldName="xState", fieldCaption="<b>State:</b>",
    fieldIsOptionList=1, isInfoOnly=#active.isHcsp -->
<!--$include std_display_field-->

<!--$fieldName="xCity", fieldCaption="<b>City:</b>",
    fieldIsOptionList=1, isInfoOnly=#active.isHcsp -->
<!--$include std_display_field-->

...
<!--$include std_page_end-->
```

The includes (std_page_end, std_doc_page_definitions, and std_html_head_declarations) were already present in the original Comments Maker HCSF. So adding support for the standard Country/State/City dependent choice list is very easy.

We can even create custom ResultSets with IdocScript and use them for option lists. For example, let's say we have only three product names: alpha, beta, and gamma. They aren't from a custom metadata field and they do not exist as an option list. To add a totally custom option list on the fly, create a comma-separated string of the option list values. Then use rsMakeFromString to create a new named result set, which creates an option list with one field named row. All the values in the string are put into separate rows in the result set.

By setting the flag optionListKey="row", we can iterate over it in nearly the same way as for Content Types:

```
<!--$productNameString="alpha,beta,gamma"-->
<!--$rsMakeFromString("PRODUCT_NAME_RSET", productNameString)-->
<!--$fieldName="productName", fieldCaption="<b>Product Name:</b>",
    fieldIsOptionList=1, noSchema=1, optionListKey="row",
    optionListResultSet="PRODUCT_NAME_RSET",
    isInfoOnly=#active.isHcsp -->
<!--$include std_display_field-->
```

The end result is a form with input fields in option lists (see Figure 5-7).

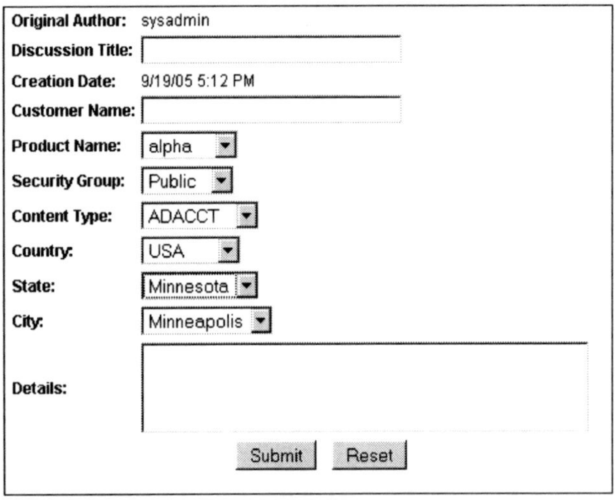

Figure 5-7. *Comments Maker HCSF with option lists*

Updating and Deleting Values on a Form

In addition to simply adding new values to the form, the existing values can be updated or deleted. Unlike a database, when this happens the old content does not disappear. Instead, a new revision of the HCSP is generated with the new values.

Updating standard values on an HCSP is simple. Until the flag `isFormFinished` is passed in the request, an HCSP can be resubmitted multiple times. Each submit creates a new HCSP, with updated values in the XML data island. For example, you could update the Customer Name or Product Name on the previous HCSPs. All that is required is an HTML `INPUT` tag with the proper name from the `idcbegindata` section:

```
<input type="text" name="productName"
    value="<!--$productName-->">
<input type="text" name="customerName"
    value="<!--$customerName-->">
```

Updating or deleting values that are in result sets is more difficult. We can use code like this to append a new row to the result set:

```
<input type="text" name="comment"
    value="<!--$comment-->">
<input type="text" name="comment!title"
    value="<!--$comment!title-->">
```

However, to update a specific field, we need to also indicate the result set row number in the request parameter. The Content Server uses the # character in an HCSP to indicate a specific row. For example, to modify the values for `comment` and `title` in the first row, we need form data like this:

```
<input type="text" name="comment#0"
    value="new comment">
<input type="text" name="comment!title#0"
    value="new title">
```

To delete a row, all the values must be set to blank. For example, to delete the first row entirely, use the following code:

```
<input type="hidden" name="comment#0" value="">
<input type="hidden" name="comment!title#0" value="">
<input type="hidden" name="comment!date#0" value="">
<input type="hidden" name="comment!author#0" value="">
```

In practice, we can add both update and delete functionality with a handful of JavaScript functions. The new Comments Maker HCSF now looks like the following:

```
<html>
<head>
<!--$if title-->
    <!--$PageTitle=title-->
<!--$else-->
    <!--$PageTitle="Comments Maker Form"-->
<!--$endif-->

<!--$isCheckin=1-->
<!--$include std_doc_page_definitions-->
```

```
<!--$include std_html_head_declarations-->

<script>
var g_suffix = "";
function resetFields(frm, index, comment, title, date, author)
{
    var field = frm.elements["comment" + g_suffix]
    field.name = "comment#" + index;
    field.value = comment;
    var field = frm.elements["comment!title"  + g_suffix]
    field.name = "comment!title#" + index;
    field.value = title;
    var field = frm.elements["comment!date" + g_suffix]
    field.name = "comment!date#" + index;
    field.value = date;
    var field = frm.elements["comment!author" + g_suffix]
    field.name = "comment!author#" + index;
    field.value = author;
    g_suffix = "#" + index;
}
function deleteFields(frm, index)
{
    resetFields(frm, index, "", "", "", "");
    frm.submit();
}
function updateFields(frm, index, comment, title, date, author)
{
    resetFields(frm, index, comment, title, date, author);
    frm.elements["Submit"].value = "Update Entry";
}
function sortFields(list)
{
    var index = list.selectedIndex;
    if (index < 0)
        return;
    var sortField = list.options[index].value;
    var newUrl = window.location.toString();

    var extIndex = newUrl.indexOf(".hcsp");
    newUrl = newUrl.substring(0, extIndex+5) +
        "?SortField=" + sortField;
    window.location.replace(newUrl);
}
</script>
```

```
<!--$idcbegindata-->
<idcformrules resultsets="comment" />
<title></title>
<originalAuthor></originalAuthor>
<creationDate></creationDate>
<customerName></customerName>
<productName></productName>
<details></details>
<!--$idcenddata-->
</head>

<!--$include body_def-->
<!--$include std_page_begin-->

<!--$c="Determine if this is the original HCSF or the HCSP, and if so
        make every field read only. Otherwise, if it's the original HCSF,
        only make the date and author fields read only."-->
<!--$if ref:dExtension like "hcsp" -->
    <!--$isHcsp = 1-->
<!--$endif-->
<!--$if isTrue(getValue("#active", "idcformrules:isFormFinished"))-->
    <!--$isFormFinished=1-->
<!--$endif-->

<!--$if isHcsp -->
    <h3>Comments Page</h3>
<!--$else-->
    <h3>Comments Page Creator</h3>

    <p>This page will create a new discussion thread page based on some
    information about a specific customer and product.</p>
<!--$endif-->

<form name="CommentsPageForm" method="POST" action="<!--$HttpCgiPath-->">
<input type=hidden name="IdcService" value="SUBMIT_HTML_FORM">
<input type=hidden name="dID" value="<!--$SourceID-->">
<table>

<!--$fieldName="originalAuthor", fieldCaption="<b>Original Author:</b>",
    fieldValue=UserName, isInfoOnly=1 -->
<!--$include std_display_field-->

<!--$fieldName="title", fieldCaption="<b>Discussion Title:</b>",
    isInfoOnly=#active.isHcsp-->
<!--$include std_display_field-->
```

```
<!--$fieldName="creationDate", fieldCaption="<b>Creation Date:</b>",
    isInfoOnly=1, fieldValue=dateCurrent()-->
<!--$include std_display_field-->

<!--$fieldName="customerName", fieldCaption="<b>Customer Name:</b>",
    isInfoOnly=#active.isHcsp -->
<!--$include std_display_field-->

<!--$fieldName="productName", fieldCaption="<b>Product Name:</b>",
    isInfoOnly=#active.isHcsp -->
<!--$include std_display_field-->

<!--$fieldName="details", fieldCaption="<b>Details:</b>", fieldType="Memo",
    isInfoOnly=#active.isHcsp -->
<!--$include std_display_field-->


<!--$c="If this is the original HCSF, no comments exist yet,
        so don't show the comments section"-->
<!--$if isHcsp-->

    <tr>
        <td colspan=2><hr></td>
    </tr>
    <tr>
        <td colspan=2><h3>Comments:</h3></td>
    </tr>
    <tr>
        <td colspan=2><hr></td>
    </tr>

<!--$if SortField-->
    <!--$rsSort("comment", SortField)-->
<!--$endif-->
<!--$isInfoOnly=1, index=0 -->
<!--$loop comment-->
    <tr>
        <td colspan=2><b><!--$comment!author--></b> [<!--$comment!date-->]</td>
    </tr>
    <tr>
        <td colspan=2><b><!--$comment!title--></b></td>
    </tr>
    <tr>
        <td colspan=2><!--$comment--></td>
    </tr>
```

```
    <tr>
        <td colspan=2>
            <input type="button" value="Delete This Entry"
                onClick="deleteFields(this.form, <!--$index-->);">
                <input type="button" value="Update This Entry"
                    onClick="updateFields(this.form, <!--$index-->,
                    '<!--$js(comment)-->',
                    '<!--$js(comment!title)-->',
                    '<!--$js(comment!date)-->',
                    '<!--$js(comment!author)-->');">
        </td>
    </tr>
    <tr>
        <td colspan=2><hr></td>
    </tr>
    <!--$index = index + 1 -->
<!--$endloop-->

  <!--$if not isFormFinished-->
    <!--$isInfoOnly="", isEditMode=1-->
    <!--$fieldName="comment!author", fieldCaption="<b>Author:</b>",
        fieldValue=UserName, isInfoOnly=1 -->
    <!--$include std_display_field-->

    <!--$fieldName="comment!title", fieldCaption="<b>Title:</b>"-->
    <!--$include std_display_field-->

    <!--$fieldName="comment", fieldCaption="<b>Comment:</b>", fieldType="Memo"-->
    <!--$include std_display_field-->

    <!--$fieldName="comment!date", isHidden=1, fieldValue=dateCurrent()-->
    <!--$include std_display_field-->

    <!--$fieldName="isFormFinished", isHidden=1, fieldValue=0-->
    <!--$include std_display_field-->
  <!--$endif -->

<!--$endif -->

<!--$if isFormFinished-->
    <tr>
        <td colspan=2>Discussion on this topic is now closed.</td>
    </tr>
<!--$else-->
    <tr>
        <td colspan=2 align=center>
```

```
        <input type=submit name="Submit" value="Submit">  
        <input type=reset>  

    <!--$c="If this is a HCSP, show a button to allow the discussion
        to be ended"-->
    <!--$if isHcsp-->
        <input type=button value="Close Discussion"
        onClick="this.form.isFormFinished.value=1; this.form.submit();">
        Sort By:
        <select name="SortOrder" onChange="sortFields(this);">
            <option>
            <option value="comment">comment
            <option value="comment!title">title
            <option value="comment!date">date
            <option value="comment!author">author
        </select>
    <!--$endif -->
    </td>
 </tr>
<!--$endif-->

</table>
</form>

<!--$include std_page_end-->

</body>
</html>
```

This code uses essentially the same IdocScript as the previous example. The main additions are the Delete This Entry and Update This Entry buttons present on each comment. Both of them call the resetFields function, which changes both the names and the values for the input fields.

When you click the Delete This Entry button for the first post, the deleteFields function resets the names of the form INPUT fields. Specifically, it appends the suffix #0 to the names. It also sets their values to blank and submits the form. Because all the fields are blank, the row will be deleted entirely from the HCSP.

When you click the Update This Entry button for the first post, a similar process occurs. The updateFields function changes the names of the form fields by appending the suffix #0 and then updates their values with the values from the first post. It also changes the text of the Submit button to Update Entry. After the user modifies the values and clicks Update Entry, the new HCSP will contain updated values for that one row.

This form also contains a sorting feature (see Figure 5-8). By using the rsSort IdocScript function, you can sort the comment result set on any of its fields in many different ways. In this case, we pull the value for SortField out of the URL and do a simple sorting on that field. At the bottom of the page there is a Sort By drop-down list that sets the proper value and reloads the page.

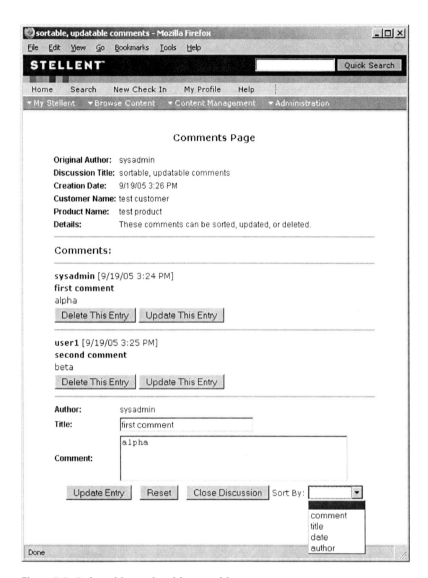

Figure 5-8. *Deleteable, updatable, sortable comments page*

Summary

HTML forms can be used as a simple tool for business process management. A person does not need extensive programming experience to create complex forms that then are processed through workflows or subscriptions. The fact that it uses XML as its core data storage means that it can easily be used by external applications for data processing.

It is also highly advantageous to place the form data into your full-text search index, which enables you to execute one search to look for a word in any one of the form fields.

For example, to search for the word `alpha` in all of the forms, you simply need the following QueryText:

```
alpha
```

If you want to narrow the search to just find instances of `alpha` in the `title` field, you can use the following Verity search query:

```
"alpha" <IN> title
```

Note that the preceding HTML forms contain both XML data and business logic. This is undesirable because it doesn't allow for a sufficient separation of layers. What if at some point in the future you want to change the look and feel of the HTML form? Because the display logic is embedded with the form data, it would require the updating of every HCSP and HCSF in the system.

A better approach is to use resource includes as much as possible, which can be accomplished with a component or with an IDOC file. The latter approach is common for HCSPs and is the subject of Chapter 6.

Leveraging IDOC Resources

An IDOC file cannot be used by itself to render HTML code; instead, it is used to define HTML and IdocScript resources that can be included on other Dynamic Server Pages. These resources take the form of `dynamichtml` includes and are formatted the same as component resource files.

A Dynamic Server Page can use includes defined in the core, and ones defined in a component. So why define includes with IDOC files? The main advantage is that you do not need to be an administrator to check-in an IDOC file—any contributor can. For example, an ordinary user can create an IDOC file with resources and then reference them on custom Hypertext Content Server Pages (HCSPs).

Another advantage is that IDOC files are not global; they are included dynamically on an HCSP, after which any defined resources become available. An HCSP can define the same include differently on separate pages. For example, it might not be desirable to override `std_page_begin` on all pages, but it can be vital for one specific HCSP. A developer then redefines `std_page_begin` in an IDOC file and loads the IDOC when needed.

An IDOC file is structured the same as a standard resource definition file. These files are then checked-into the Content Server with a verbose Content ID. Then a Dynamic Server Page executes the function `docLoadResourceInclude` with that Content ID. After that, those resources can be included on the page.

IDOC Pages and Portals

To begin, let's start with a simple HCSP:

```
<html>
<head>
    <!--$include std_html_head_declarations-->
</head>

<!--$include body_def-->
<!--$include std_page_begin-->

<p>Content of the portal page</p>
```

```
<!--$include std_page_end-->
</body>
</html>
```

This code includes the resources defined in the core and displays a page with the standard look and feel, like the one in Figure 6-1.

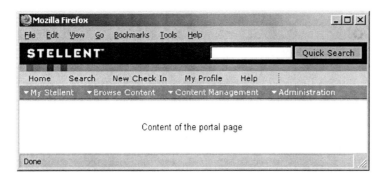

Figure 6-1. *Basic HCSP portal*

To rebrand this page with a different look and feel, we need to redefine the includes std_page_begin and std_page_end. Create the file user_portal_page.idoc with the following contents:

```
<html>
<body>

<@dynamichtml std_page_begin@>
<table width="100%" cellpadding=0 cellspacing=0>
<tr>
    <td style="background:red"> 
    </td>
    <td style="background:red;color:white">
        <h1>USER PORTAL PAGE</h1>
    </td>
</tr>
<tr>
    <td style="color:red">
        link1<br>link2<br>link3<br>link4<br>link5
    </td>
    <td>
<@end@>

<@dynamichtml std_page_end@>
    </td>
</tr>
```

```
</table>
<@end@>

</body>
</html>
```

This example overrides the resources std_page_begin and std_page_end with some generic HTML. Check this into the Content Server with the Content ID user_portal_includes.

Next, modify the HCSP to load the IDOC resource by placing the following line above the body_def include:

```
<!--$docLoadResourceIncludes("dDocName=user_portal_includes" join
    "&amp;RevisionSelectionMethod=LatestReleased")-->
```

Notice again that we use XML IdocScript on the HCSP. To be completely XML-compliant, we use the join operator and & string instead of using the & character, which ensures that any XML parser can view the HCSP.

The syntax of the docLoadResourceIncludes function is the same as the syntax for the GET_FILE service. It will accept a dID or a dDocName with a corresponding RevisionSelectionMethod. This function locates the most recently released content item with the Content ID user_portal_includes and loads the resources inside it.

Refreshing the HCSP returns a page like Figure 6-2 instead of the standard look and feel.

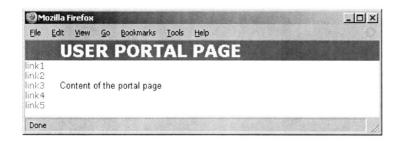

Figure 6-2. *User portal page*

Note that this change affects only the HCSP we created; it does not affect in any way the standard look and feel of the rest of the Content Server.

To rebrand this portal once more, all we need is another IDOC file. For example, we have one page for standard users and another for administrators. Create the file admin_portal_includes with the following contents:

```
<html>
<body>

<@dynamichtml std_page_begin@>
<table width="100%" cellpadding=0 cellspacing=0>
<tr>
    <td style="background:blue"> 
```

```
        </td>
        <td style="background:blue;color:white">
            <h1>ADMIN PORTAL PAGE</h1>
        </td>
    </tr>
    <tr>
        <td style="color:blue">
            link1<br>link2<br>link3<br>link4<br>link5
        </td>
        <td>
<@end@>

<@dynamichtml std_page_end@>
        </td>
    </tr>
    </table>
<@end@>

</body>
</html>
```

Check this IDOC file into the Content Server with the Content ID admin_portal_includes. Then modify the HCSP to conditionally load just one of the IDOC files, based on which user is viewing the page:

```
<html>
<head>
    <!--$include std_html_head_declarations-->
</head>

<!--$ if UserIsAdmin-->
  <!--$docLoadResourceIncludes("dDocName=admin_portal_includes" join
      "&amp;RevisionSelectionMethod=LatestReleased")-->
<!--$ else -->
  <!--$docLoadResourceIncludes("dDocName=user_portal_includes" join
      "&amp;RevisionSelectionMethod=LatestReleased")-->
<!--$ endif -->

<!--$include body_def-->
<!--$include std_page_begin-->

<p>Content of the portal page</p>

<!--$include std_page_end-->
</body>
</html>
```

Standard users see the same red page as shown in Figure 6-2, but administrators see a page like that displayed in Figure 6-3.

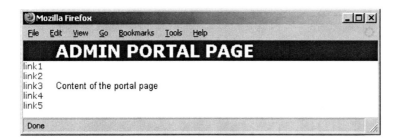

Figure 6-3. *HCSP portal for administrators*

IDOC files can also be loaded from a Java Server Page (JSP) with the docLoadResourceIncludes function. To make a similar portal page with JSPs, use the following code:

```
<%@ page import="idcserver.*" %>
<jsp:useBean id = "serverbean" scope="page" class="idcserver.ServerBean" />
<%
    serverbean.init(request);
    String isAdmin = serverbean.evalIdcScp("UserIsAdmin");
    if (isAdmin.equals("1"))
    {
        serverbean.evalIdcScp("docLoadResourceIncludes(" +
            "'dDocName=admin_portal_includes" +
            "&RevisionSelectionMethod=Latest')");
    }
    else
    {
        serverbean.evalIdcScp("docLoadResourceIncludes(" +
            "'dDocName=user_portal_includes" +
            "&RevisionSelectionMethod=Latest')");
    }
%>
<html>
<head>
    <%= serverbean.evalResInc("std_html_head_declarations")%>
</head>

<%= serverbean.evalResInc("body_def")%>
<%= serverbean.evalIdcScp("include std_page_begin") %>

<p>Content of the portal page</p>
```

```
<%= serverbean.evalIdcScp("include std_page_end") %>
</body>
</html>
```

Unfortunately, if JSP syntax is embedded in a `dynamichtml` include, it is not rendered. Standard JSP syntax supports the inclusion of entire files, but not JSP fragments. So includes in IDOC files must contain only IdocScript or HTML. If you want to include JSP fragments, you need to save each JSP fragment to a separate file and use standard JSP syntax to include them. Or use an additional framework, such as Java Server Faces, in your application.

IDOC and HTML Forms

Encapsulating your includes in IDOC files makes your code more modular. As we just saw, switching one set of includes for another is as simple as using a different IDOC file. This has additional benefits when dealing with HTML forms. IDOC files allow us to separate the form data from the display logic.

Recall the Hypertext Content Server Form (HCSF) from Chapter 5 that allowed us to create new comment forms. Every time you submit it, the Content Server generates a new HCSP for comments on a specific topic. That HCSP can be submitted multiple times to add new comments to the topic.

Now assume that at a later date, the developer needs to change the look and feel of the comments forms. By updating the HCSF, all future HCSPs will have the new look and feel. However, all existing HCSPs have the old look. To completely change all old HCSPs, you need to modify each one individually.

In contrast, assume that all the display logic was coded in an IDOC file. The HTML forms would contain XML data and a reference to the IDOC file. To change the look for all forms, all you need is to update the referenced IDOC file.

With this in mind, let's redo the HCSF using IDOC files. First copy all the source code from the HCSF into the file `comments_builder_includes.idoc`. From here, split the template into two includes: one for the HEAD section of the HTML, and one for the BODY section. We also need to change the XML IdocScript syntax back into standard IdocScript by using search and replace on the page, but take care to not destroy any valid HTML comments.

When the IDOC file is completed, it looks like this:

```
<html>
<head></head>
<body>

<!-- the header for the comments maker form -->
<@dynamichtml comments_maker_form_head_declarations@>
<$if title$>
    <$PageTitle=title$>
<$else$>
    <$PageTitle="Comments Maker Form"$>
<$endif$>
<$isCheckin=1$>
<$include std_doc_page_definitions$>
```

```
<$include std_html_head_declarations$>
<@end@>


<!-- the body of the comments maker form -->
<@dynamichtml comments_maker_form_body@>
<$include body_def$>
<$include std_page_begin$>

<$c="Determine if this is the original HCSF or the HCSP, and if so
    make every field read only. Otherwise, if it's the original HCSF,
    only make the date and author fields read only."$>
<$if ref:dExtension like "hcsp"$>
    <$isHcsp = 1$>
<$endif$>
<$if isTrue(getValue("#active", "idcformrules:isFormFinished"))$>
    <$isFormFinished=1$>
<$endif$>

<$if isHcsp$>
    <h3>Comments Page</h3>
<$else$>
    <h3>Comments Page Creator</h3>

    <p>This page will create a new discussion thread page based on
        some information about a specific customer and product.</p>
<$endif$>

<form name="CommentsPageForm" method="POST" action="<$HttpCgiPath$>">
<input type=hidden name="IdcService" value="SUBMIT_HTML_FORM">
<input type=hidden name="dID" value="<$SourceID$>">
<table>

<$fieldName="originalAuthor", fieldCaption="<b>Original Author:</b>",
    fieldValue=UserName, isInfoOnly=1$>
<$include std_display_field$>

<$fieldName="title", fieldCaption="<b>Discussion Title:</b>",
    isInfoOnly=#active.isHcsp$>
<$include std_display_field$>

<$fieldName="creationDate", fieldCaption="<b>Creation Date:</b>",
    isInfoOnly=1, fieldValue=dateCurrent()$>
<$include std_display_field$>

<$fieldName="customerName", fieldCaption="<b>Customer Name:</b>",
    isInfoOnly=#active.isHcsp$>
```

```
<$include std_display_field$>

<$fieldName="productName", fieldCaption="<b>Product Name:</b>",
    isInfoOnly=#active.isHcsp$>
<$include std_display_field$>

<$fieldName="details", fieldCaption="<b>Details:</b>",
fieldType="Memo", isInfoOnly=#active.isHcsp$>
<$include std_display_field$>

<$c="If this is the original HCSF, no comments exist yet,
    so don't show the comments section"$>
<$if isHcsp$>
    <tr>
        <td colspan=2><hr></td>
    </tr>
    <tr>
        <td colspan=2><h3>Comments:</h3></td>
    </tr>
    <tr>
        <td colspan=2><hr></td>
    </tr>
<$isInfoOnly=1$>
<$loop comment$>
    <tr>
        <td colspan=2><b><$comment!author$></b>
[<$comment!date$>]</td>
    </tr>
    <tr>
        <td colspan=2><b><$comment!title$></b></td>
    </tr>
    <tr>
        <td colspan=2><$comment$></td>
    </tr>
    <tr>
        <td colspan=2><hr></td>
    </tr>
<$endloop$>

  <$if not isFormFinished$>
    <$isInfoOnly="", isEditMode=1$>
    <$fieldName="comment!author", fieldCaption="<b>Author:</b>",
        fieldValue=UserName, isInfoOnly=1$>
    <$include std_display_field$>

    <$fieldName="comment!title", fieldCaption="<b>Title:</b>"$>
```

```
    <$include std_display_field$>

    <$fieldName="comment", fieldCaption="<b>Comment:</b>",
        fieldType="Memo"$>
    <$include std_display_field$>

    <$fieldName="comment!date", isHidden=1,
        fieldValue=dateCurrent()$>
    <$include std_display_field$>

    <$fieldName="isFormFinished", isHidden=1, fieldValue=0$>
    <$include std_display_field$>
  <$endif$>

<$endif$>

<$if isFormFinished$>
    <tr>
        <td colspan=2>Discussion on this topic is now closed.</td>
    </tr>
<$else$>
    <tr>
        <td colspan=2 align=center>
            <input type=submit value="Submit">  
            <input type=reset>  

        <$c="If this is a HCSP, show a button to allow the
            discussion to be ended"$>
        <$if isHcsp$>
            <input type=button value="Close Discussion"
            onClick="this.form.isFormFinished.value=1;
                    this.form.submit();">
        <$endif$>
        </td>
    </tr>
<$endif$>

</table>
</form>

<$include std_page_end$>

</body>
<@end@>

</body>
</html>
```

This IDOC file defines comments_maker_form_head_declarations and comments_maker_form_body, based on the original HCSF. The new HCSF can be greatly simplified into the following:

```
<html>
<head>
<!--$docLoadResourceIncludes("dDocName=comments_maker_includes" join
    "&amp;RevisionSelectionMethod=Latest")-->
<!--$include comments_maker_form_head_declarations-->

<!--$idcbegindata-->
<idcformrules resultsets="comment" />
<title></title>
<originalAuthor></originalAuthor>
<creationDate></creationDate>
<customerName></customerName>
<productName></productName>
<details></details>
<!--$idcenddata-->

</head>
<!--$include comments_maker_form_body-->
</html>
```

When this HCSF is viewed from a web browser, it looks exactly like Figure 6-4.

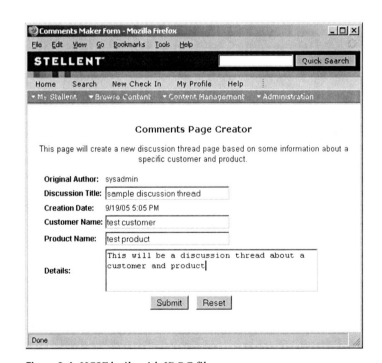

Figure 6-4. *HCSF built with IDOC files*

Because this HCSF contains only XML data and a handful of code to define page behavior, it is much more compact than the original HCSF. Additionally, all HCSPs that it generates are equally compact. As an added bonus, any time the IDOC file changes, not only do all revisions of the HCSF reflect the changes; old revisions of all generated HCSPs are likewise altered.

With this in mind, be careful with backward compatibility when modifying IDOC files. The names of includes should never be changed; otherwise, older revisions of HCSPs do not display properly. Also, keep IDOC files small—loading extremely large IDOC files can cause performance problems. If large resource files are needed, consider creating a component instead.

Overriding Metadata Display

Using an IDOC file allows us to do several other interesting things. For example, in the previous example, we use the include `std_display_field` to render form fields, which requires us to display every form field in a two-column table, in which the left column is the name of the field, and the right column is the field value.

This include is somewhat restrictive. It gives control over what data to display and how to display it, but no control over how the fields are arranged on the page. For example, it cannot be used to put two input fields in the same table row. What are our options if we want to do that?

The first option is to hard-code the form fields with HTML. Hard-coding is easy, but it has serious drawbacks (covered in Chapter 5). It is difficult to use existing Stellent features, such as Content Profiles or schema option lists, without using the `std_display_field` include. It is also more difficult to hide a field, fill it with default data, make it required, or make it read-only. If this is not a problem, hard-coding the HTML might be an option. However, for forward-compatibility reasons, it is not recommended.

The second option is to make a component that alters the way `std_display_field` works. The problem here is that it will be a global change. The customization is used on the check-in, search, and content info pages as well. If this is undesirable, you need to use special flags to control when the custom code is used. For example, set the special flag on your HCSP and look for it in your component. If the flag is not present, we default to the standard behavior. However, because this is a global change, there is always the possibility of unintended side effects.

The third option is to create an IDOC file that overrides the way `std_display_field` works. This option causes changes only on HCSF/Ps that reference the IDOC file. We need not worry about unintended side effects because the change is very local. The following example explores this third option in greater detail.

Now we must determine the best way to customize the metadata field display. The process for determining which include to override is covered in greater detail in Chapter 9. Basically, we need to open up the standard include definitions and analyze the include `std_display_field`. We must inspect the includes referenced by it and find the ones that create the table rows. After a bit of searching, we discover that the include `std_nameentry_row` contains the table row code:

```
<@dynamichtml std_nameentry_row@>
<tr <$strTrimWs(inc("std_nameentry_row_attributes"))$>>
    <td width="<$captionFieldWidth$>"
```

```
<$if isInfo$>align=right<$endif$>
<$strTrimWs(inc(fieldCaptionInclude))$></td>
    <td width="<$captionEntryWidth$>">
<$inc(fieldEntryInclude)$></td>
</tr>
<@end@>
```

Notice that this include places the form fields between TR table tags. The includes for the caption and the field are referenced by the variables fieldCaptionInclude and fieldEntryInclude, respectively. These flags are covered in more detail in Chapter 9 and Appendix C.

For maximum flexibility, we will replace this include with one that doesn't use table rows. Instead, we will place the field caption and the field entry in separate SPAN tags inside one DIV. Then we can use Cascading Style Sheets (CSS) styles to position the form data whichever way we want. This way, the display of form fields and captions is more flexible and can be placed anywhere on the page.

To continue, modify the comments_builder_includes IDOC resource in the previous example to be this:

```
<html>
<head>
</head>
<body>
<xmp>

<!-- added some CSS to control layout -->
<@dynamichtml comments_maker_form_head_declarations@>
<$if title$>
    <$PageTitle=title$>
<$else$>
    <$PageTitle="Comments Maker Form"$>
<$endif$>

<$isCheckin=1$>
<$include std_doc_page_definitions$>
<$include std_html_head_declarations$>
<style TYPE="text/css">
div.formRow {
  clear: both;
}
div.formRow span.formCaption {
  float: left;
  width: 120px;
  text-align: right;
}
div.formRow span.formEntry {
  float: left;
```

```
  text-align: left;
  padding-left: 5px;
}
</style>
<@end@>


<!—- added table rows when needed -->
<@dynamichtml comments_maker_form_body@>
<$include body_def$>
<$include std_page_begin$>

<$c="Determine if this is the original HCSF or the HCSP, and if so
    make every field read only. Otherwise, if it's the original HCSF,
    only make the date and author fields read only."$>
<$if ref:dExtension like "hcsp"$>
    <$isHcsp = 1$>
<$endif$>
<$if isTrue(getValue("#active", "idcformrules:isFormFinished"))$>
    <$isFormFinished=1$>
<$endif$>

<$if isHcsp$>
    <h3>Comments Page</h3>
<$else$>
    <h3>Comments Page Creator</h3>

    <p>This page will create a new discussion thread page based
on some information about a specific customer and product.</p>
<$endif$>

<form name="CommentsPageForm" method="POST" action="<$HttpCgiPath$>">
<input type=hidden name="IdcService" value="SUBMIT_HTML_FORM">
<input type=hidden name="dID" value="<$SourceID$>">
<table>

    <tr>
        <td colspan=2>
<$fieldName="title", fieldCaption="<b>Discussion Title:</b>",
    isInfoOnly=#active.isHcsp$>
<$include std_display_field$>
        </td>
    </tr>

    <tr>
        <td>
```

```
<$fieldName="originalAuthor", fieldCaption="<b>Original Author:</b>",
    fieldValue=UserName, isInfoOnly=1$>
<$include std_display_field$>
        </td>
        <td>
<$fieldName="creationDate", fieldCaption="<b>Creation Date:</b>",
    isInfoOnly=1, fieldValue=dateCurrent()$>
<$include std_display_field$>
        </td>
    </tr>

    <tr>
        <td>
<$fieldName="customerName", fieldCaption="<b>Customer Name:</b>",
    isInfoOnly=#active.isHcsp$>
<$include std_display_field$>
        </td>
        <td>
<$fieldName="productName", fieldCaption="<b>Product Name:</b>",
    isInfoOnly=#active.isHcsp$>
<$include std_display_field$>
        </td>
    </tr>

    <tr>
        <td colspan=2>
<$fieldName="details", fieldCaption="<b>Details:</b>",
    fieldType="Memo", isInfoOnly=#active.isHcsp$>
<$include std_display_field$>
        </td>
    </tr>


<$c="If this is the original HCSF, no comments exist yet,
    so don't show the comments section"$>
<$if isHcsp$>
    <tr>
        <td colspan=2><hr></td>
    </tr>
    <tr>
        <td colspan=2><h3>Comments:</h3></td>
    </tr>
    <tr>
        <td colspan=2><hr></td>
    </tr>
<$isInfoOnly=1$>
```

```
<$loop comment$>
    <tr>
<td colspan=2><b><$comment!author$></b>
[<$comment!date$>]</td>
    </tr>
    <tr>
        <td colspan=2><b><$comment!title$></b></td>
    </tr>
    <tr>
        <td colspan=2><$comment$></td>
    </tr>
    <tr>
        <td colspan=2><hr></td>
    </tr>
<$endloop$>

  <$if not isFormFinished$>
    <$isInfoOnly="", isEditMode=1$>

    <tr>
        <td colspan=2>
        <$fieldName="comment!author", fieldValue=UserName,
            isInfoOnly=1, fieldCaption="<b>Author:</b>"$>
        <$include std_display_field$>
        </td>
    </tr>

    <tr>
        <td colspan=2>
        <$fieldName="comment!title", fieldCaption="<b>Title:</b>"$>
        <$include std_display_field$>
        </td>
    </tr>

    <tr>
        <td colspan=2>
        <$fieldName="comment", fieldCaption="<b>Comment:</b>",
            fieldType="Memo"$>
        <$include std_display_field$>
        </td>
    </tr>

    <$fieldName="comment!date", isHidden=1,
        fieldValue=dateCurrent()$>
    <$include std_display_field$>
```

```
            <$fieldName="isFormFinished", isHidden=1, fieldValue=0$>
            <$include std_display_field$>
        <$endif$>

<$endif$>

<$if isFormFinished$>
        <tr>
            <td colspan=2>Discussion on this topic is now closed.</td>
        </tr>
<$else$>
        <tr>
            <td colspan=2 align=center>
                <input type=submit value="Submit">  
                <input type=reset>  

            <$c="If this is a HCSP, show a button to allow the
                  discussion to be ended"$>
            <$if isHcsp$>
                <input type=button value="Close Discussion"
                onClick="this.form.isFormFinished.value=1;
                            this.form.submit();">
            <$endif$>
            </td>
        </tr>
<$endif$>
</table>
</form>

<$include std_page_end$>

</body>
<@end@>


<!--override the standard name entry row with a DIV based one -->
<@dynamichtml std_nameentry_row@>
<$include div_based_nameentry_row$>
<@end@>


<!-- the custom DIV based name entry row -->
<@dynamichtml div_based_nameentry_row@>
<div id="<$#active.fieldName$>_div" class="formRow">
<span class="formCaption">
<$strTrimWs(inc(fieldCaptionInclude))$></span>
    <span class="formEntry">
```

```
<$inc(fieldEntryInclude)$></span>
</div>
<@end@>

</xmp>
</body>
</html>
```

This IDOC file contains four resources. The includes comments_maker_form_body and comments_maker_form_head_declarations are slightly modified from the originals from the previous example. Since the form fields use DIV tags as containers, the comments_maker_form_body include must contain the TR and TD tags. The comments_maker_form_head_declarations include is modified to contain the CSS classes used on the form.

The std_nameentry_row include is overridden on the page, and replaced with div_based_nameentry_row. The latter is a simplification of the former and wraps a form field in a DIV tag. In the DIV based include, SPAN tags wrap the includes referenced by the variables fieldCaptionInclude and fieldEntryInclude. The values of these vary upon what type of data is being displayed, but they are typically std_field_caption and std_field_entry, respectively.

After making the necessary modifications, check the IDOC file back into the Content Server and refresh the original HCSF. You should see it change into the form shown in Figure 6-5.

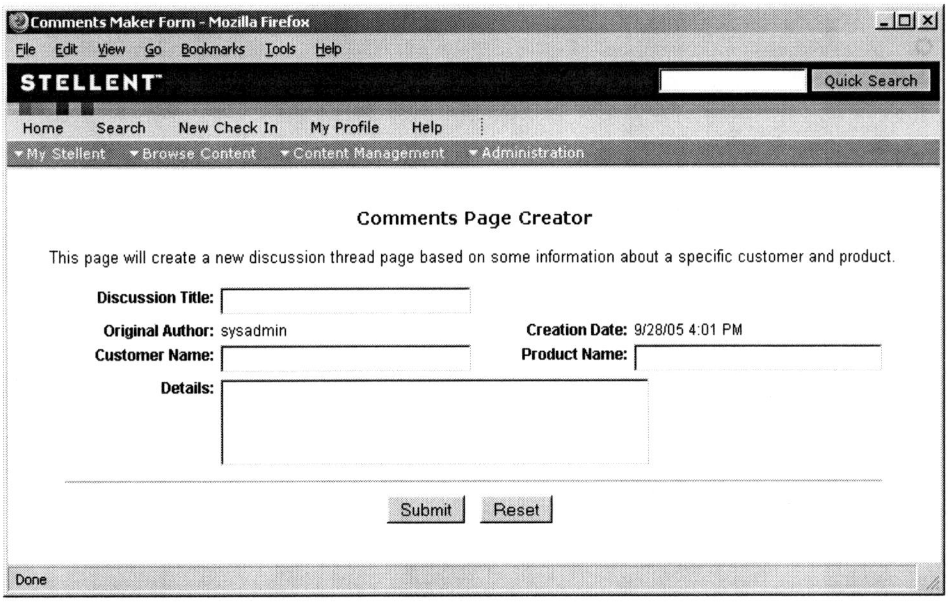

Figure 6-5. *Two-column Comments Maker form*

The width and positioning of these fields is now controlled by CSS styles. To change them, modify the include comments_maker_form_head_declarations. For example, some fields can be hidden by default but appear when a checkbox is selected.

Summary

IDOC files are extremely useful when creating Dynamic Server Pages. They give an ordinary contributor the power to create IdocScript resources and include them on other pages.

IDOC files are especially useful when creating HCSPs and HCSFs. It is a standard best-practice to define all the display logic with resource includes in IDOC files, instead of on the HCSP itself. You then call the `docLoadResourceIncludes` function on the HCSP to load those resources and display the form data. This procedure enables you to completely separate the data in the form from the logic that displays it. It also enables you to change the look and feel of the HCSP by simply checking in a new revision of the IDOC file.

You can also override standard resources with IDOC files. In doing so, you can completely override common resources (such as `std_page_begin` and `std_page_end`), but your modifications show only on the pages in which you explicitly load the IDOC resource. All other pages remain unaffected.

CHAPTER 7

■ ■ ■

Introduction to Custom Components

As mentioned in Chapter 2, the Content Server is a framework for creating functionality through components. New components can be used to modify the interface or to add new services. In fact, most Stellent products are written (at least in part) as components; for example, Site Studio, Dynamic Converter, and Records Management. In this chapter, we will cover the components you can create to modify the web interface.

A component that changes the web interface must contain HTML and JavaScript resources. Most of the time, but not always, IdocScript resources are also needed. Java and SQL resources are rarely needed for simple interface changes; they are required only when altering the Content Server's behavior (covered in Chapters 10 and 11). In both cases HTML and HDA configuration files are required to define the resources used by the component.

This chapter discusses how to create a component. You will see a handful of examples showing how to create new resources and modify existing resources. In Chapters 8 and 9, you will apply this information to make specific modifications.

Tools and References

Throughout these examples, we use the Component Wizard utility, which ships with the Content Server. We also make extensive use of the Firefox browser with the Web Developer extension. It is important to test new functionality in all browsers, but Firefox has a richer environment for debugging, so it is the preferred tool for initial testing.

In most cases, the Component Wizard is the best tool for creating the initial component and adding resources. The next few sections cover the basic use of the Component Wizard for component creation.

For more information on how to use the Component Wizard and on the structure of components, please refer to the *Working with Components* guide that ships with the Content Server. For more information on the structure of services and the list of all available services, please refer to the *Services Reference Guide* or Appendix E. See Appendixes A through D for a description of the IdocScript language as well as lists of useful IdocScript flags, functions, and includes.

Hello User Include

The most common resource is a `dynamichtml` include, which contains HTML and IdocScript code and is used on template pages. Most of the look and feel of the Content Server is contained in `dynamichtml` includes, instead of being coded directly on template pages. Resource includes allow for more portable display logic and make the Content Server much easier to customize.

The format of a resource include is the same as an IDOC resource (covered in Chapter 6). However, an include defined in a component is available on all pages, provided that the component is enabled.

To create a custom include, follow these steps:

1. Open up the Component Wizard.

2. Click Add to add a new component.

3. Name the component `HelloUser`, and click OK in all open dialog boxes.

4. Wait for the Component Wizard to create and open the `HelloUser` component.

5. In the Resource Definitions tab, click Add.

6. Select Resource–HTML Include/String and click Next.

7. Name the include `hello_user`, and in the text box type the following code:

   ```
   <h1>Hello <$UserName$>!</h1>
   ```

8. Click Finish.

9. In the menu, select Options ➤ Enable to enable the component.

10. Restart the Content Server.

During these steps, you might be prompted to open this file with a text editor on your system. Most people prefer third-party text editors to the minimalistic one provided in the Component Wizard. You can set a default text editor from Options ➤ Configuration on the menu bar.

After the preceding steps, we have a basic component with one resource and one HDA file containing the configuration information for the component:

```
stellent/custom/HelloUser/HelloUser.hda
stellent/custom/HelloUser/resources/hellouser_resource.htm
```

The file `HelloUser.hda` is called the Component Definition File, and the file `hellouser_resource.htm` is a resource file containing the include `hello_user`.

```
<html>
<head>
<meta http-equiv="Content-Type"
  content="text/html; charset=iso-8859-1">
<title>
HelloUser htmlIncludeOrString
</title>
```

```
</head>
<body>

<@dynamichtml hello_user@>
<h1>Hello <$UserName$>!</h1>
<@end@>

</body>
</html>
```

The definition of the hello_user include begins with a dynamichtml tag, which contains the name of the include. The definition ends with the end tag. As with definitions in IDOC files, the beginning and ending of resources are controlled with keywords delimited with <@ and @> characters. The IdocScript in the include must use standard IdocScript, delimited with <$ and $> characters. XML IdocScript is not supported in resource definitions.

The next step is to create a template page so we can display the resource. Several kinds of pages can display dynamichtml includes, such as core Content Server templates, Hypertext Content Server Templates (HCSTs), Java Server Pages (JSPs), Hypertext Content Server Pages (HCSPs), and Hypertext Content Server Forms (HCSFs). These pages include pages used by Site Studio and Dynamic Converter because they typically output HCSPs.

For a quick test, we will create an HCST that includes the following resource:

```
<html>
<body>

<$include hello_user$>

</body>
</html>
```

Check this HCST into the Content Server. When viewed from a web browser, the page looks like Figure 7-1.

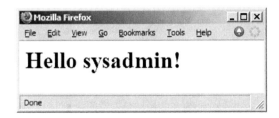

Figure 7-1. *Hello user with component include*

Includes can be modified on the fly without a Content Server restart. You can modify the existing hello_user resource, and the changes will be reloaded the next time the sample HCST is refreshed. This enables faster debugging of existing pages so you can generate the user interface more quickly.

If you alter the structure of the component by adding a new include in a new resource file, the Content Server has to be restarted.

Hello User Service and Template

Instead of using an HCST to display the include, we can create a custom template for the include. To display a custom template, we also need a custom service. To do this, follow these steps:

1. Open the Component Wizard and the HelloUser component.

2. In the Resource Definitions tab, click Add.

3. Select Template and click Next.

4. Click Next.

5. Set the name to HELLO_USER_PAGE.

6. Set the Class to Pages.

7. Set the Form Type to HelloUser.

8. Set the File Name to hello_user_page.htm.

9. Click Finish.

10. In the Resource Definitions tab, click Add.

11. Select the Service button and click Next.

12. Click Next.

13. Name the service HELLO_USER.

14. Set the Service Class to Service.

15. Click Finish.

16. Restart the Content Server.

After these steps, you have the following files in your component:

```
stellent/custom/HelloUser/resources/hellouser_service.htm
stellent/custom/HelloUser/templates/hellouser_template.hda
stellent/custom/HelloUser/templates/hello_user_page.htm
```

The hellouser_service.htm resource contains the HTML table defining the HELLO_USER service. It does very little besides display the HELLO_USER_PAGE:

```
<html>
<head>
```

```
<meta http-equiv="Content-Type" content="text/html;
   charset=iso-8859-1">
<title>
HelloUser service
</title>
</head>
<body>

<@table HelloUser_Services@>
<table border=1><caption><strong>Scripts For Custom Services</strong></caption>
<tr>
     <td>Name</td><td>Attributes</td><td>Actions</td>
</tr>
<tr>
     <td>HELLO_USER</td>
     <td>Service
         0
         HELLO_USER_PAGE
         null
         null<br>
         null</td>
     <td></td>
</tr>
</table>
<@end@>
</body>
</html>
```

The hellouser_template.hda resource contains a table with descriptive information about each template. The template HELLO_USER_PAGE is defined in hello_user_page.htm:

```
<?hda version="7.5.1 (050317)" jcharset=Cp1252 encoding=iso-8859-1?>
@Properties LocalData
blFieldTypes=
blDateFormat=M/d/yy {h:mm[:ss] {aa}[zzz]}!mAM,PM!tAmerica/Chicago
@end
@ResultSet HelloUser_
5
name
class
formtype
filename
description
HELLO_USER_PAGE
Pages
HelloUser
hello_user_page.htm
null
@end
```

The generated `hello_user_page.htm` template initially has very little in it. We should change it so that it looks more like the HCST we used for testing in the previous section:

```
<html>
<head>
<meta http-equiv="Content-Type" content="text/html;
  charset=iso-8859-1">
<title>
HelloUser HELLO_USER_PAGE
</title>
</head>
<body>
<$include hello_user$>
</body>
</html>
```

The Component Definition File `HelloUser.hda` was also changed to include the new resources in the `ResourceDefinition` result set. The `MergeRules` result set has also changed to merge the custom templates into the core templates:

```
@ResultSet MergeRules
4
fromTable
toTable
column
loadOrder
HelloUser_
IntradocTemplates
name
1
@end
@ResultSet ResourceDefinition
4
type
filename
tables
loadOrder
resource
resources/hellouser_resource.htm
null
1
service
resources/hellouser_service.htm
HelloUser_Services
1
template
templates/hellouser_template.hda
```

```
null
1
@end
```

To test your new page, manually enter a URL to your Content Server to execute the service:

```
http://localhost/stellent/idcplg?IdcService=HELLO_USER
```

This code displays a page similar to Figure 7-1. You can also create custom services that execute custom Java or SQL. See Chapter 11 for examples.

Like resource includes, templates can be modified without restarting the Content Server. However, if a new template is added, you need to restart the Content Server. Any change to the service definition also requires a server restart.

You can place IdocScript in a `dynamichtml` resource or directly into the template. Which is the better choice?

In general, `dynamichtml` resources are more flexible and should be used to encapsulate as much code as possible, which eases portability because your code can now be reused by other templates. Resource includes also ease compatibility with existing components and make your code more forward compatible. Resource includes can be customized many times in many different components, whereas a template page can be customized only once. These differences are discussed in the next section.

Overriding an Include

Most Content Server components involve overriding an existing resource—for example, adding extra HTML to a check-in form or altering the way the content info page displays its fields. To accomplish either customization, you need to override an existing include.

In a component, you can create a resource (`dynamichtml` include, service, template) that overrides an existing resource. The existing resource is typically defined in the core, but it can also be defined in a different component. Which component is used depends on how each is loaded.

When the Content Server starts, it first loads all known resources in the core and then loads all resources in each component. It loads them based on the `loadOrder` value in the `ResourceDefinition` result set of the `Component Definition` file. Resource files with higher `loadOrder` are loaded later. Whichever resource is loaded last is the one that the Content Server uses.

Therefore, to override a resource in the core, you simply need to redefine that resource in a component. Copy the exiting include to your resource file and alter it as needed.

The process is similar to overriding a resource from another component. However, in this case you must pay close attention to the `loadOrder`. You need to know which component is overriding the include and in which resource file. You need to make certain that the `loadOrder` for your resource file is higher than the `loadOrder` in the other component.

Most resources, such as templates, services, and SQL queries, can be overridden only once. For example, if two components both override the `CHECKIN_NEW` service, only one succeeds—the one with the highest `loadOrder`. The Content Server completely ignores the modifications in the component with the lower loadOrder. The same is true if they both override the same template, the same SQL query, or the same localization string.

However, overriding dynamichtml includes is different. An include is unique in that it can use the IdocScript super tag to recall the previous definition of that include. So if two components modify the std_page_begin include and they both use the super tag, both customizations will work.

For example, assume that a component with a loadOrder of 1 overrides the std_page_begin include like this:

```
<@dynamichtml std_page_begin@>
<$include super.std_page_begin$>
<!-- first component's code -->
<@end@>
```

The current definition of std_page_begin is inserted into this definition with the code `<$include super.std_page_begin$>`. The previously defined code becomes a part of this new definition.

Now assume that you need to modify the include again. In some cases, you can modify the original component. However, if you did not generate the original component, it is best to not change it. Instead you should create a second component to modify the original component.

In this second component, make sure that you create a resource file with a loadOrder of 2. In the file, create the following include:

```
<@dynamichtml std_page_begin@>
<$include super.std_page_begin$>
<!-- second component's code -->
<@end@>
```

Again, the super tag inserts the previous definition for std_page_begin into this definition. It is the equivalent of modifying the original component to have the following code:

```
<@dynamichtml std_page_begin@>
<$include super.std_page_begin$>
<!-- first component's code -->
<!-- second component's code -->
<@end@>
```

The super tag enables small changes to be made easily and in a forward compatible way. If std_page_begin is changed in the next version of the product, both customizations still work. If the first component is updated separately from the second, both customizations still work.

As a result, the use of the super tag is always encouraged. Unfortunately, this is not always possible. It is mostly useful for adding custom code immediately before or after the previously defined resource. In the preceding examples, we added custom code immediately after std_page_begin, which meant that using the super tag was possible.

However, what if you need to modify the resource in the middle? What if you do not want to simply add new HTML to the page, but instead want to radically change the display logic of the existing include? When you need to create such an invasive customization, you have fewer options.

This situation can sometimes cause component conflicts when upgrading to a newer version of the Content Server. However, if you plan for this possibility, it is still possible to create components that upgrade cleanly.

For example, assume that the hello_user include contains a reference to the date as well:

```
<@dynamichtml hello_user@>
<h1>Hello <$UserName$>!</h1>
<p>Today is <$dateCurrent()$></p>
<@end@>
```

You want to modify this include from a second component and insert an additional greeting. If you want to insert it *after* the date, the modification is simple:

```
<@dynamichtml hello_user@>
<$include super.hello_user$>
<p>Have you seen our new company newsletter?</p>
<@end@>
```

Even if the first component changes, this customization always works to add the greeting after the date.

But what if you need to insert the greeting *before* the date? In this case, the super tag cannot be used; you need to override the entire include from the first component. This is unfortunate, because now every time hello_user changes in the first component, you are forced to update the second component as well. This unfortunate code would look like this:

```
<@dynamichtml hello_user@>
<h1>Hello <$UserName$>!</h1>
<p>Have you seen our new company newsletter?</p>
<p>Today is <$dateCurrent()$></p>
<@end@>
```

Is there a better way? Thankfully, there is. You must still override the entire include in the second component, but there is a way to still benefit from the super tag. Instead of putting the custom code directly in hello_user, you can put it in hello_user_greeting and then include the customization in hello_user:

```
<@dynamichtml hello_user@>
<h1>Hello <$UserName$>!</h1>
<$include hello_user_greeting$>
<p>Today is <$dateCurrent()$></p>
<@end@>
```

```
<@dynamichtml hello_user_greeting@>
<p>Have you seen our new company newsletter?</p>
<@end@>
```

Why the extra effort? The reasoning is simple: because you needed to modify hello_user before the timestamp, it is likely that somebody else might need to do the same. Now they can benefit from your hard work. They can now override the include hello_user_greeting with the super tag, which is much easier than trying to maintain compatibility between three components.

Additionally, the extra effort makes your customization more forward compatible. Because your modification is a one-line change to `hello_user`, it is easy to maintain. If `hello_user` changes in the future, you only need to copy the new resource and change one line. Also, if you notify the original component's author about your change, it is highly likely that you will not need to modify the second component at all; with luck, your change will be added to the next version of the original component.

There are other ways to accomplish forward compatibility with resource includes. In general, the rule is to modify the original include as little as possible: create an include where you need it and then override it.

Summary

The two ways to create new pages in the Content Server are components and Dynamic Server Pages. To add new interfaces to existing services, sometimes it is easier to use Dynamic Server Pages, but components are required to customize the core look and feel.

Creating components is simple. The tricky part is to know which includes to use, which IdocScript flags to use, and how to use each of them. The next few chapters cover this topic in detail.

Chapter 8 covers how to make modifications to the color scheme, layout, and navigation links. Chapter 9 covers more-advanced web customizations, including altering the check-in form itself and finding the correct include to customize. Chapters 10 and 11 cover advanced modifications with Java code.

Customizing Layouts and Skins

In Content Server 7.0, we added a new API (sometimes called the Layout Manager API) for creating *skinable* layouts. It controls which navigation links are shown in the HTML menus, as well as how the menus are laid out and the color scheme. The resources for the Layout Manager are based on HTML, XML, Cascading Style Sheets (CSS), images, and JavaScript.

No knowledge of IdocScript is required to make changes to the general look and feel of the Content Server. However, knowledge of how to create a component is still required. The following examples demonstrate how to create these components and alter the basic look and feel of the Content Server.

Architecture

The Layout Manager API is comprised of JavaScript, CSS, and image files in the `weblayout` directory:

```
stellent/weblayout/resources/layouts/
stellent/weblayout/resources/layouts/Top Menus/
stellent/weblayout/resources/layouts/Trays/
```

A handful of JavaScript files are located in the `layouts` directory. The file `common.js` contains functions and objects used on all layouts, whereas the file `commonNav.js` contains all default navigation nodes. This folder contains two subfolders: `Top Menus` and `Trays`, which are the names of the layouts.

Each layout folder contains a file named `layout.js`, which contains all the JavaScript required to draw the HTML menus to the page. The folder also contains at least one subfolder, which contains the definition for the skins. In version 7.5, four skins are available out of the box: `Collegiate`, `Stellent`, `Stellent05`, and `Windows`:

```
stellent/weblayout/resources/layouts/Top Menus/Collegiate
stellent/weblayout/resources/layouts/Top Menus/Stellent05
stellent/weblayout/resources/layouts/Top Menus/Stellent
stellent/weblayout/resources/layouts/Top Menus/Windows
```

The skin folders contain at least the file `skin.css`, which contains the CSS information. We define all the colors and borders used on the page in the skin folder, which also contains several images specific to the skin. For example, all the graphics for the menu background images are different for different skins.

The layouts and skins are drawn to the page by using IdocScript `dynamichtml` includes. The include `std_js_bootstrap_vars` links to the JavaScript and CSS resource files. The include `std_page_begin` calls JavaScript functions in `layout.js` to draw the beginning of the layout, along with navigation menus. The include `std_page_end` draws the ending HTML for the layout.

Creating a New Skin

You can greatly change the look and feel of the Content Server by modifying an existing skin. However, it is preferable to instead create a custom skin, based on an existing skin, and modify it. You can do this without a component and without knowledge of IdocScript.

The first step is to create a copy of an existing skin folder. In this case, choose the Windows skin:

```
stellent/weblayout/resources/layouts/Top Menus/Windows
```

Give it a different name. In this case, call it Xalco:

```
stellent/weblayout/resources/layouts/Top Menus/Xalco
```

This folder will contain all of the images and CSS files needed to define a new skin. After you restart the Content Server, this new skin will become available, but only for the Top Menus layout.

Next, navigate to the user profile page, and select the Xalco skin (see Figure 8-1).

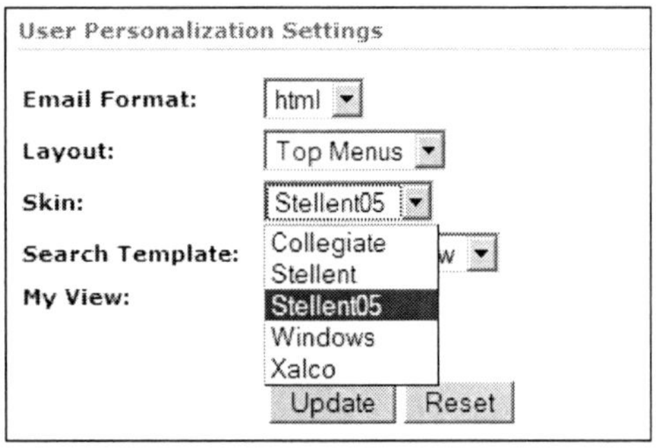

Figure 8-1. *Selecting the newly created skin*

Initially this skin should look exactly like the Windows skin. To modify it, you need to customize the `skin.css` file. For example, to replace the company logo in the upper left, replace this file with a custom company logo:

```
stellent/weblayout/resources/layouts/Top Menus/Xalco/HeaderLogo.gif
```

For this example, a custom graphic for the fictional Xalco Company is inserted (see Figure 8-2).

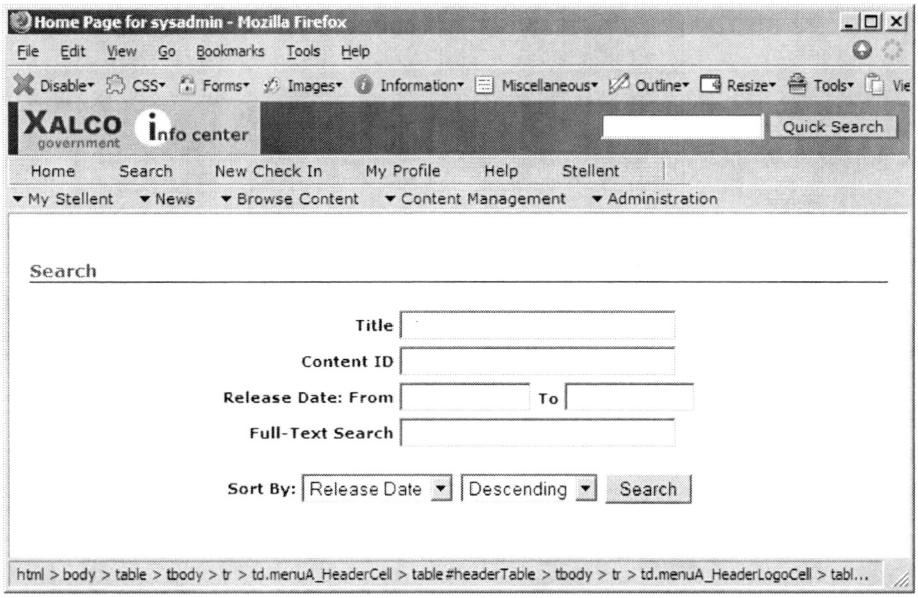

Figure 8-2. *Xalco skin, step 1*

This skin looks terrible because the yellow logo is against a blue background. To clean it up, change the CSS settings for that background to match the logo. The challenge here is to determine which of the 200 styles to change. The Firefox browser with the Web Developer toolbar becomes extremely valuable for this process.

As you can see in Figure 8-2, the Web Developer toolbar can display CSS-style information in the status bar at the bottom of the window. To begin, select the CSS menu in the Web Developer Toolbar, and click View Style Information. Next, point the mouse to the graphic or element that you want to learn more about. This information is then presented in the status bar at the bottom of the browser.

From this information, you can see that there are only three styles that can be making the blue background for the logo's table cell: menua_HedareCell, headerTable, and menuA_HeaderLogoCell. Inspect the following style file for these CSS classes:

```
stellent/weblayout/resources/layouts/Top Menus/Xalco/skin.css
```

The offending style is this:

```
.menuA_HeaderLogoCell
{
    background: url(header_bg.gif) repeat-y #A6CAF0;
}
```

This class causes the image header_bg.gif to be repeated as the background image for the header cell. You can change it by creating a new repeatable background or by simply modifying the background color. To do the latter, change the code to this:

```
.menuA_HeaderLogoCell
{
    background: #FFC435;
}
```

After a refresh, the skin now looks like Figure 8-3.

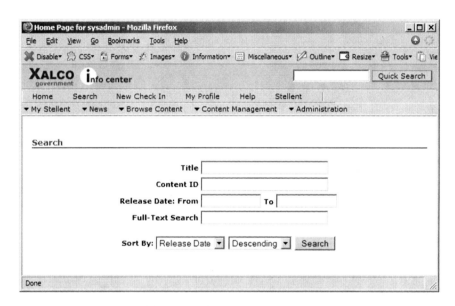

Figure 8-3. *Xalco skin with better header*

Additional CSS values can be changed in the same way to further customize the Xalco skin. For example, you might want to modify the styles for the color of drop-down menus and popup actions.

To make your skin more portable, you should bundle it inside a component. To do this open the Component Wizard and add a new component called XalcoSkin. This component doesn't need any resources; it just needs to be configured to bundle the skin:

1. Select Build ➤ Build Settings.

2. Click Add.

3. Set the Entry Type to Resources.

4. Set the Sub Directory or File to layouts/Top Menus/Xalco.

5. Click OK.

6. If you created a skin for the `Trays` layout as well, repeat steps 2–5 for the skin `layouts/Trays/Xalco`.

7. Click OK in the Build Settings window.

Now when you build this component, it packages up your skin as well. The same applies to packaging custom layouts or any other web resource you need.

Adding and Modifying Navigation Nodes

The navigation menus and link are stored in JavaScript as XML nodes. All the default navigation nodes are defined in `commonNav.js`. Each layout has its own `nav.js` file to modify the common nodes, but this is not where you should make customizations. Instead, developers should make components to add new links and menus.

The include `std_js_bootstrap_vars` is present on every Content Server page that has navigation menus. In this include, we define JavaScript flags based on existing IdocScript flags. These flags, such as `isLoggedIn`, `userName`, and `httpCgiPath`, are important for knowing which menus to display and what to put in them:

```
<@dynamichtml std_js_bootstrap_vars@>
<script>
// bootstrapping strings and flags for all users
var allowIntranetUsers = <$if AllowIntranetUsers$>true<$else$>false<$endif$>;
var coreContentOnly = <$if coreContentOnly$>true<$else$>false<$endif$>;
var httpAdminCgiPath = "<$HttpAdminCgiPath$>";
var httpBrowserFullCgiPath = "<$HttpBrowserFullCgiPath$>";
var httpCgiPath = "<$HttpCgiPath$>";
...
function finishLayoutInit(navBuilder)
{
    <$include custom_finish_layout_init$>
}
...
<@end@>
```

Please note that these flags are JavaScript, not IdocScript. The JavaScript flags have slightly different capitalization than their IdocScript equivalents: `userName` instead of `UserName`.

This include also contains the JavaScript function `finishLayoutInit`, which includes the resource `custom_finish_layout_init`. This function is called immediately before the navigation menus are drawn to the page. It gives you one final opportunity to add, remove, or modify menu items before they are drawn. To do so, you need to override the include `custom_finish_layout_init` and call methods inside the passed `navBuilder` object.

This `navBuilder` parameter is a JavaScript object that contains all the information about the navigation nodes. It contains an XML node for each navigation item, helper functions for adding new items, and functions to draw the nodes on the page as HTML. See Appendix G for a complete list of the methods and variables this object contains.

For this example, you will add a new link to the Content Management menu that will be a custom check-in form for sales people. This form will use the standard CHECKIN_NEW_FORM service with a handful of additional parameters in the URL. These parameters will preset metadata values and hide unused fields.

Each menu item has a unique ID. If you want to add a new menu item to the existing Content Management menu, you must first determine the ID for the Content Management menu. Inspect the following files to determine the unique ID:

```
stellent/weblayout/resources/layouts/commonNav_listing.txt
stellent/weblayout/resources/layouts/commonNav.js
```

The first file is a document containing a list of the nodes, their IDs, and where they occur in the tree hierarchy. If you cannot find the node of interest there, you can check the second file, which contains the actual JavaScript code. If neither file has the ID information for the node of interest, it might be defined in a different component. In this case, you might need to scan all components that override the custom_finish_layout_init include to find the one of interest.

In this case, by checking commonNav_listing.txt you will discover that the node has an ID of CONTENT_MANAGEMENT. Now you are ready to make the customization.

Use the Component Wizard to create the component CustomNavigation. Add an HTML resource to the component. In this resource file, define the include custom_finish_layout_init to look like this:

```
<@dynamichtml custom_finish_layout_init@>
<$include super.custom_finish_layout_init$>
navBuilder.addChildNodeTo("CONTENT_MANAGEMENT",
  "item",
  "id==SALES_CHECKIN",
  "label==Sales Check In",
  "url==<$HttpCgiPath$>?IdcService=CHECKIN_NEW_FORM&dDocType=ADSALES");
<@end@>
```

This JavaScript is displayed on every Content Server page inside the finishLayoutInit function described previously. Notice that the first line in the resource is this:

```
<$include super.custom_finish_layout_init$>
```

This line is essential to make sure that your component will be compatible with other components that attempt similar customizations.

The function addChildNodeTo creates a new XML node and appends it to the node CONTENT_MANAGEMENT. The first parameter is item, which means that this menu is a link to another page. The other parameters are attributes that define the data in this node. The node must contain an id attribute. The label is what is displayed when the menu is drawn to the page. When the link is clicked, the user is taken to url. See Appendix G for a list of all possible attributes.

Next, enable the component and restart the Content Server. You should see your new link in the drop-down menu for Content Management (see Figure 8-4).

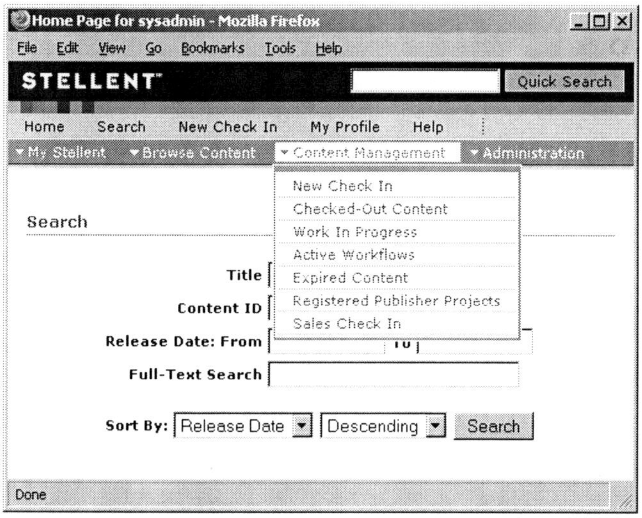

Figure 8-4. *New Sales Check In menu item*

When you click this link, it takes you to a standard check-in page, with the value for Content Type (dDocType) prefilled to ADSALES. If you want to hide this field as well, append the following flag to the previous URL attribute:

```
dDocType:isHidden=1
```

Additional flags to hide and preset metadata fields are covered in Chapter 9 and Appendix C.

If you have a component with several navigation links, the HTML source code can become cluttered with too many calls to modify the navigation. In those cases, it might be a better idea to create a static JavaScript file to contain your modifications. Static JavaScript cannot contain IdocScript, so you need to refer to the JavaScript variables created in the include std_js_bootstrap_include.

The first step is to create a JavaScript file in the weblayout directory. This item can be checked into the Content Server, but for this example you will manually create the file:

```
stellent/weblayout/resources/layouts/staticLinks.js
```

Create the following function in that file:

```
function initStaticLinks(navBuilder)
{
    navBuilder.addChildNodeTo("CONTENT_MANAGEMENT",
        "item",
        "id==SALES_CHECKIN",
        "label==Sales Check In",
```

```
        "url==" + httpCgiPath +
            "?IdcService=CHECKIN_NEW_FORM&dDocType=ADSALES");
}
```

Notice that the JavaScript variable `httpCgiPath` is used instead of the IdocScript flag `<$HttpCgiPath$>`. Now change your resource file to this:

```
<@dynamichtml custom_layout_script_links@>
<$include super.custom_layout_script_links$>
<SCRIPT LANGUAGE="JavaScript"
    src="<$HttpWebRoot$>resources/layouts/staticLinks.js">
</SCRIPT>
<@end@>


<@dynamichtml custom_finish_layout_init@>
<$include super.custom_finish_layout_init$>
initStaticLinks(navBuilder);
<@end@>
```

The include `custom_layout_script_links` is included toward the bottom of `std_js_bootstrap_vars`. It is the place to add links to JavaScript resources that are needed on all pages. You can create a `SCRIPT` node in it that points to the JavaScript resource. In `custom_finish_layout_init` you call the function that defines the new nodes.

In the custom JavaScript function, you can trigger off of flags such as `isAdmin` and `isLoggedIn`; however, these flags should not be considered secure. They should be used only as a convenience to display relevant links. They should not be used to conditionally display secure information. Such code should be restricted to server-side execution to prevent giving away secure information in your JavaScript resources.

It is possible to add more security to link nodes. Instead of a global static resource, check the JavaScript file into a secure group inside the Content Server. Then conditionally link to that resource in `custom_layout_script_links` with IdocScript. For example, to make certain your administrative links are shown only to administrators, use something like this:

```
<@dynamichtml custom_finish_layout_init@>
<$include super.custom_finish_layout_init$>
<$if AdminAtLeastOneGroup$>
    initStaticLinks(navBuilder);
<$endif$>
<@end@>


<@dynamichtml custom_layout_script_links@>
<$include super.custom_layout_script_links$>
<$if AdminAtLeastOneGroup$>
    <SCRIPT LANGUAGE="JavaScript"
        src="<$HttpWebRoot$>groups/secure/documents/adacct/staticLinks.js">
    </SCRIPT>
<$endif$>
<@end@>
```

This way, only administrators have any knowledge of the names of those links or even the existence of the JavaScript file.

Custom navigation menus work well with all kinds of customizations. You can create quick links to any content item in the server. They are generally used to create links to custom check-in and search pages. It is also used to create links to departmental portal pages or links to completely different websites.

Custom Action Popup Menus

Action popup and drop-down menus are additional user interface (UI) enhancements for version 7.0. The popup menus are used on the search results, workflow, and subscription pages to allow specific actions for single content items. For example, on the search results page you can jump to the content information page for the current item, you can check-out the current item, or you can prefill a new check-in page with metadata similar to the current item. From the workflow pages, the popup menus allow you to approve or reject the item, as well as obtain additional workflow history information.

Action drop-down menus are slightly different. They exist on the content info page as well as the search results page and are used for actions that are relevant to the entire page. For example, on the content info page you can check-in, check-out, or subscribe. On the search results page, you can save the search you just ran, or refine it and add new search terms.

To create a new action popup menu on the search results page, you need to override the include custom_search_results_action_popup. In this include we can add a link to another Content Server page based on the metadata in this content item. You could even make a link to a remote server based on the current item's metadata. In this example, you will create a link so the user can run a Google search based on the title of the current content item.

To do this, open the resource file from the CustomNavigation component you created in the previous example and add this resource:

```
<@dynamichtml custom_search_results_action_popup@>
<$include super.custom_search_results_action_popup$>
<tr><td class="xuiPopupLink" nowrap
        onMouseOver="glowPopupRow(this,'xuiPopupLink_over','xuiPopupLink')"
        onMouseOut="fadePopupRow(this,'xuiPopupLink')"
        onClick="linkItem_onclick(event, this)">
    <a class="menuA_ChildLinkText"
        href="http://www.google.com/search?q=<$url(#active.dDocTitle)$>">
    Google '<$dDocTitle$>'</a>
</td></tr>
<@end@>
```

The structure of this include is based on the original resource. To make the links highlight properly, they must be in specially formatted table rows. The row must also have specific onMouseOver, onMouseOut, and onClick events. The link itself must use the class menuA_ChildLinkText, like the other links.

Next, run a search and click the action icon to trigger the popup menu (see Figure 8-5). You should see your link in the popup menu. Clicking it runs the search against Google and displays the results in the current page.

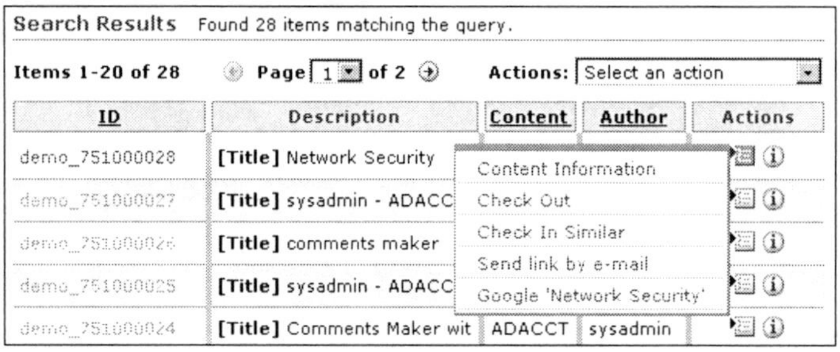

Figure 8-5. *Action popup menu to run a Google search*

Action drop-down menus are slightly different. They are designed to be used for a single content item on the content info page. On the search results page, their purpose is to apply to the entire page, for example, to save the search or to process all documents in the search in some way.

For this example, we will use some unusual IdocScript functions to allow the user to download the search results as a spreadsheet.

To do this, add the following two resources to the CustomNavigation component:

```
<@dynamichtml custom_searchapi_result_options@>
<$include super.custom_searchapi_result_options$>
<option value="window.location='<$HttpCgiPath$>?<$QUERY_STRING
    $>&IsJava=1&MergeInclude=spreadsheet_search_results'">
Download Spreadsheet</option>
<@end@>


<@dynamichtml spreadsheet_search_results@>
Title,Author,Date,Security Group,Content ID,Content Type
<$loop SearchResults$><$dDocTitle$>,<$dDocAuthor$>,<$dInDate
    $>,<$dSecurityGroup$>,<$dDocName$>,<$dDocType$>
<$endloop$>
<$setContentType("text/csv")$>
<$setHttpHeader("Content-Disposition",
    "attachment;filename=search_results.csv")$>
<@end@>
```

Action drop-down menus are much more straightforward than action popup menus. They are all contained in OPTION elements in HTML. The value attribute is a string of JavaScript to execute when the option is selected. In most cases, it submits a hidden form on the page. In this case, it performs a JavaScript redirect to a URL that will render these results into a spreadsheet.

The URL is basically the same URL of the current page. The following string is exactly the same as the current URL:

```
<$HttpCgiPath$>?<$QUERY_STRING$>
```

The other parameters appended to this URL will render the search results in a different manner. Specifically, we use the MergeInclude flag to cause the results of a service to be rendered in a dynamichtml include instead of a full template page. The flag IsJava=1 is required to make the MergInclude function properly. When viewed from a web browser, the drop-down menu looks like Figure 8-6.

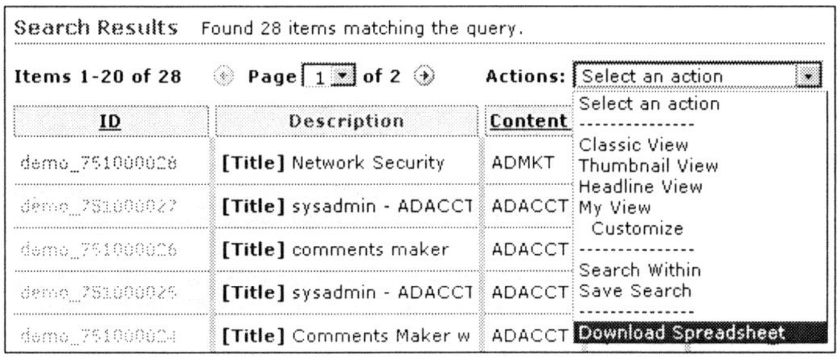

Figure 8-6. *Drop-down menu for a search results spreadsheet*

When this link is followed, the search results are rendered with the include spreadsheet_search_results, the first line of which is the names of the columns for the spreadsheet: Title, Author, Date, and so on. Notice that the column names are separated by commas.

Next, the include loops over the SearchResults. For each item in the results, it outputs a comma-separated list of the fields corresponding to the column names: dDocTitle, dDocAuthor, dInDate, and so on.

Finally, the include calls the functions setContentType and setHttpHeader. Together, these set a handful of HTTP header flags that tell the browser that it is downloading a comma separated value (CSV)–formatted spreadsheet instead of an HTML page. The browser does what it is told and opens the spreadsheet file with the appropriate application (this application is usually Microsoft Excel, but it might also be Open Office or Lotus 1-2-3).

Custom Layouts

You can create a custom layout in the same way you create a custom skin. You simply copy an entire layout folder and rename it. Then you can edit it so that it displays the page in a different way.

For example, assume that you always want a copyright footer at the bottom of the page. Although you can do this by overriding std_page_end, if you need more control over the positioning, you might want to do it as a custom layout.

To begin, copy the existing Top Menus layout folder, and rename it My Layout. You should have the following folders:

```
stellent/weblayout/resources/layouts/My Layout/
stellent/weblayout/resources/layouts/Top Menus/
stellent/weblayout/resources/layouts/Trays/
```

Next, restart the Content Server. Your user profile page should contain the new layout. Select it, and click Update (see Figure 8-7).

Figure 8-7. *My Layout is now available.*

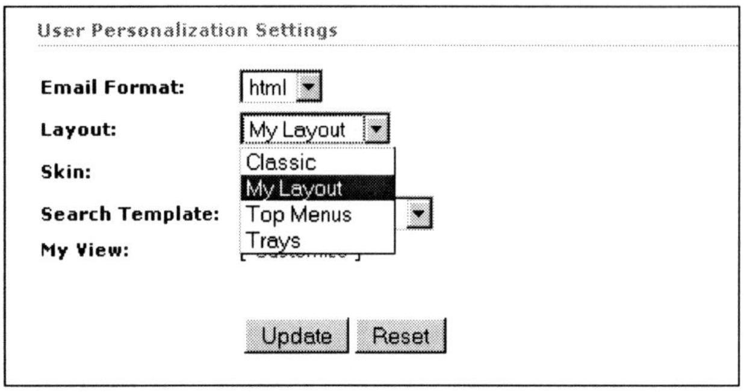

Now, open this file in a text editor:

```
stellent/weblayout/resources/layouts/My Layout/layout.js
```

There are a handful of functions of interest here (explained in more detail in Appendix G). The functions writeLayoutPageBegin and writeLayoutPageEnd draw the HTML wrappers for Content Server pages. To add a copyright footer, you need to modify the function writeLayoutPageEnd:

```
function writeLayoutPageEnd()
{
    var endHtml = "";

    /* Generate closing core content area markup. */
    endHtml +=
    '                    </center>\n' +
    '                </td>\n' +
    '            </tr>\n' +
    '    </table><!-- End main display area table -->\n';

    /* Generate closing navigation shell markup. */
    endHtml +=
    '   </td>\n' +
    '</tr>\n' +
    '<tr>\n' + // add custom footer
    '   <td>\n' +
    '       <div>Copyright 2005 Nunya Business Dot Com</div>' +
    '   </td>\n' +
    '</tr>\n' + // end custom footer
    '</table><!-- End Navigation Shell container -->\n';

    document.write(endHtml);
    document.close();
}
```

This function draws the closing TABLE tags for the page. Your modification adds an extra table row, outside of the main content area, to contain the footer. This footer can be any HTML you desire. After refreshing the web page, you should see it (see Figure 8-8).

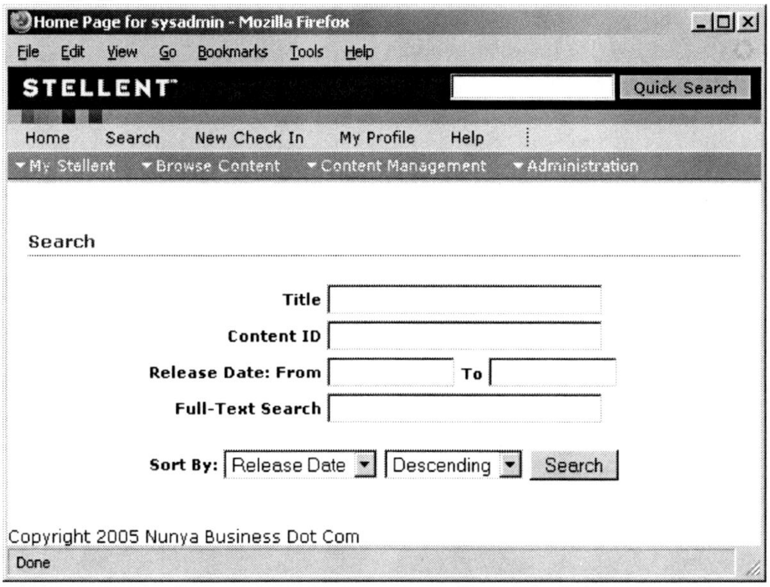

Figure 8-8. *New layout with custom footer*

If you want to change the way the beginning of the page is drawn, you should also modify writeLayoutPageBegin. If you want another group of menus somewhere, you should modify generateNavigation. To change the framework of the top-level menu, you need to modify the functions that begin with menuA_MenuItem. Likewise, to modify the framework for the second layer of menus, modify the functions beginning with menuB_MenuItem. Or create entirely new functions, and configure the Layout Manager to use them in the generateNavigation function.

Writing new layouts is much harder than writing new skins because it is difficult to debug HTML code that is drawn to the page dynamically—especially complex DHTML with drop-down menus containing cross-browser CSS. One misplaced HTML tag can cause the menus to fail or the entire layout to disappear. To make matters worse, the View Source option in browsers does not return the HTML source that is drawn by JavaScript.

I recommend that you make changes in very small increments and test constantly on multiple browsers. It is not overkill to refresh your browser every time you change one line of code. The DOM Inspector extension to Firefox is also extremely useful for inspecting the HTML that is drawn by JavaScript. Make absolutely certain that your browser cache is disabled. There is nothing more frustrating than when your browser renders an old version of layout.js when you are trying to test your changes.

Summary

Using the Layout Manager API is the most common way to change the general look and feel of the Content Server interface. Because it uses nothing more than JavaScript and XML, it is easy for web developers to modify the appearance without needing IdocScript. However, some kinds of advanced customizations require a small amount of IdocScript.

You can create new skins for the Content Server with nothing more than custom CSS code. You can change the existing images or add new ones. Custom layouts are more difficult because you need to know advanced JavaScript to create and debug them.

You can also use this API to add links to popup and drop-down menus. The popup menus are useful to add actions specific to one single content item on the search results, workflow, or subscription pages. The drop-down menus differ from the popup menus in that they are specific to an entire page. On the search results page you can use it to save or refine the search results. On the content info page you can use the drop-down menus to run services with the content item on that page.

The main limitation of the Layout Manager API is that you can modify only navigation menus with it; you cannot use it to modify fields or buttons on standard template pages. Such customizations require other kinds of components, which are covered in Chapter 9.

■■■

Customizing Forms and Core Templates

Besides adding new navigation nodes and actions, you can modify the web user interface (UI) in many other ways. Some examples include adding an additional button on a specific page, modifying the mail templates, and modifying the search results pages.

Modifications of this type are more complicated. It involves searching through the resources to locate the correct include or template. It also requires altering the code in a way that maximizes its forward compatibility.

We should emphasize here that when developing custom forms or templates, you frequently need to add debugging flags to the URL. If you are using Stellent Content Server version 7.0 or later, you cannot do this easily when using the Trays layout. You should always use the Top Menus or Classic layout for initial development. Switch to the Trays layout only for final testing.

Finding the Template Resource

The first thing that we need to do is determine which template is used by the service (by inspecting the definition for the service). Although this can be done by overriding the service and its template with the Component Wizard, it is most efficiently done by inspecting the definition files directly.

The list of all core services and their templates can be found in these resources:

```
stellent/shared/config/std_services.htm
stellent/shared/config/workflow.htm
```

Assume that we want to modify how the page looks after executing the CHECKIN_NEW service. The definition of this service follows:

```
<tr>
  <td>CHECKIN_NEW</td>
  <td>DocService
    2
    REDIRECT_TEMPLATE
    null
  documents<br>
```

```
    !csUnableToCheckIn(dDocName)</td>
  <td>3:prepareCheckinSecurity::0:null
      3:checkSecurity::0:null
      3:doSubService:CHECKIN_NEW_SUB:12:null
      3:prepareRedirect:IdcService=CHECKIN_CONFIRM_FORM&dID=<$dID$>&➡
      dDocTitle=<$url(dDocTitle)$>&dDocName=<$url(dDocName)$>&➡
      dDocAuthor=<$url(dDocAuthor)$>:0:null</td>
</tr>
```

According to this definition, the template that is used after a check-in is REDIRECT_TEMPLATE, which is misleading because that page is a fallback page for causing a redirect. What actually happens is that the action prepareRedirect forwards a successful request to the CHECKIN_CONFIRM_FORM service. The REDIRECT_TEMPLATE is not important. Therefore, we need to modify the template for the CHECKIN_CONFIRM_FORM service instead, which is the template named CHECKIN_CONFIRM.

After we know the name of the template, we need to locate it, which must be done by looking at the template definition file, located here:

```
stellent/shared/config/templates/templates.hda
```

This file contains tabular data containing the template name and the Hypertext Markup Language (HTML) file in which it is defined. In this case, the CHECKIN_CONFIRM template is defined here, which is approximately the filename that we would expect, given the template name:

```
stellent/shared/config/templates/checkin_confirm.htm
```

After opening it, we can inspect it for the resources it contains and see if there are any useful includes we can modify. If not, we need to modify the entire template, which is best done with the Component Wizard, as discussed in Chapter 8.

It is also possible that the service and template that you need does not exist in the core (in that case, it probably exists in a separate component). Tracking them down is trickier because you need to recursively search this directory for service and template resources:

```
stellent/custom/
```

Luckily, in most cases this process is not necessary.

Finding the Correct Include

In most cases you don't need to modify an entire template to customize the look and feel. Overriding a handful of resource includes is usually sufficient. However, finding the correct include to modify can be complicated. There are more than 500 includes in the Content Server core. Even with additional tools, finding the correct include entails a bit of trial and error.

The first step is to use a web browser to run the service, for example, the CHECKIN_NEW_FORM service or the SEARCH_RESULTS service. Using the browser, do a View Source from your browser to obtain the source HTML. Save this for later.

Next, add the flag ScriptDebugTrace=1 in the URL of the web page, which produces a trace log at the bottom of the page. It lists all the includes used to create the page, such as std_page_begin, std_html_head_declararions, and std_page_end, to name a few. It also lists the files and line numbers in which each include is defined.

Next, open up the files that contain all the resource includes and all the localized web strings:

```
stellent/shared/config/resources/std_page.htm
stellent/shared/config/resources/lang/ww_strings.htm
```

In your component, copy over the include that you suspect is the correct one and insert some custom code into it. For example, add some custom HTML comments.

Finally, reload the web page. You can inspect the HTML source directly or turn on the ScriptDebugTrace to see whether your include was used.

Your include might not appear for a handful of reasons. If you add a new resource file to a component, the data in it will not be loaded until the Content Server restarts. Another problem might be that the loadOrder of your resource is too low. If you are overriding a popular include, there is a good chance that somebody has set the loadOrder flag to a number higher than 1.

In the latter case, the ScriptDebugTrace indicates which component's resource is being used instead of yours. You then have to inspect its component definition file to determine which loadOrder it is using. Finally, set your loadOrder to be a higher number and then restart. Your custom include should now be visible.

The important and frequently overridden includes are described in Appendix D.

Finding Includes and Templates in Other Components

Assume that you want to modify the Folders component or a core include or template is overridden by another component. In addition to searching the core include resource files, you also need to search custom components for their resources.

Luckily, the ScriptDebugTrace outputs the filenames and line numbers to where an include is defined. It should be clear immediately which additional files need to be inspected for resource definitions.

Adding Search Feedback Buttons

On the Google search results pages, the user gets feedback and can see the search terms. If there is a typo, Google suggests an alternative spelling for the search and offers a link to run it. Similar functionality is also possible in the Content Server by making a modification to the Search Results page and taking advantage of the <TYPO> parameter for the Verity search engine.

The first step is to determine which include we need to modify. By applying the method described previously, you must first determine the service name and its template. By running a search, we can inspect the URL to determine that the service called is GET_SEARCH_RESULTS. By inspecting this service definition, we can determine that the template name used is

StandardResults. By inspecting the `templates.hda` file, we see that this template is associated with the file `search_results.htm`:

```
<!DOCTYPE HTML PUBLIC "-//IETF//DTD HTML//EN">
<html>
<head>
<$if isTraySearch$>
    <$include std_html_head_declarations$>
    <script language="JavaScript">
        <$include trays_search_script$>
    </script>
<$else$>
    <$include searchapi_result_html_head_declarations$>
<$endif$>
</head>

<$if isTraySearch$>
    <$include trays_searchapi_result_body_def$>
    <$include trays_searchapi_result_page_content$>
<$else$>
    <$include searchapi_result_body_def$>
    <$include searchapi_result_page_content$>
<$endif$>

</body>
</html>
```

This template is fairly straightforward. Most of the display logic is contained in the `searchapi_result_page_content` include, which is similar to the update, check-in, and search pages as well. Because these pages are customized so often, most of the code is placed in `dynamichtml` resource for easier modification.

However, looking through `searchapi_result_page_content` to determine all included references is tedious. A quicker approach entails searching for HTML or strings that are nearby where you want to modify. There are two approaches: we can view the source HTML or look for the localization key.

We want to modify the search results page near the top, where it says Found XXX Items Matching The Query. Searching for the string `Matching The Query` in the string files yields the localization key `wwFoundMatchesForQuery`.

Next, we search `std_page.htm` to find where this key is used. There are only three hits, so we have narrowed the field considerably. The `xui_result_nav_links` include looks correct, but we need to verify. To do that, we add `ScriptDebugTrace=1` to the URL of the search results page. The include `xui_result_nav_links` is indeed referenced in the right place, whereas the others are not.

There is another problem: what if this include is used on multiple pages? Do we want to customize all those pages or just the Search Results page? We need to run another search of `std_page.htm`, along with all templates, to see where else it is referenced. Because it doesn't appear anywhere else, we can safely modify it without concern.

If this include were used on multiple pages, you might want to control whether or not your modifications should be displayed. For example, what if this include were also used to display results in the Library or Folders pages? These pages use strict predefined queries and do not alter based on user input. Therefore, giving feedback would be superfluous.

In general, each template sets specific IdocScript flags, such as isCheckin and isSearch, among others. If you want your modifications to appear on only one page, you need to control whether to display your customizations based on the value of these flags. As a last resort, you can use the value for IdcService to control the display.

Now that you know which includes to override, you can make the component. To begin, open the Component Wizard and create the component SearchFeedback. Add an HTML resource and override the include xui_result_nav_links.

In most situations, you should never override a core include without using the super tag. This component is one of the exceptions. Because we need to modify the include in the middle, we cannot use the super tag. Instead, this include is an exact copy of the core include, but with the addition of three lines:

```
<@dynamichtml xui_result_nav_links@>
<table style="width:100%" border="0" cellspacing="0" cellpadding="0">
    <tr>
        <$if FromPageUrl and not isTrue(>
            #active.HideParentLinkForQueries)$
        <td width="75" align="center">
            <a href="<$FromPageUrl$>"><$strTrimWs(
                inc("open_folder_image"))$></a>
        </td>
        <$endif$>

        <td class="xuiPageHeadingCell"
            style="padding-right:15px;white-space:nowrap" nowrap>
            <span class="xuiPageTitleText"
                style="padding-right:10px"><$eval(pageTitle)$></span>
            <span class="xuiDisplayText_XSm"
                style="white-space:nowrap" nowrap>
            <$if not (TotalRows like "-1")$>
                <$if IsLoggedIn and IsSavedQuery and ResultsTitle$>
                    <$lc("wwFoundMatchesForNamedQuery",
                        TotalRows, ResultsTitle)$>
                <$else$>
                    <$lc("wwFoundMatchesForQuery", TotalRows)$>
                <$endif$>
            <$else$>
                <$if EmptyResult$>
                    <$lc("wwNoResultsForQueryPlain")$>
                <$endif$>
            <$endif$>
            </span></td>
```

```
    </tr>
</table>

<!-- custom modifications here -->
<$include custom_search_results_header$>
<!-- end custom modifications -->

<br style="line-height:10px">

<table style="width:100%" border="0" cellspacing="0" cellpadding="0">
  <tr>
<$if IsMultiPage$>
    <td class="xuiDisplayText_Sm_Bold"
        style="width:50%;vertical-align:middle;
          padding-right:15px;white-space:nowrap" nowrap>
          <$if not EndRow or EndRow < StartRow$>>
            <$EndRow = StartRow +
              getValue("SearchResults", "#numRows") - 1$>
          <$endif$>
          <$if TotalRows < 0$>>
            <$lc("wwXuiItemsShownNoTotal", StartRow, EndRow)$>
          <$else$>
            <$lc("wwXuiItemsShown", StartRow,
              EndRow, TotalRows)$>
          <$endif$></td>
        <td style="width:auto">
<$include xui_results_page_nav_controls$>
        </td>
<$else$>
        <td class="xuiDisplayText_Sm_Bold" style="width:50%">
           </td>
<$endif$>
        <td class="xuiDisplayText_Sm_Bold"
          style="width:50%;text-align:right;padding-left:15px;
            vertical-align:middle;white-space:nowrap" nowrap>
          <table style="width:100%" border="0" cellpadding="0"
            cellspacing="0">
            <tr>
              <td class="xuiDisplayText_Sm_Bold"
                style="width:auto;text-align:right;
                padding-left:15px;padding-right:
                4px;vertical-align:middle;
                white-space:nowrap" nowrap>
                <$lc("wwActionsLabel")$></td>
              <td style="width:10px;text-align:left;
                vertical-align:middle">
```

```
            <$include xui_searchapi_results_action_form$>
                </td>
            </tr>
        </table>
    </td>
  </tr>
</table>
<br style="line-height:9px">
<@end@>
```

The only difference is the addition of the hook custom_search_results_header, which doesn't exist in the core, along with two comments. There are two advantages to doing it this way:

- If the core include changes in the next version of the product, it's easier to make your component compatible with the changes.

- If another person wants to add a custom search header, they can take advantage of your new hook with the super tag.

Next, we need to create the include for our custom code. We want some feedback about what the search terms were. In addition, we want links to redo the search for terms that sound the same or are possible correct spellings of the term. The custom code looks like this:

```
<@dynamichtml custom_search_results_header@>
<!-- only show this if full text search was used -->
<$if ftx$>
<table style="width:100%" border="0" cellspacing="0" cellpadding="0">
    <tr>
        <td style="padding-right:15px;white-space:nowrap" nowrap>
            <span class="xuiDisplayText_XSm"
                style="white-space:nowrap" nowrap>
            <$exec inc("determine_query_display_strings")$>
            Searched For: <$xml(displayQueryText)$>
            <$if expandSearchUrl$>
                | <a href="<$expandSearchUrl$>">Expand search</a>
            <$endif$>
            </span></td>
    </tr>
</table>
<$endif$>
<@end@>

<@dynamichtml determine_query_display_strings@>
<$displayQueryText = QueryText$>
<$if TranslatedQueryText$>
    <$displayQueryText = TranslatedQueryText$>
<$endif$>
```

```
<!-- don't do this if it's already a typo search -->
<$if not (displayQueryText like "*<typo>*")$>

    <!-- a full text query will look like "term" or
        "...(term)" or "...%3eterm%3c". Determine the
        correct place to add the <typo> tag -->
    <$index = strIndexOf(displayQueryText, "(") + 1$>
    <$if index == 0$>
        <$index = strIndexOf(displayQueryText, "%3e") + 3$>
        <$if index == 2$>
                <$index = 0$>
        <$endif$>
    <$endif$>

    <!-- insert the TYPO tag into the query -->
    <$expandedQueryText = strSubstring(displayQueryText, 0, index)
        & "<typo> " & strSubstring(displayQueryText, index)$>

    <!-- generate a search url based on the include
        searchapi_navigation_common_url. This needs the query
        to be in the QueryText variable, so we must store it
        and reset it after -->
    <$oldQueryText = QueryText$>
    <$QueryText = expandedQueryText$>
    <$expandSearchUrl = inc("searchapi_navigation_common_url")$>
    <$QueryText = oldQueryText$>
<$endif$>
<@end@>
```

Finally, enable the component and restart the Content Server. Let's try this out by running a search for items with *test* in the title and full text. However, we accidentally run it with the typo *tset*, which yields a search results page like that shown in Figure 9-1.

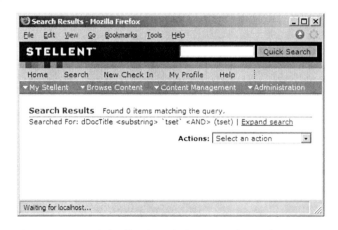

Figure 9-1. *Search feedback with the Expand Search option*

Notice that there are no results. However, if we expand the results, we will obtain documents that have *test* in the title, and something spelled like *test* in the full text.

Note that the <SOUNDEX> and <TYPO> modifiers work only on the full text of the document.

Personalized Quick Links

The Content Server stores personalization data for every user. The workflow queue, saved searches, and personal URLs are all stored with the personalization engine. They are stored as name value pairs or ResultSets in HyperData (HDA) files on the file system. These HDA files are called topics. For example, the personalization data for the sysadmin user is stored in HDA topic files in this directory:

```
stellent/data/users/profiles/sy/sysadmin/
```

The personal URLs and saved searches are stored in the file pne_portal.hda, whereas workflow information is stored in wf_in_queue.hda. The topics for these files are pne_portal and wf_in_queue, respectively.

These values are cached inside the Content Server and can be loaded up from any IdocScript page with the functions utLoad, utGetValue, and utLoadResultSet. For example, to obtain the preferred email format for a user, this code is used:

```
<$exec utLoad("pne_portal")$>
<$format = utGetValue("pne_portal", "emailFormat")$>
```

This code loads up the data in the file pne_portal.hda for this specific user and caches it. Then the value for emailFormat is pulled from the HDA file and assigned to the variable format. In general, the call to utLoad is unnecessary because it is called in the include std_js_bootstrap_vars, which is included on most Content Server pages.

Services can read personalization data, but more important, they can write it. For example, the service SAVE_USER_TOPICS is the most basic service that saves personalization data and then redirects to the home page:

```
<tr>
  <td>SAVE_USER_TOPICS</td>
  <td>UserService
      17
      REDIRECT_TEMPLATE
      null
      null<br>
      null</td>
  <td>3:prepareTopicEdits::0:null
      3:prepareRedirect:IdcService=GET_DOC_PAGE&Action=GetTemplatePage&
            Page=HOME_PAGE:0:null</td>
</tr>
```

In the method prepareTopicEdits, the value for numTopics is pulled from the request. Based on that number, a number of personalization topic strings (topicString1, topicString2,

... topicStringN) are pulled from the request and processed. For example, to add a new row to a result set in a personalization topic, the following data is sent in a request:

```
topicString1=addMruRow:topicName:resultSetName:column1,column2
numTopics=1
column1=data1
column2=data2
```

The topic string contains four entries separated by colons. The first entry is the addMruRow action to add a row. The second entry is the name of the topic (such as pne_portal or wf_in_queue). The third entry is the name of the result set in the topic file. The fourth entry is a comma-separated list of column names. The order is important because the first column is considered the unique lookup key for the result set.

Based on this topic string, the values for column1 and column2 are pulled from the request. The values are then placed in the proper result set in the proper topic file.

To delete this same row from the personalization topic, send the following data:

```
topicString1=deleteRows:topicName:resultSetName:data1
numTopics=1
```

This data is similar to the topic string for adding entries. The first entry is the deleteRows action. The second and third are the same as before. The fourth gives the value for the unique key used to delete the row. In this case, the name column is the unique key because it occurs first, and the value for name must be passed along in the string.

Most personalization data takes the form of simple name-value pairs. To add one, use the following topic string:

```
topicString1=updateKeys:topicName:paramName:paramValue
numTopics=1
```

For this sample component, we use the personalization engine to display a set of quick links for each user. The PersonalURLs is presented in a sidebar on the right of the screen. Because this list is most useful if presented on every page, we need to modify an include that is used on every page. Typically, we should make a modification to the include std_page_begin because it is present on every page in the HTML body.

To begin, open the Component Wizard and create the component QuickLinks. Add a HTML include resource to the component and then add three includes to this resource:

```
<@dynamichtml std_page_begin@>
<$include super.std_page_begin$>
<$include quick_links_sidebar$>
<@end@>

<@dynamichtml quick_links_sidebar@>
<div id="quickLinksSidebar" class="quickLinksHidden"
    onClick="slideTray('quickLinksSidebar')">
<div class="menuB_HeaderMenuCell"
    style="width:100%;height:100%;padding-left:20;">
```

```
<table>
<tr>
    <td><a class="menuB_TopCollectionItem"
        href="javascript:addSidebarLink()">
        Add Current Page...</a></td>
</tr>
<tr>
    <td> </td>
</tr>
<$loop PersonalURLS$>
<tr>
    <td style="white-space: nowrap">
        |<a class="menuB_TopCollectionItem"
        href="javascript:deleteSidebarLink('<$js(title)$>')">X</a>|
        <a class="menuB_TopCollectionItem"
        href="<$website$>"><$PersonalURLS.title$></a>
        </td>
</tr>
<$endloop$>
</table>
</div>
</div>
<@end@>


<@dynamichtml std_style_declarations@>
<$include quick_links_style_declarations$>
<$include super.std_style_declarations$>
<@end@>

<@dynamichtml quick_links_style_declarations@>
DIV.quickLinksHidden
{
    width: 20;          // 20 px wide at first
    height: 200;        // 20 px high
    position: absolute;     // absolute control over position
    right: 0;           // place it all the way on the right edge
    top: 200;           // place it 200px from the top
    overflow:hidden;        // hide any HTML that doesn't fit
}
<$include super.std_style_declarations$>
<@end@>
```

The first include just adds a hook to std_page_begin for a separate include named quick_links_sidebar. As before, the modification to the core std_page_begin include is kept as simple as possible to maximize forward compatibility.

The include `quick_links_sidebar` contains a few DIV containers and a TABLE for the quick links. The list of custom URLS are pulled from the `PersonalURLS` result set in the `pne_portal` topic. To load them with IdocScript, the following code is used:

```
<$exec utLoad("pne_portal")$>
<$utLoadResultSet("pne_portal", "PersonalURLS")$>
```

It is not necessary to have this code in the custom includes because it is already called in `std_js_bootstrap_vars`. After the result set `PersonalURLS` is loaded to the page, we can loop over it and then pull the values title and website from it. With them we create a link to the page, along with a label. For convenience, there is also an X character to the left of the link so the user can delete it. There is another convenience link that allows the user to add the current page to the list of quick links.

In addition to the HTML, we need custom Cascading Style Sheet (CSS) code on each page. For this, we modify the include `std_style_declarations` and add custom CSS. This include is present on almost all Content Server pages, similar to `std_page_begin`. In our case, we want absolute control over the size and position of the sidebar, and we want only a little bit of it to stick out of the right side. The full sidebar should be visible only when the user clicks it.

Finally, we need some custom JavaScript. To add some style, the sidebar rolls out instead of simply appearing. In addition, we need the support functions to allow the adding and deleting of rows in the personalization result set. Because we need these functions on every page, we must modify the include `std_javascript_header_functions`:

```
<@dynamichtml std_javascript_header_functions@>
<$include super.std_javascript_header_functions$>
<$include quick_links_javascript_header_functions$>
<@end@>

<@dynamichtml quick_links_javascript_header_functions@>
var quickLinksHidden = true;
function slideTray(id)
{
    var elem = document.getElementById(id);
    if (quickLinksHidden)
    {
        // slide out the links
        slideWidth(id, 200, 20, 10);
    }
    else
    {
        // slide in the links
        slideWidth(id, 20, -20, 10);
    }
    quickLinksHidden = !quickLinksHidden;
}
function slideWidth(id, targetWidth, step, wait)
{
    var elem = document.getElementById(id);
```

```
    // determine if conflicting elements should be hidden or
    // shown after the slide is complete
    var conflictDisplayStyle = "hidden";
    if (step < 0)
        conflictDisplayStyle = "visible";

    // if the slide is not yet complete
    if ( (step > 0 && elem.offsetWidth < targetWidth) ||
         (step < 0 && elem.offsetWidth > targetWidth) )
    {
        // modify the width by a small amount
        elem.style.width = elem.offsetWidth + step;

        // hide/show any conflicting elements
        setConflictingElements(conflictDisplayStyle, elem);

        // create a timeout callback to this same function again
        // after a few milliseconds have passed
        var timeout = "slideWidth('" + id + "', " + targetWidth +
            ", " + step + ", " + wait + ")";
        setTimeout(timeout, wait);
    }

}
function addSidebarLink()
{
    // obtain the URL of the current page, and prompt for a title
    var website = document.location;
    var title = prompt("Select a title for this link:",
        document.title);

    if (title != null)
    {
        // this is a URL to save this link, then redirect back
        // to the current page
        var submitUrl = httpCgiPath +
            "?IdcService=SAVE_USER_TOPICS" +
            "&topicString1=addMruRow:pne_portal:PersonalURLS:" +
              "title,website" +
            "&numTopics=1" +
            "&website=" + escape(website) +
            "&title=" + escape(title) +
            "&RedirectUrl=" + escape(document.location);

        document.location.replace(submitUrl);
    }
}
```

```
function deleteSidebarLink(title)
{
    // this is a URL to delete this item, then redirect back
    // to the current page
    var website = document.location;
    var submitUrl = httpCgiPath +
        "?IdcService=SAVE_USER_TOPICS" +
        "&topicString1=deleteRows:pne_portal:PersonalURLS:" +
            escape(title) +
        "&numTopics=1" +
        "&RedirectUrl=" + escape(document.location);
    document.location.replace(submitUrl);
}
<@end@>
```

When you click the sidebar, the function slideTray is executed. This in turn calls the function slideWidth, which changes the width of the sidebar by a few pixels. After this, the function calls setTimeout to run slideWidth again in a few milliseconds. Eventually, the sidebar will be fully extended, and the sliding stops. This is a commonly used DHTML trick to create simple animation on web pages.

We also need to use the setConflictingElements function, which is a part of the Layout Manager libraries. Because of bugs with the SELECT and APPLET tags in Internet Explorer, it is necessary to hide such elements when doing DHTML animations. The function setConflictingElements will automatically hide misbehaving elements when it detects an overlap.

The functions addSidebarLink and deleteSidebarLink call Content Server services to modify the personalization. The constructed URLs contain all the parameters needed to save or delete an entry from the personalization topic and then redirect back to the current page.

Finally, enable the component and restart the Content Server. The quick links are barely visible as a rectangle on the right side (see Figure 9-2). By clicking the rectangle, the links slide out onto the page.

There are several possible extensions to this component. For example, it can be used as a shopping cart to contain recently viewed items. Or context-sensitive links can be placed on the sidebar, directing the user to related content.

Another modification is to have it automatically save the most recent 10 searches. To do this you need to modify the service GET_SEARCH_RESULTS to include the prepareTopicEdits action, which enables us to prepare topic strings and save the results of the QueryText parameter automatically.

Additional personalization information can also be displayed and edited on the User Profile page. See the following resources on the USER_INFO template: user_profile_personalization, user_info_extra_topics_script, and user_info_submit_form. Modify these includes to allow a user to manually alter the personalization settings.

You can also modify this component to optimize the performance of the page loads. Because the JavaScript and CSS are included on every Content Server page, it makes sense to offload them to static JS and CSS files, and reference them with a link. See "Adding and Modifying Navigation and Nodes" in Chapter 8 for an example.

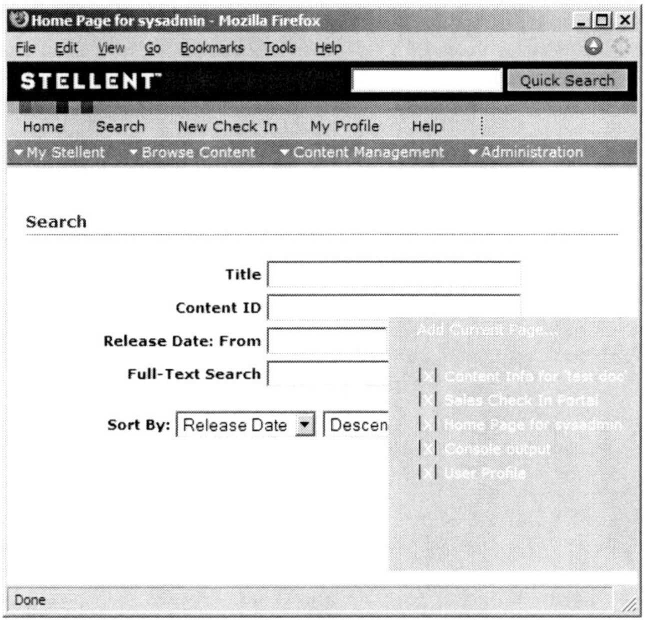

Figure 9-2. *Quick links after sliding onto the page*

Hidden and Preset Metadata Fields

The display of metadata fields on the check-in and search pages is controlled by flags inside IdocScript includes. These flags can be triggered by parameters in the URL, in the configuration files, or in a custom IdocScript include.

The includes of most interest for metadata display are `std_display_field`, `std_meta_field_display`, `compute_std_field_includes`, and `compute_std_field_overrides`. These includes are covered in earlier chapters and in Appendix D.

The include `std_display_field` controls the majority of the display of all metadata fields. This include outputs a combination of HTML and JavaScript to display a field based on flags set with IdocScript or in the URL. The include `compute_std_field_includes` sets the majority of these flags, which are as follows:

fieldName: Name of the field, such as `dDocTitle` or `xComments`

fieldCaption: Visible caption for the field

fieldType: Format of the data (`Text`, `BigText`, `Int`, `Memo`, or `Date`)

fieldIsOptionList: True if the field is an option list

fieldOptionListType: Type of option list (`choice`, `chunval`, `strict`, `combo`, `multi`, or `multi2`)

isRequired: True if this field is required for check-ins

requiredMsg: Message to display if a check-in is attempted with this required field unset fieldCaptionInclude: Include used to display the metadata caption in std_display_field, such as std_field_caption

fieldEntryInclude: Include used to display the FORM input for this field in std_display_field, such as std_field_entry

You can override these flags with a customization of the include compute_std_field_overrides. You can also manually set these flags before including std_display_field. For example, the std_document_title_field include displays the Title field with the following code:

```
<@dynamichtml std_document_title_field@>
<$fieldName = "dDocTitle", fieldCaption = lc("wwTitle"),
  isRequired = 1, fieldType = "BigText",
  requiredMsg = lc("wwSpecifyTitle")$>
<$if isPublicationMetaData$>
    sHidden="1"$
<$endif$>
<$include std_display_field$>
<@end@>
```

At the end of std_display_field, the include std_field_cleanup sets these flags to null. This prevents data pollution and enables you to call std_display_field immediately again with another field.

In addition, the output of this include can be controlled by global flags that are scoped to specific metadata fields, which enables you to pass parameters in a URL that affect only one metadata field. Some commonly used flags are the following, where xFieldName is the name of the affected metadata field:

xFieldName:isExcluded: This field is completely excluded from the page.

xFieldName:isHidden: The field is present but hidden on the page.

xFieldName:isInfoOnly: The field is present, but its value is presented in a read-only format.

xFieldName:isRelocated: The field has been manually moved to a different place on the page.

xFieldName:isRequired: The field is required.

xFieldName:include: Set this to an include to use instead of std_display_field to completely override how this field is displayed.

For example, to hide the Comments and Content ID fields, set these flags in IdocScript or in the URL:

```
xComments:isHidden=1
dDocName:isHidden=1
```

Because these flags are scoped to the specific metadata field, they are more portable and safer to use.

The `std_display_field` include is used on most pages in which metadata fields are displayed, including the search, check-in, content info, and update pages. It displays the include differently based on the following global flags, which are usually set on the templates or in `std_doc_page_definitions`:

`isCheckin`: True on a check-in new or check-in selected page

`isNew`: True on a check-in new page

`isUpdate`: True on an update content info page

`isInfo`: True on the content info page

`isQuery`: True on a search page

`isDocPage`: True if any of the above flags are set

`isUploadFieldScript`: True when the include should output JavaScript instead of HTML; used to generate code for check-in and search forms

`isFormSubmit`: True on a page in which metadata form submission is possible, for example, update, check-in, or search pages

`isEditMode`: True on a check-in or update page

In practice, most people design their resource includes to be as flexible and reusable as possible. Flags such as the preceding help you display the same include differently on multiple pages. For example, the `std_document_title_field` is displayed as a form input on the check-in page, but a simple display field on the content info page. The flags `isCheckin` and `isInfo` control which HTML the resource include outputs. Other includes are displayed differently based on the credentials of the current user, flags in the URL, or the metadata of the current content item.

For this example, we use these flags and includes to make the following modifications to the metadata display:

1. Preset the value for xComments on the check-in page.

2. Hide the xComments field on the check-in page.

3. Make the xComments field read only on the update page.

4. Add JavaScript validation to the Content Name field to block illegal characters.

5. Replace the Content Type drop-down list with a button that pops open a separate web page to allow metadata selection.

To begin, open the Component Wizard and create the component CustomMetadata. Add an HTML Include resource to it and open it up in a text editor.

The first three modifications can be done with two includes:

```
<@dynamichtml std_doc_page_definitions@>
<$include super.std_doc_page_definitions$>
<$include custom_modify_comments_definitions$>
```

```
<@end@>

<@dynamichtml custom_modify_comments_definitions@>
<$if isCheckin$>
    <$xComments:isHidden = 1$>
    <$xComments = "some preset and hidden comments"$>
<$elseif isUpdate$>
    <$xComments:isInfoOnly = 1$>
<$endif$>
<@end@>
```

This include is fairly straightforward. If it is a check-in page, set two flags. One makes the Comments field hidden; the other sets a default value for it. If it is an update page, the Comments field is read-only, so it cannot be changed on the form. Also notice the use of the super tag.

The include std_doc_page_definitions is used because it is present on all document pages (check-in, search, content info, and so on) and occurs before much HTML or JavaScript is drawn to the page. It is very important to always place global flags in this include because it occurs before any metadata fields are drawn.

This is a common customization for check-in pages that have several dozen custom metadata fields. You can modify this include to control metadata display based on the user or the current content item. Content Server version 7.5 added a feature called Content Profiles, which makes these kinds of customizations easier.

The fourth modification is more difficult and cannot be done with Content Profiles. It also cannot be done with global flags. We must override a core include for this customization:

```
<@dynamichtml std_upload_validation@>
<$include super.std_upload_validation$>
<$include validate_doc_name_script$>
<@end@>

<!-- override to check for spaces in the doc name field -->
<@dynamichtml validate_doc_name_script@>
<$if fieldName like "dDocName"$>

    // obtain the value from the current form
    value = form.dDocName.value;

    // use a Regular Expression to look for any non legal character
    var regex = /[^A-Z,a-z,0-9,_]/;

    // if there's a match, stop the checkin
    if (value.match(regex))
    {
        alert("The Content ID '"+ value + "' is invalid.\n" +
            "Only numbers, letters, and underscores are allowed.");
        return;
```

```
    }
<$endif$>
<@end@>
```

The Content Server creates JavaScript validation code for check-in and update pages by looping over the known metadata fields and including std_display_field. When isUploadFieldScript is set, the include std_upload_validation outputs the validation JavaScript for this field.

By default, if a field is a validated option list, it extracts the current value and validates it against the option list. If it's a required field, and the value is left blank, an error message appears. The field dDocName is sometimes required, but we want to also validate its value. So we must override this include to add our custom validation.

Notice that the include validate_doc_name_script does not output anything unless the fieldName equals dDocName, which prevents the validation code from executing for other fields, such as title or primary file.

The JavaScript validation itself is nothing particularly complicated. Using a regular expression, we determine whether the dDocName field contains anything other than letters, numbers, or underscores. If a match is found, we alert the user that the field is incorrect and then return from the function. This process prevents the validation from completing and therefore stops the check-in.

The final modification is the most difficult. It entails completely overriding how the HTML appears for the dDocType field on a check-in page. It also requires a custom template to hold the list of values and allow a user to select one.

In this case, there is no global flag that can help us alter the presentation of this field. We could use the flag dDocType:include to completely override the field, but that requires more customization than is needed. The best option is to use the existing includes as much as possible:

```
<!-- this does the same thing as above, but using different
     flags and a different include -->
<@dynamichtml compute_std_field_includes@>
<$include super.compute_std_field_includes$>
<$if fieldName like "dDocType"$>
    <$if isCheckin or isUpdate$>
        <$fieldEntryInclude = "custom_doc_type_popup_field_entry"$>
    <$endif$>
<$endif$>
<@end@>


<!-- this creates the input field, with a popup -->
<@dynamichtml custom_doc_type_popup_field_entry@>
    <input type="text" name="dDocType" value="<$fieldValue$>">
    <input type="button" value="Select..."
        onClick="popupMetadataSelect(this.form.name,
            'dDocType', 'docTypes')">
```

```
<script language="JavaScript">
function popupMetadataSelect(formName, fieldName, viewName)
{
    // open up a popup window to select a content type
    window.open("<$HttpCgiPath$>?IdcService=GET_DOC_PAGE" +
        "&Action=GetTemplatePage&Page=TREE_POPUP" +
        "&formName=" + formName + "&fieldName=" + fieldName +
        "&viewName=" + viewName, fieldName + "_popupWindow",
        "width=500,height=500,toolbar=0,location=0");
}
</script>
<@end@>



<!-- this is needed so that during metadata validation, the
    JavaScript will look for an INPUT field, and not a SELECT
    field named 'dDocType' -->
<@dynamichtml std_upload_field@>
<$if fieldName like "dDocType"$>
    sStrictList = ""$
<$endif$>
<$include super.std_upload_field$>
<@end@>
```

In the preceding code, we customize compute_standard_field_includes and set the flag fieldEntryInclude, which allows us to override just the HTML FORM element that is displayed on check-in and update pages. Specifically, we replace the standard include with custom_doc_type_popup_field_entry.

This include contains everything that we need: some JavaScript to pop open a window, a HTML INPUT element to contain the content type, and a button to click to execute the popup. The URL for the popup is a simple Content Server request to obtain the template page TREE_POPUP, which we will define in a moment. It also contains information about the metadata field, the form it's on, and the Schema View that was used to generate the option list.

Finally, we need a bit of code to override how the Content Type field is validated in JavaScript. The core includes generate JavaScript validation code that expects the Content Type field to be in an option list. Because this is not the case, we need to reset the local flag isStrictList to be blank, which prevents the default validation.

Next, we need to use the Component Wizard to create a template resource named TREE_POPUP. The minimum requirement for this page is a list of the possible options. These options should have links or buttons that allow the user to select one of them, fill in that value on the original check-in page, and close the popup window.

The JavaScript to fill in values and close the page is simple to create. Displaying the entries is a bit harder, and there are several possibilities.

The easy way is to loop over the ResultSet DocTypes and display all entries with a link to a JavaScript function. This is made simple because that data is present on all pages that execute the GET_DOC_PAGE service as well as all Dynamic Server Pages.

Alternatively, we can use a custom service instead of the GET_DOC_PAGE service. Such a custom service should execute a predefined SQL query and store the values in a ResultSet. Then we can loop over that ResultSet and display the values to the page. This query can even be executed against a remote database.

Instead of either of these options, this popup page uses the JavaScript APIs that are a part of Content Server 7.5. We use the Schema API to obtain option lists and the Layout Manager API to display the values in a tree format.

By using the Schema API for Content Server 7.5, administrators can create complex option lists based on database tables with the Configuration Manager applet. These option lists can be made so that the values they display are dependent on selected values. They can be filtered based on the user's security credentials or they can be localized based on the user's language.

When a metadata field is configured with an option list, its values are stored in the database as a Schema View, which is simply a database table with associated rules for filtering and displaying fields. This data is published out to static JavaScript files or delivered dynamically. Either way, on all metadata pages in Content Server 7.5, the Schema API is used to display the option lists.

In this example, we use this API to load all the option list values for Content Type and then generate an XML node for each option. Using this data, we then generate a tree control with Layout Manager APIs:

```
<html>
<head>

<$include std_html_head_declarations$>

<!-- include this just in case the 'Classic' layout is being used -->
<SCRIPT LANGUAGE="JavaScript"
    src="/dev7/resources/layouts/commonNav.js"></SCRIPT>

<script>

var g_viewName = "<$viewName$>";

// called by the navigation nodes to fill a value into the form
function setTreeValue(value)
{
    document.treeValueForm.treePath.value = value;
}

// set the proper value on the checkin form, and close the popup
function submitTreeForm()
{
    var value = document.treeValueForm.treePath.value;
    window.opener.document.<$formName$>.<$fieldName$>.value = value;
    window.close();
}
```

```
// using the option lists from schema or elsewhere, create XML
// nodes, and draw them to the page in a tree control
function drawPopupTreeNodes()
{
    // create the coreNav object to hold data about nodes
    var popupNavBuilder = new navBuilder();

    // use the standard tree drawing JavaScript functions
    // to draw this navigation to the page
    popupNavBuilder.makeCoreHtml = tree_control_CoreHtml;
    popupNavBuilder.makeOpeningHtml = tree_control_OpeningHtml;
    popupNavBuilder.makeClosingHtml = tree_control_ClosingHtml;

    // obtain the view definition, which contains a chunk of a
    // database table, along with label & value column names
    var viewDef = getViewDefinition(g_viewName);
    var labelIndex = viewDef.schLabelColumn;
    var valueIndex = viewDef.schInternalColumn;

    // loop over the row entries
    for(var i=0; i<viewDef.rows.length; i++)
    {
        // extract the value and label
        var value = viewDef.rows[i][valueIndex];
        var label = viewDef.rows[i][labelIndex];

        // create a navigation node for it
        popupNavBuilder.addChildNodeTo("NAVTREE", "item",
            "id==" + value, "label==" + label,
            "url==javascript:setTreeValue('" + value + "');");
    }

    // build the XML tree for navigation purposes
    mapXMLTree(popupNavBuilder.xmlRoot, popupNavBuilder.xmlNodeMap);

    // select an XML node to be the root display node
    var node = popupNavBuilder.getNodeById("NAVTREE");

    // select a HTML element to write the new nodes into
    var htmlElem = document.getElementById("popupTreeMenuDiv");

    // build up the 'htmlString' for this popupNavBuilder, and insert
    // it into the appropriate HTML element
    generateChildNodeDisplayCode(popupNavBuilder, node, htmlElem);
```

```
    // a workaround to help the layout manager find the correct frame
    var name = window.frames.name;
    if (!window.frames[name])
        window.frames[name] = window.frames;
}

// load up the schema data for this specific view
function loadPopupViewData()
{
    // determine the location of the script file for this schema
    // view. It could be a static file, or a dynamic page
    var viewInfo = constructViewPathInfo(g_viewName);
    var srcPath = viewInfo.path;
    if (viewInfo.url != null)
        srcPath = viewInfo.url;

    // load the script file
    loadViewValues(new Array(null, srcPath, null));
}

// initialize the schema JavaScript objects that contain the
// option lists. These must be done as callbacks, since they're
// requesting a JS file over the web might take several seconds
function initSchema()
{
    // execute the function 'loadPopupViewData' when schema is loaded,
    // so we can load up the view data
    registerGlobalCallback(new Array(loadPopupViewData));

    // execute the function 'drawPopupTreeNodes ' when the view data
    // is fully loaded
    var encodedViewName = jsFilename(g_viewName);
    registerViewCallback(encodedViewName,
        new Array(drawPopupTreeNodes));
}
</script>

</head>

<$include body_def$>

<h4 class="pageTitle">Select A Node</h4>

<div style="text-align:center;">
```

```
<div style="width:100%; height:350px; border:1px solid black; overflow: auto"
    id="popupTreeMenuDiv">
</div>

<br><br>

<form name="treeValueForm" action=""
    onSubmit="return false;">
Value: <input name="treePath" value=""><br><br>
<input type=button value="  OK   " onClick="submitTreeForm();">
<input type=button value=" Cancel " onClick="window.close();">
</form>

</div>

<script>
initSchema();
</script>
<$include std_schema_footer$>

</body>
</html>
```

The first thing to notice is that there is not much IdocScript on this page. The include
std_html_head_declarations is needed to generate the links to the Schema JavaScript files.
And the std_schema_footer is needed to initialize the Schema API after the page is loaded.
Other than that, it's entirely JavaScript—although it is very complex JavaScript.

Advanced JavaScript code looks quite strange to people accustomed to other programming languages. In JavaScript, libraries and resources are loaded with web requests, which is
extremely risky because you do not know how much time such web requests require. There is
no guarantee that the JavaScript resources will be available quickly—or ever. We also must be
careful not to use JavaScript to modify the HTML until we know for certain that the browser
has fully rendered the HTML.

In most cases, these load times are negligible. So it is not uncommon to find web pages
that load resource files and then use them immediately. Alternatively, some pages use the
onLoad event handler for the BODY tag to make sure that resources are loaded prior to using
them. However, neither method works if you need to dynamically load large JavaScript files
after the page is fully loaded.

In the Schema architecture, all option lists are contained in JavaScript files, which are
either statically published or dynamically generated. These files might contain hundreds of
options, and the browser might need to load several of them. Therefore, these load times are
not negligible, and the JavaScript needs to be more robust.

Therefore, all Schema API calls are *asynchronous* in nature. This means that when you
call a function, there is no immediate effect. Instead, the function executes when a certain

requirement has been satisfied. In this case, our custom functions do not run until Schema is ready to run them.

The Schema architecture uses `callbacks` to enable asynchronous JavaScript, so you must inform a global object that you desire to execute some code after the proper resource is loaded. This global object is `g_schemaDefinition`, which is present on all pages in which the Schema API is used.

These `callbacks` are present at the bottom of every Schema resource file. They notify the global Schema object that the resource has been loaded. Schema then runs any method that is dependent on that resource being present.

For example, after loading the view data for `dDocType`, this is called:

```
registerDefinition("doctypes", 1);
```

After which, any callback that was registered to run when this resource was loaded is executed. Now, assume that we want to run a function after this view resource is loaded. To do this, we use the `registerViewCallback` function in the following way:

```
registerViewCallback("doctypes", new Array(myFunctionName, param1, param2));
```

In this example, we need to register two callbacks. One of them loads the view data after Schema is initialized; the other one draws HTML to the page after that view is loaded. This is what the function `initSchema` does. As you can see, it is called soon after being defined to register the callbacks.

First, it registers a global callback, which means that as soon as schema is initialized, it executes the function `loadPopupViewData` without any parameters. We must first allow schema to initialize itself before we can ask it to load specific view data. The function `loadPopupViewData` does precisely that: it loads the view data for the view that corresponds to the JavaScript variable `g_viewName`, which is set to the name of the view passed in the URL (in this case, the `doctypes` view for the `dDocType` field).

The second thing `initSchema` does is register a view callback. This means that after the view data for `dDocType` has all been loaded, it calls the function `drawPopupTreeNodes`. This function extracts the values in this view with the function `getViewDefinition` and iterates over the rows.

To draw the rows as a tree, this function uses the Layout Manager API. It creates a new `navBuilder` object, and for each row in the view, it adds a new node. The ID and label for the node are extracted from the values in the view. The URL for each node is a call to `setTreeValue`, which populates the value in an input field at the bottom of the page.

After the nodes are all created, we call `mapXMLTree` to generate a navigation map for the XML nodes, which helps us find nodes more quickly in a complex XML structure and is required before drawing the nodes to the page.

Finally, we call `generateChildNodeDisplayCode` to generate HTML code based on those XML nodes. It also inserts the rendered HTML into the element with the id `popupTreeMenuDiv`.

We are now finally ready for testing. Enable this component with the Component Wizard, and restart the server. The check-in page now looks like Figure 9-3.

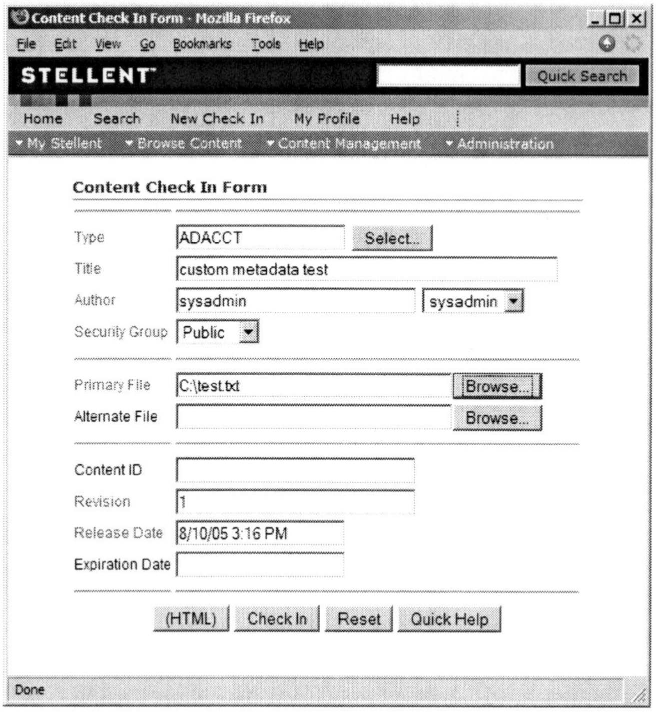

Figure 9-3. *Content Check In Form with Select button for content type*

Notice that the Comments field is now hidden from the page. It still exists on the page as a HIDDEN input element, so its value is passed along in the check-in. Also notice that the content type field is a text field with a Select button next to it. Clicking this button displays a popup that looks like Figure 9-4.

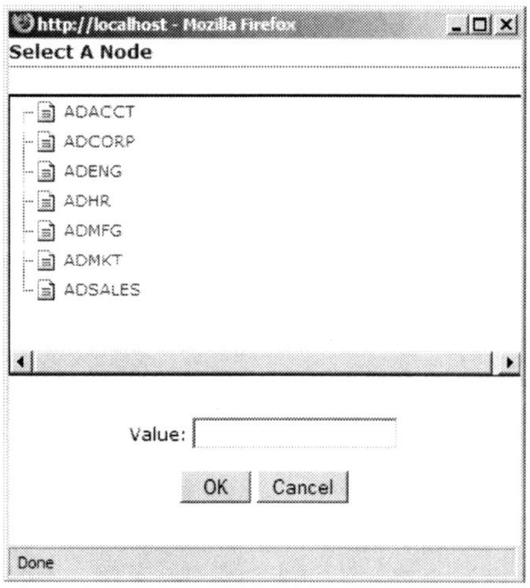

Figure 9-4. *Popup window to select a content type*

After selecting a content type, the value is populated in the input field on the bottom of the page. Click OK. The value you selected is now filled in on the check-in page.

Next, fill in the title and select a primary file to check-in. To test the Content ID validation, set it to my test document and click Check In. This is not a valid value because it contains spaces. So the check-in should be immediately halted with an error message about an invalid Content ID.

Change the Content ID to something without spaces and execute the check-in. After a successful check-in, navigate to the Info Update page for this document. It should look like Figure 9-5.

Figure 9-5. *Info update page with Select button for content type*

Notice that the Content Type looks the same on this page as it does on the check-in page. Also notice that the Comments field is now visible, but its value is read only. Its value is the one configured in the custom include std_doc_page_definitions.

JavaScript validation and read-only fields are only a convenience. They help the user input the correct values and prevent them from accidentally changing metadata values. They should not be considered secure against malicious contributors.

To guarantee 100 percent data integrity, you also need server-side validation of the data, which can be done with Content Profiles or with a Java component.

Component Best Practices

Creating a Content Server component generally requires very little custom code. The primary trick is locating the core resources to override. A good component developer follows several basic rules to make components as flexible and as easy to maintain as possible.

Use the IdocScript super Tag When Overriding Includes

This tag should always be used when overriding a core include or an include from another component.

It helps keep your code forward compatible. When a new version of the include is released, your component needs only minor modifications to be compatible.

Avoid Extensive Modifications to Core Resources: Create a Hook and Then Use It

Sometimes the super tag cannot be used—for example, when modifying another include in the middle or when altering a template page. In these cases, it is ideal to create a new resource. Place your customization inside the new include and reference the include where you want to make your modification.

Creating and using hooks help keep your code more maintainable and more forward compatible. It also enables other components to reuse your newly created resource with the super tag.

Use IsJava or IsSoap in the URL to View Raw Response Data

To see which variables, result sets, and option lists are returned by a service call, place IsJava=1 or IsSoap=1 in the URL to the web page. This process returns a dump of all data that is available after a service call, which is vital for debugging your customizations.

Note that this is only a dump of what is returned by the service, not the variables that are defined on the page. IdocScript functions such as loadDocMetaDefinition and executeService are run after the service is finished, during page rendering. These functions can place additional Result Sets onto the page. Additionally, many resource includes define important flags that affect page display.

To obtain a dump of all data available on the page at any time, you can use the trace function.

Use ScriptDebugTrace to Locate Includes

To see which includes are being used on a page, place ScriptDebugTrace=1 in the URL, which outputs a trace of every include used on the page and where that include is defined. This process is useful to get an idea of which include you need to modify to customize a core page and where it is defined. It is also useful to make certain that your include is being referenced after you have made the modification.

Note that this trace is present only on pages that use the std_debug_report include, which is referenced in the std_page_end include. Nearly all Content Server pages use std_page_end, but not all HCSTs or custom pages do.

Use trace to Debug IdocScript

IdocScript debugging is possible with the trace function. In its most basic form, it can be used to write data to the ScriptDebugTrace output:

```
<$trace("my variable = " & myVar)$>
```

In version 7.5, this function was expanded to support logging to the Java console, to the web logs, or to a named IdocScript string. You can use it to get a dump of all data in the response, including all currently defined IdocScript variables.

```
<$trace("#all", "myScriptTrace")$>
<$myScriptTrace$>
```

The trace function is useful for determining which IdocScript variables are currently defined, as well as which ResultSets and OptionLists are available.

Scope Resources to the Name of the Component

Although the names for tables, templates, and includes exist in different namespaces, they are all flat namespaces. Therefore, if one component creates a template called COMPONENT_ADMIN, no other component can do the same without overriding it.

To avoid namespace collisions, scope all tables, templates, and includes to the name of your component.

If you intentionally want to override the resource used in another component, simply redefine that resource in your component. Make certain that the loadOrder for your resource file is higher than the other component's loadOrder. This value is set in the component definition file.

Use a Development Instance to Test Components

It is always a good idea to test components on a development instance before deploying them to a production instance because doing so helps avoid the downtime that is usually involved when upgrading components. Small conflicts become more probable for systems with multiple components.

It is also helpful to use a staging server between your development server and your production server, which helps you test whether your deployment strategy from development to production works as planned.

Internationalize Your Strings

None of the previous examples used internationalized strings. This simplicity is fine for demos, but it is not a good standard practice for enterprise-level deployments. It is generally good practice to define all string in resources like this:

```
<@wwHelloWorld=Hello World!@>
```

You then display them with this code:

```
<$lc("wwHelloWorld")$>
```

This procedure allows you to localize your component into other languages more quickly. All that is needed is another resource file for each language pack. If there is a remote possibility that you will need to support multiple languages, it is worthwhile to internationalize your strings.

Avoid Excessive Usage of Slow IdocScript Functions

When pages include a great deal of IdocScript, sometimes performance can become a problem. When a page is slow, look for overuse of the functions executeService and eval.

In the first case, people sometimes create pages in which they display a list of items and then execute a service request for each one. Depending on what service you execute, a call might take several milliseconds or several seconds, which can rapidly cause serious performance problems if you are not careful. Try to limit the number of requests to only those that are absolutely essential.

In the second case, advanced users sometimes place IdocScript code into IdocScript variables. These variables can then be executed with the eval function, which is an extremely powerful way to create dynamic code (but it can be slow). Instead, the functions getValue, setValue, and setResourceInclude can be used to do anything that eval can do, and they are much faster.

In either case, you can use certain IdocScript functions to boost performance. For example, the cacheInclude function allows you to render an include and then cache the results for as long as you like. The next time you include the resource, the data is pulled instantly from the cache. You can also use the setExpires or setMaxAge functions to cache entire pages for even better performance. See Appendix B for more information about these functions.

Summary

A custom component is frequently the best way to modify the Content Server interface. It requires less code than re-creating the pages in Hypertext Content Server Pages (HCSPs) or Java Server Pages (JSPs). However, it requires more familiarity with the Content Server. You need to know how to find the correct template, the correct resource include, and the best way to add your customization so it is forward compatible.

The IdocScript super tag is the best way to make components compatible with each other. Place your custom code entirely in a custom resource. Use the super tag to insert your code immediately before or after an existing resource. If you need to insert your code in the center of a resource, create a copy of the include and insert one line of IdocScript to include your custom resource.

Most metadata fields are displayed with a small handful of resource includes: std_display_field, std_meta_field_display, compute_std_field_includes, and compute_std_field_overrides. If you become familiar with them and the flags that affect their behavior, you can create flexible and portable components with ease.

CHAPTER 10

■ ■ ■

Advanced Component Architecture

This chapter introduces Advanced Component Architecture using Java, which is used to modify the core Content Server behavior, and add new features.

As mentioned in Chapter 2, the Content Server is a Service-Oriented Architecture (SOA). Almost all functionality is exposed with services, which are defined internally as sequences of actions: security checks, Java code, SQL queries, and template pages. Stellent uses formatted HTML resources to define these services, which makes them flexible and extensible. It is relatively easy to create custom services that call custom Java code or custom SQL queries.

Java components are very similar to components mentioned in the previous chapter, which changed IdocScript includes and templates to alter the user interface. This chapter shows how to go one step further to modify the services themselves with custom Java code.

By default, most Stellent services are focused on content management or server administration. Check-in, check-out, search, conversion, and workflow are examples of core Content Management services. You can modify them to run custom code in addition to the default code. You can also add new services to run entirely custom Java code.

It is also possible to use a different SOA framework, such as an application server, and run custom code from it. In this case, you are limited to executing existing Content Server services and running custom code with the results. For example, you could execute a Stellent search from an application server and then run a SQL query on a remote database based on the data returned. The advantage of this approach is that you need not understand the inner working of the content server to run custom Java code.

However, there are advantages to running such code as a Java component instead of in an application server:

Higher Performance: The business logic is closer to the data so content management services are always faster if written as Java components.

Flexible Security: The existing content security model is used to control access to custom services and content.

Database Support: Your component uses the existing Java Database Connectivity (JDBC) connection pools and predefined SQL statements, which enables immediate and secure support for multiple databases.

Automatic Service Oriented Architecture: When the code is placed in the Content Server, it acts as part of the core. The code automatically gains the benefits of SOA, including a Simple Object Access Protocol (SOAP), J2EE, COM, and command-line interface.

Modify Existing Behavior: Only a Java component can modify existing Content Server services or integrate fully with all future customizations to the server.

A good rule of thumb is this: if your custom application retrieves content during the item's life cycle, it is reasonable to run your code in a remote application server. For example, if all you need to do is search for existing items, check-in new revisions, or process them through workflows, an application server is a fine front end.

However, if your application adds new states to the life cycle of a content item, then it should almost always be tightly integrated with the Content Server framework. For example, the only way to ensure that your business logic is compliant with Records Management is to write your code in a custom Java component. Only then can you execute your custom code when important life-cycle events occur inside the Content Server. For example, you might need to clean up additional database entries when the item expires or when it is archived.

This chapter gives an overview of which kinds of Java customizations are possible. It will also discuss how to set up a Java development environment for creating the components. It also presents some best practices on how to create and debug Java components. Step-by-step examples of Java components are presented in Chapter 11.

After reading this chapter you will understand how Java components are important to all advanced customizations. Even if the majority of your code resides in an external application server, a small Java component could save weeks of a developer's time as well as perform significantly faster.

For more in-depth information on the component definition file, refer to Chapter 2. You may also want the HowToComponents, which is a set of tutorials on how to make a Java component. These tutorials, which contain JavaDoc-based documentation of several core Stellent Java classes can be downloaded from the Stellent support site or from the author's website: http://bexhuff.com/books/stellent-dev.

Finally, you may also find the *Customizing Content Server Guide* and *Services Reference Guide* useful for more information about services and service actions. They are both included with the standard Content Server documentation.

Advanced Component Architecture

Java components have the same resources as all other components. They contain text-based resource and configuration files. Services and queries are defined in specially formatted HTML tables. The root Component Definition File is a HyperData (HDA)–formatted text file.

In addition, any custom Java code must be in the classpath of the Content Server. To do this, you can place all your compiled Java classes in this directory:

```
stellent/classes/
```

If you are using version 7.0 or later, the classpath also includes the local `classes` directory of enabled components. For example, consider a component named `HelloWorld`. The Java classes could be placed here instead:

```
stellent/custom/HelloWorld/classes
```

There are five primary ways in which custom Java code is used in a component:

Service Classes: A limited way to add new services

Service Handlers: A way to add new services or modify existing services with more portable code

IdocScript Extensions: Used to create custom IdocScript functions and variables

Filters: Used to execute custom Java code when specific events occur, such as when the server is started or when a new content item is checked-in

Class Aliases: Override core Content Server objects with custom objects

The most commonly used Java components are Filters and Service Handlers. IdocScript extensions are used slightly less often, but are still typical. Service Classes are discouraged, and Class Aliases are rarely used. They are described in greater detail in the following sections.

Service Classes

Using a Service Class is the easiest way to add a new service to the Content Server, although it lacks flexibility. A custom service's configuration can reference custom Java objects and execute methods within those objects. However, it is difficult to execute methods defined elsewhere in the core. For example, it would be extremely difficult to use a new Service Class to create a new kind of check-in service. It is mostly suitable for completely new services that do not perform content management–related functions.

For an example of how to configure a custom Service Class, recall how the core GET_SEARCH_RESULTS service is defined in `std_service.htm`:

```
<tr>
    <td>GET_SEARCH_RESULTS</td>
    <td>SearchService
        33
        StandardResults
        null
        null<br>
        !csUnableToRetrieveSearchResults</td>
    <td>3:getSearchResults::0:null</td>
</tr>
```

This code defines a service with the following characteristics:

```
Name:              GET_SEARCH_RESULTS
Service Class:     SearchService
Access Level:      33 (Read, Scriptable)
```

```
Template:              StandardResults
Service Type:          null
Subjects Notified:     null
Error Message:         csUnableToRetrieveSearchResults
Action 1:
    Type:              Java Method
    Action:            getSearchResults
    Parameters:        none
    Control Mask:      0
    Error Message:     null
```

Two things are of particular interest in this definition. The first is the Service Class; it is the classpath of the Java object that the Content Server creates to run this service. The full classpath is intradoc.server.SearchService, which extends the class intradoc.server.Service. The classpath prefix intradoc.server is assumed unless a full path is given in the definition.

As mentioned in Chapter 2, the most important part of the service definition is the list of actions. All services contain a list of actions, which execute either Java code or SQL queries. In this case, there is only one action. It is a Java method named getSearchResults.

This Java method exists in the class intradoc.server.SearchService. It might be defined there or in the super class intradoc.server.Service. In this case, it is defined in SearchService.

It is not an absolute requirement that a Java method be defined in the Service Class object. It can also be defined in a ServiceHandler object, as shown in later sections. In this simple case, SearchService has no registered Service Handlers. Therefore, it must exist in the Service Class object.

Not all Java methods can be referenced from a service definition. Private and protected methods are not available. Nor is any method that takes parameters. All accessible Java methods have the following signature:

```
public void myMethod() throws ServiceException, DataException;
```

To create a custom Service Class you need three things. A custom Java object that extends intradoc.server.Service, a Java method with the correct signature, and a custom service definition. For example, a custom service definition could look like this:

```
<tr>
    <td>HELLO_WORLD</td>
    <td>helloworld.CustomService
        0
        MSG_PAGE
        null
        null<br>
        null</td>
    <td>3:helloWorld_sayHello:::null</td>
</tr>
```

This code defines a service with one Java method, named helloWorld_sayHello. This method is contained in the Service Class, located in the object helloworld.CustomService. It is executed with a URL similar to this:

```
http://localhost/stellent/idcplg?IdcService=HELLO_WORLD
```

The custom Java code should look something like this:

```
package helloworld;

import intradoc.common.ServiceException;
import intradoc.data.DataException;
import intradoc.data.DataBinder;
import intradoc.server.Service;

public class CustomService extends Service
{
    public void helloWorld_sayHello()
        throws DataException, ServiceException
    {
        m_binder.putLocal("StatusMessage", "Hello World!");
    }
}
```

The member variable m_binder is a DataBinder object. This object is very important and is used throughout the Content Server because it contains all the data for the request and the response. In the preceding method, it sets the variable StatusMessage to the string Hello World! This variable is now a piece of the response data. Other Java methods can view or change this variable, and it can be displayed on a template page with IdocScript:

```
The message is: <$StatusMessage$>
```

If the helloWorld_sayHello method takes no parameters, how can you modify its behavior? For example, displaying a different status message for different people? There are three ways to do this.

The first option, to pass the parameter in the URL, is extremely flexible but less controllable. For example, to add a prefix to the StatusMessage, you first alter the Java method like this:

```
public void helloWorld_sayHello()
    throws DataException, ServiceException
{
    String prefix = m_binder.getLocal("prefix");
    m_binder.putLocal("StatusMessage", prefix + "\nHello World!");
}
```

And then alter the URL like this:

```
http://localhost/stellent/idcplg?IdcService=HELLO_WORLD&prefix=foobar
```

The value for the variable `prefix` is extracted from the `DataBinder` with the `getLocal` method, which is used to alter how the method works. The inherent flexibility makes this the most common method to modify how Java code works in the core. However, because these parameters can be manually set by your users, it is not always the best option when you need to restrict the possible parameters.

The second method is to place action parameters in the services definition itself. Only a component developer can set those parameters, but because they are not hard-coded in the Java code you can easily change them. This method can enhance security and prevent data pollution.

For example, we could alter the action list in the `HELLO_WORLD` service to look like this:

```
<td>3:helloWorld_sayHello:foo,bar::null</td>
```

As discussed in Chapter 2, this action has two parameters: `foo` and `bar`. They can be extracted with Java code like so:

```
String param1 = m_currentAction.getParamAt(0);
String param2 = m_currentAction.getParamAt(1);
```

The third method is to extract parameters from the context, which includes extracting user security data or flags set in the `config.cfg` for the Content Server. User data is contained in the `m_userData` object, mentioned in Table 10-1. Configuration information for the server, including cached tables and variables, are obtained with the `intradoc.shared.SharedObjects` class.

In general, the `Service` super class does not contain any methods that should be called directly. It mainly has support functions for running service actions in the correct order, initializing a user's security, running database queries, and creating the context for the request. The member variables of importance are shown in Table 10-1.

Table 10-1. *Important Service Class Objects*

Variable	Description
`intradoc.data.DataBinder m_binder`	The request and response data
`intradoc.data.Workspace m_workspace`	A connector object to the database
`intradoc.server.Action m_currentAction`	The current service action
`intradoc.server.PageMerger m_pageMerger`	IdocScript rendering object
`intradoc.server.ServiceData m_serviceData`	The current service's definition
`intradoc.shared.UserData m_userData`	The user running the service

Some functionality is not available with custom Service Classes. The service actions are limited to the methods defined in the custom `Service` object. It is not an easy task to execute service actions in other classes, such as `DocService` or `UserService`, and should not be attempted.

In practice, you should consider a Service Class to be a logical collection for a group of services. For example, `DocService` is a logical collection for document-related services, and `UserService` is a collection for user-related services. However, these Service Class objects should contain as little code as possible. For maximum flexibility, customizability, and forward compatibility, all service actions should be placed in `ServiceHandler` objects.

Service Handlers

These are similar to Service Classes, but more portable and flexible. Java code inside a custom Service Handler can be called from either a custom service or an existing service. Also, custom services that have Service Handlers can execute core Content Server methods. The Java code for a Service Handler is nearly identical to a Service Class, but it requires some additional configuration.

A Service Class can have one or more Service Handlers. In addition, code in a Service Handler can be called by services with different Service Classes. For example, code used in a DocService can also be used in a WorkflowService or a CollaborationService. Additional configuration is required to associate a Service Handler with each Service Class. Out of the box, this entire configuration is in the table ServiceHandlers in std_resources.htm. A small snippet of the table is as follows:

```
<@table ServiceHandlers@>
<table border=1><caption><strong>ServiceHandlers</strong></caption>
<tr>
    <td>serviceName</td>
    <td>handler</td>
    <td>searchOrder</td>
</tr>
<tr>
    <td>DocService</td>
    <td>DocCommonHandler</td>
    <td>10</td>
</tr>
<tr>
    <td>DocService</td>
    <td>DocServiceHandler</td>
    <td>20</td>
</tr>
...
```

This table shows the configuration for services that have DocService as their Service Class. This Service Class includes a significant number of core services, including CHECKIN_NEW and DOC_INFO. These services can execute Java methods defined in intradoc.server.DocService. The preceding configuration allows them to also execute methods defined in intradoc.server.DocCommonHandler and intradoc.server.DocServiceHandler, which enables code sharing between services with different Service Classes.

To demonstrate, assume that you need the HELLO_WORLD service to be able to execute check-in actions, as well as custom actions. To do this, first change the custom Service Class to DocService:

```
<tr>
    <td>HELLO_WORLD</td>
    <td>DocService
        0
        MSG_PAGE
        null
```

```
        null<br>
        null</td>
    <td>3:helloWorld_sayHello:::null</td>
</tr>
```

Now, define your Java method in a ServiceHandler instead of a Service:

```
package helloworld;

import intradoc.common.ServiceException;
import intradoc.data.DataException;
import intradoc.data.DataBinder;
import intradoc.server.ServiceHandler;

public class CustomServiceHandler extends ServiceHandler
{
    public void helloWorld_sayHello()
        throws DataException, ServiceException
    {
        m_binder.putLocal("StatusMessage", "Hello World!");
    }
}
```

As you can see, this code is very similar to the code for a Service.

Next you need a configuration table that makes your custom code available to all DocServices. This table is similar in structure to the ServiceHandlers table:

```
<@table HelloWorld_ServiceHandlers@>
<table border=1><caption><strong>
<tr>
    <td>serviceName</td>
    <td>handler</td>
    <td>searchOrder</td>
</tr>
<tr>
    <td>DocService</td>
    <td>HelloWorld.CustomServiceHandler</td>
    <td>100</td>
</tr>
</table>
<@end@>
```

Notice that the searchOrder is set to 100. Because it is custom code and it will not be executed very often, the searchOrder is set to a high number. If it were executed frequently for multiple services, a lower one would be more appropriate.

It is important to note that searchOrder behaves in a very different fashion than loadOrder. Both numbers dictate the order in which the resources are discovered—resources with low orders are discovered before resources with high orders. However, for resources with a loadOrder, the one with the *highest* order number is used by the Content Server, which allows component developers to override existing resources.

In contrast, if two Service Handlers contain the same methods, the Content Server uses the Service Handler with the *lower* searchOrder. In the previous example, the Content Server searches all known Service Handlers for DocService until it finds one that contains the Java method helloWorld_sayHello. It will search according to the searchOrder, from lowest to highest; then execute the first method it finds. If another method named helloWorld_sayHello exists in a different Service Handler with a higher searchOrder, this other method is ignored.

Finally, the data in the Table 10-1 must be merged into the core ServiceHandlers table by using MergeRules in the Component Definition File:

```
@ResultSet MergeRules
4
fromTable
toTable
column
loadOrder
HelloWorld_ServiceHandlers
ServiceHandlers
null
1
@end
```

Now any DocService can call your custom code, which is an ideal way to allow existing DocServices to execute custom service actions. It is also essential for making custom services that execute core code.

The ServiceHandler object is structured in a similar fashion to the Service object. The most important member variables are described in Table 10-2.

Table 10-2. *Important ServiceHandler Objects*

Variable	Description
intradoc.data.DataBinder m_binder	The request and response data
intradoc.data.Workspace m_workspace	A connector object to the database
intradoc.server.Action m_currentAction	The current service action
intradoc.server.Service m_service	Pointer to the parent Service object

The pointer to the parent Service object is used to obtain cached objects, user data, and the PageMerger object for rendering IdocScript (described in the previous section). The DataBinder and Workspace objects point to the original objects in the parent Service object.

When a Service has a Java method as its action, the Content Server scans the appropriate Service and ServiceHandler objects in a specific order looking for the method. The order is this:

1. The specific Service object for this Service Class (for example, intradoc.server.DocService).

2. All registered ServiceHandler objects for this Service Class according to the searchOrder, from lowest to highest.

Starting in Content Server version 7.5, Service Handlers have the additional feature of *chaining*, which enables two components to create a custom Service Action with the same name. When that action is referenced in a service definition, both pieces of code are executed instead of just the one with the lowest searchOrder.

For example, assume that you want to create a component that modifies what happens during a check-in after the files are added to the system. Because you want this to occur after the files are added, you cannot use the addFiles Filter, described in Appendix H. What are the options?

One option is to create a component with a modified version of the CHECKIN_NEW_SUB service, with a new action for the custom code. The following definition shows how you can customize this service to call myCustomAction right after the call to addFiles:

```
<tr>
<td>CHECKIN_NEW_SUB</td>
<td>DocService
    2
    null
    SubService
    null<br>
    !csUnableToCheckIn(dDocName)</td>
<td>3:setLocalValues:isCheckin,1,isNew,1,isInfoOnly,,isEditMode,1::null
    3:checkDocRules:changeAuthor,newDoc:0:null
    3:makeNewRevClass::0:null
    3:validateStandard::0:null
    3:mapResultSet:QnextRevID,dNextIndex,dID:0null
    2:UnextRevID::0:null
    3:checkCriteriaWorkflow::0:null
    3:validateCheckinData:Irevision,newRev:0:null
    2:Irevision::34:!csFailedToInsertRevision(dDocName)
    2:Imeta::2:!csUnableToCheckIn(dDocName)
    3:addFiles:Idocument:0:null
    3:myCustomAction::0:null
    3:setStatusMessage:checkin:0:null
    3:docHistoryInfo:Checkin,IdocHistory:1:null
    3:docRefinery::0:!csCheckInUnableToInitiateRefinery(dDocName)</td>
</tr>
```

The method myCustomAction is then defined in a custom ServiceHandler object, as demonstrated earlier. The problem here is that it is not completely forward compatible. The CHECKIN_NEW_SUB service is an important one and it might change in the future. Plus, only one component is allowed to override this service definition. What if another component also needs to modify CHECKIN_NEW_SUB? That is not possible—only one component is allowed to override a full service definition.

In version 7.5, two components can both modify the same service by *chaining* Service Handlers. The first step is to locate the service that you want to modify. Next, locate an action in that service that is executed at a point where you want to execute custom code. In this example, we want to execute custom code right after the addFiles action.

Next, create a custom `ServiceHandler` object that reimplements the `addFiles` method. Place your custom code in this new `addFiles` method. In this method, you can execute the original `addFiles` method at any time with a call to `doCodeEx`:

```
package helloworld;
import intradoc.common.ServiceException;
import intradoc.data.DataException;
import intradoc.data.DataBinder;
import intradoc.server.ServiceHandler;

public class CustomAddFilesHandler extends ServiceHandler
{
    public void addFiles() throws
        ServiceException, DataException
    {
        // custom code before 'addFiles' is called

        // call the core 'addFiles' method, or the next one
        // in the searchOrder
        m_service.doCodeEx("addFiles", this);

        // custom code for after 'addFiles' is called
    }
}
```

The `doCodeEx` method is very similar to the `super` keyword in IdocScript. It executes the code previously defined by either the core or another component. In this way you can execute your custom code either before or after calling the existing `addFiles` code. In addition, any other component can also do the same. You can create a new `ServiceHandler` with yet another method named `addFiles`. When it calls `doCodeEx`, the previous code is executed, which subsequently calls the `addFiles` method defined in the core.

The order in which these methods are executed depends entirely on the `searchOrder` set in the configuration table for the Service Handler. As mentioned earlier, the Content Server executes the `addFiles` method in the handler with the lowest `searchOrder`. A call to `doCodeEx` causes the Content Server to continue searching for more methods named `addFiles` in other handlers. If another method is found, it is executed. If not, the Content Server throws an error.

Therefore, to make the code work, the Service Handler must have a lower `searchOrder` than the one you want to override. All core Service Handlers have a minimum `searchOrder` of 10, so set yours to 5 to ensure that it is found first:

```
<@table AddAltFileHandlers@>
<table border=1><caption><strong>ServiceHandlers</strong></caption>
<tr>
    <td>serviceName</td>
    <td>handler</td>
    <td>searchOrder</td>
</tr>
```

```
<tr>
    <td>DocService</td>
    <td>helloworld.CustomAddFilesHandler</td>
    <td>5</td>
</tr>
</table>
<@end@>
```

Now any time the addFiles method is called, your custom Java code will be executed, which subsequently calls the original addFiles method.

In some cases, it might not be desirable to execute your custom code every time that addFiles is called. Perhaps you do not wish to execute it during batch check-ins, or archive check-ins. This can be easily fixed by triggering off the value for IdcService:

```
// only execute custom code for CHECKIN_NEW_SUB
String idcService = m_binder.getLocal("IdcService");
if (idcService.equals("CHECKIN_NEW_SUB")
{
    // put custom code here
}
```

In general, all new services added to the Content Server should be created as ServiceHandler objects. When modifying a custom service, use chained Service Handlers if possible. Service Handlers maximize flexibility and forward compatibility without much additional effort.

The example Hello World service in Chapter 11 contains step-by-step information on how to create custom Service Classes and custom Service Handlers.

Filters

Filters are used to trigger the execution of custom code when specific events occur in the Content Server. Some filter events occur for every service, some occur only for specific services, and others occur during events deep in the core of the product. The workflow, indexer, and subscription engines all have custom filter hooks. See Appendix H for a list of all filter events.

Filters are the easiest and most portable way to customize the Content Server's behavior. Filters are usually forward compatible, and any number of components can execute code for the same filter event. This allows two components to both hook into one filter event, and all custom code for that event will be executed according to the loadOrder in the component.

Because filters are the preferred way to customize core behavior, most of the examples in the next chapter use them. In addition, in the HowToComponents there are four other examples of filters:

DynamicPrefix: Uses the filter validateStandard, which occurs during check-in to change the AutoNumberPrefix

ScheduledEvent: Uses the filter scheduledEvents to hook into the internal scheduling system of the Content Server to run custom code at specific times

DataAccess: Uses the filter extraBeforeCacheLoadInit to create a database table upon the startup of the server

SecurityFilter: Uses the filter alterUserCredentials to boost a user's security access for one single request

Filter hooks are called from inside the core with this method:

```
intradoc.shared.PluginFilters.filter("validateStandard",
    workspace, binder, service);
```

The string validateStandard is the name of the filter event. This call executes all filters registered with that event. The context of the event is also passed to the filter, including a Workspace object, the current DataBinder, and the Service object. If the event does not occur within the content of a service request, such as startup events or background processes, a generic ExecutionContext object is passed instead. In rare situations, the ExecutionContext is null.

The return value of a filter can be CONTINUE, FINISHED, or ABORT. Each filter event deals with return values slightly differently.

All custom filters must implement the method doFilter and implement the interface intradoc.shared.FilterImplementor:

```
package mypackage;
import intradoc.common.ExecutionContext;
import intradoc.common.ServiceException;
import intradoc.data.DataBinder;
import intradoc.data.DataException;
import intradoc.data.Workspace;
import intradoc.shared.FilterImplementor;

public class MyFilter implements FilterImplementor
{
    public int doFilter(Workspace ws, DataBinder binder,
        ExecutionContext cxt)
        throws DataException, ServiceException
    {
        // put code here
        return CONTINUE;
    }
}
```

To register this filter, modify the Filters result set in the component definition file:

```
@ResultSet Filters
4
type
location
parameter
loadOrder
validateStandard
mypackage.MyFilter
null
1
@end
```

The `type` is set to the name of the filter event. The `location` is the full classpath to the custom object. The `loadOrder` controls when your code is executed if several components use this filter. Lower `loadOrder`s are executed first. The `parameter` value is a simple way to pass configuration information into the Java filter. Its value can be obtained with this code:

```
String parameter = (String)cxt.getCachedObject("filterParameter");
```

The `DataBinder` object contains the majority of the context of the filter event. However, in some cases the filter event uses additional *cached objects* to establish the context (for example, the `UserData` object, which describes who the user is and the credentials). Each filter has a different list of available cached objects. Refer to Appendix H for a complete list.

Unlike a Service or Service Handler, the important variables in a filter are not member variables; they are passed directly into the `doFilter` method or they are defined in the `FilterImplementor` interface. Using the names from `MyFilter`, the important variables are shown in Table 10-3.

Table 10-3. *Important Filter Objects*

Variable	Description
`intradoc.data.DataBinder binder`	The request and response data.
`intradoc.data.Workspace ws`	A connector object to the database.
`intradoc.common.ExecutionContext cxt`	A context for this request. This is typically a `Service` object, but not always.
`int CONTINUE`	Return this object if everything went well.
`int FINISHED`	Return this object to prevent running any more of this type of filter. Rarely used.
`int ABORT`	Return this object to halt execution entirely. Rarely used.

Filters usually return `CONTINUE` when finished. Occasionally, the `FINISHED` flag is returned, which stops the execution of any more filters for that event. The `ABORT` flag is returned very rarely.

Which flag to return depends on how the filter is called. In general, if everything finished successfully, return the `CONTINUE` flag. If a serious error occurs, throwing a `ServiceException` is generally done.

Filters are the quickest, easiest, and least-intrusive way to alter the Content Server's behavior with Java. People who write large Java components are encouraged to add custom hooks, so that others can easily modify their work. However, there are situations in which a filter might not exist exactly where you need one. When you cannot use a Filter or chain a Service Handler, your only option may be a Class Alias.

Custom IdocScript

IdocScript is the scripting language that is used throughout the Content Server. And like most things in the Content Server, it is customizable with Java code.

For simplicity and to enforce a strong separation between display logic and business logic, IdocScript does not allow you to define functions with IdocScript code; you must use custom Java. It is possible to obtain similar behavior with cleverly formatted resource includes, but typically custom functions are defined with Java code. Such functions are available on any template page or Dynamic Server Page (HCSP/T/F). They are useful for anybody who uses IdocScript extensively on rendered pages or workflows and want to extend the functionality. New computed variables, such as HttpCgiPath, can also be added.

In general, modifications to IdocScript should focus on page generation and display, and should be limited to read-only requests. IdocScript should never be used to write data on the Content Server or database; otherwise, data pollution and security holes might become a problem. The exception to this is IdocScript that is constrained with additional security to execute only in the context of a workflow.

There are two ways to add custom IdocScript. One method is to use the filter event computeFunction. Another method requires a custom Java object that extends intradoc.common.ScriptExtensionsAdaptor. The former is the easiest method and is covered in Chapter 11. The latter has better performance, but is beyond the scope of this book. Refer to the NewIdocScript component in the HowToComponents for an example.

Class Aliasing

A Class Alias is the most drastic option for customizing the Content Server. In many situations, a developer might want to significantly modify Content Server behavior deep in the core, where no Java Filter is available. Workflow, subscription, schema, and the indexer all have filter hooks, but sometimes they are not in the place you need.

Several, but not all, Java objects in the Content Server are instantiated using Java reflection. Every Service and ServiceHandler object, as well as important core objects, are created in this way. The Content Server framework uses Class Aliases to allow you to instantiate custom objects instead of the default objects.

For example, the SecurityImplementor object, which is used to set the security credentials for a user at the beginning of a service request, is instantiated like so:

```
Object obj = intradoc.shared.ComponentClassFactory.createClassInstance(
    "SecurityImplementor",
    "intradoc.upload.UploadSecurityImplementor",
    "!csUploadSecurityImplementorError");
```

This code creates the SecurityImplementor object with a default classpath of intradoc.upload.UploadSecurityImplementor. However, if you need to customize the SecurityImplementor object, you can create a Class Alias of it to override its behavior. The first step is to create a custom class that extends the default class and overrides individual methods:

```
package mypackage
import intradoc.upload.UploadSecurityImplementor

public class MySecurityImplementor extends UploadSecurityImplementor
{
    // override specific methods here
}
```

Next, configure the ResultSet ClassAlias in the component definition file. This ResultSet contains only the name of the object to implement and its new classpath:

```
@ResultSet ClassAliases
2
classname
location
SecurityImplementor
mypackage.MySecurityImplementor
@end
```

Starting in version 7.5, this ResultSet also supports the loadOrder feature. Similar to the loadOrder for resource files, it enables one component's ClassAlias to supercede another by having a higher loadOrder.

Because Class Aliases cause the component's class to override the default class, no Content Server can run two components that alias the same class. Therefore, it should be done only if no other option is available. In most cases, a Java Filter can be used instead. For example, in the previous situation, the filter alterUserCredentials might be a useful alternative to a Class Alias.

Class Aliases should be avoided at all cost. But if there is no other way, use the following guidelines:

- Keep all Class Aliases in one component that contains just Class Aliases for that version of the Content Server.

- Do not put any custom code in the Class Alias object. Instead, create a new Filter event and call it from the custom class. Then call the original code with the Java super keyword, if possible.

- Execute custom Java by leveraging the new filter events from a second component.

For example, in the preceding situation you need to Class Alias the SecurityImplementor object. Assume that you need to modify the determineUser method immediately before it is executed. To accomplish this, you can make a small Class Alias with just the following code:

```
package mypackage
import intradoc.upload.UploadSecurityImplementor

public class MySecurityImplementor extends UploadSecurityImplementor
{
    public String determineUser(Service service, DataBinder binder)
    {
        intradoc.shared.PluginFilters.filter("securityImplementorDetermineUser",
            workspace, binder, service);
        super.determineUser(service, binder);
    }
}
```

Now you should create a separate component and use the new filter hook that you invented (`securityImplementorDetermineUser`) to modify the behavior of this object.

In this way, it is easier to create components with Class Aliases that are forward compatible and can be modified by multiple components simultaneously. The only time this approach is not desirable is when a class is used so frequently that the overhead of calling a filter causes performance problems. Luckily, those cases are rare.

For the most part, these kinds of customizations require access to the original source code, especially if you need to modify code in the middle of a Java method. For a list of all possible Class Aliases, see Appendix I.

Setup of a Java Development Environment

The recommended Java development environment is Eclipse 3.0 or later:

`http://www.eclipse.org/downloads/`

This application is the de facto standard for Java compiling and debugging. It is supported by the Eclipse Foundation, which is a nonprofit corporation sponsored by Hewlett-Packard, IBM, Intel, and others. The application is free and open source. It has a thriving developer community with hundreds of free and commercial plug-ins. These plug-ins enable functionality such as VI or Emacs editors, JUnit for testing, XML/XSL editing, source control, syntax highlighting, JSP debugging, performance analysis, and many more.

To begin, download and install Eclipse 3.0 or later on the same server as a developer version of the Content Server. If you want, you should download and install the sample Java components for this book, which are available at the author's website for this book: `http://bexhuff.com/books/stellent-dev`.

This site offers downloads for the `HowToComponents` in addition to the samples from this book. They are a collection of small examples of all the major ways to create Java customizations. Some of the examples in the next chapter are simplified versions of the `HowToComponents`. They also come with the public JavaDocs for the Content Server's Java classes. Some of these components require additional steps beyond installing and enabling the components. Refer to the `readme.htm` contained within for any additional steps.

IDE Setup

After installing the `HowToComponents` and after installing Eclipse, you are now ready to set up a project. If you use an integrated development environment (IDE) different from Eclipse 2.x or 3.0, these steps will be slightly different.

■**Caution** Eclipse has a nasty habit of deleting compiled class files. This is a problem because some components do not ship with the Java source, so Eclipse cannot recompile them. If this happens, the only option is to reinstall the component. This is mainly a problem with components that need to retain backward compatibility with older versions of the Content Server.

To avoid problems, be sure to make a copy of all `classes` directories before attempting this setup. You can also configure Eclipse to not delete old class files in the first place:

1. Select Window ➤ Preferences from the top menu.

2. Select Java ➤ Compiler in the left menu.

3. Click the Build Path tab.

4. Uncheck the Scrub Output Folders box.

The side effect of this setting is that any time you move or rename a Java source file, you must manually delete its old class files. This limitation is generally not a problem because most Java customizations use relatively few class files.

Additionally, some Java developers have reported problems when compiling a component with a newer Java Virtual Machine (JVM) than the one that ships with the Content Server. For example, Eclipse 3.x uses JVM 1.5 by default, but the Content Server uses JVM 1.4.2. Stellent needs to interact with multiple third-party Java libraries (Java Database Connectivity [JDBC] drivers, XML parsers), some of which are not compatible with the 1.5 JVM. Therefore, it is always advisable to use the JVM that ships with Stellent when creating new components. You can easily configure this in Eclipse:

1. From the menu select Window ➤ Preferences.

2. In the left navigation, select the Java menu.

3. Click Installed JREs and click Add.

4. Set the JRE Name to `Stellent JVM`.

5. Click the Browse button and browse to Stellent's Java home directory. It should have a path similar to `stellent/shared/os/win32/j2sdk1.4.2_04`.

6. Click OK.

Any project for custom Java components must contain the Stellent Java libraries. When set up correctly, you can run the Content Server in a debugger so you can test your components. To do this, you need at least a base Stellent project containing all necessary Java libraries, native code, and configuration. Create this base project like so:

1. From the menu select File ➤ New ➤ Project.

2. Select Java Project and click Next.

3. Name it `Stellent` and click Next.

4. In the Source tab, click Add Folder.

5. Name the folder `classes`.

6. Click the Advanced >> button and the Link to File System.

7. Click Browse and browse to the `stellent/classes` directory for this instance. You might need to create this directory first.

8. Click OK on the remaining popup windows. If prompted to move source folders, select No.

9. At the bottom, under Default Output Folder, click Browse.

10. Expand the `Stellent` folder and select the `classes` folder, which places any newly compiled class files in the same folder as the Java source files.

11. In the Libraries tab, click Add External Jars, and add at least this library:

```
stellent/shared/classes/server.zip
```

12. Click Finish.

In step 11, there are about a dozen more JAR files in the `stellent/shared/classes` directory that you might need, depending on how your server is configured. For example, you might need `jtds.jar` if you use this JDBC driver for Microsoft SQL Server. You might need `ldapjdk.jar` if you use LDAP or `jspserver.jar` if you enabled JSP rendering. Some trial and error might be required for this step.

If you are using Content Server version 7.0 or later, each component could also have its own libraries and class folder. These are the folders named `classes` and `lib` in each component's directory. To add them to the classpath, do the following:

1. Under Project, click Properties.

2. Click the Libraries tab.

3. If the component has JAR files bundled with them, click Add External Jars to add them, similar to step 9 above.

4. If the component has a `classes` folder, click Add Class Folder to add them. You will need to create a new folder for this project, similar to the preceding steps 4–7.

Your base Content Server project is now set up, and you can now create new class files in the directory `stellent/classes/`. They will be automatically added to this project, and compiled along with the Content Server. Alternatively, you can place your Java files anywhere you want and add them to this project from the menu bar with File ➤ New ➤ Source Folder. You might need to use File ➤ Refresh to refresh the Java classes from the file system.

The settings for this project can be modified later from Project ➤ Properties ➤ Java Build Path. If you are using Eclipse 3.1, you must create the project first and then add source files to it from the Java Build Path dialog box.

Projects for Custom Components

Now that you have the primary Stellent project created, you can add new projects for your components. The process differs depending on your Content Server version and how you set up your component.

1. From the Eclipse menu, select File ➤ New ➤ Project.

2. Select Java Project.

3. Click Next.

4. Name the project the same as your component, such as `HelloWorld`.

5. Click Next.

6. In the Projects tab, select the Stellent project, which ensures that all Java classes in the Stellent project are available for your project.

7. Click Finish.

If your version is older than version 7.0, you might want to set the default output folder to the directory:

```
stellent/classes/
```

If your version is 7.0 or later, you should store your Java source files and output your class files to a specific component directory. For a component named `HelloWorld`, it would be here:

```
stellent/custom/HelloWorld/classes/
```

This code ensures a more discreet packaging of the component resources. More step-by-step examples are included in Chapter 11.

Compiling and Debugging

To compile, first click the `classes` folder in the Package Explorer on the left. Then from the menu, click Project ➤ Rebuild Project from the menu bar. You can configure the compiler from Project ➤ Properties ➤ Java Build Path.

To run or debug the server, you must do some initial configuration:

1. From the menu, go to Run ➤ Run or Run ➤ Debug.

2. Highlight Java Application and click New.

3. Name it `Stellent-IdcServer`.

4. In the Main tab, under Project, browse to the custom project you created, such as `HelloWorld`. Alternatively, you can select the main `Stellent` project. If you do so, make sure that the class files from your custom project are available to the `Stellent` project.

5. Under Main Class, enter **IdcServer**.

6. In the Arguments tab, uncheck the box Use Default Working Directory.

7. Click File System and browse to the directory `stellent/bin`.

8. In the Environment tab, click New.

9. Set the name to `PATH`.

10. Set the value to include the following directories, separated by semicolons, where *** is a name specific for your operating system, such as `linux` or `win32`:

    ```
    stellent/shared/os/***/lib
    stellent/shared/os/***/lib/htmlexport
    stellent/shared/search/vdk4/***40/bin
    stellent/shared/search/vdk4/***40/filters
    ```

Be sure to use full path names. This step enables the search engine and other non-Java features to function while running inside Eclipse. You might need to add additional native libraries depending on which components you have enabled.

11. Click Apply.

12. Click Run or Debug.

The Content Server should now start up in the Eclipse IDE. When running the debugger, you cannot debug into Content Server classes unless you have the source code. However, you can still set and hit breakpoints in your custom code.

Remote Debugging

Java has a built-in feature that allows you to attach to a remote running Java process and begin debugging it. This feature is well-integrated into Eclipse and easy to use with the Content Server. Remote debugging enables you to attach to a server running in production and step through breakpoints in the code. For performance reasons this method is not always advisable, but sometimes it's the only way to diagnose exotic problems.

Remote debugging is also a quick and easy way to attach to a running Content Server if you have difficulties launching it from Eclipse. If you have difficulties putting the correct JAR files in the library or the correct directories in the `PATH` variable, you can launch the Content Server in the normal way and then attach to it.

The primary difficulty is in making certain that you synch the Java and class files between your Eclipse project and your Content Server. Every time you make a change to a Java file and recompile it, you need to synch them up again.

To set up remote debugging, follow these steps:

1. Add the following single line to the file `stellent/bin/intradoc.cfg`:

```
JAVA_EXE=java.exe -Xdebug➥
    -Xrunjdwp:transport=dt_socket,server=y,address=8000,suspend=n
```

This line tells the JVM to launch in debug mode and allow remote debugging over port 8000. You might need to change java.exe to the full path to the Java executable running your Content Server.

2. Restart your Content Server.

3. Create a new Eclipse project for your component.

4. In the Eclipse menu, select Run ➤ Debug.

5. In the left menu, select Remote Java Application.

6. Click New.

7. Name it `Stellent-IdcServer-Remote`.

8. For Project, browse to the project that you created in step 3.

9. Under Connection Properties, fill in the hostname or IP address of the remote Content Server. If it is running on your machine, you can leave it as `localhost`.

10. Leave the Port number as 8000.

11. Click Debug.

You have now attached to the remote Content Server. You might set breakpoints in your code just as if it were launched from Eclipse. If you have any problems, make sure that the source code has been fully synched, restart the Content Server, and restart debugging from Eclipse. You might need to change the port number from 8000 to something else if that port is already in use. Also make sure that there is no firewall blocking access of that port between your workstation and the server.

Summary

When you need to customize the behavior of the Content Server or add new behavior, you frequently need to create custom components with Java code. Even if you are using an application server as a front end to the Content Server, you might need to create a small Java component to boost performance or modify existing behavior.

If you are creating new functionality, the preferred method is to use Service Handlers, which are extremely flexible and enable you to reuse existing Content Server code if needed. Even if you do not reuse existing Content Server code, you should create a Service Handler to make your code as forward compatible as possible. You might need to create a custom Service Class as a logical container for your Service Handler code, but you should minimize the amount of code in that Service Class.

If you instead want to modify core Content Server behavior, the best option is to use a Java filter. This is not always possible because the Content Server might not have a filter hook in the exact location you need. In this case, you can sometimes use a chained Service Handler to execute your code during a service request. As a last resort, you can create a Class Alias to modify the core behavior. However, to make sure that your code will be forward compatible, do not put any custom code into a Class Alias. Instead, use the Class Alias to add a custom Filter hook and then use that hook from a separate component.

Now that you know the basics of creating Java components, you are ready to create advanced customizations to the Content Server. The next chapter provides step-by-step examples of how to create the most common types of components.

Custom Java Components

This chapter contains step-by-step tutorials on how to create components that contain custom Java code. These components include simple Java filters, custom Service Handlers, and custom IdocScript functions. It also includes more-advanced samples, such as how to execute a service call from a filter, how to generate content items during the check-in process, and how to run database queries in Java.

Before continuing with any of these samples, be sure that you are familiar with the basics of the Component Wizard and that you have set up your Eclipse integrated development environment (IDE), as discussed in Chapter 10.

Dynamic AutoNumber Prefix

The simplest way to add custom Java code to the Content Server is with a Java filter. For this example, we will demonstrate how to automatically generate a Content ID with custom Java. This example shows, step by step, how to use the Component Wizard and Eclipse together to create your first Java component.

The auto numbering feature in the Content Server is a way to automatically generate Content IDs when items are checked-in. This ID is set to the next number in a counter, sometimes with an alphanumeric prefix. If you set these flags in the `config.cfg`, the Content ID is no longer a required field on the check-in page.

```
IsAutoNumber=true
AutoNumberPrefix=stel_
```

If the ID is not specified, the Content Server generates one. With the preceding value of `AutoNumberPrefix`, the generated ID looks like `stel_000001`. But what if you need additional information in that field (for example, the name of the user who checked it in, the language it is written in, or the department it came from)?

It is possible to put IdocScript in the `AutoNumberPrefix` flag, but sometimes it isn't sufficient. A more complete solution is to create a custom Java filter that executes when new items are checked-in. This Java code can then dynamically change the value of `AutoNumberPrefix` to whatever is needed.

To begin, create the component `AlterPrefix`:

1. Open the Component Wizard.

2. Click Options ➤ Add.

3. Select Create New Component and name it `AlterPrefix`.

The next step is to create a Java Project in Eclipse to contain your Java code. If your system is older than version 7.0, you can skip this step. Otherwise, do this:

1. Open Eclipse.

2. Select File ➤ New ➤ Project.

3. Select Java Project and click Next.

4. Name the Project `AlterPrefix` and click Next.

5. In the Source tab, click Add Folder.

6. Name the folder `classes`.

7. Click the Advanced >> button and the Link to File System box.

8. Click Browse and browse to the following directory:

   `stellent/custom/AlterPrefix/classes`

   You might need to create this folder first.

9. Click OK.

10. Set the output folder to `AlterPrefix/classes`.

11. In the Projects tab, click to add the `Stellent` project that you created in Chapter 10.

12. Click Finish.

All Java classes for this project will be placed in this folder:

`stellent/custom/AlterPrefix/classes`

This folder is the preferred place for component classes for version 7.0 and later. You can also build JAR files and place them here:

`stellent/custom/AlterPrefix/lib`

See the Component Wizard documentation for more details.

If your system is older than version 7.0, you do not need a new project. You can instead reuse the Stellent project that was created in Chapter 10. In this case, you should place your custom class files in the typical Stellent classpath:

`stellent/classes`

Now, in the appropriate classpath folder on the file system, create the folder `alterprefix`. In this folder, create the source file `CustomFilter.java` with the following contents:

```
package alterprefix;

import intradoc.common.ExecutionContext;
import intradoc.common.ServiceException;
import intradoc.data.DataBinder;
import intradoc.data.DataException;
import intradoc.data.Workspace;
```

```
import intradoc.shared.FilterImplementor;

public class CustomFilter implements FilterImplementor
{
    public int doFilter(Workspace ws, DataBinder binder,
        ExecutionContext cxt) throws DataException, ServiceException
    {
        // obtain the dDocType
        String type = binder.getLocal("dDocType");

        // if it exists (which it always should) set the
        // autonumber prefix to that value
        if (type != null)
        {
            binder.putLocal("AutoNumberPrefix", type + "_");
        }

        // filter executed correctly, return CONTINUE
        return FilterImplementor.CONTINUE;
    }
}
```

This class is an extension of a standard FilterImplementor (discussed in Chapter 10). It obtains the value for dDocType out of the request with the binder.getLocal function. It then sets the value for AutoNumberPrefix to be that value, plus an underscore.

Next, refresh the Eclipse project. The CustomFilter class should be visible and it should compile without any errors. If not, make sure that the Stellent project was created properly and all important JARs are in the build path.

Next, configure the component definition file with the name and classpath for this filter. In our case, we want this filter to execute during a check-in. A good filter hook for this is validateStandard, which is executed every time an item is checked-in or updated. Open the AlterPrefix component definition file, located here:

stellent/custom/AlterPrefix/AlterPrefix.hda

This file has several ResultSets listed. The one we're interested in is Filters. Configure this ResultSet to look like this:

```
@ResultSet Filters
4
type
location
parameter
loadOrder
validateStandard
alterprefix.CustomFilter
null
1
@end
```

This code tells the Content Server to execute the filter `alterprefix.CustomFilter` when the `validateStandard` event is triggered. Now we are ready for testing.

Enable the component and then restart the Content Server. Next, open a browser and navigate to a check-in page. For this example, we will set the content type to the default accounting document type, or ADACCT (see Figure 11-1).

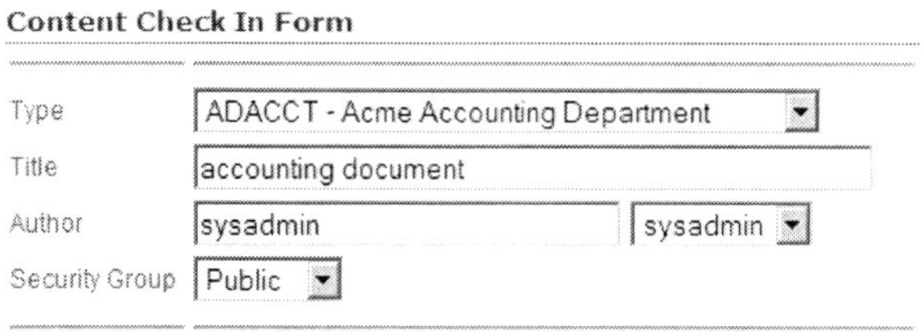

Figure 11-1. *Standard check-in form*

Fill in the appropriate metadata, and check-in a content item. After the check-in is complete, you should see a check-in confirmation page that looks similar to Figure 11-2.

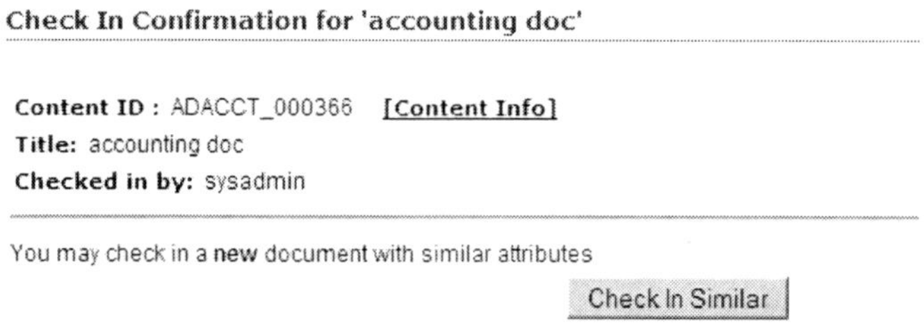

Figure 11-2. *Check-in confirmation page showing custom prefix*

As expected, the Content ID is now a number, with the Content Type as a prefix. There are several variations on this kind of component. You can use it to set the Content Type prefix to have a locale, such as en_ for English content, and fr_ for French content. Or it can be modified to be set to the department that the user came from.

If you receive an error message about your class not being found, make sure that your Java classes are in the correct directory. Sometimes Eclipse builds the class files into a local workspace instead of the component class folder. You might also need to disable and reenable the component if the class folders were not present when you first enabled the component.

In general, these kinds of filters are used for server-side validation of check-in metadata. For example, they can ensure that custom metadata fields have the proper format, or they can restrict metadata values based on security roles. For security reasons, metadata validation should be done with server-side Java code, not with client-side JavaScript.

For example, if you want to restrict the content type ADACCT to just people with the accounting role, your code looks like this:

```java
package alterprefix;

import intradoc.common.ExecutionContext;
import intradoc.common.ServiceException;
import intradoc.data.DataBinder;
import intradoc.data.DataException;
import intradoc.data.Workspace;
import intradoc.server.Service;
import intradoc.shared.FilterImplementor;
import intradoc.shared.SecurityUtils;
import intradoc.shared.UserData;

public class CustomFilter implements FilterImplementor
{
    public int doFilter(Workspace ws, DataBinder binder,
        ExecutionContext cxt)
        throws DataException, ServiceException
    {
        // obtain the dDocType
        String type = binder.getLocal("dDocType");

        // if it exists (which it always should) set the
        // autonumber prefix to that value
        if (type != null)
        {
            if (type.equals("ADACCT") && cxt instanceof Service)
            {
                UserData user = ((Service)cxt).getUserData();
                if (!SecurityUtils.isUserOfRole(user, "accounting"))
                {
                    throw new ServiceException("User '" +
                        user.m_name + "' is not an accountant.");
                }
            }
            binder.putLocal("AutoNumberPrefix", type + "_");
        }

        // filter executed correctly.  Return CONTINUE
        return FilterImplementor.CONTINUE;
    }
}
```

Now, if somebody who is not an accountant tries to check-in an accounting document, the check-in fails. By throwing a ServiceException, the Content Server is alerted that something went wrong in the filter. This exception halts the request, and causes the Content Server to roll back the database transaction and redirect to an error page.

To check this user's security, we need to cast the ExecutionContext object into a Service object. Then we can extract the UserData object from it, which contains all the information about who is running the request. We can then use the SecurityUtils.isUserOfRole function to inspect the user's access rights and throw an exception if the accounting role is not present.

Not all Filter events have a Service object as their ExecutionContext object. Some filters run deep inside the Content Server as background events. They are run anonymously and therefore have no UserData present. Sometimes the ExecutionContext object is null. It's generally a good idea to do instanceof tests before scoping the ExecutionContent object, as discussed previously.

The final step is to package the component so it can be deployed on another Content Server, which is important if you need to move the component from your development workstation to the testing server or the production server. To do this, we must configure the Component Wizard to package Java class files along with the component:

1. Open the component AlterPrefix with the Component Wizard.

2. Select Build ➤ Build Settings.

3. Click Add.

4. If you placed the class files in the directory stellent/custom/AlterPrefix/classes:

   a. Set the Entry Type to Component Class.

   b. Click OK.

5. Otherwise, if your class files are in the directory stellent/classes:

   a. Set the Entry Type to Classes.

   b. Set the Sub Directory to alterprefix.

   c. Click OK.

6. Set the version number for your component and increment it with each build.

7. Click OK.

8. Select Build ➤ Build.

9. Click OK.

This procedure creates a package of the component at this location:

stellent/custom/AlterPrefix/AlterPrefix.zip

This component package can now be deployed and installed on another Content Server with the Admin Server or the Component Wizard. You can also package extra resource files into this component, such as documentation and prepackaged JAR libraries. If your code requires additional Java libraries, the convention is to place them in a component folder named lib:

```
stellent/custom/AlterPrefix/lib/
```

These JAR files are placed in the Content Server's classpath when this component is enabled. Use the advanced build settings to include each JAR file. See the Component Wizard documentation for more details.

Hello World Service

In the previous example, we altered the behavior of an existing service. But it is also possible to create completely new services that execute custom Java code. This example shows the bare minimum that is required to create a new Content Server service. It demonstrates how to integrate custom Java code into a new service by creating a new Service Class. We will then expand upon the example and turn it into a Service Handler.

To begin, we should create a new component and Eclipse project named HelloWorld. Refer to the previous example for step-by-step instructions.

Now, in the appropriate classpath folder, create the folder helloworld. In it, create the file CustomService.java containing the following code:

```
package helloworld;

import intradoc.common.ServiceException;
import intradoc.data.DataException;
import intradoc.data.DataBinder;
import intradoc.server.Service;

public class CustomService extends Service
{
    public void helloWorld_sayHello()
        throws DataException, ServiceException
    {
        m_binder.putLocal("StatusMessage", "Hello World!");
    }
}
```

This Java Code is written as a Service Class, which is the simplest possible way to create a custom service. Any public method that takes no parameters is available as a service action. To define a custom service that executes this method, do the following:

1. Create a component named HelloWorld with the Component Wizard, and open it.

2. In the bottom-left pane of the Resource Definition tab, click Add.

3. Click Service and then click Next.

4. Click Next.

5. In the Add Service dialog box, set the Name to HELLO_WORLD.

6. Set the Service Class to helloworld.CustomService.

7. Set the template page to MSG_PAGE.

8. Under Actions, click Add.

9. In the Add Action dialog box, set the Type to Java Method.

10. Type helloWorld_sayHello in the action box.

11. Click OK.

12. Click Finish.

This code creates a service resource file at this location:

stellent/custom/HelloWorld/resources/helloworld_service.htm

This file contains a table resource formatted like this:

```
<@table HelloWorldServices@>
<table>
<tr>
    <td>Name</td><td>Attributes</td><td>Actions</td>
</tr>
<!-- This is a bare minimum service that executes custom Java code -->
<tr>
    <td>HELLO_WORLD</td>
    <td>helloworld.CustomService
        0
        MSG_PAGE
        null
        null<br>
        null</td>
    <td>3:helloWorld_sayHello:::null</td>
</tr>
</table>
<@end@>
```

Note that the Service Class used in this service is the fully qualified Java class name of the object we just created: helloworld.CustomService. The only service action in this definition is the Java method helloWorld_sayHello. The IdocScript template page used to render the response is MSG_PAGE. This is a standard Content Server template used to display the contents of the StatusMessage variable.

Finally, enable the component and restart the Content Server. We can then connect to the web page for this service with a URL similar to this:

http://localhost/stellent/idcplg?IdcService=HELLO_WORLD

The result of this service looks similar to Figure 11-3.

Figure 11-3. *Hello world message page*

This service now behaves as if it is part of the Content Server core. It can be executed from a web browser or from a remote application. For example, a Simple Object Access Protocol (SOAP) request for this service returns the following XML response:

```
<?xml version='1.0' encoding='iso-8859-1' ?>
<SOAP-ENV:Envelope xmlns:SOAP-ENV="http://schemas.xmlsoap.org/soap/envelope/">
<SOAP-ENV:Body>
<idc:service xmlns:idc="http://www.stellent.com/IdcService/"
    IdcService="HELLO_WORLD">
<idc:document dUser="sysadmin">
<idc:field name="StatusMessage">Hello World!</idc:field>
</idc:document>
</idc:service>
</SOAP-ENV:Body>
</SOAP-ENV:Envelope>
```

Next we will add more features to this example. Specifically, we will create a custom template page that allows the user to input data into a form. Then we will modify the code to send back a message based on the submitted data.

Start by adding a custom template page to the component:

1. Open up the `HelloWorld` component in the Component Wizard.

2. In the bottom-left pane, click Add.

3. Click Template and click Next.

4. Click Next.

5. Set the name to `HELLO_WORLD_FORM`.

6. Set the Class to Pages.

7. Set the Form Type to Form.

8. Set the name to `hello_world_form.htm`.

9. Click Finish.

This code creates a template file here:

`stellent/custom/HelloWorld/templates/hello_world_form.htm`

Edit this template to contain the following IdocScript:

```
<!DOCTYPE HTML PUBLIC "-//IETF//DTD HTML//EN">
<html>
<head>
<$defaultPageTitle="Hello World Form"$>
<$include std_html_head_declarations$>
</head>

<$include body_def$>
<$include std_page_begin$>

<h3>Hello World Form</h3>

<$if helloMessage$>
    <p><$helloMessage$></p>
    <p><a href="<$HttpCgiPath$>?IdcService=HELLO_WORLD_2">
        again...</a></p>
<$else$>
    <form method="GET" action="<$HttpCgiPath$>">
    <input type="hidden" name="IdcService" value="HELLO_WORLD_2">
    Enter Your Name: <input name="name">
    </form>
<$endif$>

<$include std_page_end$>

</body>
</html>
```

This template page is fairly simple. In the event that the variable `helloMessage` exists, the page displays it. Otherwise, it displays an HTML form. When submitted, the form executes the service `HELLO_WORLD_2`, with the parameter `name`.

Next, we must define the service `HELLO_WORLD_2`. This service is very similar to `HELLO_WORLD`, except that it uses `HELLO_WORLD_FORM` for its template and uses `helloWorld_sayHello2` as its action. Open the service definition HTML and add the following code for the service definition:

```
<tr>
    <td>HELLO_WORLD_2</td>
    <td>helloworld.CustomService
        0
        HELLO_WORLD_FORM
        null
        null<br>
```

```
        null</td>
    <td>3:helloWorld_sayHello2:::null</td>
</tr>
```

Finally, add this method to the CustomService class:

```
public void helloWorld_sayHello2()
    throws DataException, ServiceException
{
    String name = m_binder.getLocal("name");
    if (name != null && name.length() > 0)
    {
        String helloMessage = "Hello " + name + "!";
        m_binder.putLocal("helloMessage", helloMessage);
    }
}
```

Unlike the previous code sample, this method sets the helloMessage based on the request parameter name. To test this new service, navigate to the URL:

```
http://localhost/stellent/idcplg?IdcService=HELLO_WORLD_2
```

It should return a page similar to Figure 11-4.

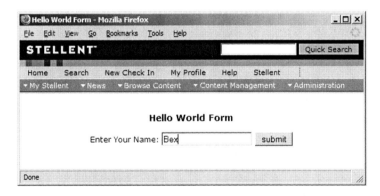

Figure 11-4. *Hello user form*

Upon first load, this page displays a data entry form in which users can input their name. When the user presses the submit button, the HELLO_WORLD_2 service is executed by the Content Server. This service executes the method helloWorld_sayHello2, which generates a value for helloMessage based on the form data. The method then places this value into the DataBinder and the service renders the response template HELLO_WORLD_FORM.

Because helloMessage is present in the response, the result template page will be rendered differently (see Figure 11-5).

Figure 11-5. *The hello world form displaying a hello message*

This service is also accessible from a SOAP request. If you pass the value for name in an external request, you receive a response with helloMessage:

```
<?xml version='1.0' encoding='iso-8859-1' ?>
<SOAP-ENV:Envelope xmlns:SOAP-ENV="http://schemas.xmlsoap.org/soap/envelope/">
<SOAP-ENV:Body>
<idc:service xmlns:idc="http://www.stellent.com/IdcService/"
     IdcService="HELLO_WORLD_2">
<idc:document dUser="sysadmin">
<idc:field name="name">Bex</idc:field>
<idc:field name="helloMessage">Hello Bex!</idc:field>
</idc:document>
</idc:service>
</SOAP-ENV:Body>
</SOAP-ENV:Envelope>
```

Service classes are easy to make, but are not very flexible. For example, what if you want to use this custom Java code in several different services? What if, instead of adding new services to the Content Server, you simply want to modify existing services such as CHECKIN_NEW or GET_SEARCH_RESULTS?

To make it more flexible, we need a ServiceHandler object. As mentioned earlier, a service definition can reference methods from only one Service Class. However, that Service Class can be configured to have multiple Service Handlers, so that the code in a Service Handler is more portable and can be shared between services. The code is almost exactly the same, but it requires slightly more configuration.

The first thing to do is create a new class, called CustomServiceHandler.java, with the following code:

```
package helloworld;

import intradoc.common.ServiceException;
```

```
import intradoc.data.DataException;
import intradoc.data.DataBinder;
import intradoc.server.ServiceHandler;

public class CustomServiceHandler extends ServiceHandler
{
    public void helloWorld_sayHello3()
        throws DataException, ServiceException
    {
        String name = m_binder.getLocal("name");
        if (name != null && name.length() > 0)
        {
            String helloMessage = "Hello " + name + "!";
            m_binder.putLocal("helloMessage", helloMessage);
        }
    }
}
```

This code is almost exactly like the previous code sample, except that it extends the intradoc.server.ServiceHandler object.

Note again that in this code we name the method helloWorld_sayHello3, which is used instead of something short like sayHello to preserve global uniqueness. Verbose method names are important in all custom Java methods, but especially so in Service Handlers.

The reason is this: after parsing the definition of a service and finding a Java action, the Content Server scans for a method matching that name. It executes the first method it finds. So if two components want to have different methods, both named sayHello, there is a problem. Only one of them will be executed.

As a result, you should take care to use verbose method names by scoping the name of the method to the name of the component.

Next, we need to add a new static table to this resource to register our code as a Service Handler. In this example, we will make it a handler for the DocService class so it can be called from the CHECKIN_NEW service. We need to first do the following:

1. Open the HelloWorld component in the Component Wizard.

2. Click Add in the bottom-left pane of the Resource Definition tab.

3. Click Resource – Static Table and click Next.

4. Name the table HelloWorld_ServiceHandlers.

5. Click Merge To and select the table ServiceHandlers.

6. Click Finish.

This process should create the following file:

```
stellent/custom/HelloWorld/resources/helloworld_resource.htm
```

This file contains the table resource you just created. The first row in the table is the list of column names, and the second row is sample data that you need to overwrite. Delete the sample row and modify the resource to look like this:

```
<@table HelloWorld_ServiceHandlers@>
<table border=1><caption><strong>
<tr>
    <td>serviceName</td><td>handler</td><td>searchOrder</td>
</tr>
<tr>
    <td>DocService</td>
    <td>helloworld.CustomServiceHandler</td>
    <td>100</td>
</tr>
</table>
<@end@>
```

This resource table has the same structure as the core `ServiceHandlers` table. The `serviceName` is the name of a Service Class, such as `DocService` or `UserService`. The `handler` is the Java path to the new `ServiceHandler` object to register with this service type. The `searchOrder` is the order in which this handler is sorted with the other handlers. As mentioned in Chapter 10, a handler with a lower `searchOrder` takes precedence over one with a higher `searchOrder`. Because it is custom code that does not override any existing service actions, we should set it to 100.

Adding this resource also changes the component definition file: `HelloWorld.hda`. The Component Wizard modified the `ResultSet` named `MergeRules` to contain information about this new table:

```
@ResultSet MergeRules
4
fromTable
toTable
column
loadOrder
HelloWorld_ServiceHandlers
ServiceHandlers
null
1
@end
```

This code means that the table we defined, `HelloWorld_ServiceHandlers`, will be merged into the core table `ServiceHandlers`. This is an essential step; otherwise, the core cannot locate the new `ServiceHandler`.

Finally, we need to make a change to our services to create the third iteration of the `HELLO_WORLD` service call. This one is a `DocService` and it calls the method `helloWorld_sayHello3`:

```
<tr>
    <td>HELLO_WORLD_3</td>
    <td>DocService
```

```
     0
     HELLO_WORLD_FORM
     null
     null<br>
     null</td>
   <td>3:helloWorld_sayHello3:::null</td>
</tr>
```

Notice that this is now a DocService and it doesn't require the fully qualified Java class name in the definition. Likewise, any service that is a DocService can have the method helloWorld_sayHello3 in its service definition.

For example, assume that we want to run custom code at the end of the CHECKIN_NEW service. This check-in service is a DocService. Therefore, we can place custom code in a Service Handler for DocService, exactly as we did previously.

The next step is to customize the CHECKIN_NEW service definition in our component. We can copy the standard definition and place it in our custom services resource table. Then you can modify the action list to contain a reference to the custom code from the Component Wizard with the following steps:

1. In the Resource Definition tab, in the left pane, click the service resource.

2. In the right pane, click Add.

3. Click the Select button at the top of the page.

4. Click the CHECKIN_NEW service in the list, and click OK.

5. In the Actions list, click Add.

6. Set the Type to Java Method.

7. Set the Action to helloWorld_sayHello3.

8. Click OK.

9. Click OK.

This procedure creates a copy of the CHECKIN_NEW service in our component, which overrides the behavior of the standard CHECKIN_NEW service. If you inspect the definition file, you see this extra service action:

3:helloWorld_sayHello3:::null

Now any time the CHECKIN_NEW service is executed, our custom code is also executed.

This is not the ideal way to modify the CHECKIN_NEW service. The custom code runs only when checking-in new content items; it does not execute when checking-in new revisions of existing items or for archive-based check-ins. It is also less forward compatible. If a future version of the Content Server changes the list of service actions, your component is no longer compatible.

As stated in Chapter 10, Java filters are the ideal way to customize existing services. The other option, new to version 7.5, is *chaining* Service Handlers (covered in the next example).

Add Alternate File

The *alternate file* is a rarely used feature that allows you to check-in two files at once. Typically, users check-in only the primary file. If they specify an alternate file, the primary file is stored in the vault, whereas the alternate file is indexed by the search engine and appears in the weblayout directory. This feature is mainly used when contributing large files that have no relevant text, such as images, video, or ZIP archives. To save space and facilitate finding the documents with the search engine, some users opt to create *alternate files* containing descriptions of the content.

In the previous example, you might have noticed that ServiceHandlers are more flexible than Services, but they still have a drawback: global namespaces. For example, take the method addFiles in DocServiceHandler, which is used to add files to the repository during a check-in. No other custom ServiceHandler can create a method named addFiles without causing conflicts. By default, only one of them is called. Whichever ServiceHandler is registered with the lowest value for searchOrder is discovered first and then executed.

This all changed in version 7.5. A new method was added to the root Service class that allows components to give their methods the same name as an existing method. Instead of executing only the first method, the Content Server can execute them both. This behavior is similar to the <$super$> syntax in IdocScript, and is called *chaining* Service Handlers.

In essence, chaining Service Handlers is like having a filter hook before and after every Java method in every ServiceHandler object. As such, using chained handlers is a far superior method for plugging-in custom code. They allow multiple components to modify the behavior of the same service action, but without conflicting with each other. Additionally, they allow your components to be more forward compatible.

To start out, use the Component Wizard to make the component CustomAddFiles, and use Eclipse to make the project CustomAddFiles, as in the previous examples.

Now, in the proper class folder, create the folder customaddfiles. In it, create a Java source file named AddFileHandler.java with this code:

```
package customaddfiles;

import intradoc.common.FileUtils;
import intradoc.common.ServiceException;
import intradoc.common.StringUtils;
import intradoc.data.DataBinder;
import intradoc.data.DataException;
import intradoc.server.ServiceHandler;

import java.io.File;
import java.io.IOException;
import java.io.Writer;


public class AddFileHandler extends ServiceHandler
{
    public void addFiles() throws ServiceException, DataException
    {
```

```java
    // pull the alternate file name, if any, from the request
    String altFile = m_binder.getLocal("alternateFile");

    // pull the flag from the request data
    String makeAltFileStr =
        m_binder.getLocal("createAlternateFile");

    // if no alternate file exists, and the above flag
    // is 'true' in the request, generate the file
    boolean makeAltFile = StringUtils.convertToBool(
        makeAltFileStr, false);
    if ((altFile == null || altFile.length() == 0) && makeAltFile)
        createAlternateTextFile();

    // call the next method called 'addFiles' in the load order.
    m_service.doCodeEx("addFiles", this);
}

/**
 * Creates an alternate file for this content item.
 */
protected void createAlternateTextFile() throws ServiceException
{
    Writer writer = null;
    try
    {
        // set the format of the alt file to just text
        m_binder.putLocal("alternateFile:format", "text/plain");

        // determine a name for the alternate file
        String docName = m_binder.getLocal("dDocName");
        String name = docName.toLowerCase() + "_alt.txt";
        m_binder.putLocal("alternateFile", name);

        // determine a temp location to build the alternate file
        String fullName = DataBinder.getTemporaryDirectory() +
            DataBinder.getNextFileCounter() + ".txt";
        m_binder.putLocal("alternateFile:path", fullName);

        // add the temp file to the binder
        m_binder.addTempFile(fullName);

        // generate some IdocScript to render as the file string.
        // This can also be pulled from an include, or a template
        String fileString = "Alt file for <$dDocTitle$>:\n" +
            "Author: <$dDocAuthor$>\n" +
```

```
                "Comments: <$xComments$>\n\n" +
                "<$HttpCgiPath$>?IdcService=DOC_INFO_BY_NAME&" +
                "dDocName=<$dDocName$>";

            // render the IdocScript string above with the data
            // currently in the binder
            fileString =
                m_service.getPageMerger().evaluateScript(fileString);

            // open a file object, and write to it
            writer = FileUtils.openDataWriter(
                new File(fullName), FileUtils.m_javaSystemEncoding);
            writer.write(fileString);
        }
        catch (IOException e)
        {
            throw new ServiceException("Unable to generate" +
                " the alternate file.", e);
        }
        finally
        {
            // close the write object
            FileUtils.closeObject(writer);
        }
    }
}
```

This class extends ServiceHandler. It contains two methods: the public addFiles method and the protected createAlternateTextFile method. As mentioned in the previous chapter, only the addFiles method is available as a Service Action because it is public and takes no parameters. We will discuss this method first.

When the Content Server tries to run the addFiles Service Action, it runs our custom method instead of the one defined in DocServiceHandler. At the end of our custom code is the following line:

```
m_service.doCodeEx("addFiles", this);
```

This code causes the Content Server to keep searching for methods named addFiles. It then runs the next one it finds. If it cannot find another, it throws an error. In our case, we want the Content Server to run our code first and then continue and run the addFiles method defined in DocServiceHandler.

Naturally, the Content Server needs to find our custom code before it finds the default addFiles method. This is entirely dependent on setting the searchOrder correctly, which is described later.

The custom addFiles method checks the flag createAlternateFile. If it is true, the method createAlternateTextFile is called. This method extracts a handful of metadata from the request and uses it to create a temporary alternate file.

We must create this generated file in the standard `temp` directory for the Content Server. The following code:

```
String fullName = DataBinder.getTemporaryDirectory() +
        DataBinder.getNextFileCounter() + ".txt";
m_binder.putLocal("alternateFile:path", fullName);
```

reserves a temporary file in this directory and puts the location of that temp file into the binder:

```
stellent/vault/~temp
```

The parameter `alternateFile:path` can be set only by server-side Java code and represents the relative path to this file.

Next, we need to create this temp file. For flexibility, we render the IdocScript in the variable `fileString` to generate the contents of the file. By calling the method `m_service.getPageMerger().evaluateScript()`, we can render script based on the parameters in the request. In this case, we use the metadata for the content item to generate the page.

For even greater flexibility, we can change the `fileString` to include a custom resource, like this:

```
String fileString = "<$include generate_alternate_file$>";
```

Then we can define resource `generate_alternate_file` in the component and use it to generate the temporary file. In this way, we significantly modify what the alternate file looks like without having to recompile the Java code.

Next, we need to register the `ServiceHandler`, as in the previous example. Use the Component Wizard to add a new static table resource. Name it `CustomAddFiles_ServiceHandlers` and merge it into the `ServiceHandlers` table, similar to the previous example. Edit the generated HTML file to look like this:

```
<@table CustomAddFiles_ServiceHandlers@>
<table border=1><caption><strong>
<tr>
    <td>serviceName</td>
    <td>handler</td>
    <td>searchOrder</td>
</tr>
<tr>
    <td>DocService</td>
    <td>customaddfiles.AddFileHandler</td>
    <td>5</td>
</tr>
</table>
<@end@>
```

During the `CHECKIN_NEW` service, the Content Server notices the `addFiles` method in the service definition. Then it scans the known handlers for this specific method. The original method is defined in `DocServiceHandler`, which has a `searchOrder` of 20 for the `DocService` service type. You can find this by inspecting the table `ServiceHandlers` in `std_resources.htm`. Also notice that all `ServiceHandlers` in that resource have a `searchOrder` of 10 or higher.

We need to make certain that our custom code is executed before all other similarly named methods by setting our searchOrder to 5.

Finally, we need to have a checkbox on the check-in page that enables the user to decide whether to generate an alternate file. Do this by adding the following include in the resource file we just created:

```
<@dynamichtml std_document_file_fields@>
<$include super.std_document_file_fields$>
<$if allowsFileUpload$>
    <$checkboxFieldName = "createAlternateFile",
      fieldCheckValue = "1",
      checkboxValue = #active.createAlternateFile,
      checkboxFieldCaption = "Create Alternate File"$>
    <$include std_checkbox_field$>
<$endif$>
<@end@>
```

This include is used to display the fields Primary File and Alternate File on the check-in page. We can use the std_checkbox_field resource include to draw a custom checkbox for the flag createAlternateFile. To properly draw the HTML resource, we need to define the variables checkboxFieldName, fieldCheckValue, checkboxValue, and checkboxFieldCaption with IdocScript before including std_checkbox_field. The allowsFileUpload flag ensures that this checkbox appears only on the check-in pages.

Finally, enable the component and restart the server. The check-in page now looks like Figure 11-6.

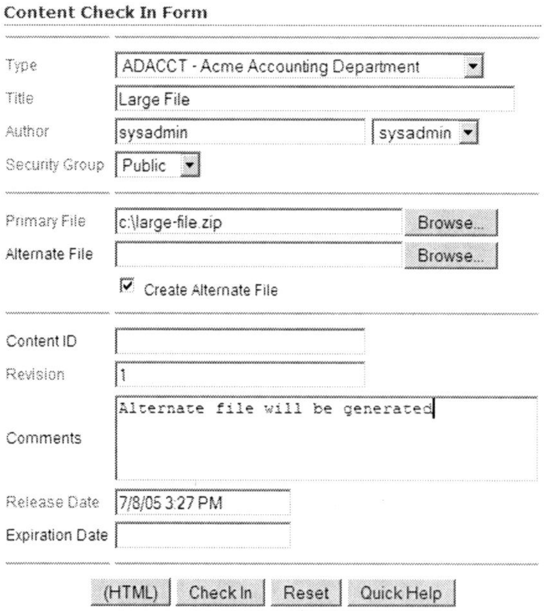

Figure 11-6. *Check-in form with alternate file checkbox*

If we click the checkbox and submit the check-in, the alternate file is automatically generated. We can see it by clicking the web viewable link from either the search results page or the content information page. This alternate file contains metadata about the author, the comments, and a URL to the content info page (see Figure 11-7).

Figure 11-7. *Generated plain text alternate file*

Instead of an ordinary text file, we can instead generate an XML file or an HTML file with links, images, and more metadata. Another option is to generate a Hypertext Content Server Page (HCSP) that includes the standard look and feel of the Content Server. For a more advanced modification, extract additional information from the primary file and place it in the alternate file. For example, extract the first file named readme.txt from a ZIP archive and use it for the alternate file. Or extract size and resolution information out of an image file and place that data in the alternate file.

You can even extend this sample to generate a primary file upon a check-in. To do this, you should set the parameters primaryFile and primaryFile:path, instead of alternateFile and alternateFile:path. You can generate this file based on the metadata of the item or other data in the request.

In conclusion, the best way to add new services to the Content Server is by using Service Handlers. If a Java filter is not available, the best way to modify core services, is to chain Service Handlers. Another approach that is less flexible is to create a copy of the service definition and include your custom action directly.

At all costs, avoid cobbling together a custom service using actions from different core services. This procedure is dangerous because the actions might interact in totally unpredictable ways. If you cannot use filters or chained Service Handlers, copy one entire service and add only custom code to it. Do not mix and match existing service actions; unless you have the original source code, doing so will end only in tragedy.

Creating Custom IdocScript Functions

After the last few examples, you should have a fairly clear understanding of how to add new services and modify core services with filters and Service Handlers. However, there are other ways to plug Java code into the Content Server. Another commonly used method is to create custom IdocScript functions.

IdocScript is designed to be a very simple text display–oriented language. So much so that it doesn't support the ability to create custom functions with IdocScript. Instead, custom functions must be written with Java, which helps to enforce a firm separation between page display and business logic.

All IdocScript functions exist in a global namespace. Most core IdocScript functions are in Java classes that extend `intradoc.common.ScriptExtensionsAdaptor`. The paths to these class files are referenced in the table `IdocScriptExtensions`. When the Content Server starts up, it loads and caches all these script extension definitions.

There are two ways to create custom IdocScript functions. The simple way is to create a Java filter that triggers off of the `computeFunction` event. The other way is to create a new class file that extends `ScriptExtensionsAdaptor`, along with a resource table, and merge that resource table into the core `IdocScriptExtensions` table. This procedure requires more complex Java code, but it is the preferable method because it results in faster IdocScript rendering. For this example, we will use the simpler Filter-based approach.

The first step is to make a component and an Eclipse project named `MyIdocScript`. Then, in the appropriate class folder, create the folder `myidocscript` with the Java source file `ComputeFunctionFilter.java`:

```java
package myidocscript;

import intradoc.common.ExecutionContext;
import intradoc.common.ScriptUtils;
import intradoc.common.ServiceException;
import intradoc.data.DataBinder;
import intradoc.data.DataException;
import intradoc.data.Workspace;
import intradoc.shared.FilterImplementor;

public class ComputeFunctionFilter implements FilterImplementor
{
    /**
     * This filter will be called every time ANY IdocScript function
     * is evaluated. It's an early hook that can allow us to add
     * custom IdocScript functions.
     * @param ws The workspace object for database connectivity
     * @param binder The databinder object for request and response
     * @param cxt The user/service context of this request
     */
    public int doFilter(Workspace ws, DataBinder binder,
        ExecutionContext cxt) throws DataException, ServiceException
    {
        // pull out the function name and the arguments out
        String function = (String)cxt.getCachedObject("function");
        Object args[] = (Object[])cxt.getCachedObject("args");
        int argLen = args.length;
        Object oResult = null;
        boolean foundIt = false;

        if (function.equals("factorial"))
        {
            if (argLen != 2)
```

```java
        {
            throw new DataException(
                "'factorial' requires one argument.");
        }
        long arg1 = ScriptUtils.getLongVal(args[0], cxt);

        long factorial = 1;
        for (long i=1; i <= arg1; i++)
            factorial = factorial * i;
        oResult = new Long(factorial);
        foundIt = true;
    }
    else if (function.equals("strMin"))
    {
        if (argLen != 3)
        {
            throw new DataException(
                "'strMin' requires two arguments.");
        }
        String arg1 = ScriptUtils.getDisplayString(args[0], cxt);
        String arg2 = ScriptUtils.getDisplayString(args[1], cxt);

        // compare the two strings lexicographically
        int result = arg1.toLowerCase().
            compareTo(arg2.toLowerCase());

        // set the result value to the one that occurs first
        if (result <= 0)
            oResult = arg1;
        else
            oResult = arg2;
        foundIt = true;
    }

    if (foundIt)
    {
        // the return value is placed at the end of the result
        args[argLen-1] = oResult;

        // evaluated the function, so this filter is finished
        return FINISHED;
    }

    // keep looking for the function in the core
    return CONTINUE;
    }
}
```

This filter is executed every time an IdocScript function is called. The name of the function called, along with any parameters, is stored in the ExecutionContext object. The function name is stored as a string named function in the CachedObjects. The arguments and the return value for the function are stored as an Object array named args. The last entry in the array args is the return object for the function, if one exists. Therefore, the length of the args array is always at least one.

Our custom filter adds support for two new IdocScript functions. One is called factorial, and the other is called strMin. A *factorial* is a mathematical function that multiplies an integer with all positive integers smaller than it. For example, 5 factorial is 5*4*3*2*1, or 120. Therefore, the factorial function takes a long integer parameter and returns a long integer result. The strMin function is used to alphabetize strings. It takes two string parameters and returns the one that comes first in alphabetic order.

In the filter code, we first inspect the value for function to see whether it is one of our custom functions. If it equals factorial, there should be only one long integer argument. To run a factorial, we must extract the first argument and convert it to a Long object with ScriptUtils. Then we can run the multiplication. Finally, we set oResult to be a new Long object containing the result. Recall that because this is an Object array, Java dictates that we must store the result in a Long object instead of a long primitive type.

If the function name is strMin, we extract two objects from args and cast them to Strings. Then we do a case-insensitive comparison of the two strings. Finally, we set oResult to be the string that occurs first in alphabetical order.

At the end of the filter, we check for the flag foundIt, which is set to true if we executed one of our custom functions. In this event, the result object oResult is placed at the end of the parameter array args. We then return the value FINISHED to signal that the function was found and evaluated. If the function was not found, we return CONTINUE to signal that the server should continue looking for the definition of that function.

Next we need a component to register our custom filter code for the proper event. Using the Component Wizard, create the component MyIdocScript. Next, edit the component definition file:

```
stellent/custom/MyIdocScript/MyIdocScript.hda
```

Make the ResultSet named Filters look like this:

```
@ResultSet Filters
4
type
location
parameter
loadOrder
computeFunction
myidocscript.ComputeFunctionFilter
null
1
@end
```

Finally, you need to enable the component and restart the Content Server. You can test your new IdocScript functions by checking in a sample Hypertext Content Server Template (HCST):

```
<html>
<body>
<h3>IdocScript test</h3>
strMin("aaa", "BBB") = <$strMin("aaa", "BBB")$> <br />
factorial(5) = <$factorial(5)$>
</body>
</html>
```

Making a component like this is an easy way to add new functions, but it is also the easiest way to override existing functions. Recall that the `computeFunction` filter is executed at the very beginning of when the Content Server is looking for the function definition. Therefore, you can override the behavior of any existing function by redefining it in Java code and passing `FINISHED` after executing it.

The primary disadvantage of using a filter instead of a `ScriptExtensionsAdaptor` is that your pages will render slowly. Because this filter is executed every time an IdocScript function is called, it runs several hundred times for each page load. Therefore, it is vital to make sure that your filter executes quickly. The previous code is fairly fast because it does almost nothing if the function name is not `factorial` or `strMin`.

Additionally, you are limited to defining IdocScript functions with a Java filter; you cannot create new computed variables. For example, the variable `<$BrowserFullCgiPath$>` is not a normal IdocScript variable—it is calculated on the fly based on the data from the user's browser. Even if you set this flag to a value on a page, it is always generated with Java code.

Therefore, the best approach is usually to create a `ScriptExtensionsAdaptor` to maximize the performance of your custom IdocScript functions and variables. Covering these adaptors is beyond the scope of this book, so refer to the `NewIdocScript` component in the `HowToComponents` for a tutorial.

It is also important to keep in mind that any contributor can check-in an HCST and evaluate your script. So be aware of possible abuses of your code. It is generally a good idea to make sure that all IdocScript functions evaluate quickly and do not alter any data in the Content Server or the database.

You might be tempted to make an IdocScript function that queries the database, but this needs to be done with caution. Be sure to execute only predefined SQL queries because they get automatically checked for malicious code. Also, restrict the queries to read-only activities. Do not create IdocScript functions that write data to the database. A malicious or poorly written HCSP could flood your server with bad data or overwrite important data.

The primary exception is for IdocScript functions that evaluate only within the context of a workflow because only administrators are allowed to write such scripts, and most workflow IdocScript functions do not run on HCSTs. To see whether the code is being run inside the context of a workflow, use the condition variable `allowWorkflowIdocScript` like so:

```
if (cxt instanceof Service)
{
    boolean isSafe = ((Service)cxt).isConditionVarTrue(
        "allowWorkflowIdocScript");
}
```

Then check the isSafe flag before doing anything that might need to update database tables or write to files on the file system.

Another possible security check is to restrict the execution of custom functions to specific users. For example, you can inspect the UserData object, as in the previous example, and throw an exception if the user running it is not an administrator.

Executing a Service Call from a Filter

Because so much of the Content Server's functionality is available as services, it is frequently useful to run them from Java code. Depending on the context, this process might be very simple or very difficult.

For example, on a content information page, you might want to execute a search to obtain a list of related content items. As shown in Chapter 3, you can do this by modifying the template page and running the IdocScript function executeService. However, this is not a perfect solution: the data is not available until after the IdocScript template page is rendered, which means the data is not available to users who connect with SOAP. To make sure that all your users benefit from this customization, you need to place this functionality in a Java customization.

The optimal approach is to customize the DOC_INFO service with a filter or chained service handler and then execute the search with Java. Luckily, the GET_SEARCH_RESULTS service has a security flag that makes it Scriptable, so it can be executed from IdocScript or Java with little effort. In Java, we can use the executeServiceEx method in the intradoc.server.Service object:

```
m_binder.putLocal("QueryText", "dDocType <matches> `ADACCT`");
m_service.executeServiceEx("GET_SEARCH_RESULTS", true);
```

This code executes the service request with the current parameters in the m_binder object. The ResultSet named SearchResults will be available in the m_binder object after the service returns. You can extract the ResultSet for additional processing in Java or display it with IdocScript on the template page.

This sounds easy. When we want to execute a service from Java code, we can customize the service and make it Scriptable, right? Wrong.

Remember, it is not safe to make a service scriptable if it changes data in the repository. The Scriptable flag should be set only for read-only services, such as searching or content information.

Well, what about a check-in? It is frequently useful to execute additional services when checking-in a new content item. For example, when one item is checked-in, you might want to create several copies of that item in the repository. After multiple copies are available, you can process each one in a different way. For example, each copy can be placed in a separate workflow for translation, or each copy might need to be redacted for different audiences.

Although a check-in service cannot be made Scriptable for security reasons, it can be easily executed from Java as a SubService.

Recall the discussion about SubServices in Chapter 2. If a service is defined as a SubService, it can be called from another service. In this case, most of the logic for a check-in is in the SubService named CHECKIN_NEW_SUB. This is used for workflow check-ins, archive check-ins, batch check-ins, and others.

A `SubService` is also easy to execute inside Java code, which is similar to executing a `Scriptable` service (as described previously). In this case, use the `executeService` function in the `intradoc.server.Service` object:

```
m_service.executeService("CHECKIN_NEW_SUB");
```

This code executes the `CHECKIN_NEW_SUB` service with the data in the current request binder. To run this service correctly, you need to generate temporary files for the check-in, as well as other related parameters. This process is covered in detail later.

There are several limitations to the previous methods. First, you need to be wary of data pollution. The request data from the first check-in might pollute the request data for the second check-in. Likewise, the response data from the second check-in pollutes both the request and response data for the first check-in. You must use caution to clear or reset the data in the binder to avoid problems with data pollution.

Second, executing a service in these ways means that the service must be defined as `Scriptable` or as a `SubService`. Although it is not difficult to create a copy of an existing service and set one of these flags, it is not always the best option. It can make things difficult to maintain if two components want to customize that service, or if the service definition changes in a future version of the Content Server.

Finally, both methods require a fully initialized `Service` object. This is not a problem if you want to execute an additional service during a check-in or content info request, but it is a problem if you need to execute a service during a background process. In those situations, you must manually create and initialize a `Service` object before you can call methods in it.

The rest of this example demonstrates how to work around all these limitations. Specifically, it will execute a `CHECKIN_NEW` service in a background process for every item in a watched folder. Modifications to the `CHECKIN_NEW` service are not required, and a `Service` object does not have to be available. However, more Java code is needed than in the previous two examples.

For this example, we will check-in all items in the watched folder when the Content Server starts up. We want to execute this filter as early as possible, but we cannot do so until the service definitions have been loaded. After checking Appendix H, the filter event `extraAfterServicesLoadInit` seems to be the best choice.

Begin as usual by creating the component `StartupService` with the Component Wizard and a similarly named project in Eclipse. In the proper class folder, create the folder `startupservice`, and in that folder create the source file `StartupCheckinFilter.java`:

```java
package startupservice;

import intradoc.common.ExecutionContext;
import intradoc.common.LocaleUtils;
import intradoc.common.ServiceException;
import intradoc.data.DataBinder;
import intradoc.data.DataException;
import intradoc.data.Workspace;
import intradoc.provider.Provider;
import intradoc.provider.Providers;
import intradoc.server.Service;
import intradoc.server.ServiceData;
```

```java
import intradoc.server.ServiceManager;
import intradoc.server.UserStorage;
import intradoc.shared.FilterImplementor;
import intradoc.shared.UserData;
import intradoc.shared.SharedObjects;
import java.io.File;

public class StartupCheckinFilter implements FilterImplementor
{
    /**
     * Run this filter after the services are all loaded
     */
    public int doFilter(Workspace ws, DataBinder binder,
        ExecutionContext cxt)
        throws DataException, ServiceException
    {
        // prepare a binder for the service requests
        DataBinder serviceBinder = new DataBinder();
        serviceBinder.setEnvironment(SharedObjects.getEnvironment());

        // load up all the files in the watched directory
        String checkinDirStr = "c:/checkin/";
        File checkinDir = new File(checkinDirStr);
        String files[] = checkinDir.list();
        for (int i=0; i<files.length; i++)
        {
            // prepare the checkin metadata
            serviceBinder.putLocal("IdcService", "CHECKIN_NEW");
            serviceBinder.putLocal("dDocTitle", "auto check in");
            serviceBinder.putLocal("dDocType", "ADACCT");
            serviceBinder.putLocal("dDocAuthor", "sysadmin");
            serviceBinder.putLocal("dSecurityGroup", "Public");

            // set some parameters so we do not need to specify
            // a unique dDocName
            serviceBinder.putLocal("IsAutoNumber", "true");
            serviceBinder.putLocal("AutoNumberPrefix", "batch_");

            // add metadata about the file's location. Note: these
            // files will be deleted from the watch directory
            serviceBinder.putLocal("primaryFile", files[i]);
            serviceBinder.putLocal("primaryFile:path",
                    checkinDirStr + files[i]);

            // run the checkin
            executeService(serviceBinder, "sysadmin", false);
```

```java
            // reset the binder for the next item
            serviceBinder.clearResultSets();
            serviceBinder.getLocalData().clear();
        }

        // success: return continue
        return CONTINUE;
    }


    /**
     * Obtain the workspace connector to the database
     */
    public Workspace getSystemWorkspace()
    {
        Workspace workspace = null;
        Provider wsProvider =
            Providers.getProvider("SystemDatabase");
        if (wsProvider != null)
            workspace = (Workspace)wsProvider.getProvider();
        return workspace;
    }


    /**
     * Obtain information about a user. Only the 'userName' parameter
     * must be non-null.
     */
    public UserData getFullUserData(String userName,
        ExecutionContext cxt, Workspace ws)
        throws DataException, ServiceException
    {
        if (ws == null)
            ws = getSystemWorkspace();
        UserData userData = UserStorage.
            retrieveUserDatabaseProfileDataFull(userName,
                ws, null, cxt, true, true);
        ws.releaseConnection();
        return userData;
    }


    /**
     * Execute a service call based on the data in the binder using
     * the credentials of the supplied user
     */
    public void executeService(DataBinder binder, String userName,
        boolean suppressServiceError)
            throws DataException, ServiceException
    {
```

```java
    // obtain a connection to the database
    Workspace workspace = getSystemWorkspace();

    // check for an IdcService value
    String cmd = binder.getLocal("IdcService");
    if (cmd == null)
        throw new DataException("!csIdcServiceMissing");

    // obtain the service definition
    ServiceData serviceData = ServiceManager.getFullService(cmd);
    if (serviceData == null)
        throw new DataException(LocaleUtils.encodeMessage(
            "!csNoServiceDefined", null,  cmd));

    // create the service object for this service
    Service service = ServiceManager.createService(
        serviceData.m_classID, workspace,
        null, binder, serviceData);

    // obtain the full user data for this user
    UserData fullUserData = getFullUserData(userName,
        service, workspace);
    service.setUserData(fullUserData);
    binder.m_environment.put("REMOTE_USER", userName);

    ServiceException error = null;
    try
    {
        // init the service to not send HTML back
        service.setSendFlags(true, true);

        // create all the ServiceHandlers and implementors
        service.initDelegatedObjects();

        // do a security check
        service.globalSecurityCheck();

        // prepare for the service
        service.preActions();

        // execute the service
        service.doActions();

        // do any cleanup
        service.postActions();

        // store any new personalization data
```

```
            service.updateSubjectInformation(true);
            service.updateTopicInformation(binder);
        }
        catch (ServiceException e)
        {
            error = e;
        }
        finally
        {
            // Remove all the temp files.
            service.cleanUp(true);
            workspace.releaseConnection();
        }

        // handle any error
        if (error != null)
        {
            if (suppressServiceError)
            {
                error.printStackTrace();
                if (binder.getLocal("StatusCode") == null)
                {
                    binder.putLocal("StatusCode", String.valueOf(
                        error.m_errorCode));
                    binder.putLocal("StatusMessage",
                        error.getMessage());
                }
            }
            else
            {
                throw new ServiceException(error.m_errorCode,
                    error.getMessage());
            }
        }
    }
}
```

This code contains four methods. The first, doFilter, is executed when the filter is called. This first method creates a DataBinder object to store the request and response data for the service. It initializes the binder with environment data from the SharedObjects, so the server's configuration settings are available. It then checks the folder c:/checkin/ for any entries. For each item found, it sets specific request parameters and calls the executeService function, defined later. These parameters include a service name (CHECKIN_NEW) and the parameters required to run it. In practice, you should extract these metadata values from a separate HDA file or XML file, or the Content Server's configuration data.

You saw most of these metadata fields used in previous examples. The two most interesting parameters are primaryFile and primaryFile:path. The first is used to determine the original name of the checked-in file. The latter is the actual path to the file, which is moved to the vault after the check-in is complete. For security reasons, the Content Server enables you to set `primaryFile:path` only in server-side Java code.

At the end of the loop, all variable data and `ResultSet`s are cleared from the `serviceBinder` object, which prevents the data pollution problems mentioned previously.

The second and third methods are utility functions used to support the fourth method. The `getSystemWorkspace` obtains a `Workspace` object by asking for the `SystemDatabase` provider. Recall that the `Workspace` object is needed to connect to the database and execute SQL statements. The `SystemDatabase` provider is a pool of these database connections. People who are familiar with Java should be familiar with the concept of database resource pools; they allow a fast and safe way for multiple users to all connect to the same database (discussed in more detail in later examples).

The third method, `getFullUserData`, obtains the `UserData` object based on a user name, including all security access rights. This object is needed so that we can execute the service as that specific user.

The last and most complex method is `executeService`, which takes a `DataBinder` object, a user name, and a `boolean` flag to suppress errors in the service. At first, this method obtains the database connection and extracts the name of the `IdcService` from the binder. It then loads the definition for this service and initializes it with the user's data and the database connection.

Next, it sets a handful of flags to make sure the service knows it's being executed from inside Java code. It then initializes the supporting objects, and runs a check to make sure that the user has sufficient rights to execute the service.

Then it prepares to execute the service actions with the `preActions` method. After which it runs all the service actions in order and performs any necessary cleanup after a minor error. In reality, the `preActions` and `postActions` methods do almost nothing—they are reserved for future versions of the Content Server, so you should call them to maintain forward compatibility.

After the service is complete, it is sometimes necessary to save changes to the user's personalization settings. In this case, we must call `updateSubjectInformation` and `updateTopicInformation` to save these changes.

If an error occurs, the Java stack trace is printed to the console, and the method might throw a Java `Exception`, depending on how it was called. Regardless, the last steps are to clean up the service and all temporary files and then release the database connection back to the provider pool.

To test this, refresh the Eclipse project to compile the Java code. Next, edit the component definition file located here:

```
stellent/custom/startupservice/StartupService.hda
```

Modify the `ResultSet` named `Filters` to look like this:

```
@ResultSet Filters
4
type
location
parameter
loadOrder
```

```
extraAfterServicesLoadInit
startupservice.StartupCheckinFilter
null
1
@end
```

Finally, create the watch folder `c:/checkin/`, and fill it with a few test files. Enable the component and restart the server. As the Content Server starts, it scans that watched folder and checks in all files located in it.

Ideally, you should not hard-code the watched folder directory; instead, you can set the parameter `WatchedCheckinFolder` in your `config.cfg` file and obtain it with Java code like so:

```
String checkinDirStr =
    intradoc.shared.SharedObjects.getEnvironmentValue("WatchedCheckinFolder");
```

You can also create a check-in folder relative to your Content Server's install directory and read files from there. For example, if you want to watch this folder for items:

```
stellent/auto-checkin/
```

your code would look like this:

```
String checkinDirStr = intradoc.server.DirectoryLocator.getIntradocDir() +
    "auto-checkin/";
```

As an enhancement, this component can be modified to scan the text in the files to set appropriate metadata. For example, the first line of the file can be used as the title, or you can use a taxonomy engine to extract keywords from the file. Alternatively, you can have a description file for each item that contains the necessary metadata for it.

You can also modify this sample to scan the check-in folder every five minutes, instead of when the server restarts, by using the `checkScheduledEvents` filter. This event triggers every five minutes and is used to schedule background processes, which include monitoring items in workflows or maintaining the database. Many component developers use this event to execute their code on a roughly timed basis.

Potential Problems

The main pitfall of executing multiple services is data pollution. For example, each time the `executeService` call is made, the `DataBinder` must be cleared of all result sets and local data because some of the data from the first response could affect the data for the second request. In our sample, the Content ID and Document ID would be present in the response after a successful check-in. If you attempted another check-in with this polluted data, it would fail: a new content item cannot be checked-in with an existing Content ID. Only new revisions of the same item are allowed to share the Content ID.

It is usually sufficient to clear the result sets and the binder. For maximum safety, you could create a new `DataBinder` object for each call to `executeService` method, but this is not necessary.

Another issue is database transactions. For example, when a service stores data in the database, it must do so from within a database transaction. That way, if an error occurs, the request can be "rolled back" and the integrity of the database is maintained.

For those unfamiliar with databases, it's a fundamental rule that you cannot begin a new transaction when you already have one open. You must first commit the existing transaction before beginning another.

For example, assume that you want to update the metadata of one item when a related item is checked-in. You could create a check-in filter, but there is a problem. The CHECKIN_NEW service begins a transaction before it calls the CHECKIN_NEW_SUB subservice and commits the transaction when the subservice returns. Also, most of the check-in filters occur in this subservice.

To update the metadata of the other item, you typically call the UPDATE_DOCINFO service. But this service also begins a transaction, so you cannot run it.

Luckily, the UPDATE_DOCINFO service calls the UPDATE_DOCINFO_SUB subservice, which does not begin a transaction. So we can execute this one instead. In other situations, you might need to make a copy of the service you want to call and remove all transaction flags. But doing so is also problematic.

Assume that you perform two check-ins with one service request. What should you do if an error occurs? Should you roll back both transactions or roll back just one? By default, both check-ins are invalidated if an error occurs. If you are just checking-in one additional item, this is fine, but might be undesirable if you want to perform several dozen check-ins and log any errors.

Another pitfall is performance. Using the previous method, it is possible for one service request to launch a dozen others, which can be problematic if these multiservices are offered to users over the web. Users might become impatient if the service takes more than a few seconds and cancel the request. Or if running a batch of services takes more than two minutes, the browser might time out and then stop the request. Use caution if you decide to run multiservices and try to make sure that they cannot be abused to the point that performance suffers.

Finally, debugging such a service can be complicated. If you generate the additional requests in Java code invisibly to the user, it might be difficult to understand why a request failed. Be sure to report all errors as completely as possible and log as much as you can.

Database Connections

As mentioned earlier, the Content Server has an abstraction layer between it and the database, which enables the server to validate the SQL data and support multiple databases with greater ease.

Your component does not need to contain Java code if it is just running database queries. Recall that a service action can be either a database query or a Java method. To run these queries, you simply need a query resource and a service that includes it as an action. Having a template page for the query results can also be useful, but this is optional.

For this example, we will show how to execute SQL queries in a service request. We will then expand on this example and use Java to execute SQL on remote databases.

To start, create a component named DatabaseConnections with the Component Wizard and add a query resource to it:

1. In the bottom-left pane of the Component Wizard, click Add.

2. Select Query, and click Next.

3. Click Next.

4. Name the query `Qconfig`.

5. Set the query text to `SELECT * FROM Config`.

6. Click Finish.

This query resource is generated here:

`stellent/custom/DatabaseConnections/resources/databaseconnections_query.htm`

It contains the following resource table:

```
<@table DatabaseConnections_Queries@>
<table border=1>
<caption><strong>Query Definition Table</strong></caption>
<tr>
    <td>name</td>
    <td>queryStr</td>
    <td>parameters</td>
</tr>
<tr>
    <td>Qconfig</td>
    <td>SELECT * FROM Config</td>
    <td></td>
</tr>
</table>
<@end@>
```

This is a very simple query that returns all rows in the `Config` table in the database. This table is used to store information about components and core features that have altered the database schema since Content Server version 3.0. Advanced components that add new managed tables or modify existing tables should place a configuration flag here. Keeping this table updated helps prevent multiple components from altering the database in the same way and gives the Content Server an idea of how the database is structured. It contains the following columns as `varchar` fields:

dSection: The section of the product that was modified

dName: The specific feature name that was added

dVersion: The Content Server version in which this feature was added

dValue: A number representing the version number for the feature

The query we just created is not very sophisticated. It only gets a dump of all rows in the `Config` table, with no control over which items to return. A better option is to allow the query to be built based on parameters in the request:

1. In the left pane of the Component Wizard, select the query resource you just created.

2. In the right pane, click Add.

3. Name the query `QconfigByVersion`.

4. Set the query text to `SELECT * from Config WHERE dVersion=?`.

5. Next to the Parameters pane, click Add.

6. Set the Name to `dVersion`.

7. Set the Type to `varchar`.

8. Click OK.

9. Click OK.

This process creates a new query resource that looks like this:

```
<tr>
    <td>QconfigByVersion</td>
    <td>SELECT * FROM Config WHERE dVersion=?</td>
    <td>dVersion varchar</td>
</tr>
```

Notice that the query contains a question mark character, which tells the Content Server to assemble this query based on data in the request. A query can have multiple parameters, but each must be on a new line. The first word in the parameter is the name of the field in the request data. The second word is the data type. The name of the field in the request data usually corresponds to the name of the column, but this is not required. For example, we could have a two parameter query defined like this:

```
<tr>
    <td>QconfigByVersion</td>
    <td>SELECT * FROM Config WHERE dVersion=? AND dValue=?</td>
    <td>foo varchar
        bar varchar</td>
</tr>
```

In this case, the server extracts the value for `foo` from the request data and validates that it is a SQL string. The validation will escape any quotes and check for extra parentheses. It then places this encoded value in the `WHERE` clause for `dVersion`. In a similar way, the server extracts the value for `bar` and sets it in the `WHERE` clause as the value for `dValue`.

Predefined queries are naturally not limited to `SELECT` statements. You can execute `INSERT`, `UPDATE`, `DELETE`, and any advanced feature supported by your database. In general, we recommend that component developers limit their queries to standard SQL so the queries are more likely to support multiple databases.

The next step is to include this query in a service definition, and create a template page to display the results:

1. In the left pane on the Component Wizard, click Add.

2. Select the Service button and click Next.

3. Click Next.

4. Set the Name to GET_DB_CONFIG.

5. Set the Service Class to Service.

6. Set the Template to DB_CONFIG_PAGE.

7. Under Access Level, check the Admin and Global boxes, limiting this service to users who are administrators of at least one group.

8. Under Actions, click the Add button.

9. Set the Type to Select Cache Query.

10. Set the Action to Qconfig.

11. Set the Parameters to CONFIG_RSET.

12. Click OK.

13. Click Finish.

This process creates a resource at this location:

```
stellent/custom/DatabaseConnections/resources/databaseconnections_service.htm
```

The location contains the following resource table:

```
<@table DatabaseConnections_Services@>
<table border=1><caption><strong>Scripts For Custom Services</strong></caption>
<tr>
    <td>Name</td><td>Attributes</td><td>Actions</td>
</tr>
<tr>
    <td>GET_DB_CONFIG</td>
    <td>Service
        24
        DB_CONFIG_PAGE
        null
        null<br>
        null</td>
    <td>5:Qconfig:CONFIG_RSET::null</td>
</tr>
</table>
<@end@>
```

Because the action type is Select Cache Query, the Content Server executes the query and caches the results in a ResultSet object. In this case, the results are saved in the object named CONFIG_RSET because that name is the first (and only) parameter in the action parameter list.

Next, we need a template page to display the results of this query:

1. In the left pane on the Component Wizard, click Add.

2. Select Template, and click Next.

3. Click Next.

4. Set the Name to `DB_CONFIG_PAGE`.

5. Set the Class and Form Type to `Administration`.

6. Set the File Name to `db_config_page.htm`.

7. Set the Description to `Database Configuration Page`.

8. Click Finish.

From the right panel of the Component Wizard, click this new template and then Launch Editor. Modify the template to look like this:

```
<html>
<head>
<$defaultPageTitle="Database Config Page"$>
<$include std_html_head_declarations$>
</head>

<$include body_def$>
<$include std_page_begin$>

<div class="xuiPageHeadingCell">
    <h4 class="xuiPageHeadingText"><$defaultPageTitle$></h4>
</div>

<br />

<table border="2">
<tr style="font-weight:bold;">
    <td>Section</td>
    <td>Name</td>
    <td>Version</td>
    <td>Value</td>
</tr>
<$loop CONFIG_RSET$>
    <tr>
        <td><$dSection$></td>
        <td><$dName$></td>
        <td><$dVersion$></td>
        <td><$dValue$></td>
    </tr>
<$endloop$>
</table>

<$include std_page_end$>

</body>
</html>
```

Finally, enable the component and restart the Content Server. Then navigate to the configuration page with a URL like this:

```
http://localhost/stellent/idcplg?IdcService=GET_DB_CONFIG
```

A page similar to Figure 11-8 returns. It shows a simple table with the standard Content Server look and feel and also the results of the database query.

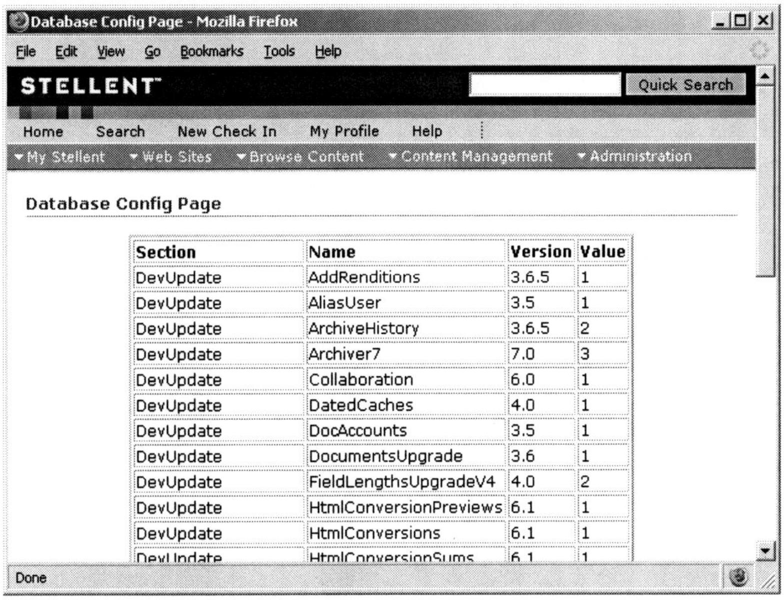

Figure 11-8. *Database config page*

To obtain configuration for one specific version, we can change the service definition to use the QconfigByVersion query. We then need to pass in the value for dVersion every time we run this service. We can do this one of two ways. First, we can pass it in the URL:

```
http://localhost/stellent/idcplg?IdcService=GET_DB_CONFIG?dVersion=7.0
```

Second, we can set it in the service definition. We can use the core Java method setLocalValues to set parameters prior to calling queries. These parameters overwrite any parameter passed in the URL, which allows us to have the flexibility of predefined queries and the security of setting the parameters in the definition file. To do so, edit your service definition to look like this:

```
<@table DatabaseConnections_Services@>
<table border=1><caption><strong>Scripts For Custom Services</strong></caption>
<tr>
    <td>Name</td><td>Attributes</td><td>Actions</td>
</tr>
<tr>
    <td>GET_DB_CONFIG</td>
```

```
<td>Service
    24
    DB_CONFIG_PAGE
    null
    null<br>
    null</td>
<td>3:setLocalValues:dVersion,7.0:0:null
    5:QconfigByVersion:CONFIG_RSET::null</td>
</tr>
</table>
<@end@>
```

You need to restart the Content Server to reload the new service definition.

Either way, the result page is now much smaller (see Figure 11-9): it contains only those entries that have a dVersion equal to 7.0.

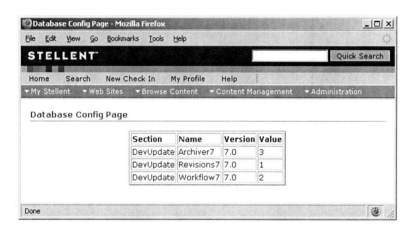

Figure 11-9. *Database config page for version 7.0*

Connecting to Remote Databases

Making a request to a remote database is slightly more difficult. First, we must set up a connection to the remote database and create some Java code to execute the queries. This topic is covered in the rest of this example.

As mentioned in Chapter 2, the Content Server has an API for connecting to remote applications. These connectors are called *providers*. By default, the Stellent has only two providers: one for the connection to the web server and another for the database. You can configure additional providers to other databases or to user repositories such as Lightweight Directory Access Protocol (LDAP).

The first step is to create a new database provider. The Content Server uses Java Database Connectivity (JDBC) to connect to databases and has several helper classes to maintain these connections. We must use these helper classes to make new connections.

For this example, we will create a second provider to the default database used by the Content Server (this is done for simplicity—you do not need to set up another database to test this code because you have one database and its configuration already available):

1. Open a web browser and navigate to the providers administration page.

2. The first provider on the list is the default SystemDatabase provider you configured during the install. In the table row for that provider, click Info. This page contains the configuration information needed for the second provider.

3. Open a second browser and navigate to the providers page again.

4. Under Create a New Provider, locate the Database row. Click Add.

5. On the next web page, set the Name and Description fields to TestProvider.

6. For the remaining fields, enter the configuration values from the other provider. Leave any unused fields blank. You might need to ask your administrator for the database password.

7. Click Add.

The provider should now be in the list, but it is not available until you restart the server; you can then can check the connection state and test the provider from this page.

If you want to connect to a different database, you need a different JDBC connection string that contains the hostname and database name from the other database server. You might also need to change the JDBC driver if the database versions are different. Most likely, the JDBC user name and JDBC password are also different.

In most cases, your remote database does not have the same tables, columns, or schema as the standard Content Server database. For example, you might use a custom provider to integrate with a remote Customer Relationship Management (CRM) database to extract the names of projects, products, employees, or customers.

The Content Server thus does not load the standard predefined queries for custom database providers (there is no point because the database tables are almost always different). However, with a little additional configuration, we can make our TestProvider load our custom queries.

Start by opening the TestProvider definition file, located here:

```
stellent/data/providers/testprovider/provider.hda
```

This file contains all the information needed to initialize and use this provider. Right before the line @end, add the following three lines:

```
ProviderConfig=intradoc.server.DbProviderConfig
QueryResourceFile=stellent/custom/DatabaseConnections/resources/➥
        databaseconnections_query.htm
QueryResourceTables=DatabaseConnections_Queries
```

The ProviderConfig variable is a classpath to an object that performs additional configuration for a provider. In this case, we set it to a standard Content Server object

that loads predefined queries. This code uses the parameters QueryResourceFile and
QueryResourceTables to locate the file and resource table for the queries.

Note that the QueryResourceFile needs to be the *full path* to the query definition file and
is all on one line. In this case, the path is to the query resource file we created earlier in this
example. The QueryResourceTables parameter is a comma-separated list of table names to
load. In our case, we set the table list to just the name of our custom query resource table:
DatabaseConnections_Queries.

After setting up the connection, we need some custom Java code to execute the queries.
Create an Eclipse project named DatabaseConnections. In the classpath, create the folder
dbconnections; in that folder, create the Java source file DatabaseProviderHandler.java:

```java
package dbconnections;

import intradoc.common.ServiceException;
import intradoc.data.DataBinder;
import intradoc.data.DataException;
import intradoc.data.DataResultSet;
import intradoc.data.DataSerializeUtils;
import intradoc.data.ResultSet;
import intradoc.data.Workspace;
import intradoc.provider.Provider;
import intradoc.provider.Providers;
import intradoc.server.ServiceHandler;

import java.io.IOException;
import java.io.StringWriter;

public class DatabaseProviderHandler extends ServiceHandler
{
    /**
     * Executes a named query against a named database provider,
     * and stores the results into a named result set.
     */
    public void dbconnections_executeProviderQuery() throws
        ServiceException, DataException
    {
        // obtain the provider name, the query, and the result set
        // name from the action definition in the service
        String providerName = m_currentAction.getParamAt(0);
        String resultSetName = m_currentAction.getParamAt(1);
        String queryName = m_currentAction.getParamAt(2);

        // validate the provider name
        if (providerName == null || providerName.length() == 0)
        {
            throw new ServiceException(
                "You must specify a provider name.");
        }
```

```java
    // validate that the provider is a valid database provider
    Provider p = Providers.getProvider(providerName);
    if (p == null)
    {
        throw new ServiceException("The provider '" +
            providerName + "' does not exist.");
    }
    else if (!p.isProviderOfType("database"))
    {
        throw new ServiceException("The provider '" +
            providerName + "' is not for a database.");
    }

    // grab the provider, and scope it to a workspace object
    // for database access
    Workspace ws = (Workspace)p.getProvider();
    DataResultSet result = null;
    DataException error = null;
    try
    {
        // if they specified a predefined query, execute that
        if (queryName != null && queryName.trim().length() > 0)
        {
            // obtain a JDBC result set with the data in it.  This
            // result set is live, and we must copy its contents
            ResultSet temp = ws.createResultSet(queryName, m_binder);

            // create a DataResultSet based on the temp result set
            result = new DataResultSet();
            result.copy(temp);
        }

        // place the result into the databinder
        m_binder.addResultSet(resultSetName, result);
    }
    catch (DataException de)
    {
        error = de;
    }
    finally
    {
        // release the JDBC connection assigned to this thread
        // (request) which kills the result set 'temp'
        ws.releaseConnection();
    }
    if (error != null)
        throw error;
}
```

```java
/**
 * This function will execute arbitrary sql against an arbitrary
 * database provider, and store the results in a result set.
 */
public void dbconnections_executeProviderSql() throws
    ServiceException, DataException
{
    // obtain the provider name, and the result set name
    // from the action definition in the service
    String providerName = m_currentAction.getParamAt(0);
    String resultSetName = m_currentAction.getParamAt(1);

    // check for RawSql
    String rawSql = m_binder.getLocal("RawSql");
    if (rawSql == null || rawSql.length() == 0)
    {
        throw new ServiceException(
            "You must specify a value for 'RawSql'.");
    }

    // validate that the provider is a valid database provider
    Provider p = Providers.getProvider(providerName);
    if (p == null || !p.isProviderOfType("database"))
    {
        throw new ServiceException("The provider '" +
            providerName + "' is not for a database.");
    }

    // grab the provider, and scope it to a workspace object
    // for database access
    Workspace ws = (Workspace)p.getProvider();
    DataException error = null;
    try
    {
        // obtain a JDBC result set with the data in it.  This
        // result set is live, and we must copy its contents
        ResultSet temp = ws.createResultSetSQL(rawSql);

        // create a DataResultSet based on the temp result set
        DataResultSet result = new DataResultSet();
        result.copy(temp);

        // place the result into the databinder
        m_binder.addResultSet(resultSetName, result);
    }
    catch (DataException de)
    {
        error = de;
    }
```

```java
        }
        finally
        {
            // release the JDBC connection assigned to this thread
            // (request) which kills the result set 'temp'
            ws.releaseConnection();
        }
        if (error != null)
            throw error;
    }


    /**
     * For demo purposes, turn the result set into a raw string that
     * can be dumped to a web page.
     */
    public void dbconnections_convertResultSetToString() throws
        ServiceException, DataException
    {
        // obtain the result set name, and the local data value
        // that the string should be placed into
        String resultSetName = m_currentAction.getParamAt(0);
        String stringName = m_currentAction.getParamAt(1);

        // get the result set from the databinder
        ResultSet result = m_binder.getResultSet(resultSetName);
        if (result == null)
        {
            throw new ServiceException("Cannot turn the result set '" +
                resultSetName + "' into a string. The result set is null.");
        }

        // turn the resultSet into a string and place it into
        // the local data
        try
        {
            DataBinder tempBinder = new DataBinder();
            tempBinder.addResultSet(resultSetName, result);
            StringWriter sw = new StringWriter();
            DataSerializeUtils.send(tempBinder, sw, m_service);
            m_binder.putLocal(stringName, sw.toString());
        }
        catch (IOException e)
        {
            e.printStackTrace();
        }
    }
}
```

This `ServiceHandler` object has three methods that can be called as service actions. The first one, `dbconnections_executeProviderQuery`, connects to a remote database and executes a named query.

First, this method extracts the parameters for the action:

```
String providerName = m_currentAction.getParamAt(0);
String resultSetName = m_currentAction.getParamAt(1);
String queryName = m_currentAction.getParamAt(2);
```

As mentioned in Chapter 10, the service definition file allows actions to take parameters for greater flexibility. In this case, we want our code to be able to connect to any provider, run any named query, and store the results in any result set. Therefore, we need to add support for these service actions.

In practice, a service calls this method with an action parameter like so (in which case the providerName is foo, the resultSetName is bar, and the query to run is Qfoobar):

```
3:mydbprovider_executeProviderQuery:foo,bar,Qfoobar::null
```

After we know the provider name, we can extract it from the `Providers` object with the following code:

```
Provider p = Providers.getProvider(providerName);
```

Note that we can obtain the default database connection by setting `providerName` to `SystemDatabase`. For safety, we make sure that the `Provider` is non-null and is the correct provider type before casting it to a `Workspace` object:

```
Workspace ws = (Workspace)p.getProvider();
```

The `Workspace` object is a clever wrapper around standard JDBC objects. All connection pooling is done for you at the `Provider` level, and you never need to worry about creating the connection. It assembles your queries based on resource definitions and request parameters. If your database supports only uppercase column names, the `Workspace` does automatic column name-mapping for you. It even contains workarounds for bugs in known JDBC drivers, as well as database-specific query optimization hints. By using a `Workspace` you can be reasonably assured that your queries run cleanly, quickly, and safely on any supported database.

One important feature of JDBC is that after executing a query, the result data is not local. The `ResultSet` object is only a reference to the rows of data, which still reside on the database. This is a network performance optimization, which enables you to quickly iterate through the results and copies only the specific data that you need.

In this case, we are interested in copying the entire results. To do so, we must first run the query and copy the results of the query into a `DataResultSet` object:

```
ResultSet temp = ws.createResultSet(queryName, m_binder);
result = new DataResultSet();
result.copy(temp);
```

The `DataResultSet` contains a local copy of the results. To make it available for other Java methods or IdocScript templates, we must place it into the `DataBinder` object along with a name:

```
m_binder.addResultSet(resultSetName, result);
```

Finally, we need to release the Workspace object so the connection goes back into the pool:

```
ws.releaseConnection();
```

The second method, dbconnections_executeProviderSql, is very similar to the first method. First it extracts action parameters from the request, then obtains the database provider, and finally creates a Workspace object for running queries.

The main difference is in how the query is executed. The second method calls createResultSetSQL, which enables you to execute arbitrary SQL statements. The Content Server does no type checking whatsoever for queries run in this way.

Clearly, this is a powerful way to dynamically generate SQL: however, it can be more dangerous. If you hard-code the SQL into Java or a resource file, this is generally safe. But if you allow user input to add parameters to the SQL query, we advise you to limit that functionality to administrators. Otherwise, you need to manually check the SQL for unbalanced quotes, unbalanced parentheses, and bad data types to make sure that your users are not trying to abuse your code.

The last method, dbconnections_convertResultSetToString, is a convenience method that takes a ResultSet object and turns it into a string. There are several ways to do this, but here we create a temporary DataBinder object and place the ResultSet into it. Then we use this standard method to serialize the DataBinder into the HDA format:

```
DataSerializeUtils.send(tempBinder, sw, m_service);
```

The DataSerializeUtils object is used to read and write DataBinder objects to files or to generic data streams. This approach is recommended so that your output data will be a correctly formatted HDA stream.

The next step is to create the HTML configuration file for this ServiceHandler object, as we did in previous examples. Using the Component Wizard, make a static table resource and merge it into the core ServiceHandlers table. Then edit this resource table to include the preceding code as a handler for the items with a serviceName of Service. Your resource table should look like this:

```
<@table DatabaseConnections_ServiceHandlers@>
<table border=1><caption><strong>
<tr>
    <td>serviceName</td>
    <td>handler</td>
    <td>searchOrder</td>
</tr>
<tr>
    <td>Service</td>
    <td>dbconnections.DatabaseProviderHandler</td>
    <td>100</td>
</tr>
</table>
<@end@>
```

Next, we need to create the service definitions to execute these Java methods. Open the file databaseconnections_service.htm and add the following three services:

```
<tr>
    <td>EXECUTE_PROVIDER_QUERY</td>
    <td>DocService
        32
        PROVIDER_QUERY_PAGE
        null
        null<br>
        Unable to retrieve the provider query page.</td>
    <td>3:dbconnections_executeProviderQuery:TestProvider,TEST_RSET,Qconfig:0:null
        3:dbconnections_convertResultSetToString:TEST_RSET,TestResultString:0:null</td>
</tr>
<tr>
    <td>EXECUTE_PROVIDER_SQL</td>
    <td>DocService
        24
        PROVIDER_QUERY_PAGE
        null
        null<br>
        Unable to retrieve the provider query page.</td>
    <td>3:dbconnections_executeProviderSql:TestProvider,TEST_RSET:0:null
        3:dbconnections_convertResultSetToString:TEST_RSET,TestResultString:0:null</td>
</tr>
<tr>
    <td>GET_PROVIDER_QUERY_PAGE</td>
    <td>DocService
        0
        PROVIDER_QUERY_PAGE
        null
        null<br>
        Unable to retrieve the provider query page.</td>
    <td></td>
</tr>
```

Note that each service action must be on a single line.

The EXECUTE_PROVIDER_QUERY service runs the query Qconfig, so the security settings for the service depend on the security of Qconfig. Because the query is a simple SELECT statement on public data, we can give it extremely low security settings. Therefore, it is sufficient to set the access flag to Scriptable (32), which means that all users, including anonymous ones, can execute this service from a page or with the executeService IdocScript function.

The EXECUTE_PROVIDER_QUERY service runs the dbconnections_executeProviderQuery method. The action parameters dictate that the query Qconfig be run with the TestProvider and the results stored in TEST_RSET.

Conversely, because EXECUTE_PROVIDER_SQL allows the user to execute arbitrary SQL, it is very important to restrict access to it. The security flags should be both Admin (8) and Global (16), for a total of 24.

This service calls the dbconnections_executeProviderSql, which runs the SQL in the parameter named RawSql. The action parameters dictate that the query be run with the TestProvider and be stored in TEST_RSET.

These two services both call dbconnections_convertResultSetToString to convert TEST_RSET to a string, so the results can be easily displayed with IdocScript on the result template.

The service GET_PROVIDER_QUERY_PAGE is a convenience service that just returns the PROVIDER_QUERY_PAGE. This page has a data entry form that executes and displays the results of the other two services. Because this service does very little, we can leave the security access flags off.

Next we need to make the PROVIDER_QUERY_PAGE. It needs to be flexible enough to run both kinds of remote SQL queries. Using the Component Wizard, add this template with Class and Form Type set to Administration, same as DB_CONFIG_PAGE. Give it the filename provider_query_page.htm and modify it to look like this:

```
<!DOCTYPE HTML PUBLIC "-//IETF//DTD HTML//EN">
<html>
<head>
    <$defaultPageTitle="Database Provider Query Page"$>
    <$include std_html_head_declarations$>
<script>
function doSubmit(idcService)
{
    document.ProviderQueryForm.IdcService.value = idcService;
    document.ProviderQueryForm.submit();
}
</script>
</head>

<$include body_def$>

<$include std_page_begin$>

<h2>Execute Predefined Query or Raw Sql</h2>

<form name=ProviderQueryForm method=GET action="<$HttpCgiPath$>">
<input type=hidden name=IdcService value="EXECUTE_PROVIDER_QUERY">
<table>
<tr>
```

```
        <td>Query:</td>
        <td><span class="configLabel">Qconfig</span></td>
        <td><input type=button value=" Execute Query "
            onClick="doSubmit('EXECUTE_PROVIDER_QUERY')"></td>
</tr>
<tr>
        <td colspan=3> </td>
</tr>
<tr>
        <td>RawSql:</td>
        <td><$if not RawSql$><$RawSql="SELECT * FROM Config"$><$endif$>
            <input type=text size=50 name="RawSql"
            value="<$xml(RawSql)$>"></td>
        <td><input type=button value=" Execute SQL "
            onClick="doSubmit('EXECUTE_PROVIDER_SQL')"></td>
</tr>
</table>
</form>

<!-- Display the result if it exists. Use XMP tags to display
     all characters, including non-HTML compliant data -->
<$if TestResultString$>
<br><br><br>
<h2>Test Result String</h2>
<xmp style="text-align:left">
<$TestResultString$>
</xmp>
<$endif$>

<$include std_page_end$>

</body>
</html>
```

This page is fairly straightforward. It contains an HTML form that runs either the EXECUTE_PROVIDER_QUERY service or the EXECUTE_PROVIDER_SQL service with the specified SQL. Some JavaScript is used to set the parameter for IdcService depending on which button the user clicks. The value of the variable TestResultString is displayed at the bottom if it is present.

Now we are ready to run some tests. Enable the component and restart the Content Server. The TestProvider that we created should now be running.

Open a browser window to the provider query page. The URL will be similar to this

```
http://localhost/stellent/idcplg?IdcService=GET_PROVIDER_QUERY_PAGE
```

On this page you can run your predefined query by clicking the Execute Query button, or you can execute arbitrary SQL with the Execute SQL button (see Figure 11-10).

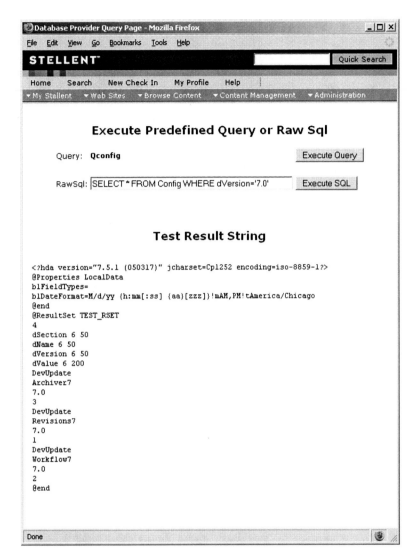

Figure 11-10. *Database provider query test page*

You can modify this component to query, insert, update, or delete any data in the remote database. For example, you can make a simple HTML form for data entry to the remote database or the Content Server database. Alternatively, you can execute this code from a check-in filter to store metadata in a remote repository. You can also modify the content info page to find links to relevant materials in an external database. The possibilities are endless.

Designing Secure Queries

If you are querying a table with secure content items, you can restrict the results according to the access rights of the user. For the standard Content Server security filter to work properly, any filtered table must have the column dSecurityGroup present. If you have accounts enabled, you can optionally specify the dDocAccount column as well.

One approach, discussed in Chapter 2, is to use a DataSource instead of a predefined query. If you query a table that contains information about content items, the DataSource automatically appends a security clause to the SQL query so that users never see items they could not ordinarily access.

Another approach is to run the query without a security clause and then filter out the items that the user cannot access. This process is usually much slower than appending a security clause to the query, but is acceptable for a small number of results. To do this, iterate over the rows in the DataResultSet and delete the rows that the user cannot access. You can validate access with the Service.checkDocAccess method:

```
int authLevel = m_service.getPrivilege();
for (resultSet.first(); resultSet.isRowPresent(); )
{
    boolean hasAccess = m_service.checkAccess(m_binder,
            resultSet, authLevel);
    if (!hasAccess)
        resultSet.deleteCurrentRow();
    else
        resultSet.next();
}
```

The authLevel flag is an integer representing the requested security access, which corresponds to the security bit-flags for the service. For example, 1 would be Read access, 2 would be Write access, and 3 would be Read and Write access. See Chapter 2 for a complete discussion of the security flags.

Even with the proper security settings, it is almost never a good idea to directly modify core Content Server database tables. The default Content Server has approximately 35 tables. With the exception of the Config table, you should never directly insert data into any of them. You should always use service requests to insert new data. Otherwise, you might accidentally modify the tables in the wrong order or in the wrong way, or not update every table you should. To preserve the integrity of your database, restrict your queries to read-only when accessing the core Content Server tables.

For more information about the names and structures of these tables, refer to Appendix A of the *Stellent Troubleshooting Guide*, which is included with the standard Content Server documentation.

Database Records Versus HCSPs

Because it is so simple to submit data to the database, you might be wondering whether it's better to use tables instead of HCSPs to store form input.

For the majority of situations, it is better to use HCSPs because HCSPs are treated as standard content items, and you gain all the benefits of life-cycle management when you use them. Specifically, your HCSP is compatible with workflows, the search engine, the Archiver, and content conversion services.

However, storing data as HCSPs does have limitations. First, it is difficult to run complex reports on data contained in an XML structure. Simple reports are easy, such as finding all forms that contain the word foo. However, if you want to find all users who submitted a form with the word foo and a separate form with the word bar, you need to execute two searches and manually assemble the results.

The optimal solution is to do it both ways: store your form data in the database as well as the HCSP. For example, when you submit your HCSP, run a SQL insert statement from a check-in filter. Design this statement to insert the form data into one or more structured tables, along with the dID of the HCSP. This method gives you the best of both worlds: you can manage the life cycle of the form as a content item, but you can also run complex reports on the data. Of course, you need to update and delete database rows whenever the content item is updated or deleted.

Another limitation to HCSPs is that they have larger storage requirements than simple database records. Each HCSP has entries in four database tables, plus two files on the file system.

For most data processing forms this limitation is not a problem because the extra storage cost gives the benefits of managing its life cycle. However, it is excessive if you are storing only a small amount of data and do not care about managing its life cycle. For example, structured configuration data, option lists for metadata, extended information about your users, and audit trails might make more sense as standard database entries. In these cases, it might make more sense to avoid the bulkiness of HCSPs and input the data directly to the database.

Summary

Adding custom Java code is the most powerful way to alter the behavior of the Content Server. In this chapter, we covered sample components that created new services, altered existing services, added custom IdocScript code, and ran queries against databases.

When modifying an existing service, the preferred approach is to use a Java filter. When no Java filter exists for your needs, you should customize the service with a chained Service Handler. If your Content Server does not support chained handlers, you should customize the service definition and add your custom methods to the definition.

Creating a custom service is extremely simple. All it takes is one definition file and your Java code. After creating them, your service behaves as if it's a part of the core. It gains all the benefits, including compatibility with the SOAP and J2EE integrations. For maximum flexibility, always add custom Java code as a Service Handler.

Use caution when creating new IdocScript code—remember that any contributor can run your code on a HCSP, so make sure that it is fast and secure.

Always use predefined queries, even when running them on a remote database. Running such queries enables you to avoid SQL-injection attacks from malicious users and helps you benefit from other query optimizations techniques built into the Content Server.

These are only a small sample of what kinds of customizations are possible. New functionality is limited only to what is possible with Java.

CHAPTER 12

■ ■ ■

Advanced Topics

This chapter discusses a handful of advanced integration tools and techniques. It covers how to integrate other applications, other web scripting languages, how to manage your websites, and some tips on metadata usage. It is beyond the scope of this book to give a comprehensive overview of each topic. Instead, this chapter gives an introduction to what is possible, some best practices, and references to where you can learn more.

Web Services and SOAP

Web Services are becoming the preferred method for integrating enterprise applications. They fit nicely into a Service-Oriented Architecture (SOA), and they are simple to implement and use. They have performance and security limitations that other integrations do not, but the correct infrastructure can address these problems.

Simple Object Access Protocol (SOAP) is an XML-based messaging protocol for executing code on remote systems. It uses the standard HTTP protocol to make the connection and uses specially formatted XML files for the request. Any application can create a SOAP interface which is both platform-neutral and language-neutral. As long as the application can make a web request and parse XML, it can use SOAP.

Web Services are a primary component of C# and other .NET technologies, and integration tools are available for almost every programming language:

- C#, VB.NET, ASPX: `System.Web.Services` in the .NET Framework

- Java: Apache SOAP, Apache AXIS

- JavaScript: `XmlHttpRequest` object (used mainly for Asynchronous JavaScript and XML [Ajax])

- PHP: `Pear::SOAP`, `nuSOAP`, and the PHP5 SOAP module

- Python: `pyWebSVCS`

- Perl: `SOAP::Lite`

- Visual Basic, ASP: `PocketSOAP`, `MSSOAP`, `XMLHTTP`, `DIME`

SOAP is even built into applications you use every day. Because Visual Basic supports it, every Microsoft Office application can run Web Services with VBScript macros. For example, you can create an Excel spreadsheet that runs SOAP searches and then update the metadata of content items.

Web Services fit in very well with Stellent's SOA. SOAP support has been offered as a free component since version 5.0 and was integrated into the core in version 7.5. As stated in Chapter 2, every service offered by the Content Server is also available through SOAP.

Architecture Overview

There are three ways to execute services with SOAP. The first is to pass the parameter `IsSoap=1` into any Content Server URL:

```
http://localhost/stellent/idcplg?IdcService=GET_USER_INFO&IsSoap=1
```

This method is extremely lightweight, but limited. It is available only in version 7.5, and it is not wise to perform check-ins or metadata updates in this way. It is mainly useful for read-only requests such as running searches or obtaining content information.

However, because you can receive a SOAP response with a simple URL, you can integrate SOAP into a web page using nothing but JavaScript. The `XmlHttpRequest` object, commonly used for Ajax integrations, can also be used to execute SOAP requests. Therefore, it is possible to run a SOAP service and display the results as HTML using nothing more than JavaScript!

The second method is to manually assemble the XML for the SOAP request and post it to the Content Server over HTTP. You can do this with custom code or with any of the dozens of SOAP toolkits available.

A SOAP-formatted request for the `GET_SEARCH_RESULTS` service looks like this:

```
<?xml version='1.0' encoding='UTF-8'?>
<SOAP-ENV:Envelope xmlns:SOAP-ENV=
  "http://schemas.xmlsoap.org/soap/envelope/">
 <SOAP-ENV:Body>
  <idc:service xmlns:idc="http://www.stellent.com/IdcService/"
    IdcService="GET_SEARCH_RESULTS">
   <idc:document>
    <idc:field name="QueryText">
      dDocTitle &lt;substring&gt; `test`</idc:field>
    <idc:field name="ResultCount">20</idc:field>
    <idc:field name="SortOrder">desc</idc:field>
    <idc:field name="SortField">dInDate</idc:field>
    <idc:field name="SortSpec"></idc:field>
    <idc:field name="StartRow"></idc:field>
    <idc:field name="PageNumber"></idc:field>
   </idc:document>
  </idc:service>
 </SOAP-ENV:Body>
</SOAP-ENV:Envelope>
```

The Content Server–specific XML is encapsulated in the `SOAP-ENV:Body` and `SOAP-ENV:Envelope` nodes, as dictated by the specification. Inside the `SOAP-ENV:Body` is the `idc:service` node, which contains all the data for the request. The `IdcService` is an attribute in this node, and all other parameters are contained in an idc:document node as idc:field nodes. Any request parameter can be passed in this manner.

Note that all parameters need to be XML-encoded. For example, the term <substring> in the QueryText must be encoded as <substring> for a SOAP request.

Both of the preceding interfaces have the same problem: you must be familiar with the names and parameters required in Content Server services to run them. You must also be comfortable assembling the XML for the request, and parsing XML data as a response, which is not difficult, but does add a learning curve.

The third method, which avoids the complexity of the above two, is to use the Web Services Description Language (WSDL) files. These XML files describe in detail what services are available, what request parameters they take, and what response data they return. Some SOAP toolkits can read WSDLs and output source code that you use to execute the request. The developer need not learn about the complexities of the Content Server or XML to begin writing applications.

The Content Server generates 8 WSDLs containing data on how to run the 20 most-common services. You can also generate new WSDLs based on custom services, which are used with SOAP toolkits to generate the necessary source code for running a service.

For example, the Apache Axis toolkit converts the Search.wsdl file into 13 Java files. One of them is called SearchSoap_BindingStub, which enables you to connect to the server and run the search. It contains methods named quickSearch, advancedSearch, and navigationSearch. These methods take different parameters and return different objects: QuickSearchResults, AdvancedSearchResults, and NavigationSearchResults, respectively. The advantage here is that you execute SOAP requests with a straightforward API, instead of manually creating and parsing XML.

In all three scenarios, the Content Server receives a HTTP request and executes a search. The response contains the search results, formatted as XML:

```
<?xml version='1.0' encoding='UTF-8'?>
<SOAP-ENV:Envelope xmlns:SOAP-ENV=
  "http://schemas.xmlsoap.org/soap/envelope/">
 <SOAP-ENV:Body>
  <idc:service IdcService="GET_SEARCH_RESULTS">
   <idc:document StartRow="1" EndRow="20" PageNumber="1"
     NumPages="1" TotalRows="8" TotalDocsProcessed="377"
     dUser="sysadmin">
    <idc:field name="SortField">dInDate</idc:field>
    <idc:field name="EnterpriseSearchMaxRows">4</idc:field>
    <idc:field name="ftx"/>
    <idc:field name="ResultCount">20</idc:field>
    <idc:field name="TranslatedQueryText">dDocTitle <substring>
      `test`</idc:field>
    <idc:field name="QueryText">dDocTitle+%3csubstring%3e+%60test%60
      </idc:field>
    <idc:field name="SortOrder">Desc</idc:field>
    <idc:field name="AdvSearch">True</idc:field>
    <idc:resultset name="NavigationPages">
     <idc:row PageNumber="1" StartRow="1" EndRow="8">
```

```
    <idc:field name="HeaderPageNumber">1</idc:field>
    <idc:field name="PageReference">1</idc:field>
   </idc:row>
  </idc:resultset>
  <idc:resultset name="SearchResults">
   <idc:row dDocType="ADACCT" dRevisionID="1" dWebExtension="txt"
     sCollectionID="" dOriginalName="test.txt"
     DOC_FN="c:/stellent/weblayout/groups/public/documents/adacct/1234.txt"
     dFormat="text/plain" dPublishType="" dDocName="1234"
     dDocAuthor="sysadmin" dOutDate="" dGif="adacct.gif"
     dExtension="txt" dInDate="8/8/05 1:49 PM"
     URL="/stellent/groups/public/documents/adacct/1234.txt"
     AlternateFormat="" dDocTitle="test document" dRevLabel="1"
     dSecurityGroup="Public" dRendition2="" dRendition1=""
     dID="554" dDocAccount="">
    <idc:field name="VDKSUMMARY">This is a test</idc:field>
    <idc:field name="SCORE">1.0000</idc:field>
    <idc:field name="AlternateFileSize">0</idc:field>
    <idc:field name="VaultFileSize">14</idc:field>
    <idc:field name="WEB-CGI-ROOT">/stellent/</idc:field>
    <idc:field name="WebFileSize">14</idc:field>
    <idc:field name="xComments"/>
   </idc:row>

   <!-- 19 rows omitted for brevity -->

  </idc:resultset>
  </idc:document>
 </idc:service>
 </SOAP-ENV:Body>
</SOAP-ENV:Envelope>
```

Both the SOAP request and response are wrapped in mandatory SOAP-ENV:Envelope and SOAP-ENV:Body XML nodes. The Content Server–specific nodes are the following:

idc:service: A wrapper for the request and response XML that contains all other nodes. Must contain the IdcService attribute.

idc:document: A wrapper for document metadata. Required metadata such as dSecurityGroup, dDocType, and dDocAuthor are present in the attributes; all others are child nodes.

idc:user: A wrapper for user metadata nodes and attributes.

idc:field: A child node for any idc:document, idc:user, or idc:service node, containing generic name-value data. Any request data can be passed in this node. Response data will be in these nodes if they do not belong in idc:document or idc:user nodes.

idc:resultset: A subnode of idc:document, idc:user, or idc:service. Contains tabular ResultSet data such as search results or a response from a SQL query.

`idc:row`: A child node of `idc:resultset` that contains name-value pairs in attributes and `idc:field`, `idc:document`, or `idc:user` nodes.

`idc:optionlist`: A child node of `idc:document`, `idc:user`, or `idc:service` that contains a list of simple options. Rarely used.

`idc:option`: A child node for `idc:optionlist`, which contains one row of data.

`idc:file`: A node containing data for file upload and download. The format of a download file is determined by the request parameter `soapResponseType`, which can be blank, `multipart/related`, or `application/dime`.

Most toolkits take the SOAP response string and turn it into an XML data object. You can use transformation languages like Extensible Stylesheet Language Transformations (XSLT) to convert the XML into HTML. If you want to extract just the data, you should use the XML Path Language (XPath) syntax to query the XML object and extract specific nodes.

The WSDL toolkits perform what is called XML Data Binding. As they parse the XML string, they create objects (such as `QuickSearchResult`) to contain the data. Parsing the XML response makes the data easier to use, but sometimes decreases the performance significantly. Executing a search from a WSDL would look something like this:

```
// create the connector to the content server
SearchLocator locator = new SearchLocator();
SearchSoap_BindingStub soapStub = (SearchSoap_BindingStub)
    locator.getSearchSoap();

// Set security settings.
soapStub.setUsername("user1");
soapStub.setPassword("idc");

// run the search
QuickSearchResult result = soapStub.quickSearch(
    "dDocTitle <substring> `test`", null);

// iterate over the results
SearchResults items = result.getSearchResults();
int numResults = items.length;
for (int i = 0; i < numResults; i++)
{
    SearchResults item = items[i];
    System.out.println("dDocName=" + item.getDDocName() +
            "\ndDocTitle=" + item.getDDocTitle());
}
```

The support for WSDLs was originally offered as a separate component. In Content Server version 7.5, SOAP serialization was merged into the core product, but WSDL support is still in a separate free component named `WsdlGenerator`.

It is highly advisable to install and enable the `WsdlGenerator` component, even if you do not intend to use WSDLs. The component contains dozens of sample code for multiple languages. You will almost certainly find something useful in these samples if you intend to use SOAP.

Limitations of SOAP

There are several limitations to SOAP that should be addressed before planning a large-scale rollout. First, there is the issue of performance. Because XML is such a verbose data format and HTTP is stateless, a request has much more overhead than other formats and protocols. This problem is compounded with WSDL toolkits because they pay the added cost of creating hundreds of data objects to store the XML response. Therefore, your SOAP clients need to do their best to optimize resource usage.

The easiest way to enhance performance is to enforce caching rules. For example, if your SOAP client executes searches frequently, and the results do not change, reuse the data for a few minutes. This rule is mainly applicable to web front ends to the Content Server. Another optimization is to make custom services that are more coarsely grained. For example, instead of calling three SOAP services, create a custom Java component that performs all three; then call just one custom service.

The second concern is security and the maintenance of users. SOAP uses standard HTTP for its protocol. Because HTTP is stateless, the authentication credentials must be passed in *every* request. It doesn't matter whether you use Active Directory, Lightweight Directory Access Protocol (LDAP), Basic HTTP Authentication, or cookie-based logins, the credentials must be present every time.

Stateless security becomes an issue if you want to create an external web application front end to the Content Server. Assume that a user logs into your web application, and you want to run a search with their credentials. You must construct an entirely new request, which means generating new authentication information for this user. To do so, you need access to the user's password or authentication cookies.

Therefore, the user has to log in *again* and give the Stellent password to your web application. This is not the best process because users do not like logging in twice, and now you have to find a way to securely store their passwords.

This problem can be solved with certain kinds of single sign-on solutions, but not all. For example, if your application and the Content Server both use the same LDAP server, the user names and passwords will be the same. It might then be possible to extract the authentication headers from the client request and assemble a new authenticated request to the Content Server without storing a password. This process works with some cookie login systems and some basic HTTP authentication systems.

However, for security reasons Active Directory does not allow your application to access the security headers, so it is always difficult to proxy these kinds of credentials. You are forced to make the users log in again. Alternatively, you can proxy the request on behalf of a super user; then have a security customization execute the request as the actual user. Security customizations are discussed later in this chapter.

Besides these drawbacks, SOAP is still an excellent choice for a service-oriented enterprise. The protocol is simple, and support is embedded in most programming languages, if not the application itself.

The maintenance of a SOAP infrastructure is simple. Because of security and performance limitations, most SOAP requests are forced to be coarsely grained and stateless, which is exactly the way a good SOA should behave. Therefore, you can upgrade features on back-end applications and have little effect on front-end interfaces when using SOAP.

It also benefits greatly from being a straightforward combination of two incredibly popular technologies: HTTP and XML.

As HTTP becomes a better protocol and integrates more advanced security features, SOAP will likewise improve. As XML toolkits become faster, easier to use, and more feature-rich, SOAP will likewise improve. Because neither HTTP nor XML are likely to be abandoned any time in the near future, SOAP is an excellent technology choice for the long term.

J2EE Application Servers

J2EE application servers and portal servers are popular tools for creating web interfaces to multiple enterprise applications. They are commonly used to create middleware to control back-end applications, such as databases and Enterprise Content Management (ECM) systems. For example, a portal server can load customer information from a Customer Relationship Management (CRM) database and then run a Stellent search to find content items related to that customer.

For middleware written in a J2EE application server, the recommended approach is to use the Stellent Content Integration Suite (CIS). An application server is recommended, but not necessary. You can also deploy the CIS in a Servlet container such as Tomcat, or from Plain Old Java Objects (POJOs).

In practice, CIS is more than just a connector to the Content Server, which differentiates it from SOAP. It's an application that adds caching, throttling, messaging, and clustering features to help boost performance. As of version 7.6.1, CIS also contains the Spring framework to help you write web applications more quickly.

If your middleware is deployed on J2EE Portal Servers, the Stellent Content Portal Suite (CPS) is a good addition to the CIS. The CPS is a collection of JSR 168–compliant portlets that execute standard Content Server requests (for example, checking-in content, searching for it, and displaying the web version to the user). These portlets are packaged for easy deployment on the JSR 168–compliant portal servers.

Architecture Overview

The CIS has two main pieces. The first is the CIS server running on an application server, which is the object that performs all communication with the Content Server. The second piece is the CIS client, which sends requests to the CIS server. This request is parsed and sent to the Content Server for processing, after which the CIS server sends the response back to the CIS client.

Because the connection to the Content Server is controlled by the CIS server, it can be used as a central point to throttle requests and cache responses during peak hours.

The method of communication between the CIS client and the CIS server depends on how the CIS application was deployed. If you installed it on a J2EE application server with a complete J2EE stack, the client-server communication uses Enterprise Java Beans (EJBs). If you installed it in a generic Servlet container, such as Tomcat, the client-server communication uses Java Remote Method Invocation (RMI). If you are using it in a Java application with no J2EE stack whatsoever, you do not create a CIS client at all; instead, you create a CIS server object and communicate with the Content Server directly.

This abstraction is hidden from the developer. You always execute services with the CISApplication object, whether it is behaving like a CIS client or a CIS server.

Unlike SOAP or Web Services, CIS connects directly to the Content Server instead of the web server (refer to Figure 2-1 in Chapter 2). This direct connection avoids the authentication step at the web server and gives a CIS developer total control over the authentication and authorization of users. Naturally, because this connection does not require a password, you must first set up a trust relationship with the server running CIS; otherwise, the Content Server will reject the connections. Alternatively, version 7.6.1 of the CIS can be configured to allow authentication at the web server.

The advantage is that you can authenticate the users at the CIS layer however you want. You can integrate with an LDAP server at the application server level, or you can ask the Content Server to validate the passwords for you. Because the connection has no password, CIS avoids some of the user maintenance problems of SOAP. However, it still requires the CIS developer to configure the authentication layer.

CIS comes with extensive samples, documentation on the Software Developer Kit (SDK), and JavaDocs of the core libraries. There are more than 1,300 classes in the CIS toolkit, so it is easy to be overwhelmed when developing your first application. However, most of these classes are for internal use and not relevant for connecting to the Content Server. The following packages are the most important for CIS integrations:

`com.stellent.cis`: Contains the root `CISApplication` object required to create all API connectors and requests.

`com.stellent.command`: Contains the CIS command façade objects as well as execution content objects that control how the request is processed.

`com.stellent.common`: Contains subpackages such as `io`, `http`, and `encode`, which are useful for Servlets and advanced integrations.

`com.stellent.context`: Contains objects for setting the user context for the service, which controls security, localization, and personalization.

`com.stellent.ucpmapi.active`: Contains all the API interfaces used to connect to a Content Server and execute services. Most functionality is here or in a subpackage.

`com.stellent.ucpmapi.active.administrative`: Contains an advanced administrative API that enables you to execute any service, including custom services.

`com.stellent.ucpmapi.active.document`: Contains document-related service objects such as check-in, check-out, and content info.

`com.stellent.ucpmapi.active.file`: Contains file-based service objects, including rendering web pages, downloading native documents, or converting the content into HTML with Dynamic Converter.

`com.stellent.ucpmapi.active.search`: Contains search-based service objects.

`com.stellent.ucpmapi.active.user`: Contains user-related service objects such as personalization, authentication, and authorization.

`com.stellent.ucpmapi.active.workflow`: Contains workflow-related service objects such as workflow information, workflow approval, and workflow rejection.

`com.stellent.web.servlet`: Contains the Servlets that ship with CIS; helps initialize the `CISApplication` object, process file downloads, and run dynamic conversions.

In each of the packages and subpackages of `com.stellent.ucpmapi`, there is usually one class that provides the API to the Content Server. The other classes are used to create objects required for the request and contain the data from the response.

For example, in the search package, there is an interface called `ISCSActiveSearchAPI`, which returns `ISCSActiveSearchResponse` and `ISCSActiveSearchResult` objects. After you install and configure CIS, you can execute a search with a Java Server Page (JSP) similar to this one:

```
<%@ taglib uri="/WEB-INF/tlds/c.tld" prefix="c" %>
<%@ page import="com.stellent.cis.CISApplication" %>
<%@ page import="com.stellent.context.ISCSContext" %>
<%@ page import="com.stellent.ucpmapi.active.
        search.ISCSActiveSearchAPI" %>
<%@ page import="com.stellent.ucpmapi.active.
        search.ISCSActiveSearchResponse" %>
<%
// create the CIS application object
CISApplication cisApp = CISApplication.initializeClient();

// create a user context
ISCSContext context = cisApp.getUCPMAPI()
    .getActiveAPI()._createSCSContext();
context.setUser ("sysadmin");

// create a search API object
ISCSActiveSearchAPI searchAPI =
    cisApp.getUCPMAPI().getActiveAPI().getSearchAPI();

// search for the first 10 documents with 'test' in the title
ISCSActiveSearchResponse scsResponse = searchAPI.search(null,
    context, "dDocTitle <substring> `test`", 10);

// dump the response to see the raw data
out.println(scsResponse);
%>
```

This JSP runs a search for all content items with `test` in their title and then prints the raw response data to the page. The `scsResponse` object contains the search results in the variable `results`. Similar to SOAP with WSDLs, the response data is available in easy-to-use Java objects. Instead of dumping the raw data to the page, you could display the results in a table with the following JSP code:

```
<table border=1>
<tr>
    <td>Content ID</td>
    <td>Title</td>
    <td>Author</td>
    <td>Security Group</td>
    <td>File Name</td>
</tr>
```

```
<c:forEach var="item" items="${scsResponse.results}">
<tr>
    <td><c:out value="${item.activeContentID}"/><br>
        <fmt:formatDate value="${item.releaseDate}"
        pattern="dd/mm/yyyy, HH:mm:ss"/></td>
    <td><a href="/scscis/getfile?dID=<c:out
        value='${item.activeDocumentID}'/>">
        <c:out value="${item.title}"/>
        </a></td>
    <td><c:out value="${item.author}"/></td>
    <td><c:out value="${item.securityGroup}"/></td>
    <td><c:out value="${item.fileName}"/>
        [<c:out value="${item.format}"/>]</td>
</tr>
</c:forEach>
</table>
```

This code uses the forEach method in the Java Standard Tag Libraries (JSTLs) to iterate over the item objects contained in the results object. Notice that the values for author and security group are stored in the variables item.author and item.securityGroup. Refer to the CIS JavaDocs for more information on variable names and how to access their values.

Active Server Pages

The Content Server can support virtually any web scripting languages available—you are not limited to using Hypertext Content Server Pages (HCSPs) or JSPs for your web application. However, if you choose another language the integration options are more limited.

Although HCSPs and JSPs are rendered by the Content Server, other web scripting languages—such as PHP, Perl, Python, and Active Server Pages (ASPs)—are rendered by the web server. You can integrate with these kinds of scripting languages in several ways, including the following:

- Configure Content Publisher or Dynamic Converter to output pages that contain web script and then render them with the web server.

- Create ASP layouts and fragments with Site Studio and render them with the web server.

- Check-in your web scripts into the Content Server repository and then render them with the web server.

- Run the web scripts on a remote web server and connect to the Content Server as needed.

In either case, if you want to execute Content Server services on these web scripting pages, you must use SOAP or CIS as a connection layer.

For example, assume that you work for one of the many organizations in which some rogue administrator has set up a PHP-based wiki application. (The odds are good that you are in this situation right now and might not know it.) If you want to integrate it with the Content

Server, one option is to write some SOAP code in PHP to check-in a new HCSP any time a user adds a new wiki entry.

If the application is written in ASPs, you have an additional integration option: an ActiveX control called IdcCommandUX, which is offered as a free product by Stellent. Similar to CIS, this module connects directly to the Content Server, bypassing the authentication at the web server. You can run it from the default web server or from a remote web server.

IdcCommandUX has features that many SOAP toolkits lack, which makes it useful on ASPs. For example, it contains the methods forwardRequest and executeFileCommand. The first helps forward check-in requests to the Content Server from the client. The second helps stream file downloads back to the client. Both are impossible to do with pure ASP code; you need a custom ActiveX control to correctly process data streams.

You can send either HDA- or SOAP-formatted data to execute a Stellent service with IdcCommandUX. For example, you could run a SOAP search from an ASP with the following code:

```
<%
    ' prepare a SOAP search
    soapRequest = _
        "<?xml version='1.0' encoding='iso-8859-1'?>" & vbcrlf & _
        "<SOAP-ENV:Envelope xmlns:SOAP-ENV=""" & _
            "http://schemas.xmlsoap.org/soap/envelope/"">" & vbcrlf & _
        " <SOAP-ENV:Body>" & vbcrlf & _
        "  <idc:service xmlns:idc=""" & _
                "http://www.stellent.com/IdcService/""" & _
                "IdcService=""GET_SEARCH_REULTS"">" & vbcrlf _
        "   <idc:field name=""QueryText"">" & _
            "dDocTitle <substring> `test`</idc:field>" & _
        "  </idc:service>" & vbcrlf & _
        " </SOAP-ENV:Body>" & vbcrlf & _
        "</SOAP-ENV:Envelope>" & vbcrlf

    ' Initialize a SOAP connection to the server
    Set idcCmd = Server.CreateObject("Idc.CommandUX")
    call idcCmd.initRemote("", "socket:localhost:4444", "sysadmin", true)

    ' execute the request, and get the XML response
    responseStr = idcCmd.executeCommand(requestStr)
%>
```

In a standard request, the name of the user is supplied to the Content Server directly in the request, similar to a CIS request.

If you want to check-in scripting pages and run them from the Content Server's default web server, you must keep several things in mind.

First, remember that ASPs are more powerful than HCSPs. They are executed by the web server, not the Content Server, and can do anything the web server is allowed to do. Depending on your web server settings, it could display secure files to the wrong user or even delete content. Therefore, it is vital that you only allow developers to check-in scripting code.

To restrict check-in of scripting pages, you should follow rules similar to the ones outlined in Chapter 4 about JSP security. You should create a special security group named `scripts` and allow only administrators to have `write` access to that group. Then you need to customize your web server to only run scripts if they belong in the correct web folder, which would be something like this:

```
stellent/weblayout/groups/scripts/
```

The configuration steps will be different, depending on the web server, and which scripting language you are using.

It is also important to remember that scripts executed by the web server will always be slower than ones rendered in the Content Server. This overhead is due to the extra steps required to create a connection, execute it across a socket, and parse the response. Because the web server is running in a separate process and perhaps on a separate physical server, the connection overhead is noticeably greater. However, with a little coding discipline and caching, you should have no trouble writing a high-performance application.

In most situations, you should execute Stellent services with SOAP. The existing SOAP toolkits are easier to install, configure, and use in comparison with IdcCommandUX. If you are running ASPs and need the extra features listed here, use IdcCommandUX. For more information, please refer to the *IdcCommand Reference Guide* that ships with your Content Server. You can also download the free `AspWebApp` module from the Stellent Support Site for ASP code samples.

Site Studio and Dynamic Converter

These applications are extensions to the core Content Server to manage websites and related items. Both applications come in two parts: the first part is a component that adds custom services to help process content; the second part is a client application that helps you design the look and feel of your web content.

The *Dynamic Converter* extracts the content from native documents and processes it into web-viewable content. For example, you can use it to extract formatted text from a Microsoft Word document and present it in a web page with the Content Server look and feel. Or it can process a very large document into multiple web pages with navigation links between them. Or it can convert the document into Wireless Markup Language (WML) so users can read the documents on their cell phones.

The Dynamic Converter template editor enables an administrator to design templates for these conversions. The Dynamic Converter analyzes the original content and looks for styles, font patterns, or even text patterns. It maps these into Dynamic Converter *elements*, which you can use to control how to display the content. You can do a simple mapping such as displaying the element in bold, or an advanced mapping that places custom HTML before and after the element.

For example, you can scan a Microsoft Word document and map a custom Word paragraph style into a Cascading Style Sheets (CSS) style. This mapping enables you to take a paragraph with the Microsoft style `CustomLeftNavigation` and display it with the `float: left` CSS style so it appears on the left. Or you can find text that is bold and red and then display it as italic and blue. You can even do an acronym conversion; look for the word SCS; then wrap it in HTML that comments out SCS and displays Stellent Content Server instead.

A user can access converted content from the search results page, the content information page, or a custom template. In practice, administrators configure processing rules so content is converted upon check-in based on their metadata. The check-in conversion allows flexibility over which conversion templates to use and boosts performance by converting the content before it's needed.

In contrast, *Site Studio* is an application for creating and managing multiple websites. It breaks the site down into reusable navigation sections, layouts, fragments, and contribution regions. It is currently the most popular way to create websites within the Content Server repository.

The purpose of Site Studio is to ease the creation and maintenance of multiple websites. For example, it simplifies the ways you can add new pages, add new content, update old content, or change the entire look and feel of the site.

Site Studio achieves this by separating the website maintainers into three groups, each with its own tools: site designers, site managers, and site contributors. The *site designers* are the HTML gurus who control the images, fonts, colors, and layout of the page. The *site managers* control the navigation structure of the site, including which layouts and which content to display. The *site contributors* have the responsibility of adding new content or editing content when it is out of date.

This separation yields numerous benefits. First, site designers do not need to be bothered if content or navigation on the site needs to be updated. They use Site Studio Designer to create reusable fragments and layouts—and then their job is done.

Second, site managers can add entirely new sections to the website without needing the design team. They can simply reuse the fragments and layouts that the designer created and then add new sections to the website. They can do this with Site Studio Designer or Site Studio Manager. The latter is a web-based application that enables you to create new sections based on existing layouts.

Finally, site contributors do not need to know HTML at all to create highly complex and attractive web pages. They can add content with native applications such as Microsoft Word or with the Site Studio Contributor. The latter is a web-based HTML editor that gives contributors a WYSIWYG environment for creating content. The site designer can still enforce a consistent look and feel by limiting what WYSIWYG options are available; for example, allowing site contributors to select only from a list of approved fonts, colors, and styles.

And of course, because the website content is managed by the Content Server, all security, revision control, workflow, and searching functionality is automatically available.

Site Studio breaks down a website into five main components:

Navigation Section: Represents one page in the navigational structure of the website. Each node has custom properties, a layout, and specific content items to display.

Layout: An HCSP/JSP/ASP that contains the basic structure of the page and information about which fragments are displayed on it.

Fragment: Contains HCSP/JSP/ASP script to run on a layout. Each fragment can have web assets (images, JavaScript files) and parameters to control their display.

Contribution Region: Used to display one or more content items on the page. Each region references an XML data file or native content in the repository. The site designer controls how the content is displayed with fragment code.

Project File: The XML file that binds all these resources together. It contains the list of navigation nodes, their custom properties, the default layout for each section, and assigned contribution regions. It also contains definitions of custom properties and additional assets.

Creating a Website

In practice, the site designer begins by creating the navigation structure for the website, which entails constructing the site hierarchy and deciding which content items belong on which page. This is the most important step in designing a website because it determines how easy it will be for your users to browse to the content they need. When you do this, be sure to focus on process instead of existing taxonomy.

In other words, think hard about how your users will look for content every day. Do not make the mistake of designing your website like an organization chart. People do not care which department created the content; they just want to find it. They might not even know that the content exists and they need an easy way to stumble upon it. Be sure to spend a sufficient amount of time in planning and be prepared to redo it after user feedback. The Site Manager tools allow you to quickly change navigation when needed.

The next step is planning the layouts of each page. Navigation sections can have two layout pages: the *primary layout* is used to display the main content for that section; the *secondary layout* is used to display the items that contributors have added to this section. For example, you design the primary layout to show a list of press releases. When you click the link to view one, the full contents are displayed in the secondary layout.

Most websites have structures that do not differ much from page to page. They contain different content, different navigation labels, and different code, but the overall layout is similar. For example, the previous two layouts would work well for press releases, recent news, calendar events, or a list of the most popular pages. By using different contribution regions and custom section properties, the same layouts and fragments can display radically different content.

As a rule, layouts contain as little code as possible. In many cases they contain nothing more than fragments and then use CSS to position those fragments where appropriate.

The next step is designing the fragments, which contain the majority of the code on a site. Fragments contain lists of content items, navigation links, graphics, as well as links to CSS and JS resources. They are also commonly used as containers for the contribution regions on the page, which gives the developer total control over how the contents of the region are displayed.

You should design your fragments to be portable between layouts, sections, contribution regions, and websites—enabling you to reuse fragments throughout the entire site. You can use fragment parameters and custom section properties to control how the fragment is displayed. For example, it is common to consolidate all CSS and JS code into one fragment and include it on all layouts. The advantage is that you can change the style and behavior of the entire site by changing one fragment. Making reusable fragments requires more planning at first, but pays off immediately if you ever change the look and feel of the site, or if you ever want to translate the site into another language.

The last step is to select contribution regions for each of the pages. These regions refer to content items in the repository and are independent of the layouts and fragments. For example, even if two navigation sections use the same layouts and fragments to render a page, they can have completely different contribution regions for the page contents.

These items are either native content or Site Studio data files. For native content, Site Studio uses Dynamic Converter to display it as HTML on the page. You can use the standard templates, which extract only the text, or a custom template that formats the output however you want.

In contrast, data files are stored as specially formatted XML in the Content Server. These data files are created with Site Studio Contributor and can contain different types of elements: images, plain text, HTML text, or custom data. One data file can contain a single item or a list of several items. For example, one XML file can contain a link to an image, a plain text label for the image, and some HTML to display with the image.

The standard procedure for site contributors is to browse the website until you find a page that needs to be updated. Then you enter contributor mode by clicking a button, a link, or a special key combination. The default key combination is `Control-Shift-F5` to enter or exit contribution mode. In this mode, you see an icon next to all the contribution regions that you are allowed to edit. From here, you can launch the contributor with one click. Or you can perform additional actions on the items, such as approve it in the workflow, open it in its native application, or view additional content information.

Additional Features of Site Studio

Remember that you can do anything on a Site Studio page that you can on a Dynamic Server Page . You can execute IdocScript functions, run services, or submit forms. The advantage of using a Site Studio page instead of a Dynamic Server Page is that the site is significantly easier to design and maintain with Site Studio.

You can even combine Site Studio pages with custom Java components to create full web applications. For example, the `SampleBlogs` and `SampleWikis` for Site Studio are two such web applications.

The first application is a sample web log, or *blog* for short. Blogs enable you to turn a section of your website into something akin to an online diary. They are useful for quickly posting informal content to your site, such as the daily thoughts of your CEO or a brief daily status report about an ongoing project.

The second application is a *wiki*, which is an extremely easy to use online knowledge base. The most popular example is `wikipedia.org`, which is a free online encyclopedia maintained by a community of thousands. In a wiki, contribution is open to all users and is made as simple as possible. The links between wiki pages are simplified to be the name of the page surrounded by brackets, such as `[[Main Page]]`. Such simplicity encourages everybody to contribute and lessens the problems with link management between pages. The Site Studio sample application adds extra support to allow quick page creation, comments, and support for wiki links.

For more information on how to set up a site, refer to the *Designer User Guide* that ships with Site Studio. Refer to the *Technical Guide* and the *Reference Guide* for tips on hidden features and the inner workings of the product. The template editor for Dynamic Converter is the same as the one for Content Publisher, an earlier product, so the best guides for creating templates are bundled with Content Publisher. Download the *Tutorials* and *Seven Easy Lessons* for Content Publisher from Stellent's support site to learn more about designing templates.

WebDAV and Folders

The ECM industry has made several attempts at making a standard protocol for web-based revision control. One of them is called Web Based Distributed Authoring and Versioning, or WebDAV. Stellent has supported this protocol since version 6.0.

This protocol exposes a small subset of content management features, which are mainly useful for editing website content. They enable documents to be created, locked, and edited; they also enable users to create new directories for new web content. WebDAV has limited support for metadata and virtually no support for processing an item through its life cycle. Its primary benefit is the same as its primary limitation: it exposes an extremely simplistic interface to a content management system.

This simplicity is good because your site contributors need almost no training in order to begin using it. WebDAV is built into many applications, including the Microsoft Office suite, Windows Explorer, and Mac OS X, so users can add new items to a content management system as easily as dragging the files into a folder. They will immediately begin placing their important content into the repository because it is so simple.

However, this simplicity is also a problem because users lose the ability to process items through workflows, obtain a conversion of the content, or supply significant metadata to the items. This deficiency will cause aggravation if processing items through workflows is a part of their day-to-day activities.

Second, if users are allowed to create their own directories, the navigation structure quickly becomes too complex to manage. WebDAV allows consumers to make their own folder structure specific to how they work, organized so they can find their content again. If you have a small number of users, this is fine. Unfortunately, this model does not scale. It quickly becomes impossible for users to locate any content that they did not create themselves.

To overcome these limitations, Stellent has two optional products that can extend WebDAV and make it more usable.

The first is the Folders component, which maps WebDAV directories into Folder objects on the Content Server. Each Folder has default metadata, so content placed into a folder can automatically inherit it. This metadata is configured by an administrator or the folder owner. Once the metadata is assigned to the item, a consumer has multiple options for finding the content. They can use the standard search interface, the standard library interface, or portal pages that display hierarchies of content based on their metadata. The Folders component also adds standard Content Server security to the creation and modification of folders, so an administrator can lock down creation privileges as needed.

The second product is the Windows Explorer Integration, which is one part of Stellent's Desktop Integration Suite. It behaves like WebDAV, but exposes more Content Server–specific functionality. By right-clicking an item you can alter its metadata, take an item offline for local editing, or view its check-out status. You can also launch a browser window to the content information page for more advanced life-cycle management. This integration gives users the simplicity of drag and drop, but doesn't restrict them to the functionality in WebDAV.

It is important to note that even with WebDAV enabled on your Content Server, you are not required to check-in content with WebDAV. All standard functionality is still available; you are not required to place an item into a folder.

Metadata Challenges for Contributor and Consumers

It is important to emphasize the difficulty of designing a system that is both easy for contributors and easy for consumers. You need to create a navigation structure that works for both groups, which is sometimes not possible. Your users typically know a lot more about the system than consumers and are fine with a department-level contribution model. But your consumers would hate such a model because they would have no idea which department created the content.

One way to ease the problem is with a rich set of metadata. You first set up a rigid folder structure that your contributors are comfortable with. Then you can use the Folders component, along with Content Profiles, to generate a rich set of metadata for each item. If this is too much effort for your administrators, the Stellent Content Categorizer integrates with third-party taxonomy engines to extract keywords and other metadata from your content.

After the item has a rich set of metadata, you have multiple options for helping consumers find it. You could construct a series of queries in either the standard library folders or on Site Studio pages to help consumers drill down into the content in whatever way they find natural.

For example, your contributors might be fine contributing content into a folder structure similar to this:

```
/division/department/employee/customer/project/
```

But your consumers are different; they are unlikely to be familiar with this aspect of your organization's taxonomy, even if they work for you. For example, if they are looking for the documentation on project Amber, they might prefer to look in these folders instead:

```
/projects/amber/
/projectType/projects/amber
/documentation/amber/
/customer/projects/amber
/index/a/amber
```

To make matters worse, frequently your users who need the Amber project documentation have no idea that they need it. Perhaps they are looking for information about a project that is related to Amber, so you need to inform them that Amber might also be relevant. You need to allow your users to learn about your taxonomy as they browse so they can stumble upon the content they need the most.

Your contributors and consumers never follow the same process for finding content, so do not force them. If you focus too much on contributors, your metadata will suffer, and it will be impossible for consumers to find content. If you focus too much on consumers, your contributors will never know where to put their content. So they will place things in the wrong folder, and give it the wrong metadata—and soon your consumers will be suffering again.

A good option is to offer a rigid but simple interface for contributors. It is much less costly to train all your contributors than all your consumers. Do not allow unsophisticated users to make bad choices with their metadata; do as much as possible for them. Nevertheless, you should give your power users as much control as they need—as long as they can be trusted to make good metadata choices.

For your consumers, it is vital to offer multiple approaches to find content. Give them several different taxonomies that allow them to browse for what they need. Enable them to find content by subject, by task, or by who they are. Place each item in multiple categories, if needed, to satisfy how consumers browse for content. Give them a simplified search that works with keywords. Track their behavior and offer related items or popular items that contain similar keywords. Be sure to use language, labels, and metadata that make sense to all visitors, not just your contributors.

You cannot set up such a system quickly and you will need to make continuous modifications after it is done. You must learn about who is in your audience and how they behave. Watch how they use the system and try to find out when and where they become frustrated. Then try to offer them hints about what to do before they give up. This is an iterative process that over time will produce a solution that works well for all your users.

Security Customizations

As mentioned in Chapter 2, the Content Server has a highly flexible security model. It is easy to integrate external user repositories, such as Active Directory or LDAP, so that the Stellent administrator does not need to manage users as well as content. However, the default integrations assume a clean mapping between the schema in the user repository and Content Server security roles. In some situations, this is not possible.

In those cases you can create a custom User Provider for the Content Server. This is similar to creating a custom Database Provider with a Java component, covered in Chapter 11. Although User Providers require only a small amount of Java code, you must be familiar with the Java LDAP libraries to write them.

You can also create a custom web server plug-in filter to perform the security check at the web server. These plug-ins must be written in C++ and are more difficult than a Java component. See the WebSecurityFilters component for sample plug-ins, source code, and a build environment.

You can also alter the security credentials for the user on the fly with a Java filter. Following are some commonly used filters for modifying the security model (see Appendix H):

- addExportedWebFilterConfiguration

- alterProviderAttributes

- alterUserCredentials

- checkExtendedSecurityModelDocAccess

- computeExtendedSecurityModelWhereClausePrivileges

- docUrlAllowAccess

- docUrlAllowDisclosure

The SecurityFilters component in the HowToComponents is a good example of how to modify security with a Java filter. This sample grants all users write access when executing a specific service. It uses the alterUserCredentials filter to boost the rights of the user for one request.

Finally, you can customize the security layer by modifying the CHECK_USER_CREDENTIALS service itself. This is the service that the web server plug-in executes when it cannot determine the security credentials for the user. The service is executed when the *Authorization Type* for the user is something besides Local. In other words, the user's credentials exist elsewhere.

They may exist in a remote LDAP repository (Authorization Type of `External`) or on another Content Server (Authorization Type of `Global`).

Because a `Local` user is authenticated by the web server, the Content Server need not be running to authenticate and authorize a user. This means that administrators should be `Local`, so they can start and stop the Content Server with the Admin Server. Also, if you want the fastest possible access to files published in the `weblayout` directory, you should be a `Local` user.

Which security customization should you use? A web plug-in runs the fastest, but requires familiarity with C++ and works only with the latest version of CIS. Web plug-ins are mainly useful if you have a cookie-based, single sign-on solution and need to integrate it with Stellent. In most cases, you can perform an integration with a relatively small amount of code. However, the plug-in environment is severely limited, and you do not have easy access to Content Server functionality.

A custom User Provider is slightly slower because the authentication step requires an additional round-trip to the Content Server. However, this cost comes with the benefits of running your authentication module in a richer environment. You have access to a database and a persistent `Hashtable` of shared objects, as well as the ability to execute custom services. If this leads to performance problems, you can always increase the `UserCacheTimeout`. The web server typically caches authentication data for one minute, but you can increase it if needed.

Modifications at the filter or service level should be avoided, if possible. Sometimes it is the only way to add the functionality that you need, but it's less intuitive for your users and administrators. If you calculate the authorization with a User Provider, it is easy to determine what a user's rights are. However, if you have multiple filters and services boosting credentials at random intervals, it is difficult to know what a user can do without analyzing the source code. This restriction makes it difficult to manage or audit your users' access rights.

The Future

The future of the Content Server depends a lot on the future of ECM. Because ECM has an extremely a nebulous definition, it's difficult to give a clear idea of what is next for the industry. However, many hope that with the right feature sets and standardization of the API, Content Management systems may one day be as commonplace as databases are now.

Similar to Content Management, databases were at first restricted to very specific enterprise-level solutions. Each application that used the database needed to be written specifically for that database. The applications worked fine, but customers hated the feeling of vendor lock-in.

Eventually, under pressure from their customers, the database vendors agreed to a standard known as SQL. After they agreed to a standard, it was possible to create applications that were database-independent. No longer were customers forced to stay with one vendor if their competition offered a better product.

The result was an explosion in new database applications, and now almost every organization in the world uses one.

Many hope Content Management systems will go through a similar standardization, followed by a popularity explosion. They look at standards such as WebDAV, BEA's Service Provider Interface (SPI), and JSR170, and hope that eventually ECM vendors will agree to one.

However, there are several stumbling blocks. The reality is that the current specifications are a good start, but have a long way to go. Several attempts were made, and none succeeded. Why? As long as the term *Enterprise Content Management* applies to so many applications, and each vendor does something radically different, these specifications will simply be too restrictive for widespread adoption.

Every specification thus far tried to restrict the Content Management problem into a simplistic search, edit, and save model. This is currently the only option because advanced features are difficult to distill into a standard that all vendors could adopt. Features such as content conversion, metadata, revision rollback, security, workflows, retention, archiving, and business process management are implemented differently by each vendor. Several vendors don't implement these advanced features at all.

Therefore, to avoid favoritism, these standards can be nothing more than the lowest common denominator. Unfortunately, that just isn't good enough for ECM customers.

These standards do not cover the functionality that some ECM vendors had *five years ago*. Nor do they have room to grow to add the features that the industry has planned. Therefore, they certainly cannot cover where the industry will be as soon as two years from today. It makes absolutely no sense for customers to standardize on an API that is seriously outdated before it is even published (and will be even worse in two years).

The good news is that the continued pressure from consumers will lead to better and better standards. The consolidation of ECM vendors in the market will lead to larger companies and probably a more coherent and complete set of ECM services. When that happens, a standard API will be much more feasible.

Many believe that companies will eventually be won over by the simplicity of blogs and wikis, and demand that they be standard components of all ECM systems. Certainly new laws, such as Sarbanes-Oxley and other compliance regulations, are forcing companies to think very hard about how they control their information, and we've seen only the beginning of laws like these. A Content Management API that does not allow the user to set retention policies simply will never work.

The future will certainly bring new security protocols and web service protocols. Perhaps somebody will invent a protocol better than SOAP, and it will be widely adopted. Perhaps one of the XML standards about workflows and business processing will gain traction, and ECM vendors will implement them. Perhaps social bookmarking or metadata extraction software will become commonplace, and all vendors will need APIs that automate lists of related content items.

Regardless of what the future holds, you can be sure that the Stellent Content Server can rise to the challenge. Stellent has the most flexible ECM system available. Its Java engine allows it to run on virtually any platform. Its data-driven service-oriented architecture allows it to quickly integrate with any remote repository or implement practically any new specification.

In short, bring it on.

APPENDIX A

■■■

IdocScript Language Basics

This appendix contains an in-depth analysis of IdocScript syntax. IdocScript is similar to other scripting languages such as PHP and VBScript. It is focused on the creation of HTML pages, and its syntax is fairly straightforward.

IdocScript is used to assemble the response page for a service request. This response is rendered with templates and resource includes, which include HTML and IdocScript. IdocScript is also used on Dynamic Server Pages such as Hypertext Content Server Templates (HCSTs) and Hypertext Content Server Pages (HCSPs). It can even be used on Java Server Pages rendered in the Servlet container.

In addition, certain request parameters support IdocScript code. For example, when running a search you can put IdocScript directly into the QueryText parameter:

```
QueryText=dDocAuthor <matches> `<$UserName$>`
```

The script in this parameter is evaluated on the fly, and the rendered QueryText will be used in the service request. This technique is particularly useful on portal pages.

For safety, some IdocScript functions are disabled unless the code is being executed in a specific context. For example, IdocScript function that alter workflows and update metadata can be used only from inside a workflow script; they do not work if used on a template page. Other functions might be available only in the content of a service request.

See Appendix B for more information of the functions available in IdocScript and Appendix C for more information about IdocScript variables.

Lexical Analysis

Case Sensitivity

All IdocScript variables, keywords, and functions are case sensitive.

Statements

A statement in IdocScript is encapsulated inside the delimiters <$$>. For example, to assign the value sysadmin to the variable myName, use the following code:

```
<$myName = "sysadmin"$>
```

This syntax is used in `dynamichtml` resource definitions, request parameters, and templates. However, it is not valid for two kinds of Dynamic Server Pages: HCSPs and Hypertext Content Server Forms (HCSFs). Because these documents must be valid XML, the IdocScript must be encapsulated within XML comments:

```
<!--$myName = "sysadmin"-->
```

Starting in version 7.0, square bracket delimiters are also supported:

```
[!--$myName = "sysadmin"--]
```

Both of the preceding code formats are called XML IdocScript. The latter format is preferred by developers who use HTML editors to design web pages because some HTML editors do not display HTML comments, whereas square brackets are usually visible.

The previous IdocScript statements do not output any characters to the page. However, the new line character at the end of the statement will be output. To output the variable `myName` to the page, use the following:

```
<$myName$>
```

Some IdocScript functions will output data to the page. To suppress the output, use the `exec` keyword:

```
<$exec myName$>
```

IdocScript supports multiple expressions in one statement if they are separated by commas. Developers typically use commas to set the values for multiple variables in one statement:

```
<$varA = "a", varB = "b", varC = "c"$>
```

Control statements cannot be comma-separated; they must always be delimited. For example, the following conditional is valid:

```
<$if (i  1)$>
    <$j=10$>
<$endif$>
```

whereas this conditional is invalid:

```
<$if (i  1), j=10, endif$>
```

Some functions return values. If you comma-separate the statements, only the last one outputs to the page. For example, the following code:

```
<$word = "Hello World!"$>
<$word$>
<$word, strLower(word)$>
<$word, strLower(word), strUpper(word)$>
```

returns the following output:

```
Hello World!
hello world!
HELLO WORLD!
```

As stated earlier, the exec keyword suppressed the output of the entire statement.

White Space and Line Breaks

As a rule, white space is not important inside an IdocScript expression. Expressions can wrap multiple lines for greater clarity:

```
<$if (i  1) and
    (i < 100) and
    (j > 1) and
    (j < 100)$>
        <$goodData = "true"$>
<$endif$>
```

Multiple expressions in one statement can also span multiple lines provided that the expressions are comma-separated:

```
<$varA = "a",
  varB = "b",
  varC = "c"$>
```

A conditional statement that wraps multiple lines outputs several new lines to the page. Each time a statement is evaluated, the following new line is output to the page. For example, the following statement outputs multiple new lines to the page:

```
<$if i == 1$>
one
<$else$>
not one
<$endif$>
```

To suppress the output of multiple new line characters, place the entire statement on one line:

```
<$if i == 1$>one<$else$>not one<$endif$>
```

However, this statement can lead to unreadable code. Alternatively, you can take advantage of how white space is ignored and write the statement like this:

```
<$if i == 1
  $>one<$
else
  $>not one<$
endif$>
```

Both statements produce one single line of output.

To control white space in an include, use the `inc` function with the `strTrimWs` function or the `exec` keyword:

```
<$exec inc("std_page_variable_definitions")$>
<$strTrimWs(inc("doc_checkout_image"))$>
```

The first statement includes the resource named `std_page_variable_definitions` but does not output it to the page. This is useful when you need to set several IdocScript variables and do not want to worry about white space.

The second statement renders the include `doc_checkout_image` but trims the leading and trailing white space from the result.

Most issues with extra white space can be addressed with IdocScript directives, which are covered at the end of this Appendix.

Comments

There is no explicit syntax for IdocScript comments. Most developers use the following convention to comment their code:

```
<$c="This is a comment"$>
```

You can also comment out blocks of code by placing them into a conditional statement that is never true:

```
<$if isTrue(0)$>
    This is a comment
<$endif$>
```

Other developers use HTML or JavaScript comments with IdocScript resource includes, but those comments will show up on the rendered HTML page. However, if you place the code in a resource and include it with the `<$exec inc()$>` method described in the previous section, all output is suppressed. However, this method is mostly useful when setting large numbers of page variables.

Strings and Encodings

A string is delimited by double quotes or single quotes. If double quotes are the delimiter, single quotes can be used inside the string without escaping them. Likewise, if single quotes are the delimiter, double quotes can be used inside the string:

```
<$myName="sysadmin"$>
<$myName='sysadmin'$>
<$myName="sys 'ad' min"$>
<$myName='sys "ad" min'$>
```

The backslash character is used to escape characters in a string, such as quotes, new lines, or tabs:

```
<$myName="sys \"ad\" min"$>
<$myName='sys \'ad\' min'$>
```

The encoding of an IdocScript string is assumed to be in the same encoding as the server. However, it is possible to have a resource pages in different encodings. Such resources must be defined in HTML pages, with the following tag in the HEAD section:

```
<meta http-equiv="Content-Type" content="text/html; charset=utf-8">
```

A resource file with the preceding header must be utf-8 encoded. You can use different values for charset if needed.

Because HCSPs and HCSFs need to be valid XML syntax, we cannot use standard math operators on them. The angle bracket characters > and < are special, so different keywords are needed.

IdocScript math operations:

```
<$ if 5 > 4$>five is bigger than four<$endif$>
```

XML IdocScript math operations:

```
<!--$ if 5 gt 4 -->five is bigger than four<!--$endif-->
```

These operations are discussed more fully in a later section.

Like the angle brackets, the ampersand character is special in XML. So string concatenation must be done with the join operator:

IdocScript string concatenation:

```
<$"Hello " & "World!"$>
```

XML IdocScript string concatenation:

```
<!--$"Hello " join "World!"-->
```

All IdocScript strings are stored in Java as Unicode, but they do not support Unicode escape sequences. On an HCSP or HCSF you can escape Unicode characters with XML encoded strings:

```
<!--$newline = "&#0013;" -->
```

In a string definition you can also escape with escaped XML syntax:

```
<@wwNewline=\&#0013;@>
```

As a rule, all IdocScript code should be restricted to the US-ASCII character set. Any string requiring Unicode characters should be stored in separate string resources, as shown previously. This is not a requirement, but it helps developers localize resources into other languages with greater ease.

String literals can span multiple lines. The following two definitions are equivalent:

```
<$myName = "my
name"$>
<$myName="my\nName"$>
```

XML IdocScript supports XML escaping inside variable definitions. The following two statements are equivalent:

```
<!--$scriptBegin="<script>"-->
<!--$scriptBegin="&lt;script&gt;"-->
```

Both statements set the variable scriptBegin to the literal string <script>. The latter is preferable because the former is not valid XML.

In contrast, standard IdocScript does not support XML escape sequences. The following statements are not equivalent:

```
<$scriptBegin="<script>"$>
<$scriptBegin="&lt;script&gt;"$>
```

The first statement sets scriptBegin to the literal value <script>. In the second case, the encoded string is taken literally. The variable then equals <script>.

When encoding a variable for display on an HTML page, the following functions are useful:

```
<$xml(myString)$>
<$js(myString)$>
<$url(myString)$>
<$urlEscape7Bit(myString)$>
```

These functions encode strings so they are appropriate for use in XML data, a JavaScript string, a URL, or a URL that might contain multibyte characters.

The function urlEscape7Bit is very helpful in that you can call it multiple times on the same string. For example, if a string had a space in it, the url function would encode it into %20. If it were run through the url function again, the % would be turned into %25, so the string would become %2520. The urlEscape7Bit function encodes a string only if it isn't 7-bit clean, so it can be used on previously URL-encoded strings:

```
<$url(" ")$>                    outputs: %20
<$url(url(" "))$>               outputs: %2520
<$urlEscape7Bit(url(" "))$>     outputs: %20
```

Identifiers and Scope

There are six kinds of identifiers for IdocScript: variables, computed variables, functions, resource includes, ResultSets, and option lists. With the exception of variables, all these identifiers are global in scope.

IdocScript variables can have four scopes: active, local, ResultSet, and environment. If a variable is defined anywhere, it is found in the active scope. If it is present in the URL or defined in the page, it will be in local scope. If it is defined in a ResultSet on the page, it is ResultSet scope. If it is defined in an environment file, such as the config.cfg, it is in environment scope. The same variable name can be defined in several different scopes.

A variable is identified by its name on a page. After setting a variable to a value, it can be referenced directly to output the value:

```
<$myName="user1"$>
<$myName$>
```

Before outputting myName to the page, IdocScript will search for its value in the following order:

1. If you are currently looping over a ResultSet, look for the value in the current row.

2. Search the local data.

3. Search all rows in all `ResultSets`.

4. Finally, check the environment settings.

After it finds the value, it is output to the page. If no value is found, an error is logged to the console. This is an expensive operation, and should be prevented.

To eliminate the possibility of these errors, specify the scope in the statement. The `getValue` function can extract a variable from a specific scope. It silently fails if the variable is not found. This function also has a shorthand equivalent, as shown here:

```
<$getValue("#env", "myName")$>
<$#env.myName$>

<$getValue("#local", "myName")$>
<$#local.myName$>

<$getValue("#active", "myName")$>
<$#active.myName$>

<$getValue("SearchResults", "dDocName")$>
<$SearchResults.dDocName$>
```

It is typical to use `#active.myName` to output the value for `myName`.

Environment variables can be overridden on the page with local variables. However, by using the #env syntax, you can pull it explicitly from the environment if necessary:

```
<$CgiFileName$>                outputs: idcplg
<$CgiFileName= "test"$>
<$CgiFileName$>                outputs: test
<$#env.CgiFileName$>           outputs: idcplg
```

Although computed variables are identified the same way as IdocScript variables, their values cannot be set—they are computed in Java dynamically when referenced on the page. As a convention, computed variables start with an uppercase letter:

```
<$HttpCgiPath$>                outputs: /stellent/idcplg
<$HttpCgiPath='test'$>
<$HttpCgiPath$>                outputs: /stellent/idcplg
```

IdocScript functions are defined in Java code. They are identified by name and can take parameters in parentheses. In general, these functions take strings as parameters. However, some of them accept date objects and numbers. If an IdocScript variable is passed, the value for it is used in the function call.

If no parameters are required, empty parentheses are used. Functions can share their names with local variables, although this is discouraged.

```
<$dateCurrent='test'$>
<$dateCurrent$>                outputs: test
<$dateCurrent()$>              outputs the current date and time
```

Resource includes can be identified in two ways. When using the `include` keyword, the name of the `dynamichtml` include is used without quotes; when using the `inc` function, the name of the include is passed as a string. The following are equivalent:

```
<$include std_page_begin$>
<$inc("std_page_begin")$>
```

Because the `inc` function takes a string, it can be used to decide dynamically which include to display.

Similar to includes, `ResultSets` can be referenced with or without quotes. When referenced with a keyword, no quotes are needed. When passed as a parameter in a function, quotes are required. The following loops are equivalent:

```
<$loop SearchResults$>
    <$dDocName$>
<$endloop$>

<$exec rsFirst("SearchResults")$>
<$loopwhile rsIsRowPresent("SearchResults")$>
    <$dDocName$>
    <$exec rsNext("SearchResults")$>
<$endloop$>
```

Option lists are mostly deprecated in version 7.5. They are referenced without quotes with the `optList` keyword. They can also be turned into a `ResultSet` with the `rsMakeFromList` function:

```
<$optList securityGroups$>

<$rsMakeFromList("GROUPS", securityGroups)$>
<$loop GROUPS$>
  <$row$>
<$endloop$>
```

Keywords

The following words are reserved and cannot be used as names for variables, includes, or functions:

break

else

elseif

endif

endloop

exec

```
directive

html

idcbegindata

idcenddata

if

include

loop

loopwhile

merge

optList
```

Data Types

There are eight kinds of data types in IdocScript: integers, floats, strings, dates, ResultSets, OptionLists, booleans, and null. All of these data types, with the exception of OptionLists, can be created on the page with IdocScript.

Integers

Can be positive or negative with the unary operator.

```
<$i = 10, j = -5$>
<$i + j$>
```

Integers are stored in Java as Long objects.

Floats

Similar to integers. They can be positive or negative with the unary operator.

```
<$i = 10.123, j = -5.678$>
<$i+j$>
```

Floats are stored in Java as Double objects.

Strings

Stored internally as Unicode Java String objects. They can be encoded as shown in the preceding "Strings and Encodings" section.

Date

Stored internally as Java `Date` objects. Use the `parseDate` function to convert a date formatted string into a date. Use the `toInteger` function to convert a date into an integer for comparisons:

```
<$dateStr = "12/31/1999"$>
<$then = toInteger(parseDate(dateStr))$>
<$now = toInteger(dateCurrent())$>
<$i<$if then < now$>>
    how was y2k?
<$endif$>
```

ResultSets

Similar to array objects found in other scripting languages. However, they are explicitly designed to encapsulate data extracted from a database table. They contain information about the column names and the type of data stored in that column. They contain zero or more rows of data.

Use the `loop` or `loopwhile` keywords to iterate over a `ResultSet`. Inside the loop, you can extract column values by name:

```
<$loop SearchResults$>
    <$dDocTitle$>
<$endloop$>
```

You can create `ResultSet` objects with IdocScript functions such as `rsCreateResultSet` and `rsMakeFromString`, among others. See Appendix B for more advanced `ResultSet` manipulation functions.

Option Lists

Mostly deprecated in Content Server version 7.5. They are stored as Java `Vector` objects containing Unicode `String` objects. They can be turned into `ResultSets` with the function `rsMakeFromList`.

Booleans

Do not exist explicitly as variables; they exist only as return values for functions. The `if` control statement is used to determine existence, not truth. Instead, the functions `isTrue` and `isFalse` are needed to convert a number or string into a `boolean`. For example, this statement always returns `true`:

```
<$test=0$><$if test$>true<$else$>false<$endif$>
```

To determine the truth of the variable `test`, use the following statement:

```
<$test=0$><$if isTrue(test)$>true<$else$>false<$endif$>
```

To guarantee a failure with the existence check, set the variable to NULL. The following statement always returns false:

```
<$test=""$><$if test$>true<$else$>false<$endif$>
```

NULL

To set a value to NULL, set it to the empty string:

```
<$isHidden=""$>
```

Variables

All local variables are stored internally in the same Hashtable. Variables in the environment scope are stored in a separate Hashtable, which is loaded once when the server starts up. ResultSets are stored as separate data objects. The getValue function checks each object in order for the existence of variables.

Variable names can have numbers in the front, middle, or end, but they must contain letters.

Expressions and Operators

IdocScript supports the standard mathematical expressions, comparisons, and operators. It also supports a handful of expressions for comparing and joining string variables.

Assignment

```
=
```
Used to assign a variable to a value, which can be a number, date, or string.

```
<$myNum = 5$>
<$myStr = "five"$>
<$myDate = dateCurrent()$>
```

Boolean

```
and, or, not
```
Used to string multiple conditionals together.

```
<$var = 5$>
<$if ((var  1) and (var < 10)) or (not (var < 100))$>
    <$var$> is between 1 and 10, or not less than 100
<$endif$>
```

Number Comparison

Each comparison operator can be represented with a symbol or two letters. The symbolic version is used on most pages. However, they cannot be used on HCSPs and HCSFs because they are not valid XML. On those pages, use the two-letter version:

```
==  eq  equality test
!=  ne  non-equality test
 >  gt  greater than
>=  ge  greater than or equal to
 <  lt  less than
<=  le  less than or equal to
```

Binary Math Operands

```
+  addition
-  subtraction
*  multiplication
/  division
%  modular division
```

Unary Math Operand

```
-  makes a number negative
```

String Concatenation

Similar to number comparisons, the concatenation operator can be represented with a symbol or a word. On HCSPs and HCSFs, use the word instead of the symbol.

    `& join` joins two strings together

String Comparison

    `like` compares two strings using the wildcard * and | as an or operator.
    Both of these expressions evaluate to true:

```
<$if "automobile" like "auto*"$>
TRUE
<$endif$>

<$if "cartoon" like "auto*|car*"$>
TRUE
<$endif$>
```

Dynamic HTML Resource Includes

Dynamic HTML resource includes are rendered on the page with the `include` keyword:

```
<$include std_page_begin$>
```

Alternatively, you can use the inc function:

```
<$inc("std_page_begin")$>
```

The latter can give you more power over the display. For example, it can be used in conjunction with strTrimWs to control white space:

```
<$strTrimWs(inc("std_page_begin"))$>
```

If the resource include contains only IdocScript, it is sometimes desirable to render it and not display any output. To accomplish it, use the exec keyword with the inc function:

```
<$exec inc("std_page_variable_definitions")$>
```

Includes are defined on resource pages inside the delimiters <@@>. The beginning of a resource definition contains the keyword dynamichtml and the name of the resource in these delimiters. The end of the include is noted with the end keyword, also inside these delimiters:

```
<@dynamichtml welcome_user@>
  Your name is <$UserName$>. Welcome!
<@end@>
```

Includes can be defined in one of four ways:

- In std_page.htm using the previous dynamichtml syntax. All core Content Server includes are defined in this file.

- In a component's resource file using the previous dynamichtml syntax. This method is used to customize core resources or add new resources.

- In an IDOC resource file using the previous dynamichtml syntax. This IDOC file must be checked-in to the Content Server. The resources in this file are loaded dynamically with the function docLoadResourceIncludes. This method is mainly useful for Dynamic Server Pages.

- On an IdocScript page with the setResourceInclude function. This is used to take a long string of HTML and IdocScript, and turn it into an include for the duration of the request. This process is used only when a resource include must be generated dynamically:

```
<$myWelcomeString = "Your name is <$UserName$>. Welcome!"$>
<$exec setResourceInclude("my_welcome", myWelcomeString)$>
<$include my_welcome$>
```

Functions

All functions are defined in Java code. If you are familiar with Java, you can create new functions with a Java Component Architecture, described in Chapter 10. Otherwise, you can create specially formatted IdocScript includes that behave like functions.

For example, you can create an include that compares two values and outputs the largest value:

```
<@dynamichtml find_max_value@>
<$if arg1  arg2$>
    <$arg1$>
<$else$>
    <$arg2$>
<$endif$>
<$arg1="", arg2=""$>
<@end@>
```

Using the inc function with strRemoveWs makes this include behave like a function:

```
<$arg1=10, arg2=20, result = strRemoveWs(inc("find_max_value"))$>
```

Instead of outputting the value, you can also set a return value:

```
<@dynamichtml find_max_value@>
<$if arg1  arg2$>
    <$arg0 = arg1$>
<$else$>
    <$arg0 = arg2$>
<$endif$>
<$arg1="", arg2=""$>
<@end@>
```

After including this resource, the value for arg0 can be used to display the result:

```
<$arg1=10, arg2=20$>
<$exec inc("find_max_value")$>
<$maxValue = arg0$>
```

In general, it is best to create custom IdocScript functions in Java.

Flow Control Statements

These statements are used to control when or if to execute specific code. IdocScript supports the standard flow statements: if, elseif, else, loop, loopwhile, and break. The if and loop statements must end with endif and endloop statements, respectively.

if, elseif, else, endif

Check the truthfulness of an expression. If the expression is true, it will evaluate the statements inside. It can be used with numeric comparisons or to check for the existence of a variable. The functions isTrue and isFalse are needed to convert a string into a boolean. The function toInteger is needed to convert a date into a number for comparison checks.

```
<$var = 5$>
<$if var < 1$>
    it's less than one
```

```
<$elseif var > 10$>
    it's more than ten
<$else$>
    it's between one and ten
<$endif$>
```

loop, endloop

Used to loop over the rows in a ResultSet. The ResultSet can be created on the page or it can be present in the response data.

```
<$loop SearchResults$>
    <$dDocName$>
<$endloop$>
```

loopwhile, endloop

Used to loop until a certain condition is met. This condition is usually used in conjunction with an IdocScript function that returns a boolean. It can also be used to loop over a ResultSet when the name of the ResultSet is available only in a variable.

```
<$resultSetName = "SearchResults"$>
<$exec rsFirst(resultSetName)$>
<$loopwhile rsIsRowPresent(resultSetName)$>
    <$dDocName$>
    <$exec rsNext(resultSetName)$>
<$endloop$>
```

It can also be used with numeric conditions:

```
<$var = 10$>
<$loopwhile var > 0$>
    <$var$>
    <$var = var - 1$>
<$endloop$>
```

break

Used to break out of a loop. Usually used in conjunction with if...endif to exit a loop when a certain condition is met.

```
<$var = 10$>
<$loopwhile var > 0$>
    <$var$>
    <$if var == 6$>
        <$break$>
    <$endif$>
    <$var = var - 1$>
<$endloop$>
```

Directives

Directives were added in Content Server version 8.0. They are used to turn on or off special IdocScript rendering options. Once a directive is specified, it is valid for the remainder of the template page. If a directive is specified in a resource include, it is valid for only that include.

Multiple directives can be specified on one line. You can also turn off directives with the minus (-) sign:

```
<@dynamichtml welcome_user@>
  <$directive trimtext,-reducews$>

  Your name is <$UserName$>. Welcome!

<@end@>
```

The following directive keywords are supported:

reducews

Enabling this directive reduces the white space output caused by IdocScript statements. It can be used instead of the IdocScript formatting tricks mentioned previously.

This directive eliminates the white space from an included resource up until the first line that contains text. If a line contains nothing but spaces or tabs, it is removed from the output. After the first newline, any remaining white space is also omitted. For example, if we modified the welcome_user resource to be this:

```
<@dynamichtml welcome_user@>
<$directive reducews$>
<$name = UserName$>
    Your name is <$name$>. Welcome!
<$foo=1$>
<$bar=1$>
<@end@>
```

and included it on a template page like this:

```
Message: "<$include welcome_user$>"
```

the output would be two lines instead of the typical six lines:

```
Message: "    Your name is sysadmin. Welcome!
"
```

Note that the four spaces are still included in the output, as in the new line. This directive is enabled by default on version 8.0 and above. It is not necessary to enable it for an include. However, in rare cases in which additional white space is important, you might need to disable it.

trimtext

This is a more aggressive white space reduction directive than reducews. It removes all white space around IdocScript constructs. This directive is mainly useful when creating HTML that all belongs on one line, but it requires several lines of IdocScript. For example, to create a URL to a search results page, you can use a resource like this:

```
<@dynamichtml my_search_url@>
<$directive trimtext$>
<$HttpCgiPath$>
?IdcService=GET_SEARCH_RESULTS&QueryText=<$myQueryText$>
   &ResultCount=<$myResultCount$>
   &SortOrder=<$mySortOrder$>
   &SortField=<$mySortField$>
<@end@>
```

and then include it on a template page like this:

```
<$myQueryString="test", myResultCount=20,
  mySortOrder="Desc", mySortField="dInDate"$>
<a href="<$include my_search_url$>">Run Search</a>
```

The output would contain one blank line, then the entire link on the second line:

```
<a href="/stellent/idcplg?IdcService=GET_SEARCH_RESULTS&QueryText=test&➡
   ResultCount=20&SortOrder=Desc&SortField=dInDate">Run Search</a>
```

The first line is blank because it is the output from setting the four IdocScript flags in my_search_url. The second line contains the entire link. If the directive trimtext was specified on the template page, the first blank line would be suppressed as well.

Eliminating white space in this manner can sometimes cause problems. For example, assume that you want to force the welcome_user resource to be on one single line. You can create an include like so:

```
<@dynamichtml welcome_user@>
<$directive trimtext$>
<$name = UserName$>
  Your name is <$name$>. Welcome!
<$foo=1$>
<$bar=1$>
<@end@>
```

If it were included on a page like this:

```
Message: "<$include welcome_user$>"
```

the output would be on one line, like so:

```
Message: "Your name issysadmin. Welcome!"
```

Notice that the space between is and sysadmin is eliminated by this directive. To force the space to exist, you need to add it inside the IdocScript itself. Alter the resource to include a space character in the IdocScript statement, like this:

```
<@dynamichtml welcome_user@>
<$directive trimtext$>
<$name = " " & UserName$>
  Your name is <$name$>. Welcome!
<$foo=1$>
<$bar=1$>
<@end@>
```

Now when included on the page, the output has the additional space character:

```
Message: "Your name is sysadmin. Welcome!"
```

Naming Conventions

All functions start with a lowercase letter. Many of them start with a prefix to describe what kind of function it is. For example, most string-manipulation functions begin with the prefix str, most workflow functions begin with wf, and most ResultSet functions begin with rs.

In general, most variables in the environment (HttpCgiPath), and all computed variables (UserName) begin with an uppercase letter. Many parameters in service request (QueryText) also begin with uppercase letters. Variables defined on the page itself are generally defined with a lowercase letter first (lmSkinName, lmLayoutName). Resources, such as dynamichtml includes, are generally all lowercase letters with underscores separating the words (std_page_begin).

The variable names in response data follow different conventions. Most of the data returned begins with a lowercase letter, but this is not always the case. The only universally applied rule is that data from a database table begins with a lowercase letter, describing where it came from. If it is a metadata field common to all systems, it begins with a lowercase d, such as dDocTitle and dDocAuthor. Custom user metadata begins with a lower case u, such as umdType. Custom metadata fields begin with a lower case x, such as xComments. Result sets are typically in all uppercase letters, such as DOC_INFO. The most common exception to this is SearchResults.

Local variables follow a different convention. To scope a variable to a specific topic or metadata field, the convention is to separate them with a colon. For example, to hide the Content Type field, set this flag:

```
<$dDocType:isHidden = "1"$>
```

This is a naming convention used throughout the core to scope flags to specific metadata fields.

Common IdocScript Functions

This appendix contains a list of the commonly used IdocScript functions. These functions are used throughout the Content Server's interface, including web pages, Content Profile rules, and workflow scripts.

These functions can use strings, integers, or dates as their parameters. They can return strings, integers, dates, booleans, or null. This return value can be set to an IdocScript variable or output directly to the page. To suppress the output of a function, use the `exec` keyword:

```
<$exec rsNext("MyList")$>
```

Some IdocScript functions can be executed only in the context of a service request, so they cannot be used on custom subscription or workflow email templates. The text of those emails is generated in a background process, not in a service request. Therefore, functions such as `executeService` or `getValueForSpecifiedUser` are not available. Other functions, such as `wfSet` and `wfGet`, can be used only from inside a workflow script. When applicable, these restrictions are noted in the following sections.

The full list of IdocScript functions is also available in the *IdocScript Reference Guide*. They are also available in the web-based help under *Developer* ➤ *Reference* ➤ *IdocScript Reference Guide*. The *Workflow Implementation Guide* contains more information on how to apply workflow functions to create workflow scripts.

IdocScript Functions

abortToErrorPage(errorMessage)
Stops the rendering of the IdocScript page or Profile Rule and redirects to an error page. The `errorMessage` message will be displayed on the error page.

Added In: 4.0
Context: Service

cacheInclude(includeName, scope, lifeSpanInSeconds [, cacheName, key])
Similar to the `inc` function and `include` keyword, it renders the resource include that corresponds to `includeName` and displays it on the page. The difference is that it will cache the rendered HTML. The next time `cacheInclude` is called for the same include, the rendered HTML will be pulled from the cache. This speeds up IdocScript rendering of slow includes.

To render the include the same for all users, set the scope parameter to application. To allow each user to render the include differently, set scope to session. Set lifeSpanInSeconds to the number of seconds that this cache should exist. A setting of 300, corresponding to five minutes, is the default. The optional parameter cacheName can be set if you need another global cache besides the application scope cache. This, along with the key parameter, can give you greater control over global caches.

```
<$cacheInclude("my_include_name", "session", 600)$>
```

Added In: 7.0
Context: Service

clearSchemaData()

The Schema API defines a large number of local variables to control field display. This function will reset all these variables to null, which prevents data pollution.

Added In: 7.0
Context: Service

computeDocUrl(isRelative)

Computes the URL to a content item, based on the data on the page. For example, when looping over a ResultSet of items, call this function to generate a URL to the item. The following information must be present on the page: dDocAccount (optional), dDocName, dDocType, dProcessingState, dRevLabel, dSecurityGroup, dWebExtension.

Added In: 6.0

computeRenditionUrl(url, revLabel, renditionLabel)

Calculates the rendition of a content item based on its URL. It is typically used on the search results page to display thumbnails and links to converted XML documents. The url parameter is usually present in the ResultSet SearchResults; otherwise, it can be calculated with computeDocUrl. The revLabel should correspond to dRevLabel. The renditionLabel is a one-character representation of the rendition: for example, t for a thumbnail rendition or x for an XML rendition. It should correspond to dRendition1 or dRendition2 in the SearchResults. The following code shows a thumbnail if present; otherwise, just the title:

```
<$QueryText = "dDocTitle <substring> `test`"$>
<$executeService("GET_SEARCH_RESULTS")$>
<$loop SearchResults$>
  <$if dRendition1$>
    <a href="<$URL$>">
      <img src="<$computeRenditionUrl(URL, dRevLabel, dRendition1)$>">
    </img></a>
  <$else$>
    <a href="<$URL$>"><$dDocTitle$></a>
  <$endif$>
<$endloop$>
```

Added In: 3.0

dateCurrent([daysFromNow])

Returns a date string formatted according to the user's locale. The optional daysFromNow parameter is used to format a date for the future or the past.

```
today = <$dateCurrent()$>
next week = <$dateCurrent(7)$>
last week = <$dateCurrent(-7)$>
```

Added In: 3.0

dcShowExportLink()

Returns true if the Dynamic Converter has been configured to convert this content item. It is based on the value for dFormat for the item and is typically used on search results pages to conditionally display a Dynamic Converter link.

```
<$QueryText = "dDocTitle <substring> `test`"$>
<$executeService("GET_SEARCH_RESULTS")$>
<$loop SearchResults$>
  <$if dcShowExportLink()$>
    <a href="<$HttpCgiPath$>?IdcService=GET_DYNAMIC_CONVERSION&dID=<$dID$>">
      HTML Conversion of <$dDocTitle$></a>
  <$endif$>
<$endloop$>
```

Added In: 5.0
Context: Service

docLoadResourceIncludes(resourceParameters)

Loads an IDOC resource file dynamically and is typically used on Hypertext Content Server Pages (HCSPs) and other Dynamic Server Pages. These IDOC files must be checked-into the Content Server. The resourceParameters is a URL-encoded string of parameters used to locate the resource file. It takes the same parameters as the GET_FILE service: dID, dDocName, and RevisionSelectionMethod. It is common to use dDocName with RevisionSelectionMethod. It allows the look and feel to automatically change when a new revision of the IDOC file is checked-in.

```
<$docLoadResourceIncludes("dID=100")$>
<$docLoadResourceIncludes("dDocName=user_portal_includes&"
    & "RevisionSelectionMethod=Latest")$>
```

The value for StatusCode is set to -1 if an error occurred when loading the resource. Use abortToErrorPage if desired to stop displaying the page. See Chapter 6 for more examples.

Added In: 4.0
Context: Service

docRootFilename(url)

Returns the final file name based on a URL. Used on Search Results pages to display short names for URLs.

```
myFile.txt = <$docRootFilename("/path/to/myFile.txt")$>
```

Added In: 5.0

docUrlAllowDisclosure(url)

Used with the Need To Know component to conditionally display URLs to content items. It parses the URL and determines whether the user can view the metadata, if not the content item itself. It returns true or false, depending on whether the user can access it.

Added In: 4.0

Context: Service

dpGet(key)

Used to set side effects in Content Profile rules. Rules are evaluated in a clean context, so setting flags in a rule does not affect other rules. You must use dpSet and dpGet to cause one rule's activation to trigger other rules.

It is useful if you have complex logic in a rule activation condition and you want to reuse it. For example, two rules could be dependent on condition1 and condition2. These conditions can be coded into one rule's activation condition with the following code:

```
(if condition1 and condition2 and dpSet("doTheRule", 1))
```

To reuse the same conditions in a later rule, trigger off of the value for doTheRule in the activation condition:

```
(if dpGet("doTheRule") == 1)
```

Added In: 7.5

dpPromote(key, value)

Similar to dpSet, it promotes a value out of the Content Profiles into the page or service request data. Typically the function dpSet is useful only to set flags to trigger other profile rules. In contrast, dpPromote can set parameters to affect page display or the way the service is executed. For example, to force the title field to be hidden on the page, you can place this script in any profile rule:

```
<$dpPromote("dDocTitle:isHidden", "1")$>
```

Added In: 8.0

dpSet(key, value)

Used with dpGet to create side effects when evaluating Content Profile rules. It sets a specific key to a specific value in a context in which profile rule data is stored.

Added In: 7.5

eval(idocScriptString)

Evaluates a string as if it were IdocScript. It is a good way to dynamically write IdocScript code with IdocScript. The parameter `idocScriptString` contains the script to evaluate, including the `<$$>` delimiters.

```
<$fieldName = "dDocTitle"$>
<$script = "<$" & fieldName & ":isHidden = '1'$>"$>
<$eval(script)$>
```

Because this function creates an entirely new context for evaluating script, it can cause performance problems. In general, its use should be avoided. The functions `getValue`, `setValue`, and `setResourceInclude` are recommended instead. For example, the preceding code is equivalent to the following code:

```
<$fieldName = "dDocTitle"$>
<$setValue("#local", fieldName & ":isHidden", "1")$>
```

Added In: 3.0

executeService(serviceName)

Executes a scriptable Content Server service. The results of the service are available as `ResultSets` and local variables on the page. The `serviceName` parameter contains the name of a scriptable service (see Appendix E for a list of scriptable services). All parameters required for the service must already be defined on the page. It is commonly used on an HCSP or other Dynamic Server Page to run a search and display the results:

```
<$QueryText = "dDocTitle <substring> `test`"$>
<$executeService("GET_SEARCH_RESULTS")$>
<$loop SearchResults$>
    <a href="<$URL$>"><$dDocTitle$></a>
<$endloop$>
```

Added In: 4.0
Context: Service

forceExpire(includeName, scope[, cacheName, key])

Used in conjunction with `cacheInclude`. It immediately expires the cached value for the include corresponding to `includeName` in the specific scope. The `cacheName` and `key` are optional parameters, same as in `cacheInclude`.

```
<$forceExpire("my_include_name", "session")$>
```

Added In: 7.0
Context: Service

formatDate(dateString)

Reformats a date string into the preferred format for this user. The `dateString` can be format-ted in one of several ways: the user's date format, the server's default date format, the display date format, or the Java Database Connectivity (JDBC) date format:

```
<$dateString = "12/31/2005 11:59 PM"$>
<$formatDate(dateString)$> = 12/31/05 11:59 PM


<$dateString2 = "December 31, 2005 11:59 PM"$>
<$formatDate(dateString2)$> = 12/31/05 11:59 PM


<$dateString3 = "{ts '2005-12-31 23:59:00.000'}"$>
<$formatDate(dateString3)$> = 12/31/05 11:59 PM
```

This step is performed automatically if the date string is stored as metadata in the Content Server. It is mainly useful for parsing date strings stored in custom database tables or HCSPs. For greater control over the format, use `parseDate` or `formatDateWithPattern`.

Added In: 3.0

formatDateDatabase(dateString)

Similar to `formatDate`, except it formats the `dateString` into the JDBC date format:

```
<$dateString = "12/31/2005 11:59 PM"$>
<$formatDateDatabase(dateString)$> = {ts '2005-12-31 23:59:00.000'}
```

Added In: 3.0

formatDateDisplay(dateString)

Similar to `formatDate`, except it displays a more user-friendly date. It is configured as the Display Date Format in the System Properties Editor. The localized name of the month is shown instead of the number:

```
<$dateString = "12/31/2005 11:59 PM"$>
<$formatDateDisplay(dateString)$> = December 31, 2005 11:59 PM
```

Added In: 7.0

formatDateOnly(dateString)

Similar to `formatDate`, but it displays only the date information. All time information is suppressed.

```
<$dateString = "12/31/2005 11:59 PM"$>
<$formatDateOnly(dateString)$> = 12/31/05
```

Added In: 3.0

formatDateOnlyDisplay(dateString)

Similar to formatDateDisplay, it displays only the date information. All time information is suppressed.

```
<$dateString = "12/31/2005 11:59 PM"$>
<$formatDateOnlyDisplay(dateString)$> = December 31, 2005
```

Added In: 7.0

formatDateOnlyFull(dateString)

An older and deprecated date formatter. It displays output similar to formatDateOnlyDisplay, but isn't fully internationalized. If you cannot use formatDateOnlyDisplay, use formatDateWithPattern.

Added In: 3.0

formatDateWithPattern(dateString, pattern)

This is the most powerful way to format a date into a display string. The pattern contains a list of date tokens. It returns the date formatted according to that pattern, regardless of the user's locale.

The date tokens in pattern are based on the Java Date object, with a handful of differences. These tokens are used throughout the Content Server to parse dates and format them for display. All supported tokens are as follows:

- **a**: Meridian (AM/PM)

- **d**: Day of month (1–31)

- **dd**: Two-digit day of month (01–31)

- **D**: Day of year (1–365)

- **E**: Day of week (1–7)

- **EEE**: Short word for the day of week (Mon–Sun)

- **EEEE**: Full word for the day of week (Monday–Sunday)

- **G**: Gregorian Era (BC, AD)

- **h**: Hour of day (1–12)

- **hh**: Two-digit hour of day (01–12)

- **H**: Hour of day in military time (0–23)

- **HH**: Two-digit hour of day in military time (00–23)

- **m**: Minute of hour (1–59)

- **mm**: Two-digit minute of hour (01–59)

- **M**: Month of year (1–12)

- **MM**: Two-digit month of year (01–12)

- **MMM**: Localized short word for month of year (Jan–Dec)

- **MMMM**: Localized full word for month of year (January–December)

- **s**: Second of minute (1–59)

- **ss**: Two-digit second of minute (01–59)

- **S**: Milliseconds

- **y**: Four-number year (2005)

- **yy**: Two-digit year (05)

- **Z**: Zulu: Military time zones, date parsing only (Alpha–Zulu)

- **z**: Time zone (America/Chicago)

These tokens can be used in any combination to display a date in a specific format.

```
<$dateString = "12/31/2005 11:59 PM"$>
<$formatDateWithPattern(dateString, "MMM d (y) H:mm:ss")$>
    = Dec 31 (2005) 23:59:00
```

They can also be used to conditionally display HTML based on the date. For example, extract the current day of the week (1-7) with the E token:

```
<$dayNumber = formatDateWithPattern(dateCurrent(), "E")$>
```

This number can be used to display different HTML based on the day of the week. Added In: 5.0

formatTimeOnly(dateString)
Similar to formatDate, but it displays only the time information. All date information is suppressed.

```
<$dateString = "12/31/2005 11:59 PM"$>
<$formatTimeOnly(dateString)$> = 11:59 PM
```

Added In: 3.0

formatTimeOnlyDisplay(dateString)
Similar to formatTimeOnly and formatDateDisplay, it uses the Display Date Format for displaying just time information. All date information is suppressed. It is usually the same as formatTimeOnly:

```
<$dateString = "12/31/2005 11:59 PM"$>
<$formatTimeOnlyDisplay(dateString)$> = 11:59 PM
```

Added In: 7.0

generateUniqueId(fieldName)

Returns a unique ID for this HTML page. It is used in conjunction with the id attribute in an HTML element to guarantee a unique ID.

Added In: 7.5

getCookie(key)

Returns a string value for the HTTP cookie with the passed key. Cookies can be set with JavaScript or with the setCookie IdocScript function. It is useful to maintain state information about the user. Cookies should not be used to store excessive amounts of data or any kind of unencrypted security information.

The following code increments a counter every time the page is refreshed. The cookie expires one year from the current date.

```
<$numVisits = getCookie("numVisits")$>
<$if not numVisits$>
    <$numVisits = 1$>
<$endif$>
You have visited this page <$numVisits$> times.
<$setCookie("numVisits", numVisits+1, dateCurrent(365))$>
```

Added In: 7.1
Context: Service

getDebugTrace()

Returns the IdocScript trace log for this page. It is available only if the request parameter ScriptDebugTrace is true. The trace logs contain information about every IdocScript include used on the page, and where it is defined. This function is called in std_debug_report, which is included in std_page_end.

Added In: 4.0

getErrorTrace()

Similar to getDebugTrace. It returns only the trace of IdocScript errors on the page; for example, trying to display a variable that is not defined. Serious IdocScript errors stop the page from being rendered. This function is called in std_debug_report, which is included in std_page_end.

Added In: 4.0

getFieldConfigValue(fieldName, configFlag, defaultValue)

Returns a configuration flag for specific field. If it does not exist, the default is returned instead.

```
<$caption = getFieldConfigValue("dDocTitle", "fieldCaption", lc("wwTitle"))$>
```

Added In: 7.5.1

getFieldViewDisplayValue(fieldName, viewName, fieldValue)

Returns the display value for an item in a Schema option list. For example, assume that you have an option list for a custom metadata field named `Customer`. In the database, you have a Schema table with the `CustomerName` and a unique `CustomerID`. Upon check-in, the `CustomerName` is visible to the user, but the `CustomerID` is what is stored in the database. The function `getFieldViewDisplayValue` is used to extract the human-readable `CustomerName` based on `CustomerID`:

```
<$customerName = getFieldViewDisplayValue("xCustomer", "Customer_View", "1234")$>
```

Added In: 7.5

getFieldViewValue(fieldName, fieldValue, schemaColumn)

Similar to `getFieldViewDisplayValue`, but it can be used to obtain any field in a Schema table. It is not necessary to know the name of the Schema view. It is mainly useful in complex Content Profile rules or complex workflows. For example, assume that you have a schema table named `Customer` that contains the column `CustomerRegion`. This function can be used to extract the region for that customer, provided that you know the unique ID for the customer:

```
<$custName = getFieldViewValue("xCustomer", "1234", "CustomerName")$>
<$custRegion = getFieldViewValue("xCustomer", "1234", "CustomerRegion")$>
```

If you do not know the unique ID for the customer, you can use `getViewValuesResultSet` to obtain a list of all customers. However, this should be avoided whenever possible to ensure high performance.

Added In: 7.5

getFreeMemory()

Returns the amount of free memory in the Java virtual machine. It is a performance auditing function used on the System Audit Information page.

Added In: 7.0

getHelpPage(helpPageName)

Returns a relative URL to a help page, based on the name of the page:

```
<input type=Button value="<$lc("wwQuickHelp")$>"
  onClick="QuickHelp('<$getHelpPage("QH_AdvancedSearch")$>', 'Search')">
```

Added In: 4.0

getOptionListSize(optionListName)

Returns the size of an option list. Used to determine whether or not to display custom user metadata fields on the user profile page.

Added In: 4.0

getParentValue(viewName, relationName, parentFieldName, internalParentValue)

Returns a parent value from a Schema view. It is needed prior to generating the dependent option list for the current field. The `viewName` is the name of the Schema view used for the current field. The `relationName` is the name of the Schema relation between this field and the parent field. The `parentFieldName` is the name of the parent field. The `internalParentValue` is the value for the parent field. It might be different from the value displayed on the page. It is frequently a unique number that is stored internally, so the display values can be localized.

In most cases, this function will return the same value as `internalParentValue` because most option lists trigger their dependency on the unique key for the parent field. However, this is not a requirement, especially for complex dependent choice lists.

```
<$parentValue=getParentValue("xState", "Country_State", "xCountry", "123")$>
```

Added In: 7.5

getRequiredMsg(fieldName, defaultRequiredMsg)

Returns the required message for a custom metadata field. A custom metadata field can be configured to be required, similar to the title and security group fields. If this field is not entered on a check-in page, the check-in fails with this message. It is needed because Content Profiles enables an administrator to have several different required messages for the same field.

```
<$requiredMsg = getRequiredMsg("dDocAuthor", "Please specify an author")$>
```

Added In: 7.5

getTextFile()

Returns the content of a text file as a string. It functions only for files checked-into the Content Server with a text format, including `text/plain` and `text/xml`. It throws an error if the user cannot access the file in question.

The parameters needed to locate the file are pulled from the local data. The results of a `GET_SEARCH_RESULTS` or a `DOC_INFO` service contain all required parameters. Otherwise, the user can set them explicitly:

```
<$dDocName="my_text_file", dWebExtension="txt", dRevLabel="1",
  dSecurityGroup="Public", dDocType="ADACCT", dDocAccount=""$>
<$fileData = getTextFile()$>
<$fileData$>
```

Because this function accesses the file system, for performance reasons it should not be used more than once per request. It is advisable to use it in conjunction with the `cacheInclude` function.

Added In: 7.5
Context: Service

getTotalMemory()

Similar to `getFreeMemory`, it obtains the amount of total memory used by the Java Virtual Machine (JVM). It is used on the System Audit Information page to determine how much memory the server is using.

Added In: 7.0

getUserValue(userFieldName)

Returns a user metadata value for the current user. For example, the email address, or the full name of the user:

```
<$fullName = getUserValue("dFullName")$>
```

> Added In: 4.0
> Context: Service

getValue(scope, key)

Returns the value for a specific key in a specific scope. If the key is not found, an empty string is returned. Using this function is similar to outputting the variable directly to the page:

```
<$getValue("#active", "QueryText")$>
<$QueryText$>
```

However, if the value for QueryText is not defined on the page, the preceding second line will log an error message. The value for scope must be the name of a ResultSet or one of the following special keywords:

- **#active**: Pulls the key from anywhere: page, environment, or a ResultSet

- **#env**: Pulls the key from the configuration environment

- **#local**: Pulls the key from the URL or variables defined on the page

The value for key is the name of a variable in that scope. For a ResultSet, additional special keys are supported:

- **#isEmpty**: Returns true if the ResultSet is empty

- **#isRowPresent**: Returns true if there is data in the current ResultSet row

- **#numRows**: Returns the number of rows in this ResultSet

- **#row**: Returns the index of the current row

These special keys are needed when manually looping over a ResultSet with loopwhile instead of loop:

```
<$QueryText = "dDocTitle <substring> `test`"$>
<$executeService("GET_SEARCH_RESULTS")$>

Results = <$getValue("SearchResults", "#numRows")$>
<$loop SearchResults$>
    <$getValue("SearchResults", "dDocTitle")$>
    <$getValue("#local", "QueryText")$>
<$endloop$>
```

This function is used so often, most developers use the shorthand version, which is simply the name of the scope, followed by a dot, and the name of the key:

```
<$QueryText = "dDocTitle <substring> `test`"$>
<$executeService("GET_SEARCH_RESULTS")$>
```

```
Results = <$SearchResults.#numRows$>
<$loop SearchResults$>
    <$SearchResults.dDocTitle$>
    <$#local.QueryText$>
<$endloop$>
```

See Appendix A for more information about IdocScript scope.
Added In: 3.0

getValueForSpecifiedUser(username, userFieldName)

Similar to getUserValue, but used to obtain user metadata for any user. It is especially helpful in workflow scripts and Content Profile rules. You can modify the behavior based on the user's type.

```
<$name = getValueForSpecifiedUser("sysadmin", "dFullName")$>
<$type = getValueForSpecifiedUser("sysadmin", "dUserType")$>
<$locale = getValueForSpecifiedUser("sysadmin", "dUserLocale")$>
```

Added In: 5.0
Context: Service

getViewDisplayValue(viewName, fieldValue)

Similar to getFieldViewDisplayValue, but the field name is not required.

```
<$customerName = getViewDisplayValue("Customer_View", "1234")$>
<$getViewDisplayValue("doctypes", "ADACCT")$>
<$getViewDisplayValue("City_View", "New York")$>
```

Added In: 7.5

getViewValue(viewName, internalValue, columnNameInView)

Similar to getFieldViewValue, but this function requires the view name instead of the field name.

```
<$custName = getViewValue("Customer_View", "1234", "CustomerName")$>
<$custRegion = getViewValue("Customer_View", "1234", "CustomerRegion")$>
```

Added In: 7.5

getViewValuesResultSet(viewName, relationName, parentValue)

Loads a Schema table and places it on the page as a ResultSet named SchemaData. The column names in the ResultSet are the same as the names in the database table. For example, assume that you have a Schema table and view for a list of countries. The view is named Country_View. To output the contents of that table to the page, use the following code:

```
<$getViewValuesResultSet("Country_View", "", "")$>
<$loop SchemaData$>
<$count = 0, num = rsNumFields("SchemaData")$>
    <$loopwhile count < num$>
        <$fieldName=rsFieldByIndex("SchemaData", count)$>
        <$fieldName$> = <$getValue("SchemaData", fieldName)$>
```

```
        <$count = count + 1$>
    <$endloop$>
<$endloop$>
```

It outputs the table even if you do not know the column names. This function is most useful to obtain a list of dependent choices based on a parent value. For example, assume that you have a Dynamic Choice List (DCL) for the fields Country and State. The list of States depends on which Country is selected. To obtain the list of States when the Country is USA, use this:

```
<$getViewValuesResultSet("State_View", "Country_State", "USA")$>
```

Although the data in Schema is cached, you should still avoid using this function for large lists of data. Whenever possible, create a Schema relation to help break down a Schema view into small manageable chunks.

Added In: 7.5

hasAppRights(applicationName)

Returns true if the user has rights to run the specified application name. It is used by the subadmin feature in the Content Server. In it, a user can be given access rights to administrative applets, even if they do not have the admin role. This function is typically used to conditionally display links to launch applets.

```
<$if UserIsAdmin or hasAppRights("WebLayout")$>
    You can run the Web Layout Editor!
<$endif$>
```

Added In: 4.0
Context: Service

inc(includeName)

Similar to the include keyword in IdocScript. It returns a rendered dynamic HTML resource as a string. It is typically output directly to the page or it can be stored as a variable.

The advantage of using inc instead of include is that you can dynamically decide which resource to use. For example, for the sysadmin user, the following lines are equivalent:

```
<$include custom_includes_for_sysadmin$>
<$inc("custom_includes_for_" & UserName)$>
```

It is also useful when you want to do post-processing of the include before displaying it to the page:

```
<$strTrimWs(inc("custom_include"))$>
```

Other useful post-processing functions include regexReplaceAll, strLower, strRemoveWs, and strUpper.

Added In: 3.0

incGlobal(globalResourceFileName)

Similar to `inc`, but references a global resource filename instead of a dynamic HTML include. This feature is used only on the main home page. These includes are created with the Web Layout editor and are stored with the rest of the web layout pages. For example, the portal message is stored here:

```
stellent/data/pages/portal_message.inc
```

> Added In: 4.0

incTemplate(templateName)

Similar to `inc`, but it includes an entire template page instead of a Dynamic HTML resource include. Because resource includes are easier to customize and maintain than templates, the use of this function is discouraged.

> Added In: 4.0

indexerSetCollectionValue(flagName, flagValue)

A rarely used function to modify the logic of the Verity search indexer. It is used only in the include `verity_indexer_params_override`.

> Added In: 6.1
> Context: Search Indexer

isActiveTrace(traceSection)

Returns `true` if the passed tracing section is enabled. This is a debugging function that enables the Content Server to output diagnostic information. Tracing sections are enabled on the System Audit Information page.

> Added In: 7.0

isComponentEnabled(componentName)

Returns `true` if a specific component is installed and enabled. It is useful for advanced components that must behave differently in the presence of other components. For example, if a resource include should be one way on a typical system, but a different way if the Folders component is enabled, use this function:

```
<$if isComponentEnabled("Folders")$>
    <$include folders_compatible_custom_include$>
<$else$>
    <$include standard_custom_include$>
<$endif$>
```

> Added In: 7.0

isFalse(variable)

Returns true if the passed variable evaluates to false. That means that the variable is either zero, or it begins with the letter f or n.

```
<$doSomething = 0$>
<$if doSomething$>
    The variable 'doSomething' exists, it's either true or false
<$endif$>
<$if isFalse(doSomething)$>
    The variable 'doSomething' is false
<$endif$>
```

Added In: 3.0

isTrue(variable)

Returns true if the passed variable evaluates to true. This means that the variable is either one or it begins with the letter t or y.

```
<$doSomething = 1$>
<$if doSomething$>
    The variable 'doSomething' exists, it's either true or false
<$endif$>
<$if isTrue(doSomething)$>
    The variable 'doSomething' is true
<$endif$>
```

Added In: 3.0

isVerboseTrace()

Similar to isActiveTrace. It returns true if verbose tracing is enabled. This means that a very large amount of tracing data will be output to the console logs.

Added In: 7.0

isZoneField(fieldName)

Returns true if the specified metadata field is present in a Verity zone. They are used to optimize the performance of Verity searches. If the field is in a zone, the search query syntax must be slightly different.

Added In: 7.5

js(string)

Returns an encoded version of string that can be placed in a JavaScript variable. White space and quote characters are escaped with backslash characters. Any non-ASCII character is encoded with the standard Unicode escape sequence. For example, this code:

```
var hello1 = "<$js("say 'hello'")$>";
var hello2 = "<$js("say 'hello' en Français")$>";
```

will render on the page like this:

```
var hello1 = "say \'hello\'";
```

```
var hello2 = "say \'hello\' en Fran\u00e7ais";
```

This function ensures that any value can be placed in a JavaScript string without adversely affecting the JavaScript code. The functions url and xml are also useful for encoding variables on HTML pages.

Added In: 3.0

jsFilename(string)

Similar to js, but it encodes a string so that it can be used in a file path. The encoding is similar to URL encoding, but not all file systems support the % character in a file path. Instead, this function uses the @ character in the escape sequence:

```
<$jsFilename("my file name")$> = my@0020file@0020name
```

This function is used mainly by Schema to determine the location of JavaScript resources.

Added In: 7.0

lc(stringResourceName[, param1, param2, param3])

Returns a localized string resource. The string is rendered in the user's preferred language. If the string has not been translated, it displays in the default language for the system. String resources are defined like this in components:

```
<@wwHello=Hello!@>
<@wwHelloUser=Hello {1}!@>
```

These web string resources can be displayed on the page with the lc function and a list of parameters:

```
<$lc("wwHello")$>
<$lc("wwHelloUser", UserName)$>
```

See Chapter 2 for more information on string resources.

Added In: 5.0

lcCaption(stringResourceName[,param1, param2, param3])

Similar to lc, except it is used to wrap a string into a caption. This typically places a colon to the right of the string. For right-to-left reading languages, such as Hebrew and Arabic, the colon is placed on the left.

Added In: 7.5

ImGetLayout()

Returns the Layout Manager layout configured for this user. For example, Top Menus or Trays. In the event that the layout is no longer enabled, it will return the default.

Added In: 7.0

ImGetSkin()

Returns the Layout Manager skin configured for this user; for example, Collegiate, Stellent, or Windows. If the skin is no longer enabled on the system, it will return the default.

Added In: 7.0

loadCollectionInfo(collectionId)

Loads the collection information for an additional search collection. It is used mostly in the Lightly Managed Content component.

    Added In: 4.0

loadDocMetaDefinition()

Loads the definition for the custom metadata fields. It creates the `ResultSet DocMetaDefinition` on the page. This `ResultSet` contains the field names, the type of field, its caption, and the name of its option list. It is generally used with the resource `std_meta_field_display` to display custom metadata fields on document pages:

```
<$loadDocMetaDefinition()$>
<$loop DocMetaDefinition$>
    <$strTrimWs(inc("std_meta_field_display"))$>
<$endloop$>
```

    Added In: 4.0

loadDocumentProfile()

Loads and evaluates the Content Profiles and global rules. They are used to allow administrators to customize document pages without a component. This function determines which rules need to be evaluated, based on the context of the page, user, and content item. It then evaluates these rules, which sets special IdocScript flags. These flags hide fields, set defaults, reorganize fields, or make fields read-only. See Chapter 9 and Appendix C for more information on these variables.

    Added In: 7.5

loadEnterpriseSearchCollections(isImplicit)

Loads the `ResultSet EnterpriseSearchCollections`. It is used to display a list of remote Content Servers that this server can query with Enterprise Search. This data is used on a search page to enable the user to select which servers to query. If the `isImplicit` flag is zero, the `ResultSet` does not include the names of servers that are automatically searched.

    Added In: 4.0

loadEnterpriseSearchResults()

Renames certain `ResultSets` on the page to support Enterprise Search. It is used when looping over the `ResultSet EnterpriseSearchResults`. It loads the `ResultSet` from the specific server and renames it to `SearchResults`. This primarily helps to simplify the IdocScript used on Search Results pages.

    Added In: 4.0

loadSchemaData(schemaTable, fieldOrViewName)

Loads Schema configuration tables. It can be used to load field configuration or view configuration. It is similar to `loadDocMetaDefinition`, but it is specific to one field and contains more information.

```
<$loadSchemaData("SchemaFieldConfig", "xCountry")$>
<$loadSchemaData("SchemaViewConfig", "Country_View")$>
```

    Added In: 7.0

loadSearchOperatorTables(searchEngineName)

Loads the search operator tables, used to construct JavaScript on the search page. Because several search engines are supported, the JavaScript needed to construct the QueryText is extremely complex. This function loads the following ResultSets: SearchIntegerField, SearchZoneField, SearchQueryOpMap, SearchDateField, SearchTextField, SearchQueryOpStrMap, and SearchSortFields. They are used to generate the HTML on the search page and the JavaScript needed to assemble the QueryText parameter.

Added In: 7.0

loadUserMetaDefinition()

Loads the custom user metadata definition. It exists in the table UserMetaDefinition, which is placed on the page as a ResultSet. It is used on LDAP administration pages to help administrators map user metadata to the Content Server.

Added In: 6.1

Context: Service

localPageType(linkData)

Returns the page type for a page in the Library Folders. It can be a directory or a query page. It is used mainly by the Layout Manager API. When Trays is the layout, it is used to construct a tree view of the library's pages.

Added In: 7.0

parseClbraProject(projectName)

Returns the Account name of a Collaboration Server project name.

Added In: 6.0

parseDataEntryDate(dateString)

Parses a dateString and returns a Date object. It is similar to parseDate, but it attempts to parse the date with all known date formats. It is the most flexible date parsing function, but it is also the slowest. It is generally used in workflow scripts to make date parsing as easy as possible. It returns a Date object that can be used with the formatDate functions to display it. If the string could not be parsed by any known date format, the returned object will be null.

```
<$dateStr = "12/31/2005"$>
<$date = parseDataEntryDate(dateStr)$>
<$if date$>
    <$date$>
    <$formatDateDisplay(date)$>
<$else$>
    The date string "<$dateStr$>" cannot be parsed.
<$endif$>
```

Added In: 7.0

parseDate(dateString)

Similar to `parseDataEntryDate`, but it checks a smaller number of date formats. It will first try to parse it with the JDBC date format, which is used when storing dates in the database. It will then attempt the date format for the specific user. It will finally attempt the default date format for the server. If none of these work, the user will be redirected to an error page.

Added In: 4.0

parseDateWithPattern(dateString, pattern)

Similar to `parseDate`, except the `dateString` is parsed with a specific pattern. Similar to `parseDataEntryDate`, except the returned object will be `null` if it cannot be parsed.

```
<$strangeDateStr = "2005/31/12 23-05"$>
<$date = parseDateWithPattern(strangeDateStr, "y/d/M H-m")$>
<$if date$>
    <$date$>
    <$formatDateDisplay(date)$>
<$else$>
    The date string "<$strangeDateStr$>" cannot be parsed.
<$endif$>
```

See `formatDateWithPattern` for a list of the supported patterns.

Added In: 7.0

proxiedBrowserFullCgiWebUrl(relativeWebRoot)

Returns the absolute web root for content items on an enterprise search page. Because these items might exist in a remote server, the calculation can be somewhat complex. It is based on the value for `HttpRelativeWebRoot` in the `ResultSet EnterpriseSearchResults`. It is also dependent on the user. It calculates the server's host name and the protocol (HTTP or HTTPS) based on the content of the user's browser.

Added In: 4.0

Context: Service

proxiedCgiWebUrl(relativeWebRoot)

Similar to `proxiedBrowserFullCgiWebUrl`, except it returns a relative URL instead of an absolute URL. As such, it is only dependent on `EnterpriseSearchResults`, not on settings in the user's browser.

Added In: 4.0

regexMatches(string, regularExpression)

Similar to `strSubstring` and the `like` operator, it returns `true` if the `string` matches the `regularExpression` parameter. A regular expression is similar to the wildcards used in the `like` operator, but is much more powerful.

A complete discussion of Java regular expression syntax is beyond the scope of this book. Briefly, commonly used regular expressions include the following:

- **x**: The character x

- ****: The backslash character

- **\uHHHH**: The Unicode character with hexadecimal value 0xHHHH

- **\t**: The tab character (`'\u0009'`)

- **\n**: The newline character (`'\u000A'`)

- **\r**: The carriage-return character (`'\u000D'`)

- **[xyz]**: The letter x, y, or z

- **[^xyz]**: Any character except x, y, or z

- **[a-zA-Z]**: a through z or A through Z, inclusive

- **.**: Any character (might or might not match \n)

- **\d**: A digit: [0–9]

- **\D**: A non-digit: [^0-9]

- **\s**: A white space character: [\t\n\x0B\f\r]

- **\S**: A non–white space character: [^\s]

- **\w**: An alphanumeric "word" character, including the underscore: [a-zA-Z_0-9]

- **\W**: A non–alphanumeric "word" character: [^\w]

- **X?**: The expression X, once or not at all

- **X***: The expression X, zero or more times

- **X+**: The expression X, one or more times

- **X{n}**: The expression X, exactly *n* times

They are used in IdocScript in the following way:

```
<$string = "this is a regex test for 2005"$>
contains the string 'test' (true)
    = <$regexMatches(string, ".*test.*")$>
contains numbers (true)
    = <$regexMatches(string, ".*\\d.*")$>
contains numbers, then at least one non-number (false)
    = <$regexMatches(string, ".*\\d*\\D+")$>
```

This function uses the regular expression syntax used in the matches method of the Java String object. This function is valid only when using JVM version 1.4.1 or later.

Added In: 7.5

regexReplaceAll(string, regularExpression, newData)

Replaces all instances of the `regularExpression` in the `string` with the `newData`. Similar to `strReplace` but has more powerful syntax. For example, the following code replaces any four-digit number with the number 2006:

```
<$string = "this is the 2nd regex test for 2005"$>
<$regexReplaceAll(string, "\\d{4}", "2006")$>
```

> Added In: 7.5

regexReplaceFirst(string, regularExpression, newData)

Similar to `regexReplaceAll` but replaces only the first match with `newData`. For example, the following code alters only the first instance of a four-digit number with 2006:

```
<$string = "this is the regex test for 2005. The first was in 2005."$>
<$regexReplaceFirst(string, "\\d{4}", "2006")$>
```

> Added In: 7.5

rptDisplayMapValue(tableName, key)

Returns a localized string representation of an internal key code. These key codes are more low-level than standard localization messages. They are used to store status and state flags for content items. It is used on the content information page and workflow pages to output descriptions of the internal state.

```
<$dID=75$>
<$executeService("DOC_INFO")$>
status = <$rptDisplayMapValue("StatusList", dStatus)$>
```

> Added In: 5.0

rsAddRowCountColumn(resultSetName, columnName)

Adds a new column to an existing `ResultSet`. This new column will have a name corresponding to `columnName`, and its value will be the index for that row. For example, in a `ResultSet` with 10 rows, this value is 0 for the first row, and 9 for the last. Similar to using `getValue` on the `ResultSet` with the `#row` keyword.

```
<$rsCreateResultSet("MyList", "fieldA,fieldB,fieldC")$>
<$rsAppendRowValues("MyList", "A,B,C,D,E,F,X,Y,Z")$>
<$rsAddRowCountColumn("MyList", "index")$>
<$loop MyList$>
    #<$index$>: <$fieldA$>, <$fieldB$>, <$fieldC$>
<$endloop$>
```

> Added In: 7.0

rsAppend(targetResultSetName, sourceResultSetName)

Appends all rows from the source `ResultSet` to the target `ResultSet`. It modifies the target `ResultSet` to contain the columns of the source `ResultSets`, if necessary. It then appends the target with all the rows in the source.

The column names between the source and target do not always match up. When this happens, the target contains blank values for empty column names.

This function can be used with ResultSets returned from a service or ones created on the page with rsCreateResultSet. For example, create a ResultSet named MyList:

```
<$rsCreateResultSet("MyList", "fieldA,fieldB,fieldC")$>
<$rsAppendRowValues("MyList", "A,B,C,D,E,F")$>
<$loop MyList$>
    <$fieldA$>, <$fieldB$>, <$fieldC$>
<$endloop$>
```

Now create another ResultSet with slightly different column names and new data. After using rsAppend, the new rows are available in MyList:

```
<$rsCreateResultSet("NewData", "fieldB,fieldC,fieldD")$>
<$rsAppendRowValues("NewData", "X,Y,Z")$>
<$rsAppend("MyList", "NewData")$>
<$loop MyList$>
    <$fieldA$>, <$fieldB$>, <$fieldC$>, <$fieldD$>
<$endloop$>
```

Added In: 7.0

rsAppendNewRow(resultSetName)

Creates a new empty row in an existing ResultSet. The values in this row are blank and must be set with the setValue function:

```
<$rsCreateResultSet("MyList", "fieldA,fieldB,fieldC")$>
<$rsAppendNewRow("MyList")$>
<$setValue("MyList", "fieldA", "X")$>
<$setValue("MyList", "fieldB", "Y")$>
<$setValue("MyList", "fieldC", "Z")$>
<$loop MyList$>
    <$fieldA$>, <$fieldB$>, <$fieldC$>
<$endloop$>
```

Added In: 7.1

rsAppendRowValues(resultSetName, data)

Appends new rows to an existing ResultSet. The data parameter is a comma-separated list of values to append. The values are appended to the columns in order. If the data string contains more values than fit in one column, additional columns are created and appended:

```
<$rsCreateResultSet("MyList", "fieldA,fieldB,fieldC")$>
<$rsAppendRowValues("MyList", "A,B,C,D,E,F")$>
<$rsAppendRowValues("MyList", "X,Y,Z")$>
<$loop MyList$>
    <$fieldA$>, <$fieldB$>, <$fieldC$>
<$endloop$>
```

This is a quick way to insert new row values if you know the order of the columns in the ResultSet. If not, you need to use rsAppendNewRow.

Added In: 7.0

rsCopyFiltered(resultSetName, newResultSetName, filterField, filterFieldValue)

Creates a new ResultSet based on the data in an existing ResultSet. Only the rows in which filterField equals filterFieldValue are placed in the new ResultSet.

```
<$rsCreateResultSet("MyList", "fieldA,fieldB,fieldC")$>
<$rsAppendRowValues("MyList", "A,B,C,A,B,C,X,Y,Z")$>
<$rsCopyFiltered("MyList", "NewList", "fieldA", "A")$>
<$loop NewList$>
    <$fieldA$>, <$fieldB$>, <$fieldC$>
<$endloop$>
```

Added In: 7.0

rsCreateResultSet(resultSetName, fieldList)

Creates a new ResultSet with the specified fields. The parameter fieldList is a comma-separated list of column names. This is used with rsAppendRowValues and rsInsertNewRow to populate a ResultSet with data.

```
<$rsCreateResultSet("MyList", "fieldA,fieldB,fieldC")$>
<$rsAppendRowValues("MyList", "A,B,C,D,E,F")$>
<$loop MyList$>
    <$fieldA$>, <$fieldB$>, <$fieldC$>
<$endloop$>
```

Added In: 7.0

rsDeleteRow(resultSetName)

Deletes the current row in the specified ResultSet. To advance the current row to the correct position, use rsSetRow or rsFindRowPrimary.

```
<$rsCreateResultSet("MyList", "fieldA,fieldB,fieldC")$>
<$rsAppendRowValues("MyList", "A,B,C,D,E,F,X,Y,Z")$>
<$exec rsSetRow("MyList", 1)$>
<$rsDeleteRow("MyList")$>
<$loop MyList$>
    <$fieldA$>, <$fieldB$>, <$fieldC$>
<$endloop$>
```

Added In: 7.0

rsDocInfoRowAllowDisclosure(resultSetName)

Validates that the user has read permission to the current row in a ResultSet. In general, it is not needed. This check is performed in the service itself. It is used mainly in the Need To Know component.

Added In: 4.0

Context: Service

rsExists(resultSetName)

Returns `true` if the named `ResultSet` exists. It can also be done with the `if` conditional. However, if the name of the `ResultSet` was dynamically generated, the `rsExists` function is easier to use:

```
<$rsCreateResultSet("MyList", "fieldA,fieldB,fieldC")$>
<$rsAppendRowValues("MyList", "A,B,C,D,E,F")$>
<$if MyList$>
    It exists!
<$endif$>
<$if rsExists("My" & "List")$>
    It exists!
<$endif$>
```

Added In: 6.0

rsFieldByIndex(resultSetName, index)

Returns the name of the field at the specific `index`. It is useful for when you need to output the data in a `ResultSet` row, but you do not know the names of the fields. It can be used with `rsNumFields` to dynamically iterate over any `ResultSet`.

```
<$rsCreateResultSet("MyList", "fieldA,fieldB,fieldC")$>
<$rsAppendRowValues("MyList", "A,B,C,D,E,F")$>
<$fieldZero = rsFieldByIndex("MyList", 0)$>
<$loop MyList$>
    fieldZero = <$getValue("MyList", fieldZero)$>
<$endloop$>
```

Added In: 7.0

rsFieldExists(resultSetName, fieldName)

Returns `true` if the specified field exists in the specified `ResultSet`.

```
<$rsCreateResultSet("MyList", "fieldA,fieldB,fieldC")$>
<$if rsFieldExists("MyList", "dDocTitle")$>
    dDocTitle is in MyList
<$endif$>
<$if rsFieldExists("MyList", "fieldA")$>
    fieldA is in MyList
<$endif$>
```

Added In: 6.0

rsFindRowPrimary(resultSetName, value)

Advances the current row in the `ResultSet` to the one in which the first column's value matches the parameter `value`. It is used to bypass fields that you might not want to display.

```
<$rsCreateResultSet("MyList", "fieldA,fieldB,fieldC")$>
<$rsAppendRowValues("MyList", "A,B,C,D,E,F,X,Y,Z")$>
<$rsFindRowPrimary("MyList", "X")$>
```

```
<$loopwhile getValue("MyList", "#isRowPresent")$>
    <$fieldA$>, <$fieldB$>, <$fieldC$>
    <$exec rsNext("MyList")$>
<$endloop$>
```

This function cannot be used with the loop statement, only the loopwhile statement because the loop statement resets the ResultSet to the first row.

Added In: 4.0

rsFirst(resultSetName)

Advances a ResultSet to the first row, which prepares it for looping. It is typically used only with the loopwhile statement.

```
<$rsCreateResultSet("MyList", "fieldA,fieldB,fieldC")$>
<$rsAppendRowValues("MyList", "A,B,C,D,E,F,X,Y,Z")$>
<$rsFirst("MyList", "X")$>
<$loopwhile getValue("MyList", "#isRowPresent")$>
    <$fieldA$>, <$fieldB$>, <$fieldC$>
    <$exec rsNext("MyList")$>
<$endloop$>
```

Added In: 3.0

rsInsertNewRow(resultSetName)

Similar to rsAppendRowValues, but more flexible. First, advance to the correct row with rsSetRow. Next, use rsInsertNewRow to insert an empty row. Finally, use setValue to set a specific field to a specific value in that row.

```
<$rsCreateResultSet("MyList", "fieldA,fieldB,fieldC")$>
<$rsAppendRowValues("MyList", "A,B,C,D,E,F")$>
<$exec rsSetRow("MyList", 1)$>
<$rsInsertNewRow("MyList")$>
<$setValue("MyList", "fieldA", "X")$>
<$setValue("MyList", "fieldB", "Y")$>
<$setValue("MyList", "fieldC", "Z")$>
<$loop MyList$>
    <$fieldA$>, <$fieldB$>, <$fieldC$>
<$endloop$>
```

Added In: 7.0

rsIsRowPresent(resultSetName)

Returns true if the current row in the ResultSet contains data. It is used when iterating over a ResultSet with the loopwhile statement. It is the same as using getValue with the key #isRowPresent.

```
<$rsCreateResultSet("MyList", "fieldA,fieldB,fieldC")$>
<$rsAppendRowValues("MyList", "A,B,C,D,E,F,X,Y,Z")$>
<$rsFirst("MyList")$>
```

```
<$loopwhile rsIsRowPresent("MyList")$>
    <$fieldA$>, <$fieldB$>, <$fieldC$>
    <$exec rsNext("MyList")$>
<$endloop$>
```

Added In: 7.0

rsMakeFromList(resultSetName, optionListName [, fieldName])

Converts an existing OptionList into a ResultSet. It is useful because ResultSets are much more flexible. By default, it creates a one-column ResultSet with the field name row. If the parameter fieldName is specified, it is used instead of row.

```
<$rsMakeFromList("Groups", "securityGroups")$>
<$loop Groups$>
    <$row$>
<$endloop$>
```

Added In: 5.0

rsMakeFromString(resultSetName, data [, fieldName])

Similar to rsMakeFromList, this creates a one-column ResultSet. The parameter data is a comma-separated list of fields to insert into the ResultSet. By default, it creates a one-column ResultSet with the field name row. If the parameter fieldName is specified, it is used instead of row.

```
<$rsMakeFromString("MyList", "A,B,C,D,E,F")$>
<$loop MyList$>
    <$row$>
<$endloop$>
```

Added In: 5.0

rsMerge(targetResultSetName, sourceResultSetName, mergeField)

Merges the data from the source ResultSet into the target ResultSet. It is similar to rsAppend except that the new rows are not automatically appended. The data is merged into existing rows, if possible; otherwise, it is appended to the end. The mergeField is used to determine when a match is found.

```
<$rsCreateResultSet("MyList1", "fieldA,fieldB,fieldC")$>
<$rsAppendRowValues("MyList1", "A,B,C,AA,BB,CC")$>

<$rsCreateResultSet("MyList2", "fieldA,fieldX,fieldY")$>
<$rsAppendRowValues("MyList2", "A,X,Y,AA,XX,YY,AAA,XXX,YYY")$>

<$rsMerge("MyList1", "MyList2", "fieldA")$>
<$loop MyList1$>
    <$fieldA$>, <$fieldB$>, <$fieldC$>, <$fieldX$>, <$fieldY$>
<$endloop$>
```

Added In: 7.0

rsMergeDelete(targetResultSetName, sourceResultSetName, mergeField)

Deletes the rows in the target ResultSet if they exist in the source ResultSet. The mergeField is used to determine when a match is found.

```
<$rsCreateResultSet("MyList1", "fieldA,fieldB,fieldC")$>
<$rsAppendRowValues("MyList1", "A,B,C,AA,BB,CC")$>

<$rsCreateResultSet("MyList2", "fieldA")$>
<$rsAppendRowValues("MyList2", "A")$>

<$rsMergeDelete("MyList1", "MyList2", "fieldA")$>
<$loop MyList1$>
    <$fieldA$>, <$fieldB$>, <$fieldC$>
<$endloop$>
```

Added In: 7.0

rsMergeReplaceOnly(targetResultSetName, sourceResultSetName, mergeField)

Replaces rows in the target ResultSet based on the data in the source ResultSet. It does not append new rows or new columns; it can be used only to update existing data values. The mergeField is used to determine when a match is found.

```
<$rsCreateResultSet("MyList1", "fieldA,fieldB,fieldC")$>
<$rsAppendRowValues("MyList1", "A,B,C,AA,BB,CC")$>

<$rsCreateResultSet("MyList2", "fieldA,fieldB,fieldC")$>
<$rsAppendRowValues("MyList2", "A,B2,C2")$>

<$rsMergeReplaceOnly("MyList1", "MyList2", "fieldA")$>
<$loop MyList1$>
    <$fieldA$>, <$fieldB$>, <$fieldC$>, <$fieldX$>, <$fieldY$>
<$endloop$>
```

Added In: 7.0

rsNext(resultSetName)

Advances a ResultSet to the next row. It is useful when iterating over the ResultSet with the loopwhile statement. It returns a boolean value, representing success or failure. Failure means that there are no more rows in the ResultSet. See rsIsRowPresent for an example.

Added In: 3.0

rsNumFields(resultSetName)

Returns the number of fields in a ResultSet. It can be used with rsFieldByIndex to iterate over the fields in a ResultSet by index rather than by name.

```
<$rsCreateResultSet("MyList", "fieldA,fieldB,fieldC")$>
<$rsAppendRowValues("MyList", "A,B,C,AA,BB,CC")$>
Number of fields = <$rsNumFields("MyList")$>
```

Added In: 7.0

rsRename(resultSetName, newName)

Renames an existing ResultSet to a new name. It is mainly useful when calling executeService multiple times. For example, to run several searches on the same page, you must rename SearchResults each time. Otherwise, the data will be overwritten the next time GET_SEARCH_RESULTS is executed.

   Added In: 5.0

rsRenameField(resultSetName, oldName, newName)

Renames a field in an existing ResultSet.

```
<$rsCreateResultSet("MyList", "fieldA,fieldB,fieldC")$>
<$rsAppendRowValues("MyList", "A,B,C,AA,BB,CC")$>
<$rsRenameField("MyList", "fieldA", "newName")$>
<$loop MyList$>
    <$newName$>, <$fieldB$>, <$fieldC$>
<$endloop$>
```

   Added In: 7.0

rsSetRow(resultSetName, rowIndex)

Advances a ResultSet to the specified rowIndex. It returns a boolean flag, representing success or failure. Failure means that no row exists at that rowIndex. It is typically used with rsDeleteRow and rsInsertRow to alter ResultSets.

```
<$rsCreateResultSet("MyList", "fieldA,fieldB,fieldC")$>
<$rsAppendRowValues("MyList", "A,B,C,D,E,F,X,Y,Z")$>
<$exec rsSetRow("MyList", 1)$>
<$rsDeleteRow("MyList")$>
<$loop MyList$>
    <$fieldA$>, <$fieldB$>, <$fieldC$>
<$endloop$>
```

   Added In: 3

rsSort(resultSetName, sortField [, sortType, sortOrder])

Sorts the rows in a ResultSet. The sortField is the column name to sort over. The sortType is the type of sorting desired. It corresponds to the field type and can be string, int, or date. The default is int. It causes an alphabetic sort with all capital letters coming before lowercase letters. For case-insensitive sorting, set it to string. The sortOrder can be asc for ascending or desc for descending. If not specified, it defaults to ascending.

```
<$rsCreateResultSet("MyList", "fieldA")$>
<$rsAppendRowValues("MyList", "A3,A1,a2,a4")$>
<$rsSort("MyList", "fieldA", "string")$>
<$loop MyList$>
    <$fieldA$>
<$endloop$>
```

   Added In: 6.0

rsSortTree(resultSetName, rowId, parentId, nestingLevel, sortField[, sortType, sortOrder])

A more advanced sorting mechanism than rsSort. Instead of sorting on just one field, it will also be sorted according to relationships between rows, which allows a ResultSet to display a tree view of the items instead of a simple list. For example, threaded discussions contain information about when a comment was added and what the comment's parent is. They can be sorted into a tree in the following way:

```
<$rsCreateResultSet("MyList", "id,parent,title,depth")$>
<$rsAppendRowValues("MyList",
    "1,,first post,0," &
    "2,,another post,0," &
    "3,1,re: first post,1," &
    "4,3,re: re: first post,2," &
    "5,2,re: another post,1")$>
<$rsSortTree("MyList", "id", "parent", "depth", "id", "string")$>
<$loop MyList$>
    <$id$> - <$title$>
<$endloop$>
```

In the preceding example, sorting by id yields the tree:

```
1 - first post
3 - re: first post
4 - re: re: first post
2 - another post
5 - re: another post
```

If sorted by title, you see a different tree:

```
2 - another post
5 - re: another post
1 - first post
3 - re: first post
4 - re: re: first post
```

Added In: 6.0

setContentType(contentType)

Sets the HTTP Content Type for the response page. It enables you to generate a text page with IdocScript and set the Content Type to something other than text/html. Common alternatives include text/plain, text/xml, and application/csv. The first is useful for downloading raw data files. The second is useful for supporting XML-based Really Simple Syndication (RSS) feeds. The third is useful for opening up tabular data in Microsoft Excel.

Added In: 7.0

Context: Service

setCookie(key, value[, expirationDate])

Sets an HTTP cookie with the specified key and value. The expirationDate for the cookie is optional but recommended. Cookies can be read with JavaScript or with the getCookie IdocScript function.

The following code increments a counter every time the page is refreshed. The cookie expires one year from the current date.

```
<$numVisits = getCookie("numVisits")$>
<$if not numVisits$>
    <$numVisits = 1$>
<$endif$>
You have visited this page <$numVisits$> times.
<$setCookie("numVisits", numVisits+1, dateCurrent(365))$>
```

> Added In: 7.1
> Context: Service

setExpires(expirationDate)

Sets the `Expires` HTTP header. This header is an expiration date for the returned HTML page. Browsers use this date to determine how long to locally cache the page. If the page is cached and the user requests it again, the browser loads it from a local cache. No web request is performed to display the HTML page. It is useful for pages that a user views multiple times before it changes. To cache a full page for a week, use the following code:

```
<$setExpires(dateCurrent(7))$>
```

> Added In: 7.0
> Context: Service

setHttpHeader(headerName, value)

Sets an arbitrary HTTP header for the response page. The functions `setExpires`, `setContentType`, and `setMaxAge` are specializations of this function.
> Added In: 7.0
> Context: Service

setMaxAge(ageInSeconds)

Similar to the `setExpires` function, it controls how long a browser will cache the response page. Instead of setting a date for when the page should be refreshed, it sets a maximum age in seconds. For example, to cache a page for 30 minutes, use this code:

```
<$setMaxAge(1800)$>
```

> Added In: 7.0
> Context: Service

setResourceInclude(includeName, idocString)

This is an advanced IdocScript function that creates resource includes dynamically. The `includeName` is the name to give the new include. The `idocString` is a string containing the full text of the include. The include is available only for the current request.

```
<$idocString = "Hello <$UserName$>!"$>
<$exec setResourceInclude("hello_user", idocString)$>
<$include hello_user$>
```

The previous functionality can also be obtained with the eval function. However, the eval function is much slower than setResourceInclude if the code is used multiple times. You can also use a Component or an IDOC file to define resource includes. However, if the include depends a lot on user personalization or dynamically loaded data, it is sometimes easiest to create it dynamically.

Added In: 4.0

setValue(scope, key, value)

Creates a new variable named key with the specified value. The scope can either be #local or the name of an existing ResultSet.

For the most, part, this function is no different from simply declaring a variable. It is useful when the value for key is generated dynamically. For example, if you are looping over a ResultSet and need to set a variable for each entry, use setValue:

```
<$key1 = "value1"$>
<$setValue("#local", "key2", "value2")$>
<$setValue("#local", "key_" & UserName, "value3")$>
key1 = <$key1$>
key2 = <$key2$>
key_<$UserName$> = <$getValue("#local", "key_" & UserName)$>
```

It is also useful when modifying values in ResultSets. See rsAppendNewRow and rsInsertNewRow for examples.

Added In: 7.0

stdSecurityCheck()

Similar to rsDocInfoRowAllowDisclosure, it runs a standard security check. It is based on the current values for dSecurityGroup and dDocAccount and the security setting for the current service. For example, on a content information page, it checks for read privileges. On a check in page, it checks for write privileges. Typically this function is not needed because the service performs all necessary checks. Components that modify the security model occasionally have a need for it.

Added In: 4.0

Context: Service

strCenterPad(string, length)

Returns the string with spaces padded to the left and right of it, so it is a minimum length. It is useful when creating HTML buttons in internationalized environments.

Added In: 5.0

strCommaAppendNoDuplicates(string, token)

Appends a new token to an existing string. It returns the string, plus a comma, plus the new token. If the token already exists in the string, it is not added:

```
<$myString = strCommaAppendNoDuplicates(myString, "A")$>
<$myString = strCommaAppendNoDuplicates(myString, "B")$>
<$myString = strCommaAppendNoDuplicates(myString, "C")$>
```

```
<$myString = strCommaAppendNoDuplicates(myString, "A")$>
<$myString = strCommaAppendNoDuplicates(myString, "B")$>
<$myString$> = A,B,C
```

Added In: 6.0

strConfine(string, maxLength)

Returns a truncated version of the passed string if it is longer than maxLength. By default, it truncates it to three characters fewer than maxLength and inserts ellipses (...) representing an overflow:

```
Hello... = <$strConfine("Hello to all the new users!", 8)$>
```

The ellipses can be changed with the StrConfineOverflowChars configuration flag.
Added In: 5.0

strEquals(stringOne, stringTwo)

Returns true if stringOne and stringTwo are exactly the same. The use of this function is discouraged in favor of the like keyword or strEqualsIgnoreCase.
Added In: 3

strEqualsIgnoreCase(stringOne, stringTwo)

Similar to strEquals, but this comparison is case insensitive.

```
<$str1 = "hello", str2 = "Hello"$>
false = <$strEquals(str1, str2)$>
true = <$strEqualsIgnoreCase(str1, str2)$>
```

Added In: 3.0

strGenerateRandom([length])

Returns a random string of hexadecimal characters. It outputs as many characters as specified by the parameter length. If length is not specified, it defaults to 16 characters long.
Added In: 7.5

strIndexOf(string, subString)

Determines whether the string subString is present in the parameter string. If so, it returns the index in which subString is located. If it is not found, it returns -1. The search is case sensitive. To perform a case-insensitive search, use strLower or strUpper prior to using strIndexOf.

```
<$haystack = "Hello world!"$>
<$needle1 = "world", needle2 = "World"$>
6 = <$strIndexOf(haystack, needle1)$>
-1 = <$strIndexOf(haystack, needle2)$>
6 = <$strIndexOf(strLower(haystack), strLower(needle2))$>
```

Added In: 3.0

strLeftFill(string, filler, minLength)

Returns a string based on the parameter `string`, at least as long as `minLength`. If the passed `string` is not long enough, it will be padded with the string `filler` to the left of the passed string.

```
.....Hello = <$strLeftFill("Hello", ".", 10)$>
```

Added In: 5.0

strLeftPad(string, minLength)

Similar to `strLeftFill`, except the space character is used by default for filler.
Added In: 5.0

strLength(string)

Returns the length of the passed string.

```
<$hello = "Hello world!"$>
12 = <$strLength(hello)$>
```

Added In: 3.0

strLower(string)

Returns the parameter `string` in all lowercase letters. It is a useful preliminary step before performing case-insensitive searches.

```
<$hello = "Hello world!"$>
hello world! = <$strLower(hello)$>
```

Added In: 3.0

strRemoveWs(string)

Returns the parameter `string` with all white space characters removed:

```
<$test=" A B C D "$>
'ABCD' = '<$strRemoveWs(test)$>'
```

It is used to eliminate excess white space present in some resource includes. Useful when used in conjunction with the `inc` function.
Added In: 3.0

strReplace(sourceString, findString, replaceString)

Replaces all instances of `findString` in `sourceString` with `replaceString` and returns the result. Similar to `regexReplaceAll`, but without regular expression support.

```
<$hello = "Hello world! I love the world!"$>
<$strReplace(hello, "world", "universe")$>
```

Added In: 4.0

strReplaceIgnoreCase(sourceString, findString, replaceString)

Similar to strReplace, except it performs the search for findString in a case-insensitive manner.

```
<$hello = "Hello world! I love the world!"$>
<$strReplaceIgnoreCase(hello, "WORLD", "universe")$>
```

Added In: 4.0

strRightFill(string, filler, minLength)

Returns a string based on the parameter string at least as long as minLength. If the passed string is not long enough, it will be padded with the string filler to the right of the passed string.

```
Hello..... = <$strRightFill("Hello", ".", 10)$>
```

Added In: 4.0

strRightPad(string, minLength)

Similar to strRightFill, except the space character is used as the filler.
Added In: 5.0

strSubstring(string, startIndex[, endIndex])

Returns a substring of the passed string. The substring begins at startIndex and ends at endIndex. If endIndex is not specified, the default is the end of the string. It is used in conjunction with strLength and strIndexOf to parse strings.

```
<$hello = "Hello world!"$>
'Hello' = '<$strSubstring(hello, 0, 5)$>'
'world!' = '<$strSubstring(hello, 6)$>'
```

Added In: 3.0

strTrimWs(string)

Returns the parameter string with all leading and trailing white space removed. Similar to strRemoveWs, except it does not remove white space between words in the string:

```
<$test=" A B C D "$>
'A B C D' = '<$strTrimWs(test)$>'
```

Added In: 3.0

strUpper(string)

Returns the passed string in all uppercase letters. It is a useful preliminary step to performing case-insensitive searches.

```
<$hello = "Hello world!"$>
HELLO WORLD! = <$strUpper(hello)$>
```

Added In: 3.0

toInteger(object)

Converts any object to an integer and returns it. It can be used to turn an integer string into an integer or a date into an integer. If the object cannot be parsed into an integer, the function logs an error. It is useful to turn dates into integers so their values can be compared.

```
<$now = dateCurrent()$>
<$then = "1/1/2000"$>
<$nowInt = toInteger(parseDate(now))$>
<$thenInt = toInteger(parseDate(then))$>
<$if nowInt > thenInt$>
    how was y2k?
<$endif$>
```

Added In: 3.0

trace(message[, location, tracingSection])

Outputs a trace message for IdocScript debugging purposes. Prior to version 7.5, the message would be visible only if ScriptDebugTrace were enabled for the request. In version 7.5, this function was augmented to accept the location and tracingSection parameters. They allow the tracing message to be output to the console or to the web logs.

The message parameter can be any of the following:

- A text string containing the message to output

- #local

- #all

When the message is #local, all local data is traced, including all parameters in the URL and all variables currently set on the page. If it is set to #all, all the request and response data is traced, including the URL being accessed, all local data, and all ResultSets.

The location parameter can be any of the following:

- null

- #console

- #log

- The name of an IdocScript variable

If the location is null, the message is logged only when ScriptDebugTrace is active. If it is #console, the message will be output to the Java console. This output is accessible from the Admin Server, or the System Audit Information page. If it is #log, the message will be output to the standard HTML-based Content Server Logs. These web logs are less volatile and are used for more important tracing messages.

For example, to log the entire page context for debugging purposes, use the following:

```
<$trace("#all", "traceDump")$>
<$traceDump$>
```

The `tracingSection` parameter is used to control when the tracing message is logged. It corresponds to the Trace Sections found on the System Audit Information page. For example, workflows frequently contain complex IdocScript. You can leave tracing messages in a workflow script and have them output only when the `workflow` tracing section is active:

```
<$trace("message", "#console", "workflow")$>
```

If the `tracingSection` is blank, the message will always be logged.
Added In: 4.0

url(string)
Returns a URL-encoded version of the parameter `string`. It is useful when creating URLs that might contain spaces or other restricted characters. It is also useful when using the `RedirectUrl` parameter for a service request.

```
<$path = "my file.txt"$>
my%20file.txt = <$url(path)$>
```

Added In: 3.0

urlEscape7Bit(string)
Returns a URL-encoded version of the parameter `string`. Similar to the `url` function, but it encodes only characters that are not seven-bit clean (ASCII). This means that the function can be called repeatedly on the same string. If the `url` function is used to double-encode a string, every % character is encoded to %25, as seen here:

```
<$path = "mÿ fïlë.txt"$>
mÿ%20fïlë.txt = <$url(path)$>
mÿ%2520fïlë.txt = <$url(url(path))$>
m%ff%20f%efl%eb.txt = <$urlEscape7Bit(url(path))$>
m%ff%20f%efl%eb.txt= <$urlEscape7Bit(urlEscape7Bit(url(path)))$>
```

Added In: 7.1

userHasGroupPrivilege(securityGroup, privilege)
Returns `true` if the user has the specified `privilege` to the specified `securityGroup`. The privilege flag is a one-character representation of the access level:

- **R**: Read
- **W**: Write
- **D**: Delete
- **A**: Administrate

```
<$userHasGroupPrivilege("Public", "R")$>
<$userHasGroupPrivilege("Secure", "A")$>
```

Added In: 7.5

userHasRole(roleName)
Returns true if the user has the specified security role.

```
<$userHasRole("admin")$>
```

Added In: 4.0

utGetValue(topicName, key)
Returns a value saved in this user's personalization. The topicName is the topic where the data is stored, typically pne_portal. The key is the name of the variable stored. It is typically used to retrieve information on how to personalize the web interface.

```
<$utGetValue("pne_portal", "emailFormat")$>
<$utGetValue("pne_portal", "XuiSearchTemplate")$>
<$utGetValue("pne_portal", "lastSortField")$>
```

Added In: 4.0

utLoad(topicName)
Loads the personalization topic corresponding to topicName. This function is no longer necessary. Any function that loads data from personalization automatically loads the topic.
Added In: 4.0

utLoadDocumentProfiles(topicName, resultSetName)
Loads the Content Profile–related ResultSet corresponding to resultSetName and places it in the page context. It returns true if the ResultSet was loaded properly.

```
<$exec utLoadDocumentProfiles("pne_portal", "PneDocumentProfiles")$>
```

Added In: 7.5

utLoadResultSet(topicName, resultSetName)
Loads a ResultSet from a personalization topic and places it in the page context. Typically, these ResultSets contain lists of saved queries, personal URLs, and the workflow in queue for the user.

```
<$exec utLoadResultSet("pne_portal", "SavedQueries")$>
<$exec utLoadResultSet("pne_portal", "PersonalURLS")$>
<$exec utLoadResultSet("wf_in_queue", "WorkflowInQueue")$>
```

Added In: 4.0

wfAddUser(userOrAlias, type)
Adds a user to the current workflow step in a workflow script. The user can be added by name, by alias, or with a workflow token. The parameter userOrAlias is the user, alias, or token. The parameter type can be user or alias.

```
<$wfAddUser("bex", "user")$>
<$theBoss = getValueForSpecifiedUser("bex", "uManager")$>
<$wfAddUser(theBoss, "user")$>
<$wfAddUser("accounting", "alias")$>
```

Added In: 5.0
Context: Workflow

wfCurrentGet(key)

Returns the value of a key set for the current step in the workflow. It returns only data that was explicitly scoped to the current step. Some data, such as entryCount and lastEntryTs, is set automatically. Any other flag must be set in a workflow script with wfCurrentSet.

```
last entry = <$wfCurrentGet("lastEntryTs")$>
number of times rejected = <$wfCurrentGet("lastEntryTs") - 1$>
```

In the Workflow Companion File, the full name of this key is scoped to the specific step name and workflow name: step_name@workflow_name.key.

Added In: 5.0
Context: Workflow

wfCurrentSet(key, value)

Stores a value in the Workflow Companion File specific to the current workflow, content item, and step. The value can be extracted later with wfCurrentGet. For example, to store the name of the original author for this step, use the following code in the entry event:

```
<$wfCurrentSet("originalStepAuthor", dDocAuthor)$>
```

In the Workflow Companion File, the full name of this key is scoped to the specific step name and workflow name: step_name@workflow_name.key.

Added In: 5.0
Context: Workflow

wfCurrentStep(stepsFromCurrent)

Returns the name of a step in the current workflow. The parameter stepsFromCurrent is an integer, representing the number of steps away from the current step.

```
this step = <$wfCurrentStep(0)$>
next step = <$wfCurrentStep(1)$>
previous step = <$wfCurrentStep(-1)$>
```

Added In: 5.0
Context: Workflow

wfDisplayCondition(workflowName, workflowStep, stringResource)

Displays the additional exit conditions for this step, if any exist. Some workflows require additional conditions to be satisfied before an item is released from a workflow step. For example, a workflow step might require two approvals, but at least one of those approvals must come from the alias accounting. This function is used on workflow information pages. It displays what else must occur before the item can move forward in the workflow.

```
<$wfDisplayCondition(dWfName, dWfStepName, "wfAdditionalExitCondition")$>
```

Added In: 6.1
Context: Workflow Service

wfExit(numJumpsToRewind, numForwardSteps)

Exits a workflow or subworkflow at any point. It is important to keep in mind that the first parameter, numJumpsToRewind, is used to go backward in the workflow. It rewinds a subworkflow to the main workflow. The next parameter, numForwardSteps, moves the item forward through the main workflow after rewinding the subworkflows. To always exit, set these numbers to values much greater than the possible number of steps.

```
move to previous jump step: <$wfExit(1,0)$>
always exit: <$wfExit(1000,1000)$>
```

> Added In: 5.0
> Context: Workflow

wfGet(key)

Returns the value for the specified key in the current workflow. Similar to wfCurrentSet, except these parameters are global for this item for all steps. It is mainly useful for extracting workflow flags or custom tokens. These values are stored in the workflow companion file.

```
<$wfGet("wfJumpName")$>
<$wfGet("originalAuthor")$>
```

> Added In: 5.0
> Context: Workflow

wfGetStepTypeLabel(stepType)

Translates an internal workflow state flag into a human readable string. Specifically, it takes the stepType parameter and translates it into a meaningful string that describes which actions are possible in this step. It is typically used on workflow information pages.

```
<$wfGetStepTypeLabel(dWfStepType)$>
```

> Added In: 7.0
> Context: Workflow Service

wfIsReleasable()

Returns true if the item has satisfied all criteria to be released from the workflow. This does not mean it is available in the search engine; simply that the workflow process is not preventing its release.

> Added In: 7.0
> Context: Workflow Service

wfLoadDesign(workflowName)

Loads the design for the specified workflow. The design file contains information about the workflow steps and jump scripts. It is used on workflow information pages to display information about what steps remain.

```
<$if wfLoadDesign(dWfName)$>
```

> Added In: 6.1
> Context: Workflow Service

wfNotify(name, userOrAlias[, emailTemplate])

Sends a workflow email message to one or more users. The name parameter is the name of a user or alias. The userOrAlias parameter must be set to user or alias. The emailTemplate parameter can be set to the name of a Content Server template to render the message. The values for wfMailSubject and wfMessage are extracted from the workflow companion file to render the email.

```
<$wfSet("wfMailSubject", "workflow item " & dDocName)$>
<$wfSet("wfMessage", "This item is still in workflow.")$>
<$wfNotify(dDocAuthor, "user")$>
```

> Added In: 5.0
> Context: Workflow

wfReleaseDocument()

Releases a workflow item for public consumption. It is used for post-release workflow items. Such items are considered available for general consumption, but they remain in the workflow. They are full-text indexed, if applicable, and released to the search engine. These post-release workflow items consume more resources than normal workflow items and should be used sparingly.

```
<$wfReleaseDocument()$>
```

> Added In: 7.0
> Context: Workflow

wfSet(key, value)

Sets a key to the specified value in the workflow companion file. It is mainly useful for preparing workflow jumps or setting custom workflow tokens.

```
<$wfSet("originalAuthor", dDocAuthor)$>
<$wfSet("wfJumpName", "jump-to-subworkflow")$>
<$wfSet("wfJumpTargetStep", "step1@sub_workflow_A")$>
<$wfSet("wfJumpEntryNotifyOff", "0")$>
```

> Added In: 5.0
> Context: Workflow

wfUpdateMetaData(fieldName, fieldValue)

Updates the value of one metadata field of a workflow content item. It executes the service UPDATE_METADATA in a new context. It updates only custom metadata in the database. It cannot be used to update standard metadata fields, such as dDocTitle or dSecurityGroup. It does not update the search collection for items in a post-release workflow.

> Added In: 6.1
> Context: Workflow

xml(string)

Returns an XML-encoded version of the passed string. It escapes restricted XML characters, such as angle brackets and ampersands. It is used to place data into HTML attributes.

```
<$dDocTitle = "Policies & Procedures"$>
<input name="dDocTitle" value="<$xml(dDocTitle)$>">
```

Added In: 4.0

APPENDIX C

■ ■ ■

IdocScript Variables

As discussed in Appendix A, IdocScript supports variables in many different scopes. These variables include configuration flags, variables defined on the page, variables defined in the URL of a page, and variables that are calculated in Java. They can be broken down into the following categories:

- Environment variables: Also called configuration variables, they are defined in the `config.cfg` and custom environment resources. For example, `SysAdminAddress`. These are accessible in IdocScript, unless they contain secure information, such as `JdbcPassword`.

- Computed variables: These variables are computed with Java inside the core; for example, `BrowserVersionNumber` and `UserRoles`.

- Local variables: These variables include flags that are set on the page in IdocScript or in the URL. Flags such as `IsJava` and `fieldName` affect how resource includes are rendered on a page.

This appendix contains a list of the 50 most common variables in each category.

Top 50 Environment Variables

Environment variables are typically set in the `config.cfg` file and mostly affect how the Content Server services function. For security, you can explicitly pull values from the environment with this code:

```
<$getValue("#env", "MyVariable")$>
<$#env.MyVariable$>
```

Some environment variables can be set dynamically in the service request. For example, `AutoNumberPrefix` can be changed on the fly in a Java component or in a profile rule. You can also enable the download applet on a search results page by setting `DownloadApplet=1` in the URL of the search results page.

There are more than 500 configuration flags, all documented in the *IdocScript Reference Guide*. Following are some of the most popular settings.

AdditionalIndexBuildParams

Used to alter the Verity search collection after each bulk load and for advanced tuning of the collection for size and speed. See the *IdocScript Reference Guide* for a complete list of options:

```
AdditionalIndexBuildParams=-repair
AdditionalIndexBuildParams=-optimize maxclean
AdditionalIndexBuildParams=-optimize maxmerge -squeeze
```

Added In: 3.0

AdditionalSubscriptionCollatedFieldList

Needed when customizing the subscription or workflow mail templates. By default, only a small subset of document's metadata is available when rendering the email templates. By adding a field to this list, it will be promoted into the email rendering context.

```
AdditionalSubscriptionCollatedFieldList=dOriginalName
```

Added In: 7.1

AuthorDelete

If set to true, allows users to delete items that they created. It is true even if users do not have delete privileges for the security group. People typically enable this setting and then restrict delete privileges to only administrators.
Added In: 3.0

AutoNumberPrefix

When IsAutoNumber is true, is used with the number to generate the content name (dDocName) upon check-in. This flag can contain IdocScript:

```
AutoNumberPrefix=<$dDocType$>_<$dDocAuthor$>_
```

Added In: 3.0

CgiFileName

The URL to the web plug-in for the Content Server. It is appended to HttpRelativeWebRoot to generate the URL prefix needed to run services.
Added In: 3.0

DefaultAccounts

The accounts everyone can access when accounts are enabled with UseAccounts. This flag is a comma-separated list of account names and permissions in parentheses:

```
DefaultAccounts#none(RWDA),general(RW)
```

Added In: 4.0

DownloadApplet

Enables the download applet on the search results page and the content information page. It is useful for downloading multiple large files in one batch. It is a global setting that affects all users. As of version 6.1, the users can disable it on their User Profile page.
Added In: 3.0

EnableDocumentHighlight

Enables highlighting of search keywords in documents. They can be PDF, text, or HTML files. When `true`, the link on the search results page executes a service that highlights the full text search keywords and returns the highlighted document to the user.

Added In: 3.0

EnableExpirationNotifier

Enables a background process to watch for documents about to expire. When a document is set to expire in a week, the author receives an email notification.

Added In: 7.0

ExclusiveCheckout

When `true`, restricts the check-out of a content item to the person who originally authored it. It prevents anybody who is not an administrator from making a new revision of this content item.

Added In: 3.0

GetCopyAccess

Restricts access to the vault rendition of a content item. If `false`, restricts access to those who have write privileges to the item's security group. Others can view only the version in the `weblayout` directory. This flag protects the original documents, such as AutoCAD drawings or Java Server Pages (JSPs), while still allowing access to the converted renditions.

Added In: 3.0

HasExternalUsers

Is `true` if the Content Server is using an external database for its user's credentials. Examples include a Lightweight Directory Access Protocol (LDAP) server, Active Directory, or Integrated Windows Authentication (IWA), formerly called NTLM.

Added In: 3.0

HasGlobalUsers

Is `true` if the Content Server is obtaining its user's credentials from another Content Server. It is `true` in the case of a proxied Content Server or a custom global user database.

Added In: 4.0

HttpRelativeWebRoot

The full relative path to the root of the Content Server's web directory. This path includes a forward slash, but not the hostname. By default, it is `/stellent/`.

Added In: 3.0

HttpServerAddress

The hostname of the web server. This name appears on all the full URLs that this Content Server displays. Therefore, it should always be a full DNS path that all users can resolve.

Added In: 3.0

IDC_Name

The unique name of the Content Server. No two Content Servers should ever have the same value for IDC_Name. Clustered servers are the exception because they are treated as nodes in the same logical server.

    Added In: 3.0

IdcAdminServerPort

The port on which the Admin Server runs. The Admin Server is used to stop and start the Content Server, as well as manage components on them.

    Added In: 4.0

IdcServerSocketQueueDepth

An advanced tuning parameter for high-volume servers, it sets the depth of the queue for TCP sockets that the Content Server will accept. By default, it is 50. By setting it higher, the Content Server does not reject requests when it gets too busy. The requests wait in the queue until the Content Server has enough resources to process them.

    Added In: 6.1

IndexVaultFile

Some items, such as ZIP archives, are not processed by the content refinery. Their conversion step is set to PASSTHRU. Typically these files are placed in both the weblayout and vault folders, which is a waste of storage for very large files.

    By setting this flag to true, these files instead have a Hypertext Content Server Template (HCST) placed in the weblayout folder. This file contains a link to download the rendition in the vault.

    Added In: 7.0

IntradocServerPort

The port on which the Content Server's Java server runs. The web server makes a connection to the Content Server on this port, which is typically 4444.

    Added In: 3.0

IsAutoNumber

When set to true, the content name (dDocName) is automatically generated for new content items. It is still an optional parameter on the check-in page. The content name is a number, which can have a prefix based on AutoNumberPrefix, mentioned previously.

    Added In: 3.0

IsDynamicConverterEnabled

Set to true to enable the Dynamic Converter. You do not need the full Dynamic Converter component to perform basic conversion, but you do need it for advanced features. You must also set DefaultHtmlConversion to the content name of an item in the server. This item must be the template that you want to use for conversion. This template is based on the Outside In HTML conversion parameters, which uses a different scripting language than IdocScript:

```html
<html>
<head>
<meta http-equiv="content-type" content="text/html;
  charset={## insert element=pragma.charset}" />
<title>
{## insert element=pragma.sourcefilename}
</title>
{## if element=pragma.cssfile}
    <link rel="stylesheet"
      href="{## insert element=pragma.cssfile}" />
{## /if}
</head>
<body>
{## repeat element=sections}
    {## insert element=bodyorimage}
{## /repeat}
</body>
</html>
```

Finally, enable the Dynamic Converter for specific formats, such as Microsoft Word, from the Administration page. Now a Dynamic Conversion link will be present on the content information page for basic conversion.

Added In: 5.0

IsJspServerEnabled

Set to true to enable the Tomcat integration engine. It causes JSPs to be rendered inside the core. See Chapter 4 for more details.

Added In: 5.0

IsOverrideFormat

Set to true to allow user to set the format of a document upon check-in. It is useful if you have several clients that use Apple or Unix workstations. Because files on these systems do not always have file extensions, setting the file type upon check-in ensures the proper conversion.

Added In: 3.0

JspEnabledGroups

A comma-separated list of security groups that are allowed to render JSPs. These groups should have highly restrictive write access but highly open read access.

Added In: 5.0

JvmCommandLine

A special configuration flag used in `intradoc.cfg` instead of `config.cfg` that is not used by the Content Server. Instead it is used by the Launcher, which is a native application that starts and stops all Stellent Java applications. It uses several other flags defined in `intradoc.cfg` to tune the Java startup parameters. Two examples follow:

```
JvmCommandLine=$JAVA_EXE -classpath $CLASSPATH $STARTUPCLASS
JvmCommandLine=$JAVA_EXE $JAVA_OPTIONS➥
  "$DEFINE_PREFIXjava.endorsed.dirs=$ENDORSEDPATH"➥
  $APPEND_CLASSPATH "$CLASSPATH" $STARTUPCLASS
```

These flags control the Java classpath, the amount of memory consumed, and specific platform options. The supported flags depend greatly on the Java version, the Content Server version, and the platform. Refer to the install documentation for more information on the Launcher. On Windows, you can obtain a debug dump by running `IdcServer.exe` with the `-debug` flag. The command line will look something like this:

```
c:\stellent\bin\IdcServer.exe -debug
```

Added In: 4.0

MailServer

Hostname for the outgoing email server. The Content Server needs to use it to send out subscription and workflow emails. It is typically something like `mail.company.com`.
Added In: 3.0

MaxQueryRows

Maximum number of rows displayed from a database query on certain pages. For example, the number of results on an Active Report, the Work In Progress page, and the Repository Manager applet are always less than this number. It defaults to 200.
Added In: 3.0

MaxResults

Maximum number of results that are returned for a Verity search. The search results page will never show more than this number. The default is 200, and you should use caution when increasing this number. Verity is limited to returning 64,000 fields. So if you have 40 custom metadata fields, this number cannot be greater than approximately 1,000.
Added In: 3.0

MaxSearchConnections

Number of connections to the Verity search engine. Increasing this number might increase the number of simultaneous searches you can support. However, this is not typical unless you have a multiple CPU server. The default is 5. For a multiple CPU server, the rule of thumb is two connections per CPU. So with 4 processors, you can set it to 8.
Added In: 4.0

MemoFieldSize

Maximum size for custom metadata fields of type Memo. It affects only the size of new fields. Increasing this has no effect on existing fields; they have to be manually resized in the database. The default is 255.

Added In: 4.0

MultiUpload

Enables the Upload Applet on the Check In page. This applet is used to bundle several items together into one ZIP file and then check it in. It has an upload progress bar, so it is also useful for checking in very large files. It is a global setting that affects all users. As of version 6.1, users can disable it on their User Profile page.

Added In: 3.0

NtlmSecurityEnabled

When set to `true`, users can automatically log into the Content Server with their IWA. For example, if your users have credentials on your local network and your web server is IIS, you can securely log into the Content Server without being prompted for your password. It is restricted to web browsers that support IWA, such as Internet Explorer and Firefox with the setting `network.automatic-ntlm-auth.trusted-uris`. You might also need to map Windows network credentials to Content Server roles and accounts, which can be done from the Administration page. Advanced integrations might require a security customization or the `UseAdsi` flag as well. See Chapter 12 for a discussion.

Added In: 3.0

NumConnections

Number of Java connections to the database, which defaults to 5. Setting it to a higher number sometimes enables a server to support more users. However, this is generally only the case for consumption-oriented servers.

If you have a contribution and consumption server, the situation is more complex. Increasing the number of connections will sometimes cause the Content Server to slow down. For example, assume that one user is querying a table at the same time another user is updating it. All databases run more slowly in this situation because it's difficult to make certain that everybody gets back the correct data. Increasing the number of connections will make the problem worse unless the database can handle the extra load.

The rule of thumb is five connections or one connection per CPU on the database server. Setting it higher should not be done without performance testing.

Added In: 4.0

PrimaryWorkQueueTimeout

Subscription and workflow emails are sent out on a schedule. Every few seconds, the server runs a few queries to determine whether new emails need to be sent. The interval corresponds to the value of this flag. The default is 600, or 10 minutes. If you are testing workflow scripts, you might want to make it lower.

Added In: 3.0

SchemaPublishInterval

The Schema API takes data from the database and publishes it out into static JavaScript files. It is based on a complex algorithm, based on how often the database changes, and a dozen tuning parameters. This flag is the absolute maximum amount of seconds between two publishings of schema. Its default is 14400, which is four hours. If you are testing your schema setup, you might want to make it much lower.

Added In: 7.0

SearchIndexerEngineName

Name of the search engine to use. The default is VERITY. Other supported values include DATABASE and DATABASEFULLTEXT. Unless you are switching to the DATABASE option, you need to perform additional steps to use another search index. Each search engine uses its own unique format for query strings. The default uses Verity syntax, whereas database search requires SQL syntax.

Added In: 7.0

SearchQueryFormat

By setting this field to Universal, you enable the search engine query translation. This means that Verity syntax is valid for all search queries, regardless of the SearchIndexerEngineName.

Added In: 7.0

ShowOnlyKnownAccounts

When accounts are enabled, the Content Server presents a list of accounts on the advanced search page, and the check-in pages. An administrator can set up a list of predefined accounts that the user has access to. However, the user can also create new accounts by using the predefined accounts as a prefix. For example, the administrator can give the user write access to the account research/. The user can then set the account to research/myproject/ for the new content item. The new account will be generated during the check-in process.

When this flag is true, the check-in page will only display the account research/. If this flag is false (the default), it will also display research/myproject/.

Added In: 3.0

SocketHostAddressSecurityFilter

A pipe-separated list of IP addresses. The Content Server allows only direct connections from a server if it is in this list. If your server is not in this list, you must access the Content Server through the web interface. It can accept the asterisk as a wildcard:

```
SocketHostAddressSecurityFilter=127.0.0.1|10.10.*.*
```

This setting is mainly useful when using CIS or IdcCommandUX to connect directly to the Content Server. Its default is localhost, or 127.0.0.1.

Added In: 4.0

SysAdminAddress

Email address of the main system administrator. It is mainly used in outgoing emails as the From field.

Added In: 3.0

SystemLocale

The default locale for the Content Server. It contains information on how to store and display dates, numbers, and translated strings. Users can specify their own locales if the system locale is not right for them. New locales can be created with components and enabled with the System Properties Editor.

Added In: 5.0

TraceSectionsList

A comma-separated list of tracing sections that are enabled when the server starts. By enabling a tracing section, an administrator can closely monitor what the Content Server is doing. For example, you can enable the `workflow` section to monitor how an item is processed through workflow or the `systemdatabase` section to monitor the raw SQL sent to the database. Tracing sections are enabled dynamically from the System Audit Information page. The default is as follows:

```
TraceSectionsList=system,indexer
```

Adding additional sections to this list is useful for debugging startup errors. It is also useful when you need to restart the Content Server several times to troubleshoot a problem.

Added In: 7.0

UseAccounts

Set to `true` to enable accounts in addition to security groups. Enabling accounts will seriously affect how your content is secured. Please read the *Managing Security and User Access* document for more information.

Added In: 3.0

UseAdsi

Forces authentication with an Active Directory server when `NtlmSecurityEnabled` is `true`.

Added In: 6.0

UseNetscape

Causes an LDAP provider to connect to an LDAP server with the Netscape Software Developer Kit (SDK). It is the recommended setting because it greatly increases performance.

An LDAP provider can be created from the *Providers* administration page. This flag is set by selecting the checkbox Use Netscape SDK.

Added In: 6.1

UseNtlm

Used in conjunction with `NtlmSecurityEnabled`. When both are `true`, the authentication will take place with the NT LAN Manager. It is an older and less-used precursor to Active Directory.

Added In: 6.0

UserCacheTimeout

Cached locally for performance when user information exists in an external database. This flag sets the length of time in milliseconds that the cache will be considered valid. The default is 60,000, or one minute. If your site has lots of users and a slow LDAP server, you might want to increase this value.

Added In: 4.0

UseSecureLdap

Causes an LDAP provider to connect to an LDAP server using the Secure Sockets Layer (SSL) protocol. It is more secure than standard authentication, but it is much slower.

An LDAP provider can be created from the Providers administration page. This flag is set by selecting the checkbox Use SSL.

Added In: 6.1

UseSelfRegistration

When enabled, exposes a link that enables users to create new accounts. New users receive the roles and accounts that correspond to SelfRegisteredRoles and SelfRegisteredAccounts. It is mainly useful for extranets or client facing servers. For internal networks, it is less useful. It is easier to maintain the users if they exist in LDAP or Active Directory.

Added In: 4.0

UseSSL

Affects how URLs are drawn in the Content Server interface. After you set up SSL in your web server, set this flag to true. Then all the full URLs will use https:// as a prefix instead of http://.

Added In: 3.0

Top 50 Computed Variables

Some variables cannot be set in the environment or on the page. Due to security concerns or due to the complexity of calculating them, they are evaluated in Java code. Computed variables are referenced on the page in the same way as other variables:

```
<$HttpCgiPath$>               outputs: /stellent/idcplg
<$HttpCgiPath='test'$>
<$HttpCgiPath$>               outputs: /stellent/idcplg
```

These variables cannot be set in the URL or in the environment files. Some computed variables depend on values in the environment, but are still calculated in Java. For example, HttpCgiPath depends on the environment values HttpServerAddress and CgiFileName.

Some variables can be computed only in specific contexts. For example, the variable BrowserVersionNumber is available only if a web browser is rendering the page. That means it cannot be used in a workflow script or on a custom email template. It can be executed only in the context of a service request. Whenever applicable, the restricted context is noted.

There are about 100 computed variables. The commonly used ones are listed in the following sections.

AdminAtLeastOneGroup

Returns true if the user has administrative privileges to at least one security group. It is mainly useful for conditional display of administrative links.

Added In: 3.0

AllowCheckin

Returns true if the user is allowed to check-in a new revision of the item in workflow. It is useful for determining which workflow links to display to a user.

Added In: 3.0
Context: Service Request

AllowCheckout

Returns true if the user is allowed to check-out the current revision of the item in workflow. It is useful for determining which workflow links to display to a user.

Added In: 3.0
Context: Service Request

AllowReview

Returns true if the user is allowed to approve or reject the item in workflow. It is useful for determining which workflow links to display to a user.

Added In: 3.0
Context: Service Request

BrowserVersionNumber

Returns the version number of the user's browser. It is used to determine whether it supports Cascading Style Sheets (CSS) and Dynamic HTML (DHTML) sufficiently.

Added In: 3.0
Context: Service Request

DelimitedUserRoles

Returns a comma-separated list of this user's role names and uses colon characters as delimiters. For example, the user sysadmin will have :admin:,:sysmanager: for its list of roles. It is used with the like operator to determine whether a user has a specific role:

```
<$if DelimitedUserRoles like "*:admin:*"$>
    You're an administrator!
<$endif$>
```

Added In: 4.0
Context: Service Request

HttpAbsoluteCgiPath

Similar to HttpCgiPath, but returns an absolute URL instead of a full relative URL.

Added In: 3.0

HttpAdminCgiPath
Returns the relative URL to the web plug-in for the Admin Server.
> Added In: 4.0

HttpBrowserFullCgiPath
Similar to `HttpAbsoluteCgiPath`, except based on the current browser's context. For example, some Content Servers have two hostnames. It might have one address for internal users, but a different name for external users. This variable assembles the full CGI path based on the hostname in the current user's browser.
> Added In: 3.0
> Context: Service Request

HttpCgiPath
Returns the relative URL to the CGI-based web plug-in for the Content Server. All service requests must begin with this URL. For a full URL, set `isAbsoluteCgi` to `true` before displaying this variable.
> Added In: 3.0

HttpCommonRoot
Returns the URL to the common directory in the `weblayout`. It is typically located here:

`stellent/weblayout/common/`

and has a URL similar to this one:

`/stellent/common/`

> It is where Java applets for the Content Server are stored.
> Added In: 3.0

HttpEnterpriseCgiPath
Used only for proxy servers. It returns the `HttpCgiPath` for the master Content Server.
> Added In: 4.0

HttpHelpRoot
Returns the URL to the help directory in the `weblayout`. It is typically located here:

`stellent/weblayout/help/`

And will have a URL similar to this:

`/stellent/help/`

> It is where the online help documentation resides. These help documents exist in several languages. This URL contains the specific language prefix needed by the current user.
> Added In: 4.0

HttpImagesRoot
Returns the URL to the images directory in the `weblayout`. It is typically located here:

```
stellent/weblayout/images/
```

and will have a URL similar to this:

```
/stellent/images/
```

It stores some of the images used by the Content Server. Images are also stored in the skin folders for specific layouts. See Chapter 8 for more examples.
Added In: 4.0

HttpSystemHelpRoot
Similar to HttpHelpRoot, except it returns the path to the help files for the default system language.
Added In: 7.1

HttpWebRoot
Returns the URL to the root weblayout directory. It is typically located here:

```
stellent/weblayout/
```

and has a URL similar to this one:

```
/stellent/
```

It has the portal.htm page and all the subdirectories for help, common, and resources.
Added In: 3.0

IsContributor
Returns true if the user has write access to at least one group. It is typically used to conditionally display navigation links.
Added In: 4.0
Context: Service Request

IsExternalUser
Returns true if the user's credentials exist in an external database, such as LDAP or Active Directory.
Added In: 3.0
Context: Service Request

IsLoggedIn
Returns true if the user is currently logged in. It is typically used to conditionally display navigation links.
Added In: 3.0
Context: Service Request

IsMac
Returns true if the browser client's operating system is an Apple.
Added In: 3.0
Context: Service Request

IsSubAdmin

Returns `true` if the user has subadministrator rights. Typically, a user is not allowed to access the Administration page without the `admin` role. If a user is a subadministrator, the user has restricted access to the Administration applets. This flag is typically used to conditionally display navigation links.

Added In: 4.0

Context: Service Request

IsSun

Returns `true` if the browser client's operating system is a Sun workstation.

Added In: 3.0

Context: Service Request

IsSysManager

Returns `true` if the user has the `sysmanager` role. The user then has access to the Admin Server. This flag is typically used to conditionally display navigation links.

Added In: 4.0

Context: Service Request

IsUserEmailPresent

Returns `true` if the user's email address is known. It is typically used on subscription pages. If the user's email address is not known, the user is prompted for one.

Added In: 4.0

Context: Service Request

IsWindows

Returns `true` if the browser client's operating system is Windows.

Added In: 3.0

Context: Service Request

IsWorkflow

Returns `true` if the content item on a check-in page is in a workflow.

Added In: 3.0

MSIE

Returns `true` if the client's browser is Internet Explorer.

Added In: 3.0

Context: Service Request

NoMatches

Returns `true` if no matches were found in the search query that was just executed.

Added In: 3.0

URL

Returns a relative URL to a content item based on the data in the results of a search.

Added In: 3.0

UserAccounts

Returns a comma-separated list of accounts to which the user has access.

> Added In: 3.0
> Context: Service Request

UserAddress

Returns the email address for the current user.

> Added In: 3.0
> Context: Service Request

UserDefaultAccount

Returns the default account for the user. It is blank unless accounts are enabled and this user has a default account configured.

> Added In: 3.0
> Context: Service Request

UserFullName

Returns the full name of the current user.

> Added In: 3.0
> Context: Service Request

UserIsAdmin

Returns true if the user has the admin role. The user then has access to the Administration applets. This flag is typically used to conditionally display navigation links.

> Added In: 4.0
> Context: Service Request

UserLanguageId

Returns the two-letter code representing the user's preferred language (for example, en for English, fr for French, and ja for Japanese). It is useful for constructing URLs to localized web resource files.

> Added In: 5.0
> Context: Service Request

UserLocaleId

Returns the full name for the user's locale. For example, English-US, English-UK, Français, or Japanese. The locale contains information on language, date, and number formatting.

> Added In: 5.0
> Context: Service Request

UserName

Returns the name of the user.

> Added In: 3.0
> Context: Service Request

UserRoles

Returns a comma-separated list of roles that the user has.

Added In: 3.0

Context: Service Request

WfStart

It is used only in a workflow script. It returns the name of the first step in the current work-flow. It can be used with other workflow script functions to return to the beginning of the workflow. For example:

```
<$wfSet("wfJumpTargetStep", WfStart)$>
```

Added In: 5.0

Context: Workflow Script

Top 50 Local Variables

Local variables can be set in IdocScript or in the URL of a web page. They are used to affect the display of the page and are most frequently used to create customized pages.

Some of these variables are scoped to specific fields. For example, to hide the Comments field on a check-in page, you can use a URL like this:

```
http://localhost/idcplg?IdcService=CHECKIN_NEW_FORM&xComments:isHidden=1
```

This flag can also be set in IdocScript by using a component. Such components typically override the include std_doc_page_definitions:

```
<@dynamichtml std_doc_page_definitions@>
<$include super.std_doc_page_definitions$>
<$include custom_modify_comments_definitions$>
<@end@>

<@dynamichtml custom_modify_comments_definitions@>
<$if isCheckin$>
    <$xComments:isHidden = 1$>
<$endif$>
<@end@>
```

Other flags are not scoped to specific fields. They are set and reset many times on the page when displaying metadata fields. For example, fieldName and fieldCaption are set to the current field's name and caption. These flags are used to render the include std_display_field.

These flags are used for modifications at a deeper level. They are trickier to use, but can alter behavior in ways that the scoped flags cannot. To use them, customize the include compute_std_field_includes:

```
<@dynamichtml compute_std_field_includes@>
<$include super. compute_std_field_includes$>
<$include custom_modify_comments_definitions$>
```

```
<@end@>

<@dynamichtml custom_modify_comments_definitions@>
<$if isCheckin and fieldName like "xComments"$>
    <$fieldCaption = "Custom Comments Caption"$>
<$endif$>
<@end@>
```

The Content Server uses thousands of local variables in its templates and includes. Most are defined and used in the same include, whereas some are used in multiple includes. The 50 most commonly used local variables are listed in the following sections.

ClientControlled
Is set when the web page has been opened by a client application, such as Publisher or Site Studio. It is used to enable additional buttons and links that affect the client application when clicked.
Added In: 4.0

coreContentOnly
Set this flag in the URL of a service request to display only the form itself. The includes std_page_begin and std_page_end will not be displayed.
Added In: 4.0

defaultFieldInclude
Is set to the name of the default include used to display a metadata field. This include renders the field along with its caption in a HTML table row. It is typically std_namevalue_field. The field is displayed with this include unless fieldInclude or xFieldName:include is set.
Added In: 4.0

fieldCaption
The string HTML to display for this field. It is set in std_prepare_metafield_include and rendered in std_field_caption. It can also be directly set before calling std_display_field to show a custom field.
Added In: 4.0

fieldCaptionInclude
The name of the include used to display the caption for a metadata field. It is set in compute_std_field_includes and used in std_nameentry_row. It is usually std_field_caption.
Added In: 4.0

fieldEditWidth
The character width of the metadata input field on the HTML page. It is set in compute_namevalue_edit_widths, which is included in the resource compute_std_field_includes.
Added In: 4.0

fieldEntryInclude

The name of the include to use to display an input field for a metadata field. It is set in
compute_std_field_includes and used in std_nameentry_row. It is usually std_field_entry.
It can also be std_memo_entry, std_file_entry, or std_checkbox_entry.

Added In: 4.0

fieldExtraScriptInclude

The name of an include containing additional JavaScript validation for the specific metadata
field. Set in compute_std_field_includes.

Added In: 4.0

fieldInclude

The name of the include used to display the metadata field. It is usually std_namevalue_field,
but it can be set to another include as a last resort. It is usually set at the top of the page with
xFieldName:include, but it can also be set by overriding the resource
compute_std_field_includes.

Added In: 4.0

fieldIsOptionList

Is true if the metadata field has an option list. It is set in the include
std_prepare_metafield_include based on the ResultSet DocMetaDefinition.

Added In: 4.0

fieldMaxLength

The maximum length of the metadata field. It is not the size of the field, but the maximum
number of characters that the field can contain. It is usually set at the top of the page with
xFieldName:maxLength, but it can also be set by overriding the resource compute_std_field_includes.

Added In: 4.0

fieldName

The internal name of the field that is being displayed, such as dDocTitle or xComments. It is set based
on the values in the ResultSet DocMetaDefinition in the include std_prepare_metafield_include.
It can also be manually set before calling std_display_field to display a custom field on a Hypertext Content Server Page (HCSP).

Added In: 4.0

fieldOptionListType

If this field is an option list, this variable is set to the type of option list. It can be strict, combo,
multi, or multi2. It is set in the include std_prepare_metafield_include based on the values in
the ResultSet DocMetaDefinition.

Added In: 4.0

fieldType

The type of metadata field being displayed, such as Date, Int, Text, BigText, or Memo. It is set in the include std_prepare_metafield_include based on the values in the ResultSet DocMetaDefinition.

Added In: 4.0

HttpLayoutRoot

The URL to the folder containing the current layout files. Useful if you have additional JavaScript resources specific to the current layout.

Added In: 7.0

isAbsoluteCgi

When this flag is set, the URL to the HttpCgiPath will be fully qualified, meaning that it will have the full URL, including the hostname. It is useful when creating URLs for email messages or similar output that is not displayed in the content of a web page.

Added In: 3.0

isAbsoluteWeb

When this flag is set, all URLs returned by IdocScript functions will be treated as absolute, meaning that it will have the full URL, including the hostname. It is useful when creating full URLs for email messages or similar output that is not displayed in the content of a web page.

Added In: 3.0

isCheckin

Set to true on a check-in new or check-in selected page.

Added In: 4.0

isDocPage

Set to true when the current page is a check-in, search, content information, or update page.

Added In: 4.0

isEditMode

Set to true on update and check-in pages.

Added In: 4.0

isFieldExcluded

Set to true when the current field is excluded from display on the HTML page. It is usually set at the top of the page with xFieldName:isExcluded, but it can also be set by overriding the resource compute_std_field_includes.

Added In: 4.0

isFieldInfoOnly

Set to true when the current field will have only its data displayed. It is usually set at the top of the page with xFieldName:isInfoOnly, but it can also be set by overriding the resource compute_std_field_includes.

Added In: 4.0

isFormSubmit

Set to `true` on pages where metadata form submission is possible, like update, check-in, or search.

Added In: 4.0

isInfo

Set to `true` if the page is the content information page. It will cause the metadata fields to display their current value instead of an input field.

Added In: 4.0

IsJava

Similar to `IsSoap` and `IsXml`. Set to `true` in the URL of a service request to obtain a raw data response in HDA format. It is useful when inspecting the service response data.

Added In: 3.0

isNew

Set to `true` on a check-in page if the content item is new. It causes the `IdcService` to be `CHECKIN_NEW` on the page.

Added In: 4.0

isQuery

Set to `true` if the metadata page contains a search form. It alters the display of the metadata input fields so they are properly named on the search page.

Added In: 4.0

isRequired

Set to `true` if the current metadata field is required. It is used in `std_display_field` to alter the HTML elements and the JavaScript validation for a metadata field. It is usually set at the top of the page with `xFieldName:isRequired`, but it can also be set by overriding the resource `compute_std_field_includes`.

Added In: 4.0

IsSoap

Similar to `IsJava` and `IsXml`. Set to `true` in the URL of a service request to obtain a raw data response in SOAP-formatted XML. It is useful to inspect the data returned from a service call and for lightweight SOAP integrations.

Added In: 7.5

isUpdate

Set to `true` if the current page is the Information Update form, which is used to modify the metadata for a content item.

Added In: 4.0

isUploadFieldScript

Set to `true` when drawing validation JavaScript for metadata fields. It is set in the `HEAD` section of check-in, update, and search pages. When set, `fieldInclude` becomes `std_upload_field`. It has the JavaScript for validating metadata fields and making sure that required fields are non-empty. After the JavaScript has been drawn, this flag is set back to `null`.

Added In: 4.0

IsXml

Similar to `IsJava` and `IsSoap`. Set this to `true` in a URL to a HCSP or HCSF to obtain a raw data dump of the HTML form. It will return just the XML data contained in the form. It is useful for extracting form data, or submitting forms, from a remote application.

Added In: 7.0

requiredMsg

The required message for a custom metadata field. If the user submits the form without setting a value for this field, this warning message is displayed. It is set in `std_prepare_metafield_include`.

Added In: 4.0

ScriptDebugTrace

Set to `true` in the URL of a page to display a debug trace of the IdocScript resources. The output contains a list of all dynamic HTML resources included and where they are defined. It is useful when making a component to help track down which resources to override. The trace is output in the include `std_debug_report`, which is included in `std_page_end`. This flag is typically set in the URL to a page.

Added In: 4.0

ScriptErrorTrace

Set to `true` in the URL of a page to display a debug trace of IdocScript errors. It is similar to `ScriptDebugTrace`, but it outputs only IdocScript errors.

Added In: 4.0

StdPageWidth

The standard fixed width of the page. It is mostly deprecated in favor of the Layout Manager CSS files, but it is still used on certain input forms.

Added In: 3.0

useLayoutManager

Is `true` if the user's browser supports JavaScript and CSS sufficiently to use the Layout Manager API.

Added In: 7

Scoped Local Variables

These are a special kind of local variable, which are used to override how metadata is drawn to the page. These variables are scoped to a specific metadata field by separating them with the colon. For example, to hide the title and comments fields, you would set the flags:

```
dDocTitle:isHidden=1
xComments:isHidden=1
```

These flags must be set early in the page—for example, in the URL or by overriding the include std_doc_page_definitions. In the following list, all flags affect the display of the field xFieldName:

xFieldName:groupHeader

Set in Content Profiles if this field is the first field in a group. If so, the group of metadata fields contains a chunk of HTML that visually separates them from the other fields. This variable contains the HTML to display for this group, which is drawn to the page immediately before the field is drawn.

Added In: 7.5

xFieldName:hasOptionList

Enables the field to contain a custom option list instead of using the default option list. Must be used with the flags xFieldName:optionListName or xFieldName:optionListScript.

Added In: 7.5

xFieldName:include

Used (rarely) to set the value for fieldInclude to the name of a custom resource include. This resource is used all over the page, including the JavaScript and the HTML. If needed, use the include std_namevalue_field as a guide for making a custom include.

Added In: 4.0

xFieldName:isExcluded

Set to true to exclude a field from the page completely. It is not displayed as a field or as a hidden input field. The field will be completely absent from the page.

Added In: 4.0

xFieldName:isHidden

Set to true to hide a field on the page. On pages with form posts, the field is still present. However, it exists only as a hidden INPUT field. The value of the field is blank unless xFieldName or fieldValue is defined. Hiding a field enables you to create pages with default values that cannot be changed with the web form.

Added In: 4.0

xFieldName:isInfoOnly

Set to true to display only the value of a field. It is used instead of xFieldName:isHidden to show the user what default values are being submitted.

Added In: 4.0

xFieldName:isRelocated

Set to true to stop the automatic display of a field on the HTML page. By default, all fields on the page have a specific order. To reorder them, you must set this flag and then display the field manually.

```
<!-- hide the comments field -->
<$xComments:isRelocated = 1$>
<$loop DocMetaDefinition$>
    <$strTrimWs(inc("std_meta_field_display"))$>
<$endloop$>

<!-- now turn off relocation, and display it -->
<$xComments:isRelocated = ""$>
<$fieldName="xComments", fieldCaption="Comments", fieldType="Memo"$>
<$include std_display_field$>
```

    Added In: 4.0

xFieldName:isRequired

Set to true to turn this field into a required field. This flag must be set in std_doc_page_definitions before the JavaScript validation code is drawn to the page.

    Added In: 7.5

xFieldName:maxLength

Similar to fieldWidth, sets the maximum length of a text input field. It is usually greater than fieldWidth and must be less than the width of the field in the database.

    Added In: 4.0

xFieldName:noSchema

Set to true to disable a schema option list for a field. Required if you want to generate option lists in a custom dynamic way.

    Added In: 7.1

xFieldName:optionListName

Can be set only if a field is an option list. You can override which option list to use to display values:

```
<$xCountry:hasOptionList = 1$>
<$xCountry:noSchema = 1$>
<$xCountry:optionListName = "securityGroups"$>
<$loop DocMetaDefinition$>
    <$strTrimWs(inc("std_meta_field_display"))$>
<$endloop$>
```

    Added In: 7.5

xFieldName:optionListScript

Similar to optionListName, except can be used to render IdocScript instead of explicitly defined option lists. It allows the option list to be drawn with a ResultSet instead:

```
<$xCountry:hasOptionList = 1$>
<$xCountry:noSchema = 1$>
<$xCountry:optionListScript =
        "<$rsMakeFromList('GROUPS', 'securityGroups')$>" &
        "<select>\n" &
        "<$loop GROUPS$>" &
        "  <option><$row$>" &
        "<$endloop$>\n" &
        "</select>"$>
<$loop DocMetaDefinition$>
    <$strTrimWs(inc("std_meta_field_display"))$>
<$endloop$>
```

Added In: 4.0

xFieldName:rowClass

Used in std_nameentry_row. It sets a CSS class for the table row that contains this field:

```
<$xComments:rowClass="xuiPageTitleText"$>
<$loop DocMetaDefinition$>
    <$strTrimWs(inc("std_meta_field_display"))$>
<$endloop$>
```

Added In: 7.5

xFieldName:rowStyle

Same as rowClass, but can be used to create inline styles. For example, to hide the Comments field with DHTML, use this:

```
<$xComments:rowStyle="display:none"$>
<$loop DocMetaDefinition$>
    <$strTrimWs(inc("std_meta_field_display"))$>
<$endloop$>
```

It is useful when you want to hide and display fields dynamically without a page reload.
Added In: 7.5

APPENDIX D

■ ■ ■

Dynamic HTML Resource Includes

The majority of the Content Server's user interface is in dynamichtml resource includes, which are defined in the resource files:

```
stellent/shared/config/resources/std_page.htm
stellent/shared/config/resources/std_schema.htm
```

Resources can be overridden in a component or in an IdocScript resource file. See Chapters 2, 6, and 7 for examples.

To alter the look and feel, the first step is to determine which include you need to modify, which can be difficult because there are more than 500 resources. The next step is to place the parameter ScriptDebugTrace=1 in the URL of the web page, which creates a dump of all the dynamichtml resources used and where they are defined. You can use this trace output, along with the definitions in std_page.htm, to determine which include to modify. The HTML source of the page is also important, as is the IdocScript function trace. See Chapter 9 for step-by-step examples of tracking down resources.

This appendix covers the most commonly used resources and in which version of the Content Server they were added. Most components override at least one of the resources in this appendix. Many components do not need to override anything else. Be sure to always use the super tag when overriding these resources.

body_def
Used on most pages to define the HTML BODY tag. Override it to add a global header.
Added In: 3.0

body_def_internal
Similar to body_def, it is used on pages in which additional attributes are needed in the BODY tag, such as onLoad event handlers on check-in pages.
Added In: 3.0

checkin_page_content

Used on the check-in new, check-in selected, and update pages, which displays the main content of these pages. Which kind of page to display is determined by the flags set in the individual templates.

Added In: 4.0

compute_std_field_includes

Called before displaying anything with std_display_field, it is used to determine which include to use to display the metadata field. It sets local variables to the names of includes to display; for example, setting fieldEntryInclude to std_memo_field for memo fields. It also sets the names of the option lists and schema views.

Added In: 4.0

compute_std_field_overrides

Used to override the default flags before compute_std_field_includes is called, it is the place to use local variables such as isFieldHidden to modify metadata display.

Added In: 4.0

custom_checkin_list_action_popup

The action popup for individual content items on the list of checked-out items page. Modify this include to add new action pop-ups, such as emailing the contributor who last checked-out the item.

Added In: 7.0

custom_docinfo_doc_options

The actions drop-down list on the content information page. It allows the user to perform actions for the item, such as check-in, check-out, or subscribe.

Added In: 7.0

custom_finish_layout_init

Used to alter the navigation items with the Layout Manager API. Override this include to add new menu items, or rearrange existing ones.

Added In: 7.0

custom_js_bootstrap_vars

Included in std_js_bootstrap_vars. This include takes IdocScript variables and places them in JavaScript variables so they can be used in the Layout Manager API to display different menus to different users.

Added In: 7.0

custom_layout_script_links

Override this to add a link to a static JavaScript resource on all pages.

Added In: 7.0

custom_query_results_options

Custom search options and buttons to add to the search page.
>Added In: 7.5

custom_search_results_action_popup

The action popup for individual content items on the search results page. Override it to add a new popup action, such as running a new service with just this content item.
>Added In: 7.0

custom_searchapi_result_options

The actions drop-down on the search results page. It allows the user to act on the search result. For example, the user can save the search or refine the search terms.
>Added In: 7.0

custom_subscription_action_popup

The action popup for individual content items on the subscription pages.
>Added In: 7.0

custom_wips_list_action_popup

The action popup for individual content items on the work-in-progress page.
>Added In: 7.0

custom_workflow_action_popup

The action popup for individual content items on the workflow pages. Override it to add new workflow actions for content items.
>Added In: 7.0

info_page_content

Contains the main content of the content info page.
>Added In: 4

query_page_content

Contains all the forms and metadata fields for displaying the search page
>Added In: 4.0

query_results_options

The options at the bottom of the search page, which specify how to sort the results and how many results to return.
>Added In: 4.0

searchapi_define_includes_for_result

Sets the flags used in `searchapi_result_section`. In Content Server 7.5, the results can be displayed in one of four views: *Thumbnail*, *Headline*, *My View*, and *Classic*. Each uses up to four different includes to display the results. Use it to see which include to override for each view.
>Added In: 7.0

searchapi_result_html_head_declarations
Included in the HTML HEAD element on the search results page. This contains JavaScript used to save the search, or refine it.
    Added In: 4.0

searchapi_result_doc_href_start
Generates the link to the content item used on the search results page. It typically links to the web viewable file. It might also link to a converted document, a service to do text highlighting, or to another server.
    Added In: 3.0

searchapi_result_page_content
Contains the bulk of the contents of the search results page.
    Added In: 4.0

searchapi_result_section
Contains the main table that displays the search results.
    Added In: 4.0

show_std_field
The standard include used to display a metadata field. The include compute_std_field_includes must be called before including it or else all the required variables must be set manually. This include takes all the flags defined in compute_std_field_includes and displays the JavaScript and HTML needed for this field to be displayed.
    Added In: 4.0

std_checkbox_field
Use instead of std_display_field to display a checkbox. It usually displays the include std_checkbox_entry.
    Added In: 4.0

std_checkin_html_head_declarations
Contains JavaScript functions and IdocScript flags needed to display a check-in page.
    Added In: 4.0

std_checkin_submit_extra_actions
Contains custom form submit buttons and parameters for the check-in and update services.
    Added In: 4.0

std_checkin_submit_html
Contains the form submit buttons on the check-in and update pages.
    Added In: 4.0

std_definitions
Contains definitions of IdocScript variables that are present on all pages, such as the known image files, and the page width. Used mainly for Classic mode. In 7.0 and higher, most of these definitions are in Cascading Style Sheets (CSS) files.
    Added In: 3.0

std_display_field
Used to display any metadata field besides the checkbox or file upload fields.
    Added In: 4.0

std_doc_page_definitions
Contains definitions of IdocScript variables that are present on all document pages, including the search and check-in pages. It is the place to set global IdocScript variables such as dDocTitle:isHidden to affect metadata display. The flags isInfo and isCheckin can be used to conditionally set global flags.
    Added In: 4.0

std_document_checkin_fields
Contains all the metadata fields displayed on the check-in and update pages. It is generally not overridden in an include. Instead, override one of the includes referenced in this include to add a custom form field.
    Added In: 4.0

std_field_cleanup
After displaying a metadata field with std_display_field, it is used to clear all temporary IdocScript flags. For example, the flags fieldName and isFieldHidden are reset to blank (NULL) so that they do not affect the display of the next metadata field.
    Added In: 4.0

std_html_head_declarations
Contains the contents of the HTML HEAD element that is present on all pages and includes several important variable definitions. It is included on almost all pages.
    Added In: 4.0

std_info_html_head_declarations
Contains code that belongs in the HTML HEAD element of the content info page. It contains JavaScript needed in the action options.
    Added In: 4.0

std_js_bootstrap_vars
Used by the Layout Manager API, it maps a handful of important IdocScript flags (HttpCgiPath, UserName) to JavaScript variables so they can be used to build the navigation with pure JavaScript.
    Added In: 7.0

std_meta_field_display
Used to display a metadata field when looping over the DocMetaDefinition result set.
> Added In: 4.0

std_meta_fields
Loops over custom metadata and displays values or form fields. It is included on search, update, check-in, and content info pages.
> Added In: 4.0

std_page_begin
Used at the beginning of every Content Server page, it draws the HTML navigation links or the beginning wrapper for the Layout Manager.
> Added In: 3.0

std_page_end
Used at the end of every Content Server page to close any tags opened in std_page_begin.
> Added In: 3.0

std_query_html_head_declarations
Contains the code in the HTML HEAD element of the standard search page. It contains all the JavaScript needed to assemble the QueryText and submit the search.
> Added In: 4.0

std_query_page_search_fields
Contains all the metadata fields displayed on the search page. It is generally not overridden in an include. Instead, override one of the includes referenced in this include to add a custom form field.
> Added In: 7.0

std_style_declarations
Contains CSS information for all pages. It is deprecated in 7.0 in favor of the Layout Manager API.
> Added In: 4.0

std_update_html_head_declarations
Contains JavaScript functions and IdocScript flags needed for the update service.
> Added In: 4.0

std_upload_validation
Contains code to validate a metadata field on a check-in page. It can be customized to add client-side JavaScript validation.
> Added In: 4.0

■ ■ ■

Stellent Services

As mentioned in Chapter 2, services are the core of the Content Server architecture. This appendix contains information about commonly used services, including a list of parameters that they require and the data they return. For a full list of services, refer to the *Services Reference Guide*.

Most services are executed with a browser request. The browser connects to a web server that runs a special plug-in that authenticates the user and forwards the request to the Content Server. For example, to run a search for all items in the system, you can use a URL similar to this:

```
http://localhost/stellent/idcplg?IdcService=GET_SEARCH_RESULTS&QueryText=
```

This URL runs the GET_SEARCH_RESULTS service. The result data is rendered with the default IdocScript template for this service. You can alter how the results are rendered with the optional parameters IsJava, urlTemplate, docTemplateName, or docTemplateID. These parameters are discussed in Chapter 2 and demonstrated in Chapters 3 and 4.

Other services require a HTML form POST to be executed. For example, a check-in request alters the state of the Content Server repository, so it must be called with a POST. The action parameter on the form is the URL to the web server plug-in:

```
http://localhost/stellent/idcplg
```

After the request is processed, the Content Server redirects the user to a confirmation page, which ensures that the user can refresh the result page without reposting the request. These services are called *redirectable*. The request parameters RedirectUrl and RedirectParams can be used to redirect to a different confirmation page. These parameters are also discussed in Chapters 2, 3, and 4.

Not all services require a specially formatted URL. Some can be executed directly on a Dynamic Server Page with the IdocScript function executeService. These services are called *scriptable*. After running the service, the page is automatically populated with the response data. For example, to run a search you can use the following script in a Hypertext Content Server Template (HCST):

```
<$QueryText = "dDocTitle <substring> `test`"$>
<$executeService("GET_SEARCH_RESULTS")$>
<$loop SearchResults$>
    <a href="<$URL$>"><$dDocTitle$></a><br>
<$endloop$>
```

A typical service request will return an HTML-formatted page. By specifying `IsJava=1` in the request, you can also obtain a raw data response. This method is used by remote applications to process requests and receive raw data responses.

Following are descriptions of the most commonly used services and the Content Server version when they were added. The returned data is important if you want to modify the result pages or execute this service from a remote application.

Top 50 Services

CHECK_USER_CREDENTIALS

Called during the authentication process. It is called by the web server if it cannot authenticate the user with NTLM. It causes the Content Server to authenticate the user with the currently enabled user providers. For example, it is used to extract a user's credentials out of LDAP before running a request. This data is cached, so it is not called for every service request.

Added In: 4.0

Required Parameter:

`username`: The name of the user

Optional Parameters:

`getUserInfo`: Boolean flag; `true` if you want the extended user info

`hasSecurityInfo`: Is `true` if the security info is present in the request

`authenticateUser`: Boolean flag; `true` if you want to authenticate the user

`userPassword`: The password to authenticate

`userExtendedInfo`: The extended info that we currently know, in an HDA-encoded string

Results:

`isAuthenticated`: Is `true` if the password is valid

`accounts`: A comma-separated list of accounts the user can access

`roles`: A comma-separated list of roles the user has

`hasSecurityInfo`: Is `true` if the security information is present in the response

`extendedInfo`: An HDA-encoded string of extended user information

CHECKIN_LIST

Displays a list of items currently checked-out. From the response page, you can undo a checkout, or check the items back in.

Added In: 3.0

Execution Flags: Scriptable

Optional Parameter:

userOnly: Boolean flag; true to show only the content items checked-out by the current user

Results:

CHECKIN_LIST: A ResultSet of all items checked-out and their metadata

CHECKIN_CACHES: A ResultSet of all items that are in a cached check-in state

CHECKIN_NEW

This common service will check-in an initial revision of a new content item. The item must have a unique value for dDocName if specified in the request. After a successful check-in, it redirects to a confirmation page. This page contains links to the content information page and a link to check-in a similar item.

Added In: 3.0

Execution Flags: Redirectable

Required Parameters:

dDocAccount: The security account for this item. This parameter is required only if accounts are enabled.

dDocAuthor: The author of this item. This parameter is set to the name of the user who processed the request. If the user has administrator privileges, it can be set to a different user's name.

dDocName: The content name for this item. If the IsAutoNumber feature is enabled, this parameter is optional.

dDocTitle: A descriptive title for this content item.

dDocType: The content type of this item.

dSecurityGroup: The security group for this content item.

primaryFile: The path to the file to check-in. This parameter is used to extract the filename and its extension. The Content Server determines how to process it after it is in the repository. For a web browser request, the file is encoded and sent in the request. For a request using IdcCommand or the Batchloader, the parameter primaryFile:path should be used instead.

Optional Parameters:

alternateFile: If present, the alternateFile will be processed by the search engine and the refinery instead of the primaryFile. The web viewable file is also based on the alternateFile. It is useful if the primaryFile is a very large binary file or contains no searchable text.

createAlternateMetaFile: This option is available if the configuration flag AllowAlternateMetaFile is enabled. If this flag is true, an alternate file will be generated upon check-in based on the metadata for this item.

createPrimaryMetaFile: This option is available if the configuration flag AllowPrimaryMetaFile is enabled. If this flag is true, the primaryFile is no longer a required parameter. Instead, a placeholder file is created based on the check-in metadata. This placeholder file can be overwritten at a future date from the Update Content Information page.

dFormat: This option is available on the HTML page if the configuration flag IsOverrideFormat is enabled. It allows the user to explicitly set the format of a content item upon check-in. It is useful for clients on Apple or Unix systems, in which file extensions are less common.

dInDate: The release date for this item, which is the date when the item will be available for public consumption. Typically it is set to the same date as the check-in.

dOutDate: The expiration date for this item. After this date, this revision is removed from the search collection, but still exists in the repository.

dRevLabel: The human readable revision label. This is usually an incrementing number, but can also contain letters.

Custom Metadata: For example, the custom metadata field comments can be set by passing the parameter xComments in the request. Custom metadata fields are optional, unless explicitly configured to be required.

Results:

dConversion: If this item was processed by the refinery, this flag contains information about what specific conversion occurred.

dID: The content ID of the new item.

IsWorkflow: This flag is true if the item went into a workflow upon check-in.

CHECKIN_NEW_FORM

Loads the metadata configuration for the Content Server and displays a page for checking in new content.

Added In: 3.0

Execution Flags: Scriptable

Results:

DocTypes: A ResultSet of all known content types in the server

DocFormats: A ResultSet of all known formats in the server, such as application/msword

OptionLists for all metadata fields that are option lists

CHECKIN_SEL

Same as CHECKIN_NEW, except it is for checking in items that were previously checked-out.
Added In: 3.0

Execution Flags: Redirectable

Required Parameters:

Same as CHECKIN_NEW

dDocName: The content name of this item is always required.

Optional Parameters:

Same as CHECKIN_NEW

isFinished: If this item was checked-out for a workflow, this flag must be passed in as true to trigger the next step.

Results:

Same as CHECKIN_NEW

CHECKIN_SEL_FORM

Same as CHECKIN_NEW_FORM, except it is for items previously checked-out. It loads the current content information for the item. The form page will be displayed with the old metadata information.
Added In: 3.0

Execution Flags: Scriptable

Required Parameter:

dID: The content ID for the checked-out item

Results:

Same as CHECKIN_NEW_FORM

DOC_INFO: A ResultSet containing the content information of the previous revision

IsWorkflow: Set to true if this item is in a workflow

DocUrl: The relative URL to this content item

CurRevCheckoutUser: The name of the user who checked-out this item

CurRevIsCheckedOut: Is true if this is the revision that is currently checked-out

CHECKIN_SIMILAR_FORM

Similar to CHECKIN_NEW_FORM. Loads up the metadata of an existing item and renders a check-in new page. This causes the check-in form to have its metadata values prefilled to match the values of the existing item.

Added In: 6.0

Execution Flags: Scriptable

Required Parameters:

dID: The content ID for the similar item

Results:

Same as CHECKIN_NEW FORM

DOC_INFO_SIMILAR: A ResultSet containing a subset of the similar item's metadata

CHECKIN_UNIVERSAL

Similar to CHECKIN_NEW and CHECKIN_SEL. This is used as a generic check-in service that runs the check-in that is appropriate for the item's current state. If an item with the same dDocName is found and is checked-out, a new revision will be checked-in. If no matching dDocName is found, a new content item is checked-in.

Added In: 6.0

Execution Flags: Redirectable

Required Parameters:

Same as CHECKIN_NEW and CHECKIN_SEL

Optional Parameters:

Same as CHECKIN_NEW and CHECKIN_SEL

Results:

Same as CHECKIN_NEW and CHECKIN_SEL

CHECKOUT

Checks out the latest revision of a content item. It then redirects with the CHECKOUT_OK service. Requires the specific dID for the item. If it is unknown, use the CHECKOUT_BY_NAME service instead.

Added In: 3.0

Execution Flags: Scriptable, Redirectable

Required Parameter:

dID: The content ID of the item to check-out

Results:

Common Metadata fields: dDocName, dDocAccount, dRevLabel, dReleaseState, dPublishState, dIsCheckedOut

CurRevCheckoutUser: The user who checked-out the current item

CurRevID: The current content ID

CurRevIsCheckedOut: Boolean flag for if the current revision is already checked-out, for error handling

IsNotLatestRev: Boolean flag, true if this item is too old to check-out, for error handling

IsWorkflow: Boolean flag for if this item is in a workflow

CHECKOUT_OK

After checking out an item, this service is called to display the check-out confirmation page. It contains confirmation information about the item, as well as links used to check it back.
Added In: 4.0

Execution Flags: Scriptable

Required Parameters:

dID: The content ID of the checked-out item

CurRevID: The ID of the current revision, usually the same as dID

CurRevCheckoutUser: The user who checked it out

Results:

DOC_INFO: A ResultSet containing metadata information about this item

DELETE_REV

Deletes a specific revision of a content item. You cannot delete an item if it is in a workflow. If all revisions of this item are deleted, it redirects to a message page. Otherwise, it redirects to the DOC_INFO service.
Added In: 3.0

Execution Flags: Redirectable

Required Parameter:

dID: The content ID of the item to delete

Results:

DOC_INFO: If more revisions of this item exist, it contains the metadata for the most recent item.

isAllRevisionsDeleted: Is true if no revisions exist for this item.

DOC_INFO

Displays the metadata and state for a specific content item. It includes information about other revisions, limited workflow information, and whether or not the user is subscribed to the item.

Added In: 3.0

Execution Flags: Scriptable

Required Parameter:

dID: The content ID for the item

Results:

DOC_INFO: A ResultSet containing metadata information about this item.

REVISION_HISTORY: A ResultSet of all revisions of this item, containing a minor amount of metadata.

WF_INFO: If this item is in a workflow, it contains information about which workflow, which step, and its status. For more complete information, run GET_WORKFLOW_INFO_BYNAME.

AuthorAddress: The email address of the original author, if known.

DocUrl: The full URL to the content item.

dSubscriptionAlias: If the user is subscribed to this item, the value is the username.

dSubscriptionID: The name of the kind of subscription. Either the content name of the item or the value of the metadata field that defines the subscription.

dSubscriptionType: The name of the subscription type: either Basic or a custom name given in the Repository Manager.

DOC_INFO_BY_NAME

Same as DOC_INFO, except that it accepts dDocName as a parameter instead of dID. It always returns the content information for the most recent item. Mainly useful for links in content items themselves. For example, it is useful when dealing with scenarios in which you only have the dDocName parameter. It is also useful to always show the content information of the most recent item.

Added In: 4.0

Execution Flags: Scriptable

Required Parameter:

dDocName: Content name of the item

Optional Parameter:

RevisionSelectionMethod: Can be Latest to get the most recent item or LatestReleased to get the most recent released item. An item is not released until it is out of workflow.

Results:

Same as DOC_INFO

DOC_INFO_SIMPLE

Similar to DOC_INFO, but does not load up the workflow information or subscription information. The service is then faster and is mostly used by external applications.

Added In: 4.0

Execution Flags: Scriptable

Required Parameter:

dID: The content ID of the item

Results:

Same as DOC_INFO, but without workflow or subscription ResultSets

DOC_SUBS_LIST

Returns a list of content items that would be included in a specific subscription. For criteria-based subscriptions, returns all items that match the criteria. For Basic subscriptions, returns the content item with a dDocName that matches dSubscriptionID.

Added In: 4.0

Execution Flags: Scriptable

Required Parameters:

dSubscriptionID: The name of the kind of subscription. This is either the content name of the item or the value of the metadata field that defines the subscription.

dSubscriptionType: The name of the subscription type. Either Basic or a custom name given in the Repository Manager.

Results:

DOCUMENT_LIST: A ResultSet of document metadata for items matching the subscription type and ID

USER_SUBSCRIPTION: A ResultSet of the subscription info for this user

EDIT_USER_PROFILE

Saves the current user's personalized settings, such as email address and password. Cannot be used to change the security credentials of the user. Any optional parameter passed in the request has its value updated. All other values remain the same. After a submission, it is typically redirected to the HOME_PAGE.

Added In: 4.0

Execution Flags: Redirectable

Required Parameter:

dName: The username of the current user.

Optional Parameters:

Layout: The Layout Manager API layout to use (7.0+).

Skin: The Layout Manager API skin to use (7.0+).

XuiSearchTemplate: The template to use for the search results pages (7.0+).

dEmail: The new email address for this user.

dFullName: The new full name for this user.

dPassword: The new password for this user.

dUserLocale: The new locale for this user.

dUserType: The customized user type. This and all other Information Fields defined in the User Admin applet can be modified in this service.

emailFormatList: Set to html for HTML-based emails or text for text-based emails.

numTopics: The number of additional personalization topics in this request.

topicString1: An encoded string of a personalization topic to update. See Chapter 9 for examples of encoded strings.

Results:

Nothing

GET_ACTIVE_WORKFLOWS

Returns the Active Workflows page. From here a user can select a workflow and view all documents in that workflow.

Added In: 4.0

Execution Flags: Scriptable

Required Parameters:

None

Results:

ClbraWorkflows: Contains the ResultSet of collaboration workflows if the collaboration server is enabled.

StdWorkflows: The ResultSet of workflows, including name, ID, and description.

GET_ADMIN_PAGE

Renders a template page in a manner similar to GET_DOC_PAGE. However, it does not load the server's configuration. In addition, it is restricted to administrative users. You must have the admin role or subadmin rights to run this service.
Added In: 3.0

Execution Flags: None

Required Parameters:

Action: The action to perform; almost always GetTemplatePage

Page: The name of the template page to load

GET_DOC_METADATA_INFO

Returns the list of custom metadata fields. Used mainly by remote applications to configure search pages.
Added In: 7.5

Execution Flags: Scriptable

Required Parameters:

None

Results:

DocMetaDefinition: A ResultSet of the metadata field definitions, including captions and field types

DocTypes: A ResultSet of all content types supported in the server

Accounts: An OptionList of default accounts for this user

SecurityGroups: An OptionList of security groups to which this user has read access

GET_DOC_PAGE

Loads some server configuration data and renders a specified IdocScript template. Used in conjunction with the IdocScript functions `loadDocMetaDefinition` and `loadDocumentProfile` to render several core pages. For example, to obtain the standard search page, use this service with the `STANDARD_QUERY_PAGE` template.

Added In: 3.0

Execution Flags: Scriptable

Required Parameters:

`Action`: The action to perform; almost always `GetTemplatePage`

`Page`: The name of the template page to load

Results:

`DocFormats`: A `ResultSet` of all content formats supported in the server

`DocTypes`: A `ResultSet` of all content types supported in the server

GET_DYNAMIC_CONVERSION

Dynamically converts a content item into text. The output is typically HTML or XML, but others are possible. It works only if a Dynamic Converter template has been created for the format of this content item, which can be done from the administration page.

This service is available if the Dynamic Converter component is installed and enabled. A limited subset is also available if the flag `IsDynamicConverterEnabled` is set to `true`. See Appendix C for a discussion of Dynamic Converter flags.

Added In: 5.0

Execution Flags: Scriptable

Required Parameter:

`dID`: The content ID of the item to convert into text (HTML or XML)

Optional Parameter:

`conversionTemplate`: The content name of an item checked-into the server that will be used as a template for dynamic conversion. If not set, the conversion is based on the resource include `conversion_template_computation`.

Results:

The result page from a browser is the converted content in text format. If executed from a remote server, the following data is available:

`DCConversions`: A result set of all supported conversions and the metadata used to trigger them

`DOC_INFO`: A `ResultSet` containing metadata information about this item

DocFormats: The content formats supported in the Content Server

DocTypes: The content types supported in the Content Server

FileFormat: The format of this item, typically application/msword

inputFilePath: The file path to the content item being converted

outputFilePath: The file path to the location where the converted file will be placed

outputRelativePath: The relative web URL used to view this item

templateFilePath: The template file used to convert the input to the output

templateName: The content name of the template file

GET_DYNAMIC_PAGE

Returns a page from the library folders. They are portal pages with links to content, database reports, and predefined queries. These pages are configured with the Web Layout Editor applet.

Added In: 3.0

Execution Flags: Scriptable

Required Parameters

PageName: The name of the library page, such as index

Results:

LinkList: A ResultSet of all the links on this page and what kind of links they are: queries, external links, reports, or local pages containing more links.

PageMap: A ResultSet containing the links this page makes to other local pages.

HeaderText: The header text for this page. It can contain IdocScript.

PageTitle: The title for this page. It can also contain IdocScript.

PageType: The type of page.

PageUrl: The URL to this page. Used for back buttons on subdirectories.

restrictByAccount: Boolean flag to restrict queries according to account.

restrictByGroup: Boolean flag to restrict queries by security group.

GET_DYNAMIC_URL

Returns an arbitrary web viewable file from the Content Server. It can return any web file in the weblayout directory for the Content Server, including content checked-into the repository, as well as any support files located in the weblayout directory.

It is typically called from the web plug-in to render a Hypertext Content Server Page (HCSP) or a Java Server Page (JSP). When the web server is on a separate machine from the Content Server, it calls this service to obtain every web file. This service is also frequently used by remote applications to obtain web files.

When used to obtain a Dynamic Server Page, the service returns a limited amount of server configuration. It also returns a small amount of content information for the Dynamic Server Page. For any other file, this information is not available.

Added In: 4.0

Execution Flags: Scriptable

Required Parameter:

fileUrl: The relative URL for the item. This item need not be checked-into the Content Server. It can be a JavaScript file for Schema or the Layout Manager. It can be an image from the images directory.

Results:

DocFormats: A ResultSet of the content formats supported in the Content Server.

DocTypes: A ResultSet of the content types supported in the Content Server.

ref:dDocAccount: The security account for this item.

ref:dDocName: The content name for this content item.

ref:dDocType: The content type of this content item.

ref:dExtension: The file extension for this item. Usually hcst, hcsp, hcsf, or jsp.

ref:dSecurityGroup: The security group for this content item.

ref:hasDocInfo: Boolean flag, set to true if the other ref: flags are set.

ref:isLatestRevision: Boolean flag, true if this item is the most recent revision.

SourceID: The content ID for this item if it is an HCSP or an HCSF.

HCSP and HCSF metadata: If the fileUrl points to an HCSP or HCSF in the Content Server, all the XML data for the file is available in the response—including any custom XML between the idcbegindata and idcenddata sections. See Chapter 5 for more examples.

GET_EXPIRED
Returns a list of expired and expiring items in the Content Server. During a check-in, a user can set an Out Date, after which the content item is no longer considered to be released. After that, it is still present in the Content Server repository, but you will not be able to find it with the search engine. This service can be used to find these expired items and to search for items that will expire soon.

Added In: 3.0

Execution Flags: Redirectable

Required Parameters:

None

Optional Parameters:

endDate: Items expiring before this date will be displayed

isExpiredQuery: Boolean flag, true if searching just for expired content

startDate: Items expiring after this date will be displayed

Results:

EXPIRED_LIST: A ResultSet containing the metadata for expired content items

GET_FILE

Returns the specified content item. Used to obtain the web viewable rendition, the native rendition from the vault.

Added In: 3.0

Execution Flags: Scriptable

Required Parameters:

dID: The content ID of the item to download. If it is set, dDocName is optional. RevisionSelectionMethod is assumed to be Specific.

dDocName: The content name of the item to download. If it is set, dID is not needed.

RevisionSelectionMethod: Decides which revision to download: Specific, Latest, or LatestReleased. For Specific, the dDocName is ignored, and the dID is used. For Latest, the most recent revision is returned. For LatestReleased, the most recent released version is returned. The last one is typically used, which ensures that you avoid downloading items still in workflow.

Optional Parameters:

allowInterrupt: Suppresses an error if the user cancels the file download.

Rendition: The name of the rendition to download. Several renditions are possible, depending on which components are enabled. Common ones are Primary, Web, and Alternate. For Primary, which is the default, it downloads the native rendition from the vault. For Web, it downloads the refined document in the weblayout directory, typically a PDF. For Alternate, it downloads the alternate file that was checked-in with the Primary file.

Results:

The requested file

GET_SECURE_PAGE

Same as GET_DOC_PAGE, but this page is restricted to users with write permission to at least one group. Useful for obtaining check-in pages.

Added In: 4.0

Execution Flags: Scriptable

Required Parameter:

Same as GET_DOC_PAGE

Results:

Same as GET_DOC_PAGE

GET_SCHEMA_VIEW_FRAGMENT

Returns a fragment of a schema-based option list. This fragment can either be the entire option list or a partial option list. The partial option lists are used when the field is part of a Dynamic Choice List (DCL). It means that the values in the list are dependent on the values of another parent field.

Unlike most services, it returns a JavaScript file instead of an HTML file. This file is used by a schema to dynamically load option list values.

Added In: 7.5

Execution Flags: None

Required Parameter:

schViewName: Name of the schema view, such as docTypes or City_View

Optional Parameters:

schRelationName: If this field is a DCL, it is the name of the schema relation used to filter the values in the schema view. For example, a view containing all cities (City_View) can use a relation with states or countries to limit the number of entries.

schParentValue: If this field is a DCL, this is the value of the parent field used with the relation to filter the option list.

Results:

A ResultSet with the same name as schViewName. Contains a data dump of the view. The parameters in this ResultSet are dependent on how the view was configured.

schInternalColumn: The name of a column in the preceding ResultSet. It corresponds to the internally stored value for the option list items.

schLabelColumn: The name of a column in the preceding ResultSet. It corresponds to the label for the option list items.

GET_SEARCH_RESULTS

Runs a search for content items that match a specific criterion (for example, all items in a specific security group or all that have the word test in their title). Depending on the search engine used, you can run searches for text inside the content items.

By default, the Content Server appends a security clause to the query passed in by the user, ensuring that the user sees only items that they have access to. For example, a guest user can be restricted to items in the Public security group.

In general, short queries run faster than long queries, and exact matches are faster than substring matches. If you have performance issues on your templates or Site Studio pages, you should consider optimizing your queries.

Added In: 3.0

Execution Flags: Scriptable

Required Parameter:

QueryText: The query string to use to run the search. It is different depending on the search engine used. For example, to search for all items with test in the title with Verity, the syntax is: dDocTitle <substring> `test`.

Optional Parameters:

dDocAccount: If present in the request, the Content Server searches only for items in this account. Use it to boost performance with slow queries if you have a complex security model.

dSecurityGroup: If present in the request, the Content Server only searches for items in this security group. Use it to boost performance with slow queries if you have a complex security model.

SortField: The metadata field to sort values with. For an alphabetized list, sort on dDocTitle. For a chronological list, sort on dInDate.

SortOrder: The order to sort the item with. It can be Asc for ascending or Desc for descending.

StartRow: Used for search results that occupy several pages. Used to determine where to start displaying results.

SortSpec: A comma-separated list of field-order pairs used to sort the data in several ways. For example, to sort items by security group and then by date, set it to dSecurityGroup Asc, dInDate Desc.

ResultCount: The number of results to display per page, usually set to about 20. It is not recommended to set it above 1000 when using Verity.

SearchEngineName: The name of the search engine to use for the request. If this value is set to DATABASE, the QueryText can be written with SQL syntax; for example, dDocTitle like '*test*'. It enables you to change search engines dynamically, if needed. For example, if a query is faster in SQL than Verity, run it in SQL with this flag.

PageNumber: Has no effect on the search itself. It is conventionally used to help display the proper data on search results that span multiple pages.

Results:

EnterpriseSearchResults: A ResultSet containing information about which Content Servers were searched in this query. It also contains the names of the ResultSets that contain the results for each search. The default name is SearchResults.

NavigationPages: A ResultSet containing information about the result pages. It is present only if multiple pages of results are available.

SearchResults: The ResultSet containing the metadata about the documents matching the criteria. Does not contain state information, such as who has the item checked-out— that requires a DOC_INFO service call. It contains all custom metadata, as well as the following fields: AlternateFileSize, AlternateFormat, dDocAccount, dDocAuthor, dDocName, dDocTitle, dDocType, dExtension, dFormat, dGif, dID, dInDate, dOriginalName, dOutDate, dPublishType, dRendition1, dRendition2, dRevisionID, dRevLabel, dSecurityGroup, dWebExtension, SCORE, URL, VaultFileSize, VDKSUMMARY, WebFileSize.

NumPages: If the results span multiple pages, the number of pages required to display the results.

SearchProviders: If this query spanned multiple Content Servers, the list of providers it used to search them.

Text1: Contains IdocScript that has a short description of the item. Sometimes used as the label for the URL to the content item. It can be set in the Web Layout Editor.

Text2: Similar to Text2, it gives a longer description of the content item.

TotalDocsProcessed: The total number of content items in the repository. It is not available for database search.

TotalRows: The total number of rows that match the criteria.

GET_UPDATE_FORM
This service will return the info update form for an existing content item. From this page the user can change the metadata for the item.
Added In: 3.0

Execution Flags: Scriptable

Required Parameter:

dID: The content ID of the item

Results:

DocFormats: A ResultSet of all content formats supported in the server

DocTypes: A ResultSet of all content types supported in the server

DOC_INFO: A ResultSet containing metadata information about this item

GET_USER_INFO

Returns the user profile page for the current user. From here, users can update their passwords, email addresses, and personalization information.

Added In: 4.0

Execution Flags: Scriptable

Required Parameters:

None

Results:

USER_INFO: A ResultSet of information about the user that is stored in the database, such as dFullName and dEmail.

UserMetaDefinition: A ResultSet containing the information about custom user metadata. The values are stored in USER_INFO. This ResultSet contains information about what those fields are like.

GET_WORKFLOW_INFO_BYNAME

Returns the workflow information page for a specific content item, which includes the history of the document, what steps remain in the workflow, and who is currently reviewing it.

Added In: 5.0

Execution Flags: Scriptable

Required Parameter:

dDocName: The content name of the item in workflow

Results:

AuthorAddress: The email address of the author of this revision

DOC_INFO: A ResultSet containing metadata information about this item

dWfStepID: The ID of the current step

RemainingStepUsers: A list of users that can approve the current step

WF_DOC_INFO: Contains information about the current state of the workflow

WorkflowActionHistory: A ResultSet of actions that have been taken on this item, such as who approved it and when

WorkflowInfo: A ResultSet containing information about this workflow

WorkflowState: A ResultSet of the users who have approved this revision

WorkflowStep: A ResultSet of information about the current step

WorkflowSteps: A ResultSet of information of all known steps

GET_WORKFLOWDOCREVISIONS

Returns all content items in a specific workflow. From here, the user can approve or reject an item, review it, or view its workflow history.

Added In: 4.0

Execution Flags: Scriptable

Required Parameter:

dWfName: The name of the workflow

Results:

WF_INFO: A ResultSet containing information about this workflow.

WfDocuments: A ResultSet of content items in this workflow, their metadata, and workflow state.

WorkflowSteps: A ResultSet containing information about the steps in this workflow. Used to determine whether the current user can approve or reject the item.

LOAD_PNE_PORTAL

Returns the raw personalization data for this user in the pne_portal topic. Includes the saved queries for this user and the personal URLs. It also includes any name-value pair stored in this topic, such as the preferred email format. Used by remote applications to obtain the user's personalization settings.

Added In: 7.0

Execution Flags: Scriptable

Required Parameters:

None

Results:

emailFormat: The preferred email format

PersonalURLS: A ResultSet of the user's bookmarked URLs

SavedQueries: A ResultSet of this user's saved queries in the Content Server

LOAD_USER_TOPIC

Similar to LOAD_PNE_PORTAL and LOAD_WORKFLOW_QUEUE, but can be used to download any personalization topic. The common ones are pne_portal and wf_in_queue, but others are possible. They are all stored in HDA files in the stellent/data/users/ directory. The exact path is dependent on the user's name. For example, the sysadmin's personalization information is stored here:

```
stellent/data/users/profiles/sys/sysadmin/
```

Added In: 7.0

Execution Flags: Scriptable

Required Parameters:

userTopic: The name of the user topic

Results:

The contents of the personalization topic

LOAD_WORKFLOW_QUEUE
Returns the raw personalization data for this user in the wf_in_queue topic. Contains a list of content items in a workflow that require action. The allowed actions are to approve or reject the item. If the item is checked-out by the current user, the only allowed action is to check it back in. Used by remote applications to obtain the workflow queue for a user.
Added In: 7.0

Execution Flags: Scriptable

Required Parameters:

None

Results:

WorkflowInQueue: A ResultSet containing limited information about the content items that require this user's attention

LOGIN
Logs in the current user. This service is one of many ways to authenticate the user with the web server. This service is automatically called if the Auth parameter is in any URL.
Added In: 3.0

Execution Flags: Redirectable

Required Parameters:

None

Optional Parameters:

Action: To redirect to a template page after a login, set this to GetTemplatePage.

Auth: Set to Internet to do Basic HTTP authentication or Intranet for Integrated Windows Authentication (IWA) logins.

Page: Set to the name of a template to redirect to after the login. The default is HOME_PAGE.

Results:

None

PING_SERVER

A lightweight service that is called to make certain that the Content Server is still running. It also forces users to log in if they haven't already.

Added In: 3.0

Execution Flags: None

Required Parameters:

None

Optional Parameters:

None

Results:

None

RESUBMIT_FOR_CONVERSION

Resubmits an item to the content refinery to be converted again. Used mainly when an item failed to convert properly. After fixing the problem, the item can be resubmitted. It is also useful after you change the settings in the content refinery. For example, if you enabled thumbnails, you need to resubmit old content to generate the new thumbnails. Existing content can be resubmitted to generate web renditions with the new settings. After a resubmit, the service redirects to the content information page. The service itself returns limited state information about the item.

Added In: 3.0

Execution Flags: Redirectable

Required Parameter:

dID: The content ID for the item to resubmit

Optional Parameter:

AlwaysResubmit: Must be set to true if you want to resubmit an item that converted successfully

Results:

Common state information about the content item: dConversion, dCurRevID, dExtension, dFileSize, dFormat, dOriginalName, dProcessingState, dPublishState, dReleaseState, dStatus, dWorkflowState

REV_HISTORY

Returns the revision history for a content item. Most of this information is also present with a DOC_INFO service.

Added In: 3.0

Execution Flags: Scriptable

Required Parameter:

dID: The content ID of the item

Results:

REVISIONS: A ResultSet containing all the revisions of this item

DOC_INFO: A ResultSet containing metadata information about this item

SAVE_USER_TOPICS

Saves general personalization information for this user. This information must be in a formatted string, called a topic string, which contains four parameters, separated by commas:

actionName:topicName:keyName:data

The actionName can be one of the following:

addMruRow: Adds a new row to a new or existing ResultSet.

deleteKeys: Deletes an existing key-value pair.

deleteRows: Deletes a row from an existing ResultSet.

updateKeys: Adds or updates a key-value pair.

updateRows: Updates a row in a ResultSet.

The topicName is the name of the personalization topic. Common ones are pne_portal for general data and wf_in_queue for the workflow items. They correspond to the names of HDA files in the following directory:

stellent/data/users/profiles/.../username/

The keyName can be the name of ResultSet in that HDA file. It can also be the key of a key-value pair in the HDA file.

The format of data depends on the action. If you are modifying a key-value pair, it is simply the value; if you are modifying a ResultSet, it contains a comma-separated list of the column names in the ResultSet. It is used to pull additional data out of the request to populate the row values. See Chapter 9 for examples of topic strings.

Added In: 6.0

Execution Flags: Redirectable

Required Parameters:

None

Optional Parameters:

numTopics: The number of topic strings in this request

topicString1–topicStringN: Contain the encoded topic strings to save to the server. The names of these strings have a number prefix, such as topicString1 and topicString2. The number of these strings corresponds to numTopics.

Additional parameters as needed for modifying ResultSets

Results:

UserTopicEdits: A ResultSet containing the parsed data that was saved

SUBMIT_HTML_FORM

Submits a Hypertext Content Server Form (HCSF) or a Hypertext Content Server Page (HCSP) for processing. These are web pages used to process HTML-based business forms (for example, filling out a purchase request form or maintaining a list of comments about a particular topic). Submitting an HCSF will generate a new content item. Submitting an HCSP generates a new revision of the submitted HCSP. The submitted data is saved as XML in the new item. After a submit, the service redirects to a confirmation page. See Chapters 5 and 6 for examples of HTML forms.
Added In: 4.0

Execution Flags: Redirectable

Required Parameter:

dID: The content ID of the form to submit

Optional Parameters:

Varies. Each form can define the XML data to store in the form.

isFormFinished: Used on HCSPs. If this flag is set, the HCSP cannot be submitted any more.

Results:

Standard Metadata for the new content item

SUBSCRIBE

Subscribes a user to a specific content item or a group of items. The user receives email notifications whenever a new revision of the item is available. By default, the only subscription type is based on the content name (dDocName), which is called a Basic subscription. Additional subscription types can be added with the Repository Manager, which allow subscriptions to be based on metadata criteria (for example, subscribing to all items with the same author or all items with the same content type). After a subscription, the user is redirected to the content information page for the item.
Added In: 3.0

Execution Flags: Redirectable

Required Parameters:

dID: The content ID of the item the user is subscribing to.

dSubscriptionEmail: The email address to use for the subscription. If blank, the default email address for this user is used.

Optional Parameters:

dSubscriptionID: A unique ID for this subscription. It corresponds to the metadata value used for the subscription. For example, it is the dDocName of the item for a Basic subscription or the dDocAuthor of the item for an author-based subscription.

dSubscriptionType: The name of the custom configured subscription type. It can be Basic or a custom defined subscription.

Results:

dSubscriptionCreateDate: The date the subscription occurred

SUBSCRIPTION_LIST
Returns a list of subscriptions for the user. It includes all Basic subscriptions and all criteria-based subscription groups.
Added In: 3.0

Execution Flags: Scriptable

Required Parameters:

None

Results:

SUBSCRIPTION_LIST: A ResultSet containing metadata for the content items that this user is subscribed to

UNDO_CHECKOUT
Undoes a check-out. It then redirects to the content information page or the page that the user was on previously.
Added In: 3.0

Execution Flags: Redirectable

Required Parameter:

dID: The content ID of the item currently checked-out

Results:

IsWorkflow: Set to true if this content item is currently in a workflow

UNSUBSCRIBE

Undoes a subscription. One content item can satisfy more than one subscription criterion; for example, the user might be subscribed to a specific item and all items by that item's author. This service removes only one subscription at a time. If the user unsubscribed from the content information page, the service redirects back there when complete.

Added In: 3.0

Execution Flags: Redirectable

Required Parameter:

dID: The content ID of the item tow which the user is subscribing

Optional Parameters:

dSubscriptionID: A unique ID for this subscription. It corresponds to the metadata value that is used for the subscription. For example, it is the dDocName of the item for a Basic subscription or the dDocAuthor of the item for an author-based subscription.

dSubscriptionType: The name of the custom configured subscription type. It can be Basic or a custom defined subscription.

UPDATE_DOCINFO

Updates the metadata of a content item. Each revision can be modified to change the security group, author, or custom metadata. Some data cannot be changed, such as the state of the document or the release date. After an update, returns to the content information page.

Added In: 3.0

Execution Flags: None

Required Parameters:

Common metadata fields: dDocAccount, dDocName, dID, dRevLabel, dSecurityGroup

Optional Parameters:

Any changed metadata fields. They can be a core field, such as dDocAuthor; or they can be a custom metadata field, such as xComments.

Results:

Metadata of the updated content item

WORK_IN_PROGRESS

Returns a list of content items that are checked-into the Content Server, but are not yet released—they are still being processed by the refinery or they have a release date set to sometime in the future. Does not show items that are currently in workflow.

Added In: 4.0

Execution Flags: Scriptable

Required Parameters:

None

Optional Parameters:

orderClause: The SQL order clause that can be used to sort the field; for example, to sort by title, it would be order by dDocTitle.

Results:

DOC_LIST: A ResultSet of content items that have not yet been released. Also contains some metadata for the items.

WORKFLOW_APPROVE

Approves an item currently in a workflow. After an approve, the user is redirected to the Workflow In Queue page or to the Workflow Content Items page.

Added In: 3.0

Execution Flags: Redirectable

Required Parameter:

dID: The content ID of the item to approve

Results:

Common metadata fields: dDocName, dDocTitle, dExtension, dOriginalName, dPublishState, dReleaseState

Common workflow fields: dWfComputed, dWfCurrentStepID, dWfDirectory, dWfDocState, dWfEntryTs, dWfID, dWfName, dWfStatus, dWfStepDescription, dWfStepID, dWfStepIsAll, dWfStepName, dWfStepType, dWfStepWeight, dWfType, dWorkflowState, wfAction, wfCurrentStepPrefix, wfUsers

entryCount: The number of times this item has entered the workflow

WORKFLOW_CHECKIN

Similar to CHECKIN_SEL, this service is used to check-in a new revision of an item that is in a workflow.

Added In: 3.0

Execution Flags: Redirectable

Required Parameters:

Same as CHECKIN_SEL

Optional Parameters:

Same as CHECKIN_SEL

isFinished: To proceed to the next step in the workflow, this flag must be set. Otherwise, the revision can be checked-out and back in again.

Results:

Same as CHECKIN_SEL

WORKFLOW_REJECT

Rejects an item currently in a workflow. After a reject, the user is redirected to the workflow in queue page or to the workflow content items page.

Added In: 3.0

Execution Flags: Redirectable

Required Parameters:

dID: The content ID of the item to reject.

dWfName: The workflow that this item is in.

wfRejectMessage: The reason for rejection. This text is emailed to the author.

Results:

Common metadata fields: dDocAuthor, dDocName, dDocTitle, dExtension, dOriginalName, dPublishState, dReleaseState

Common workflow fields: dWfComputed, dWfCurrentStepID, dWfDirectory, dWfDocState, dWfID, dWfName, dWfStatus, dWfStepDescription, dWfStepID, dWfStepIsAll, dWfStepName, dWfStepType, dWfStepWeight, dWfType, dWorkflowState, wfAction, wfCurrentStepPrefix, wfUsers

entryCount: The number of times this item has entered the workflow

Tomcat Integration Reference

The Content Server integrates with Tomcat to provide a Java Server Page (JSP) and Servlet container. Anything that can be written as a Servlet can be deployed to the Content Server. A JSP can be rendered in the Content Server simply by checking it into the repository.

These Servlets and JSPs can instantiate any Content Server Java object and run methods with them directly. To simplify integrations, the Content Server provides a small API that exposes the frequently used features. This API is contained in the Java package idcserver. It is used frequently on JSP pages checked-into the Content Server. It is also used on Site Studio JSPs.

This appendix contains documentation on the classes, methods, and variables available in this API. See Chapter 4 for information on how to enable the Servlet container and to see some sample JSPs.

idcserver.ServerBean

This class is the main entry point to interact with the Content Server. It can evaluate IdocScript code, and execute services. The response data from service calls is contained in this object in the form of Properties or ServerResultSet objects. A ServerResultSet object is a lightweight wrapper around a standard ResultSet object.

To use this object, follow these steps:

1. Create an idcserve.ServerBean object.

2. Initialize the ServerBean with the method init.

3. Set IdocScript variables and service request variables with the method putLocal.

4. Evaluate dynamichtml resources with the method evalResInc.

5. Evaluate any IdocScript with the method evalIdcScp.

6. Execute a service with executeService or parseExecuteService.

7. Retrieve the results of a service request with getLocal, getResultSet, or with evalIdcScp.

Methods

public void addResultSet(String name, ServerResultSet srs)
Adds a ServerResultSet to this bean with the given name.

public void addOptionList(String name, Vector options)
Adds an option list Vector to this bean with the given name.

public String evalIdcScp(String script)
Evaluates an IdocScript string without the <$$> delimiters; for example, HttpCgiPath instead of <$HttpCgiPath$>. Throws a ContentServerException if there is a parsing error.

public String evaluateIdocScript(String script)
Evaluates an IdocScript string, such as <$HttpCgiPath$>. Throws a ContentServerException if there is a parsing error.

public String evalResInc(String include)
Evaluates a dynamic HTML resource include, such as std_page_begin, or show_std_field. Throws a ContentServerException if there is a parsing error.

public void executeService()
Executes a Content Server service. The execution results are inserted directly into the ServerBean data objects. Result set and other data can be accessed through the get methods. To use this method, set the IdcService and all parameters with the putLocal method, or evalIdcScp. Throws a ContentServerException if an error occurred in the service.

public Object getCachedObject(String id)
Retrieves a Cached Object from the ExecutionContext by its id, such as UserData. Returns null if no match was found.

public ServerResultSet getCurrentActiveResultSet()
Returns the ResultSet that is considered active so it is currently being looped over. When looping over multiple ResultSets, the innermost loop is the active ResultSet.

public Properties getEnvironment()
Returns the Properties object that holds the environment values for this object. Contains CGI headers and configuration key-value pairs.

public String getEnvironmentValue(String key)
Returns one value from the environment by its key or null if no matches were found.

public String getLocal(String key)
Returns one value from the local data by its key or null if no matches were found.

public Properties getLocalData()

Returns the `Properties` object that holds the local data, including any parameter on the URL, any variable set with IdocScript, and any parameter returned in a service request.

public Vector getOptionList(String name)

Returns an option list from the bean according to its name; for example, the list of security groups is contained in the option list `securityGroups`. Returns `null` if no matches were found. The option list `Vector` contains string for elements.

public Enumeration getOptionLists()

Returns an `Enumeration` of the names of all option lists.

public ServerResultSet getResultSet(String name)

Returns a `ResultSet` from the bean according to its name. Returns `null` if no matches were found.

public Enumeration getResultSetList()

Returns an `Enumeration` of the names of the `ResultSet`s in the bean.

public void init(ServletRequest request)

Initializes the `ServerBean` object with the `ServletRequest`, which initializes the `ServerBean` based on the request context. This method must be called before using the `ServerBean`.

public void parseExecuteService(String serviceUrl)

Executes a Content Server service. The results of the service are stored in the `ServerBean` as parameters in the `localData` and `ServerResultSet`s. The `serviceUrl` is a URL-encoded list of service parameters, containing at least `IdcService`. For example, the following throws a `ContentServerException` if an error occurred in the service:

```
sb.parseExecuteService("IdcService=GET_SEARCH_RESULTS&QueryText=test");
```

public void parseExecuteService(String serviceString, char sep, char esc)

Executes a Content Server service. The results of the service are stored in the `ServerBean` as parameters in the `localData` and `ServerResultSet`s. The `serviceString` is a list of parameters, separated by the `sep` character. The string uses `esc` as an escape character, which enables executing a service without requiring the parameters to be URL-encoded. For example, the following throws a `ContentServerException` if an error occurred in the service:

```
String params = "IdcService=GET_SEARCH_RESULTS\n" +
    "QueryText=test\n";
sb.parseExecuteService(params, '\n', '\\');
```

public void putLocal(String key, String value)

Stores a `value` in the local data with the specified `key`, which is similar to declaring a variable in IdocScript.

public void removeLocal(String key)
Removes a value from local data according to its key.

public ServerResultSet removeResultSet(String name)
Removes a ResultSet from the ServerBean by its name.

public void setCachedObject(String id, Object obj)
Places an object into the CachedObjects with a specific id.

public void setEnvironment(Properties env)
Replaces the current environment with this Properties object. In general, it should not be used. Environment values should be set one at a time, if ever.

public void setEnvironmentValue(String key, String value)
Sets one environment key to a new value.

public void setLocalData(Properties localData)
Sets the Properties object that holds the local data, which is a good way to prevent data pollution when executing several services with the same ServerBean.

idcserver.ServerResultSet

This is a wrapper for the intradoc.data.DataResultSet object, which itself is an implementation of the intradoc.data.ResultSet interface. A ResultSet contains an ordered list of fields, also known as columns. These fields can contain several data types: Strings, Dates, or numbers. The ResultSet can have zero or many rows. Each row is stored as an ordered Vector of values, one for each column. It also maintains the concept of a current row. It is used when iterating over the ResultSet and extracting values from the current row.

This object is used to store data returned from the database, or generic tabular data.

Constructors

public ServerResultSet()
Creates an empty ServerResultSet with no rows or columns.

public ServerResultSet(DataResultSet drset)
Creates a new ServerResultSet instance from a DataResultSet object.

Methods

public void addRow(Vector vect)
Appends the specified row to the ServerResultSet. The elements in the Vector are typically String objects. The order corresponds to the order of the columns.

public void appendFields(Vector finfo)

Appends columns to the ResultSet with the passed Vector of FieldInfo objects.

public void copyFieldInfo(ResultSet rset)

Copies only the field information of the specified ResultSet into this ServerResultSet, which makes the two ResultSets have the same columns.

public void copyFiltered(ResultSet rset, String field, ResultSetFilter filter)

Copies rows from a ResultSet into this ServerResultSet. The two ResultSets must have the same columns. It only copies the rows in which the specified field matches the filter.

public void copyFilteredEx(ResultSet rset, String key, ResultSetFilter filter, boolean startAtFirst)

Same as copyFiltered, but allows you to copy from either the current row in the ResultSet or start at the first row.

public void copySimpleFiltered(ResultSet rset, String field, String value)

Copies rows from a ResultSet into this ServerResultSet. It copies only the rows in which the specified field has the specified value.

public Vector createEmptyRow()

Creates and returns an empty row with empty strings for this ServerResultSet. This row can be populated and inserted into the ServerResultSet with insertRowAt.

public ResultSetFilter createMaxNumResultSetFilter(int maxnum)

Returns a ResultSetFilter that copies all rows up to a maximum number.

public Vector createRow(Parameters params)

Returns a new row for this ServerResultSet, based on the passed params. It is easier to use than createEmptyRow because the fields are automatically populated in the correct order.

public ResultSetFilter createSimpleResultSetFilter(String lookupVal)

Returns a simple ResultSetFilter that returns a match for the passed lookupVal. It is used with copyFiltered to match a specific field to this filter.

public boolean deleteCurrentRow()

Deletes the current row. The row must be set by looping or with setCurrentRow.

public void deleteRow(int index)

Deletes the row at the specified index.

public Vector findRow(int colIndex, String val)

Finds the row whose field value at the given colIndex is equal to the given value. Returns null if no match is found.

public boolean first()
Sets the current row to the first row in the ResultSet.

public int getCurrentRow()
Returns the index of the current row.

public Properties getCurrentRowProps()
Returns the data in the current row as a Properties object. The keys correspond to the column field names.

public Vector getCurrentRowValues()
Returns the current row as an ordered Vector.

public Date getDateValue(int index)
Returns the value of the field at the specified index in the current row as a Date object. This works only for fields explicitly defined as date objects.

public int getFieldIndex(String fieldName)
Returns the column index of the specified fieldName.

public boolean getFieldInfo(String fieldName, ServerFieldInfo sfi)
Populates the passed ServerFieldInfo object with information for the specified fieldName. Returns false if the field is not present in the ResultSet.

public String getFieldName(int index)
Returns the name of field located at a particular column index.

public void getIndexFieldInfo(int index, ServerFieldInfo sfi)
Populates the passed ServerFieldInfo object with information for the field at the specified column index.

public int getNumFields()
Returns number of fields in the ResultSet.

public int getNumRows()
Returns the number of rows in the ResultSet.

public Vector getRowValues(int index)
Returns all the values of the row at the specified row index.

public String getStringValue(int index)
Returns the String value from the current row with the specified column index.

public String getStringValue(String name)
Returns the String value from the current row with the specified field name.

public void insertRowAt(Vector row, int index)

Inserts the Vector row into the ResultSet at the specified row index.

public boolean isEmpty()

Returns true if the ResultSet does not contain any rows.

public boolean isRowPresent()

Returns true if there is a row present at the current row index. It is used when looping over the ResultSet to make sure that there is still data available.

public boolean last()

Advances the current row to the last row. Returns false if there are no rows.

public void mergeFields(DataResultSet rset)

Merges the fields from a DataResultSet into this ServerResultSet. It is used to create a copy of the structure of the DataResultSet. It does not copy any of the rows. Duplicate field names are ignored.

public boolean next()

Advances the current row to the following row. Returns false if there is no next row.

public boolean previous()

Sets the current row to the preceding row. Returns false if the current row is the first row.

public void removeAll()

Removes all rows from the ResultSet, but retains the field information.

public void removeFields(String[] fieldNames)

Removes fields from this ResultSet. It completely removes the columns from the ResultSet. This is an expensive operation because it needs to iterate over every row, removing elements from all the Vectors.

public void reset()

Resets the ResultSet back to an empty ResultSet, containing no columns or rows.

public void setCurrentRow(int currentRow)

Sets the current row to the specified index.

public void setCurrentValue(int colIndex, String value)

Sets a value in the current row at the specified colIndex to the specified value. Throws an Exception if the column or row index is invalid.

public void setRowValues(Vector vect, int rowIndex)

Sets the values for the entire row at the specified rowIndex.

idcserver.ServerFieldInfo

This object contains information about a field used in the ServerResultSet. It contains information about the column index of the field and data type information.

If m_type is null, there is no field type information available beyond the index. Type information is generally available only if the data was returned from the database. If it was loaded from an HDA file, it probably does not contain field information. In this case, the field is treated as a string.

This object is a loose wrapper for the intradoc.data.FieldInfo object. It is generally not created by users of the ServerBean. Instead, it is used as a container for field information returned from service calls.

Fields

public static final short BINARY
Contains variable length binary data.

public static final short BOOLEAN
Contains a boolean flag.

public static final short CHAR
Contains a single character.

public static final short DATE
Contains a Date.

public static final short FLOAT
Contains a floating point number represented with a Java Double.

public static final short INT
Contains an integer represented with a Java Long.

public static final short STRING
Contains a Unicode String. The source of the string might not necessarily be Unicode. If m_isFixedLen is set to false, it is a variable length String.

private FieldInfo m_fi
The original FieldInfo object.

public int m_index
The column index in the ServerResultSet in which this field is located.

public boolean m_isFixedLen
Set to true if the field has a maximum length when translated to a String.

public int m_maxLen

The maximum character length of a String field; valid only if m_isFixedLen is true.

public String m_name

The name of the field.

public int m_type

The type of the field set to one of the previous static shorts.

Constructor

public ServerFieldInfo()

Constructs an empty ServerFieldInfo object.

Methods

public void copy(ServerFieldInfo sfi)

Makes this object a copy of the passed ServerFieldInfo object.

public FieldInfo getFieldInfo()

Retrieves the private FieldInfo object that this object wraps.

public void init(FieldInfo fi)

Initializes this object with the values in the passed FieldInfo object. Copies all values from the FieldInfo object into this object. It also stores the FieldInfo object as a private variable.

public void refresh()

Synchronizes the data in this object with the privately stored FieldInfo object.

idcserver.ContentServerException

This is a wrapper for any Content Server exception that is thrown, which can be due to poorly formatted IdocScript or an error in a service call.

Constructors

public ContentServerException(Exception e)

Creates a new ContentServerException from an Exception object.

public ContentServerException(String msg, Exception e)

Creates a new ContentServerException from an Exception object and a String message.

■ ■ ■

Layout Manager API

Architecture

The Layout Manager is an API that uses JavaScript and Cascading Style Sheets (CSS) to change the look and feel of the Content Server. This API does not affect the content on the pages; it is used to control the navigation menus. It also controls the Hypertext Markup Language (HTML) at the beginning and ending of every page.

The *layouts* in this API are JavaScript resources that describe which navigation menus are present and how they are drawn on the page. The *skins* are collections of CSS files and images that control the color scheme of the layouts. As demonstrated in Chapter 8, it is easy to alter the navigation nodes with a component. It is also possible to create new skins and layouts and then package them into a component.

This appendix contains information about the JavaScript API used to create new layouts or modify the navigation dynamically.

Navigation XML Schema

The XML schema for the navigation nodes is fairly simple. There are three node types: navtree, item, and collection. The root node must be a navtree node. The item node contains information about a menu link in the navigation. For example, the Check In link, which takes you to the content check-in page, is represented with an item node. A collection node represents a submenu, which can contain other item and collection nodes (for example, the My Stellent submenu contains links to personalized view of the Content Server). That menu is represented with a collection node.

All nodes must have a unique id attribute. The root node's id must be NAVTREE. All other attributes are optional:

collection_service: Valid only for collection nodes. Some collections, such as those in a Folders library, need to run a service before their child nodes can be populated. In that case, this attribute is set to the URL to run that service. When clicked, the URL is opened in an invisible IFRAME. The resulting HTML page contains JavaScript that populates the collection node with its children.

icon: A URL to an icon image for this node, which is used only when the node is shown in a tree view (for example, the left sidebar in the Trays layout). If it is not set, a default icon is used.

id: The globally unique id for this node.

label: The label displayed for this node, such as My Stellent or Check In New.

target: If the URL for the menu link should be opened in a new window, it is set to the link's target.

tray_doc: Only valid for the Trays layout. If a node in the menu should display an HTML page instead of a tree view control, set this attribute to the URL of that page. It is used for the Search Tray.

url: Only for item nodes. When this menu item is clicked, it follows this URL.

Configuration Flags

A handful of configuration flags affect the behavior of the Layout Manager:

LmDefaultLayout: The default layout used by guests and new users. It defaults to Trays but it can also be Top Menus or Classic.

LmDefaultSkin: The name of the skin used by guests and new users. It defaults to Stellent on version 7.0 and to Stellent05 on version 7.5. It can also be Collegiate or Windows.

The navBuilder Variables

The navBuilder object contains all the XML navigation nodes, as well as pointers to the JavaScript functions used to render XML into HTML. Each navigation area has its own navBuilder object, containing its nodes and functions. For example, the menu at the very top is drawn differently from the menu second from the top. The left side tray navigation is also rendered differently.

The global object coreNav contains all navBuilder objects for all navigation sections.

htmlString

Contains the generated HTML string for this navBuilder object. This HTML is generated with a call to generateChildNodeDisplayCode based on the data in xmlDocument.

menuA

A navBuilder object containing data for the topmost horizontal menu. This menu is used mostly for links (item nodes), not drop-down menus (collection nodes). It is used in the Top Menus and Trays layouts. To make a node visible here, add it to the main navBuilder object in finishLayoutInit. Then add its id to menuA.topLevelNodes with the function menuA.addTopLevelNode(...).

menuB

A navBuilder object containing data for the horizontal menu under menuA. It is used mostly for drop-down menus (collection nodes) and it is used in the Top Menus layout. To make a node visible here, add it to the main navBuilder object. It or one of its ancestors must also have its id in menuB.topLevelNodes.

topLevelNodes
A standard JavaScript Array containing an ordered list of node ids to display in this navigation section. To display a navigation node, it or one of its ancestors must have its id in the list of topLevelNodes for one of the navigation areas. The navigation areas are named menuA, menuB, and trayA.

trayA
A navBuilder object containing data for the tray-based navigation section on the left side of the window. It is used in the Trays layout. To make a node visible at the top level here, add it to the main navBuilder object. It or one of its ancestors must also have its id in trayA.topLevelNodes.

xmlDocument
The full XML Document object for this navBuilder object. It contains all collection and item nodes. This is initially empty for the menuA and trayA navigation areas. The nodes are copied into navigation areas from the main navBuilder object just prior to display.

xmlNodeMap
An Array of node ids and nodePointer objects, which contain information about the node's locations. It helps to find nodes more quickly. The value nodePointer.location is a string such as "0.1.2", which means that the node is the third child, of the second child, of the first child, of the xmlRoot object.

xmlRoot
The documentElement node for the xmlDocument object.

navBuilder Methods

addChildNodeTo(parentId, nodeType [, attribute1, attribute2, ...])
Constructs a new node and adds it as a child to an existing collection node with an id equal to parentId. The nodeType is the type of the node: either collection or an item. After this, the function can take an arbitrarily long list of attribute strings in the form of id==NEW_NODE_ID. The id attribute must be specified; all others are optional.

addPrevSiblingNodeTo(siblingId, nodeType [, attributes])
Constructs a new node, and add it as the previous sibling to an existing node. This function is similar to addChildNodeTo, except that it adds the new node as a sibling, not a child.

addTopLevelNode(nodeId [, beforeNodeId])
Adds a nodeId to the list of node ids in topLevelNodes for a specific navigation area. It forces the node to be drawn as a top-level menu item. If beforeNodeId is specified, it inserts this node before the node with that id. Otherwise, the node is added at the end. The beforeNodeId parameter is available only in version 7.5.

buildHtmlStringFromXml(node[, nodeLocation])

Generates the HTML code for one XML node and its children. The result is saved to the htmlString variable for this navigation section. The functions makeOpeningHtml, makeCoreHtml, and makeClosingHtml determine how the XML is converted into HTML. The nodeLocation is the node location string for this node, or null if node is the root node.

deleteChildrenOf(nodeId)

Deletes all children of the XML node with an id equal to nodeId. The node itself is not deleted.

deleteItem(nodeId)

Deletes the XML node with an id equal to nodeId.

deleteTopLevelNode(nodeId)

Removes a specific node from the topLevelNodes array. This function exists only in version 7.5.

getNodeById(nodeId)

Returns the XML node with a id attribute of nodeId. If the node is not found, it returns null.

makeClosingHtml(node, nodeLocation)

Renders the closing HTML code for this XML node. This function is called during generateChildNodeDisplayCode. It is usually used only for collection nodes to close the TABLE or DIV tags that contain its children. The node parameter is the XML node to draw. The nodeLocation parameter is the node location string from xmlNodeMap. By default, it is an empty function pointer. The real function is defined in the specific layout.js file for the layout and is then assigned to this navBuilder object.

makeCoreHtml(node, nodeLocation)

Renders the contents of an XML node into HTML. This function is called during generateChildNodeDisplayCode. It contains information about how to draw the HTML contents for an XML node. This is usually a hyperlink, as well as a handful of images. The node parameter is the XML node to draw. The nodeLocation parameter is the node location string from xmlNodeMap. By default, this is an empty function pointer. The real function is defined in the specific layout.js file for the layout and then assigned to this navBuilder object.

makeOpeningHtml(node, nodeLocation)

Renders the opening of a HTML container for the contents of a rendered XML node. This function is called during generateChildNodeDisplayCode. It contains information about how to draw the opening HTML for an XML node. It is usually used only by collection nodes to open TABLE or DIV tags to contain its children. The node parameter is the XML node to draw. The nodeLocation parameter is the node location string from xmlNodeMap. By default, it is an empty function pointer. The real function is defined in the specific layout.js file for the layout and then assigned to this navBuilder object.

moveItemInto(newParentCollectionId, nodeId, clone)

Moves an existing node into an existing `collection`. If the item being moved is itself a `collection`, all its children are moved with it. If the `clone` parameter is `true`, the item will be copied instead of being moved.

moveItemAbove(siblingNodeId, nodeId, clone)

Moves an existing node into an existing collection. It is similar to `moveItemInto`, except that it is used to make the node the previous sibling of an existing node.

setAttributeValue(nodeId, attrName, attrValue)

Sets an attribute for an existing node. The parameter `attrName` is the name of the attribute, such as `label` or `icon`. The parameter `attrValue` is the new value for that attribute.

Global Methods

In addition to the `navBuilder`, the Layout Manager API has several other methods that are useful for creating DHTML interfaces. Some of the more useful ones are described following:

dimensionFinder(element)

Creates an object containing the size and location of a HTML `element` or event. The object contains the following variables: `width`, `height`, `actualLeft` (X-position within browser window) `actualTop` (Y-position within browser window), `relativeLeft` (X-position within nearest CSS-positioned ancestor), and `relativeTop` (Y-position within nearest CSS-positioned ancestor).

finishLayoutInit(coreNav)

Exists on all Content Server pages that have layouts. It is the last opportunity for a developer to modify the menu nodes before being drawn to the page. The include `custom_finish_layout_init` is referenced inside this function. Override this include if you want to modify the menus from a component. The `coreNav` parameter is the `navBuilder` object containing all the known menu nodes.

generateChildNodeDisplayCode(navBuilder, node, htmlContainer)

Generates HTML based on the XML nodes in the `navBuilder` object. The parameter `node` represents the root node to start from. This HTML is then inserted into a HTML element represented by `htmlContainer`. The generated HTML is based on the function pointers in the `navBuilder` object: `makeOpeningHtml`, `makeCoreHtml`, and `makeClosingHtml`.

generateNavigation()

Generates the menu navigation and draws it to the appropriate place in the layout. It is defined in the individual `layout.js` files. This takes the global `navBuilder` object named `coreNav` and populates its top-level nodes. It then sets the XML rendering functions in `coreNav` to functions defined elsewhere in `layout.js` and then calls `finishLayoutInit` to allow a developer to do last-minute modifications of the layout. Finally, it draws the menus onto the page.

insertHtml(text, element)
Inserts HTML text into a HTML element, replacing any existing HTML in that element.

layoutInitialize()
Initializes the navigation menus after the layout has been drawn. It is called on the standard Content Server pages, which creates the coreNav object and then generateNavigation to draw the menus.

mapXMLTree(node, nodeMapObject)
Generates an XML node map based on a root node element. This map is inserted into the nodeMapObject:

```
mapXMLTree(coreNav.xmlRoot, coreNav.xmlNodeMap)
```

navBuilder([xmlString])
Returns a new navBuilder object containing the supplied xmlString.

theseElementsOverlap(element1, element2)
Returns true if the two HTML elements overlap. It is used to help position pop-up menus.

writeLayoutPageBegin ()
Draws the beginning of the layout directly to the page. The beginning of the layout contains the framework for drawing the menus and the trays. It also contains the top menu bar and all its images.

writeLayoutPageEnd ()
Draws the end of the layout directly to the page, which closes all the HTML elements opened in writeLayoutPageBegin.

APPENDIX H

Java Filter Events

The Content Server executes filters when specific events occur. For example, they run when the server starts up, when a user's security credentials are calculated, or during validation of check-in metadata. To run custom Java code when these events occur, you need to create a custom filter, and configure it to run for a specific event with a component. See Chapter 11 for more examples of creating Java components.

Your code must implement the FilterImplementor interface to run. Following is an example of a very simple filter:

```
package mypackage;
import intradoc.common.*;
import intradoc.data.*;
import intradoc.shared.FilterImplementor;

public class MyFilter implements FilterImplementor
{
    public int doFilter(Workspace ws, DataBinder binder,
        ExecutionContext cxt) throws DataException, ServiceException
    {
        System.out.println("Hello World!");
        // put code here
        return CONTINUE;
    }
}
```

A filter can return the flags CONTINUE, FINISHED, or ABORT. Each has a different behavior according to which filter you execute. You should return CONTINUE unless the filter specifies otherwise. If an error occurs, throw an exception. Some filters expect you to set a return value in the ExecutionContext object to denote success or failure:

```
cxt.setReturnValue("true");
```

To execute this code during the validation of check-in data, use the validateStandard filter, which requires a Java component with a specially formatted ResultSet in the Component Definition File:

```
@ResultSet Filters
4
```

```
type
location
parameter
loadOrder
validateStandard
mypackage.MyFilter
null
1
@end
```

The objects passed into the doFilter method contain information about the state of the process. By modifying the data in the DataBinder, you can modify the process. In addition, some filters place additional Java objects into the ExeceutionContext so they are accessible to customizations. They are stored as CachedObjects and can be obtained like so:

```
Object obj = cxt.getCachedObject("objectName");
```

You can use the cached objects to alter how your code works. In addition, you can change the cached objects to alter core behavior. For example, it is common for filters to extract the UserData object to obtain information about the user and sometimes adjust the security credentials.

If this filter is executed as part of a service request, the ExecutionContext object is an intradoc.server.Service object. You can cast it into a Service object to run methods or obtain additional information about the service request:

```
if (cxt instanceof Service)
{
    Service svc = (Service)cxt;
}
```

Some filters expect a return value, some expect you to modify values in the DataBinder, and some expect you to change the cached objects. Following is a list of filter events, along with brief descriptions. The names and classes of the CachedObjects are also listed when applicable.

addCollectionInCollectionEnd

Executed after a folders collection object is created. This is a good place to enforce additional rules about folder creation and metadata.

Added In: 6.0 (Folders component)

addCollectionInCollectionStart

Executed before a folders collection object is created. This is a good place to enforce additional rules about folder creation and metadata.

Added In: 6.0 (Folders component)

addExportedWebFilterConfiguration

Executed right before the publishing of the SecurityInfo.hda web filter configuration file. Use it to place additional data in the configuration file, so it can be accessed by the web filter plugins.

Added In: 7.1

addExtraPreviewParameters

Used to add parameters to affect how a content preview is generated. It is executed toward the end of `intradoc.preview.PreviewHandler.performPreview` in the service `PREVIEW_DOCUMENT`.

Added In: 5.0

addFiles

Executed during a check-in immediately before the uploaded files are placed into the vault folder.

Added In: 3.0

additionalImportFilter

Used during an Archiver table import to control which items are imported. Place an additional SQL `WHERE` clause into the binder variable `additionalImportFilter` to fine-tune the import.

Added In: 7.5

advanceDocumentStateMarkWorkflowFinished

Executed just before a content item in workflow is marked as finished. You can perform additional logging, or update external resources with this filter.

Added In: 7.5

Cached Objects: `intradoc.server.workflow.WorkflowStates WorkflowStates`

advanceDocumentStateStart

Executed at each step in a workflow, including check-in, check-out, and approval. Here you can store additional data into the workflow companion file. If you return `FINISHED`, you can completely override the workflow processing with custom code.

Added In: 7.5

Cached Objects: `intradoc.server.workflow.WorkflowStates WorkflowStates, boolean WorkflowUseLocal`

afterArchiveBatchFile

Executed while running an export archive after a certain number of items have been processed. The default batch size is 1000 items. This is a good place to perform additional archive logging.

Added In: 6.0

Cached Objects: `String archiveName, String batchDir, String batchFileName, String metaFileName, String fileNumber`

afterCreateTransferPackageFileSet

Executed during archive replication services, such as `REQUEST_TRANSFER`, and `TRANSFER_ARCHIVE`. It is executed just before creating the ZIP file to replicate to a remote server. This is a good place to add additional data to an archive.

Added In: 7.1

Cached Objects: `String batchDir, String archiveDir, String targetDir, String fileName, intradoc.data.ResultSet fileSet, intradoc.server.archive.ArchiveImportStateInformation importState`

afterLoadRecordWebChange

Executed during indexing of deletions, additions, or retries. If it returns ABORT, no indexing of the content item is performed. This is a good place to hook in extremely pervasive changes to the indexing engine.

> Added In: 6.2
> Execution Context: intradoc.indexer.IndexerWorkObject
> Cached Objects: intradoc.data.DataBinder WebChangeFilterParams, intradoc.indexer.IndexerInfo FilterIndexerInfo, intradoc.indexer.IndexerBulkLoader IndexerBulkLoader, intradoc.indexer.WebChange WebChange, intradoc.data.ResultSet DemotedRevisionInfo

afterImportBatch

Executed during an archive import after a certain number of items have been processed. The default batch size is 1000.

> Added In: 7.1
> Cached Objects: Vector currentImportDocs

afterInitLocale

Executed at the beginning of every service request after the locale for the user has been determined. This is a good place to override the locale for the user or perform additional initialization for the request.

> Added In: 7.5

afterPrepareSingleDoc

Executed when the archive explicitly imports one single item from an archive via the IMPORT_DOCUMENT service. It is run after the item has been processed through field maps and value maps.

> Added In: 7.1
> Cached Objects: Vector currentImportDocs

afterPreprocessImportBatch

Executed after the metadata for a batch of items in an import have been preprocessed. At this point, all field maps and value maps will have been applied.

> Added In: 7.1
> Cached Objects: Vector currentImportDocs

allowProblemReportAction

Executed at the beginning of allowProblemReportAction in UPDATE_PROBLEMREPORT and DELETE_PROBLEMREPORT to determine whether or not a user is allowed to see a Content Publisher problem report.

> Added In: 4.6
> Cached Objects: String TestProblemReportAction

alterProviderAttributes

Executed after retrieving a user's information from an external user provider, such as Lightweight Directory Access Protocol (LDAP). It is useful for altering any user attribute or mapping an organizational attribute to a security attribute.

Added In: 6.1

Cached Objects: `intradoc.provider.UserProvider TargetUserProvider`

alterUserCredentials

Executed at the end of `retrieveUserDatabaseProfileData` to allow temporary alteration of user credentials. The altered credentials are temporary; they are valid only for the current request.

Added In: 4.0

Cached Objects: `intradoc.shared.UserData TargetUserData`

ArchivableTableRelationsDefinition

Executed during an archive to obtain a list of schema tables to include with the archive. Alter the `ArchivableTables` result set in the binder to affect which tables to archive.

Added In: 7.5

archiveCheckinRevisionComparisonTest

Executed during an archive, when testing to see which service call to perform when inserting a new item. For example, if `canInsertNew` is `true`, the `INSERT_NEW` service is used. Otherwise, an error is thrown.

Added In: 7.5

archiveHistoryItem

Executed after recording the history of an archived document into the `ArchiveHistory` database table. This is a good place to store additional metadata about an archived item.

Added In: 4.0

archiveTablePostExportFilter

Executed after exporting a schema database table with the Archiver.

Added In: 8.0

auditUserAttributesStore

Executed during an update of user data. Before the new data is saved to the database, this filter can be used to perform extra validation or store the information into a different table.

Added In: 4.0

Cached Objects: `intradoc.shared.UserData TargetUserData, Boolean hasUserChanged`

beforeLoadRecordWebChange

Executed during the indexing of deletions, additions, or retries into the search engine. This is a good place to hook in extremely pervasive changes to the indexing engine.

Added In: 6.2

Cached Objects: `intradoc.data.DataBinder WebChangeFilterParams, intradoc.indexer.IndexerInfo FilterIndexerInfo, intradoc.indexer.IndexerBulkLoader IndexerBulkLoader, intradoc.indexer.WebChange WebChange, intradoc.data.ResultSet DemotedRevisionInfo`

checkDocRules

Executed in the action checkDocRules, which occurs during a check-in, check-out, or update to check which security rules apply. For example, it determines if this user has rights to change the value for dDocAuthor field for an update service. You can add additional rules as needed.

Added In: 4.0

Cached Objects: String CheckRule

checkExtendedSecurityModelDocAccess

Executed during a security check for a document. It can be used to alter which security credentials are needed to view this item. Set the securityResult to false to reject access.

Added In: 4.0

Cached Objects: Integer desiredPrivilege, intradoc.data.ResultSet securityProfileResultSet, intradoc.data.DataBinder securityProfileData, Boolean securityResult, String securityResultMsg

checkMetaChangeSecurity

Executed when the security metadata changes on an update page, including changes to security groups, accounts, and Access Control Lists (ACLs). This filter should throw an exception if the change should not be allowed.

Added In: 7.1

Cached Objects: boolean checkMeta:isNewDoc, intradoc.data.ResultSet checkMeta:priorDocInfo

checkDownloadOverride

Executed during a file download service such as GET_FILE. This is a good place to override the data that is returned in such services. If the filter returns FINISHED, the service is considered complete.

Added In: 7.5

Cached Objects: Object[]sendFileResponseParams, which contains the following entries:
intradoc.data.DataBinder binder
String fileName
String downloadName
String format

checkScheduledEvents

Executed after checking whether it is time to run scheduled events. These events include the compaction of the database or the removal of the cache, which are performed every few hours. This event fires soon after the Content Server starts, and every five minutes thereafter. It is a good place to add custom scheduled actions. Note: the server is not fully initialized when this event first occurs.

Added In: 3.0

checkUpdateDocInfo

Executed during an update of the metadata of a content item. This is a good place to add additional security checks to prevent the updating of specific fields.

Added In: 7.5

Cached Objects: `Object[] checkUpdateDocInfoParams`, which contains the following entries:
`Boolean doMoveCheck`
`ResultSet docInfo`
`String resultSetName`
`String revisionsResultSetName`

cleanOldWebViewables
Executed while a new revision of an item is checked-in, but before being processed by the content refinery. If you created web viewables for the previous revision with a custom process, this is a good place to delete them, if needed.
Added In: 7.5

createWebViewable
Executed just prior to the creation of the web viewable with the content refinery. This is a good place to dynamically change which refinery conversion to perform by altering the value `webViewableFile:format` in the binder.
Added In: 7.5

xxxComponentUninstallFilter
Executed when the Admin Server or the Component Wizard uninstalls a component. You must replace xxx with the name of your component. This is useful if you need to perform extra cleanup after the component is uninstalled.
Added In: 7.0

computeDocName
Executed during a check-in after the value for `dDocName` is computed. This is only applicable if `IsAutoNumber` is enabled for the server.
Added In: 7.1

computeExtendedSecurityModelWhereClausePrivileges
Executed during a security check for search results. It is used to augment the normal security levels to grant special access to viewing the metadata for an item, even if they do not have access to the file's contents.
Added In: 4.0
Cached Objects: `Integer desiredPrivilege, Boolean isVerity, intradoc.shared.UserData UserData`

computeFunction
Executed every time an IdocScript function is rendered. It is a quick way to add new IdocScript functions or override existing ones. The last object in the array `args` is the return value if one exists.
Added In: 3.0
Cached Objects: `String function, Object[] args`

computeOptionList
Used to compute or filter an option list for display on IdocScript pages. Place the result Vector in the cached object `optionlist`. This has been mostly deprecated by the schema functionality.
> Added In: 3.0
> Cached Objects: `Vector params`

copyCollectionInCollectionEnd
Executed after a Folders collection object is copied into another collection object.
> Added In: 6.0 (Folders component)

copyCollectionInCollectionStart
Executed before a Folders collection object is copied into another collection object.
> Added In: 6.0 (Folders component)

createProviderData
Executed after adding a new provider, or modifying the configuration of an existing provider. Executed after `validateProvider`.
> Added In: 4.0
> Cached Objects: `intradoc.data.DataBinder ProviderData`

createWebViewable
Executed in the last step of a check-in, when the web viewable file is placed in the `weblayout` directory. Executed immediately before the web files are converted.
> Added In: 7.5
> Cached Objects: `intradoc.server.WebViewableConverterOutput WebViewableOutput`

determineDocConversion
Executed in the `docRefinery` action to override the computed value for `dConversion`. This flag is used by the Content Refinery to create web viewable renditions of content items.
> Added In: 7.5.1
> Cached Objects: `Object[] DocConversionParams`, which contains the following entries:
> `intradoc.server.DocFormats docFormats,`
> `Boolean isResubmit`
> `String fileKey`
> `String format`
> `String conversionType`

doUpdateMoveCheck
Executed in the service `UPDATE_DOCINFO` to check whether a content item's metadata was modified sufficiently to force it to be moved. For example, changing the security group or content type is usually blocked if the item is in a workflow or refinery process.
> Added In: 7.5
> Cached Objects: `String doUpdateMoveCheckParams`

docUrlAllowAccess

Executed during remoteCredentialsCheck to augment the security level for external users. The DataBinder contains the ResultSet DOC_URL_INFO, which contains information about the URL that the user is trying to access. Set the cached object isAuthorized to control access.

Added In: 4.6
Cached Objects: intradoc.shared.UserData UserData

docUrlAllowDisclosure

Executed when the IdocScript function docUrlAllowDisclosure is evaluated. Similar to docUrlAllowAccess, the result set DOC_URL_INFO contains information about the URL being accessed. Set the cached object isAuthorized to control access.

Added In: 4.0

dynamicFileLoadDocEnvironment

Executed every time a Dynamic Server Page is rendered in the Content Server. This filter can be used to load up a richer environment prior to rendering pages.

Added In: 7.5

editHttpResponseHeader

Executed when building the response page to all service requests. It is used to modify the HTTP headers in the response to contain caching information or content type information.

Added In: 5.0
Cached Objects: intradoc.server.ServiceHttpImplementor HttpImplementor, StringBuffer responseBuffer

editTopic

Executed when personalization data is saved to the Content Server, including Workflow In Queue, Save Searches, and Personal URLs. If you return FINISHED, the Content Server does not change the files. This can be used to modify or extend how user preferences are saved.

Added In: 4.0
Cached Objects: Properties topicEditRowProps

evaluateGlobalRulesAndProfile

Executed before Content Profiles are evaluated. This can be used to set flags to trigger specific profiles or global rules.

Added In: 7.5

executeSubServiceCode

Executed when a SubService is executed or when a scriptable service is executed with the executeService IdocScript function.

Added In: 7.5

exportTable

Executed before exporting a schema database table with the Archiver.

Added In: 7.5

extraAfterConfigInit
Executed after the IdcSystemLoader is initialized. Executed near the beginning of the server's startup. Place code here if it's needed before the connections to the database are created or before the services are loaded.
Added In: 3.0

extraAfterProvidersStartedInit
Executed after the incoming and outgoing providers have been started. This is the earliest point at which you can connect to the database.
Added In: 8.0

extraAfterServicesLoadInit
Executed after the server loads the definitions for the services. This is a startup filter that occurs very late in the startup. Place code here if it should be run when the server starts and it requires a fully initialized server.
Added In: 3.0

extraBeforeCacheLoadInit
Executed during server initialization. It occurs after the database connections have been established, but before the data in the database has been cached. This is a good place to manipulate the tables in a database for a component.
Added In: 3.0

finishProfileEvaluation
Executed after all the Content Profiles and global rules have been evaluated. This is another place to trigger profile side effects.
Added In: 7.5
Cached Objects: Hashtable FieldMap

fixUpAndValidateQuery
Executed immediately before a search query is run. This is the last chance to modify the parameter QueryText before running the search.
Added In: 7.0

formPostSubmit
Executed at the very end of an HTML form submission.
Added In: 4.0

formPreSubmit
Executed at the very end of the action processForm. It occurs after the default data processing occurs, but before the HTML form is checked-in. This is a good place to modify metadata values before they are stored in a new HTML form.
Added In: 4.0

getDocFormats

Executed on content info pages to determine the known formats of a content item. This includes the format for any alternate files, or refined content. Examples include text/html or application/msword.

Added In: 7.1

getEnterpriseSearchResults

Executed at the end of an enterprise search.

Added In: 4.6

getnextrow

Executed any time you loop over a ResultSet with IdocScript. It can be used to filter the values displayed. This is less secure than filtering the data prior to page display and is rarely used.

Added In: 3.0

Cached Objects: String resultset

handleIndexerResult

Executed for each item that the Content Server attempted to index into a search engine repository. The index might or might not have been successful. Use this filter for custom retry logic, callbacks, or logging.

Added In: 7.5

Cached Objects: intradoc.indexer.IndexerInfo IndexerInfo, intradoc.indexer.WebChange WebChange

importTable

Executed before the Archiver imports the data from an archived database table.

Added In: 7.5

incomingSocketProviderInit

Executed when any incoming socket provider is initialized, such as the connection from the web server or from another Content Server.

Added In: 4.0

incomingSocketProxyAuth

Executed when validating an incoming socket provider from a proxy server. This is a good place to add additional authentication for connections between Content Servers.

Added In: 4.0

Cached Objects: intradoc.data.DataBinder ProxyAuthProviderData, Properties ProxyAuthParams

initDataBinderProtocol

Used to initialize a low-level serializer that can convert a data stream to a DataBinder object. The currently supported formats are HyperData (HDA), Simple Object Access Protocol (SOAP), and Web Based Distributed Authoring and Versioning (WebDAV). To support another format, you need to override this filter with a custom serializer.

Added In: 7.5

initSearchIndexer
Executed at the end of the initialization of the search indexer.
    Added In: 4.0

initSubjects
Executed after loading the cached database tables upon server initialization.
    Added In: 3.0

isDoubleLocked
Executed during an undo check-out to make sure that the item isn't locked by content refinery.
Set the return value to true if the file is locked.
    Added In: 7.5

isSimplifiedCheckin
Executed before the check-in by the Content Refinery to determine whether this is a simple
check-in, such as those executed by WebDAV. Set the return value to true if it is a simple
check-in.
    Added In: 7.5

isStateLockedDocument
Executed before the document is checked for being locked for processing by the content refinery. Set the return value to true if the file is locked.
    Added In: 7.5

isStateUnlockedDocument
Executed before the document is checked for being unlocked for the content refinery. Set the
return value to true if the file is unlocked.
    Added In: 7.5

isUseEntitySecurity
Executed to determine whether to use entity security ACLs for one specific request. The return
value from the service object determines whether to use ACLs. By not using ACLs, you can
increase performance. Set the return value to false to turn off entity security for this request.
    Added In: 8.0
    Cached Objects: intradoc.server.DocumentAccessSecurity DocumentAccessSecurity

JspExecution
Executed immediately before a Java Server Page (JSP) is rendered. This is a good place to
create a richer environment for JSP execution.
    Added In: 7.1
    Cached Objects: java.io.OutputStream OutputStream, intradoc.data.Workspace Workspace

loadDefaultInfo
Executed at the beginning of the action loadDefaultInfo. This occurs when check-in and
update forms are displayed for retrieval of doc formats, doc types, and accounts.
    Added In: 3.0

loadMetaDefaults

Executed at the beginning of the action `loadMetaDefaults` to load custom metadata and the defaults.

Added In: 3.0

loadMetaOptionsLists

Executed before loading the custom metadata option lists from the database.

Added In: 3.0

loadStateLists

Executed before the state list is loaded for a project.

Added In: 4.0

loadUserAttributes

Executed before running `QuserSecurityAttributes` to determine the security attributes for this user. This works only for Local or Global users, not External users. Return `FINISHED` to prevent the Content Server from loading the attributes.

Added In: 4.0

Cached Objects: `intradoc.shared.UserData TargetUserData`

mapToInternalUserName

Allows you to map an external user name to an internal name. For example, if users have multiple names depending on how they log in, you can extract the true name and set it to `dName` in the binder.

Added In: 7.5

Cached Objects: `intradoc.data.DataBinder CredentialsData, intradoc.shared.UserData CachedUserData`

moveCollectionInCollectionEnd

Executed after a Folders collection object is moved into another collection object.

Added In: 6.0 (Folders component)

moveCollectionInCollectionStart

Executed before a Folders collection object is moved into another collection object.

Added In: 6.0 (Folders component)

notFoundMultiSelectSchemaKey

Executed in the IdocScript function `getFieldViewDisplayValue` when the schema cannot determine how to translate an internal value into a display value for a multiselect list.

Added In: 7.5

Cached Objects: `Object[] notFoundSchemaKeyArgs`, which contains the following entries:
`String sArg1`
`String optionListType`
`String key`
`String displayString`

notFoundSchemaKey
Executed in the IdocScript function getFieldViewDisplayValue when the schema cannot determine how to translate an internal value into a display value for a standard option list.
>   Added In: 7.5
>   Cached Objects: Object[] notFoundSchemaKeyArgs, which contains the following entries:
>   String sArg1
>   String optionListType
>   String schemaValue

notifySubjects
Executed before any subject is notified. A subject is a local cache of data from the database. Once a subject is notified, it reloads its cache from the database.
>   Added In: 3.0
>   Cached Objects: Vector serviceSubjects, Boolean isNotify

notifynextrow
Executed after the getnextrow filter.
>   Added In: 3.0
>   Cached Objects: String resultset

onEndScriptSubServiceActions
Executed at the end of the IdocScript function executeService.
>   Added In: 7.5

onEndServiceRequestActions
Executed at the end of all successful service requests before the response is sent back.
>   Added In: 7.5

onServiceRequestError
Executed every time a service throws an error.
>   Added In: 7.5
>   Cached Objects: intradoc.server.ServiceException CurrentRequestError

outgoingRequestHeaders
Executed to alter the HTTP headers for an outgoing request from one Content Server to another.
>   Added In: 4.0
>   Cached Objects: Properties requestHeaders

parseDataForServiceRequest
Executed when the Content Server is parsing a URL service request into a DataBinder. This is executed only for HTTP GET requests. This is a good place to add additional security, such as blocking some services from being run with GET requests.
>   Added In: 7.5

postConversionQueueSubmit

Executed in the Content Refinery process. It occurs after the action createWebViewable, but before the workflow history is recorded.

Added In: 7.5

postDocHistoryInfo

The DocumentHistory table contains information about the life cycle of an item. Services such as delete, check-in, and update store data into this table. This filter is executed during those services after the history is recorded.

Added In: 7.1

postHtmlFormCheckin

Executed in the action postHtmlFormCheckin during the SUBMIT_HTML_FORM service.

Added In: 4.0

postIndexingStep

Executed after the indexer processes a content item, immediately before the index cleanup.

Added In: 3.0

Cached Objects: intradoc.indexer.IndexerState IndexerState, intradoc.indexer.WebChanges WebChanges

postParseDataForServiceRequest

This is similar to the parseDataForServiceRequest filter. It is executed when parsing data from an HTTP POST into a DataBinder for the request. It is a good place to modify the SOAP parser or add support for another protocol.

Added In: 7.5

postProcessBatch

Executed by the Archiver at the end of the import of an archived schema table.

Added In: 7.5

postUnpackageResultFile

Executed toward the end of a preview request, after the preview files have been unpackaged.

Added In: 6.1

postValidateCheckinData

Executed at the end of the action validateCheckinData and after the filter validateCheckinData. This is a good place for last-minute alterations of the metadata prior to a check-in.

Added In: 7.1

postWebfileCreation

Executed after the web rendition is placed into the weblayout directory.

Added In: 4.6

Cached Objects: String WebfilePath, String VaultfilePath

postWriteBatchFile

Executed after the Content Server creates a batchload file for the search indexer. Use this filter to copy the bulkload file to another place or index the content into multiple repositories. To obtain the path to the bulkload file, use the `indexerConfig` cached object and call `getValue("IndexerBulkloadFile")`.

Added In: 7.5

Cached Objects: `intradoc.indexer.IndexerConfig indexerConfig`, `intradoc.indexer.IndexerDriverAdaptor indexerDriver`, `Vector indexList`, `Hashtable docProperties`

preIndexingStep

Executed at the beginning of an indexer step after the indexer determines which files to process.

Added In: 3.0

Cached Objects: `intradoc.indexer.IndexerState IndexerState`, `intradoc.indexer.WebChanges WebChanges`

preIndexList

Executed just prior to creating the bulkload file for the search engine indexer. Some search engines require additional parameters in the batch file, so this is a good place to conditionally add them. Return `ABORT` if you are performing all bulkloading manually.

Added In: 8.0

Cached Objects: `intradoc.indexer.IndexerConfig indexerConfig`, `intradoc.indexer.IndexerDriverAdaptor indexerDriver`, `Vector indexList`, `Hashtable docProperties`

preMergeInFileInfo

Executed when building an archive, during the creation of a batch result set. It occurs before computing the names of the files to archive.

Added In: 4.0

prepareDoActions

Executed prior to the service actions being initialized or executed. This is a good place to open connections to remote resources that you might need for multiple service actions or do some initial logging.

Added In: 8.0

prepareExportQuery

Executed when the export query is generated by the Archiver to determine which content items to archive.

Added In: 7.5

prepareForFileResponse

Executed before sending a response to a file-based service request, such as `GET_FILE`. This is useful for altering the behavior of certain file-based services, such as adding extra headers, compressing the file, or decrypting the file.

Added In: 7.5

prepareHttpResponseHeader

Executed before the HTTP response is created for every service call.

Added In: 5.0

Cached Objects: `intradoc.server.ServiceHttpImplementor HttpImplementor`, `StringBuffer responseBuffer`

prepareQuery

Executed before the general search query is assembled. It is a good place to modify the `SortOrder` and `ResultCount` fields.

Added In: 7.1

prepareQueryText

This is the first opportunity to modify the parameters that will alter how the `QueryText` is normalized. Modifications to the `QueryText` belong here or in `fixUpAndValidateQuery`.

Added In: 7.1

prepareSendDataBinderData

Called when you are streaming raw data binder data back in the response. This happens when `IsJava` is specified in the request or it is called from CIS.

Added In: 8.0

prepareSendDataBinderError

Called when an error occurs and you are streaming raw data binder data back in the response. This happens when `IsJava` is specified in the request or it is called from CIS.

Added In: 8.0

prepareSubscriptionMail

Executed before information about a subscription is placed in the mail queue. If this filter returns `ABORT` or you set the cached object `isSendMail` to `false`, you can completely override the subscription email behavior. You can also use it to modify data in the `DataBinder` to render subscription emails differently.

For performance reasons, most parameters in the `DataBinder` are removed prior to rendering the subscription email. If you want to add new fields, you must specify them in the parameter `AdditionalSubscriptionCollatedFieldList` in the `config.cfg` file. This parameter is a comma-separated list of variable names that are present on subscription pages.

Added In: 7.1

Cached Objects: `Boolean isSendMail`, `Hashtable LoadedProps`, `Hashtable SubscriptionInfo`, `intradoc.indexer.WebChanges WebChanges`

preWebfileCreation

Executed before the file is put into the conversion queue. The resulting converted file will be placed into the `weblayout` directory.

Added In: 7.0

removeCollectionInCollectionEnd

Executed after a Folders collection object is deleted.

Added In: 6.0 (Folders component)

removeCollectionInCollectionStart
Executed before a Folders collection object is deleted.
　　Added In: 6.0 (Folders component)

removeCustomDatedCaches
Executed before deleting a dated cache. These are used by Dynamic Converter to store previously converted HTML content.
　　Added In: 4.0

requestAuditEndRequest
If the requestaudit tracing section is active, this filter is executed at the end of every request. This is a useful place to put extra debugging information.
　　Added In: 7.5
　　Cached Objects: `String requestAuditServiceName, String requestAuditCurNumActiveThreads`

requestAuditParsedRequest
If the requestaudit tracing section is active, this filter is executed immediately after the data for a request has been parsed.
　　Added In: 7.5

requestAuditStartRequest
If the requestaudit tracing section is active, this will be executed immediately after an incoming request has been initialized, which occurs before the data in the request is parsed. This is a very powerful hook to allow for extremely thread-specific and request-specific logging.
　　Added In: 7.5
　　Cached Objects: `intradoc.server.IdcServerThread RequestAuditIncomingThread,`
`intradoc.server.ServiceManager RequestAuditServiceManager`

requestAuditStatisticsReport
If the requestaudit tracing section is active, this will be executed during the generation of a statistics report. To customize the format of the report, you might also need the filter `requestAuditStartRequest` to store additional data. The configuration flag `RequestAuditIntervalSeconds` controls how often this report is generated and output to the console.
　　Added In: 7.5
　　Cached Objects: `StringBuffer requestAuditReportBuffer`

retrieveProviderInfo
Executed after the data about a provider is loaded. This hook is generally useful on the Provider's administration page to display additional information about a specific provider.
　　Added In: 4.0

scheduledSystemEvent
This is similar to the checkScheduledEvents filter, but more useful for modifying the behavior of existing system scheduled events. Using this filter requires additional configuration. See the

ScheduledEvents component in the HowToComponents for an example. Return FINISHED if your custom system event executed properly.

Added In: 7.0

schemaBasePublishing

Executed before the base schema files are published to the weblayout directory. They contain the definitions of the schema views, but not the lists of values. Return FINISHED to skip the default publishing step.

Added In: 7.5

Cached Objects: intradoc.server.schema.StandardSchemaPublisher SchemaPublisher

schemaFinalizePublishing

Executed before the publishing of schema is finalized. The finalizing step might include verification of the contents and moving them from the build directory to the schema directory. Return FINISHED to skip the default finalizing step.

Added In: 7.5

Cached Objects: intradoc.server.schema.StandardSchemaPublisher SchemaPublisher

schemaNewBinder

Executed after generating a new DataBinder for use with schema. This is a good place to add additional data to the binder so your published schema files can contain extra data.

Added In: 7.5

Cached Objects: intradoc.server.schema.StandardSchemaPublisher SchemaPublisher

schemaPublishingBaseFinished

Executed after the base schema files are generated.

Added In: 7.5

Cached Objects: intradoc.server.schema.StandardSchemaPublisher SchemaPublisher

schemaPublishingEntireView

Executed before the schema publishes an entire view into one JavaScript file. Return FINISHED to skip the default publishing step.

Added In: 7.5

Cached Objects: intradoc.server.schema.StandardSchemaPublisher SchemaPublisher

schemaPublishingFinished

Executed after all schema JavaScript files have been generated, verified, and moved to the correct directory. This is the last step in the schema publishing cycle.

Added In: 7.5

Cached Objects: intradoc.server.schema.StandardSchemaPublisher SchemaPublisher

schemaPublishingStart

Executed at the beginning of the schema publishing cycle after all views and configurations have been loaded.

Added In: 7.5

Cached Objects: intradoc.server.schema.StandardSchemaPublisher SchemaPublisher

schemaPublishView

Executed prior to calling the publishing steps for the schema view values. Return FINISHED to skip the default publishing step.

Added In: 7.5

Cached Objects: intradoc.server.schema.StandardSchemaPublisher SchemaPublisher, intradoc.shared.schema.SchemaViewData SchemaViewData

schemaPublishViewFragment

Executed before publishing one single schema view value file. Return FINISHED to skip the default publishing step.

Added In: 7.5

Cached Objects: intradoc.server.schema.StandardSchemaPublisher SchemaPublisher, intradoc.shared.schema.SchemaViewData SchemaViewData

sendDataForServerResponse

Executed at the end of every service request that returns raw data. This occurs when most remote applications connect to the Content Server or when IsJava=1 is passed in the URL. This is useful for modifying the way request data is sent back to application servers.

Added In: 7.5

Cached Objects: String responseString

sendDataForServerResponseBytes

This is similar to sendDataForServerResponse, but is executed first. At this point the filter can modify a raw response byte stream, such as those returned in a GET_FILE request. If the Cached Object responseBytes is non-null, it is streamed back to the remote application.

Added In: 7.5

Cached Objects: String encoding, byte[] responseBytes

serviceCleanUp

Executed during the cleanup stage of all service requests. This is sometimes useful to close any extra connections you have open that might span multiple service actions. You might want different cleanup depending on whether an error occurred.

Added In: 8.0

Cached Objects: Object[] serviceCleanUp, which contains the following entries: Boolean isError

skipAccountAndMetaDataSecurityCheck

Executed during an access check for a content item. Set the return value to true to bypass further checks. This allows you to give a user access to a document based on metadata other than dSecurityGroup and dDocAccount.

Added In: 8.0

Cached Objects: intradoc.server.DocumentAccessSecurity DocumentAccessSecurity

specialAuthGroupClause

When entity security ACLs are enabled, this filter can be used to modify the security WHERE clause used for the search engine. This WHERE clause is appended to all searches to filter out items the user cannot see.

Added In: 8.0
Cached Objects: `intradoc.server.DocumentAccessSecurity DocumentAccessSecurity`

startSendMailTo
Executed whenever an email is sent via workflow or subscription. Use this filter to alter how email is sent. To completely override how email is sent, do all email processing in custom code and return `ABORT` in the filter. If the email was sent successfully, set the return value to `true`.

Added In: 7.5.1
Cached Objects: `Object[]` `sendMailToParams`, which contains the following entries:
`intradoc.server.PageMerger pageMerger`
`intradoc.server.UserData userData`
`String emailStr`
`String mailPage`
`String subjectTmp`

submitHtmlForm
Executed at the end of the action `submitHtmlForm` in the service `SUBMIT_HTML_FORM`. At this point the submitted Hypertext Content Server Page (HCSP) is generated, but it has not yet been checked into the repository.

Added In: 4.0
Cached Objects: `String IsTemplate`

unmanagedDocCheckAccess
Executed when a user makes a request to an unmanaged document in the weblayout directory. Includes help files, images, and other resources. This filter enables you to secure access to files that are outside of the Content Server repository.

Added In: 7.5

updateCollectionInCollectionEnd
Executed after a Folders collection object has its metadata or security settings updated.

Added In: 6.0 (Folders component)

updateCollectionInCollectionStart
Executed before a Folders collection object has its metadata or security settings updated.

Added In: 6.0 (Folders component)

updateExtendedAttributes
Executed when revision information about a content item changes. It occurs when a new revision is checked-in or an old revision is deleted. It also occurs when the metadata for the item is updated, or when it is archived in or out of the system. It is a good single point of entry to process code at different points of an item's life cycle. If your component adds new life cycles to the content server, you should execute this at least this filter. This occurs before the value for `dRevRank` is calculated.

Added In: 7.5
Cached Objects: `String attributes:revAction`

updateMetaTable
Executed after a new custom metadata field is added or removed.
   Added In: 5.0

updateSubscriptionInfo
Executed at the beginning of determining how to process a subscription.
   Added In: 3.0
   Cached Objects: intradoc.indexer.WebChanges WebChanges, intradoc.indexer.IndexerState
IndexerState

updateWorkflowStateAfterChange
Executed in the action updateWorkflowStateAfterCheckin in the service WORKFLOW_CHECKIN_SUB.
It allows additional alteration of parameters for updating the state of a content item in a
workflow.
   Added In: 5.0

xxx:validate
Executed at the beginning of the action hasAllowableValueInOptionLists. This is used to validate the value for one specific metadata field upon check-in or update. Replace xxx in the
name of the filter with the name of the metadata field to validate, such as xComments:validate.
   Added In: 3.0

validateCheckinData
Executed during a check-in or update to validate the metadata fields. This is a common place
to add custom metadata validation.
   Added In: 3.0

validateProvider
Executed when adding or editing a provider. This runs after the data for the provider has been
validated by the server to allow for additional validation.
   Added In: 4.0

validateStandard
Executed during update or check-in. This runs before the core validates the metadata fields,
such as dReleaseState, dDocName, dRevClassID, dDocTitle, primaryFile, alternateFile,
dCreateDate, dInDate, and dOutDate.
   Added In: 3.0

workflowComputeDocStepInfo
Executed each time the state of an item in workflow is calculated. This translates the work-
flow state flags into the flags AllowCheckin, AllowCheckout, AllowReview, HasApproved, and
IsStaging. These are used on template pages to help the user determine what they can do in
this workflow step.
   Added In: 7.5
   Cached Objects: intradoc.shared.workflow.WfStepData WfStepData

Aliasable Java Classes

A *Class Alias* is used in Java Component Architecture to customize the server's behavior. Many Java objects used in the server are loaded with reflection at runtime. The classpath to these objects can be configured with a component, so a developer can create a custom Java object that extends the existing one, with a few modifications. A Class Alias in a component tells the server to load the custom class instead of the default.

Aliases are difficult to write without the original source code. Also, each object can only be aliased once. This means that if two components both alias the same class, those components are usually incompatible. Filters and chained Service Handlers are the recommended approach.

When Filters and chained Service Handlers are not feasible, the only option is a Class Alias. The recommended way to perform a Class Alias is to use the original source code for your Content Server version and add a custom Filter hook. Then place all custom code in a new Filter that triggers off of that event.

In this manner, multiple components can use the new Filter hook, and it is easier to update your component to future revisions of the Content Server. See Chapter 10 for more information about Class Aliases and best practices for their use.

In a component, an alias is configured with the `ResultSet ClassAlias` in the component definition file:

```
@ResultSet ClassAliases
2
classname
location
SecurityImplementor
mypackage.MySecurityImplementor
@end
```

Each aliasable class has a globally unique `classname` and a `location`, which is the classpath to the object. The `classname` is typically the name of the Java class, but not always.

All Service objects and Service Handler objects are aliasable. However, this is rarely done because their code can be modified in much easier ways. All other alias-able classes are listed here by name, along with the default location and a brief description.

Applications

Contains configuration information about the known applications (User Administrator, Archiver) and their classes.

> Added In: 3.0
>
> Location: `intradoc.apps.shared.Applications`

ArchiveCheckinHandler

The `ServiceHandler` for Archive services. Contains Archiver methods useful for the Batchloader.

> Added In: 3.0
>
> Location: `intradoc.server.ArchiveCheckinHandler`

ArchiveExportHelper

Used to create and run export queries and maintain Archiver helper result sets.

> Added In: 7.5
>
> Location: `intradoc.server.archive.ArchiveExportHelper`

ArchiveHandler

The `ServiceHandler` for Archive services. Contains most Archiver service methods.

> Added In: 4.0
>
> Location: `intradoc.server.archive.ArchiveHandler`

ArchiveImportStateInformation

This class is used mainly to maintain the value and field mapping during an archive import. It is also used to preprocess a document's information before an import and to maintain the import flags and counters.

> Added In: 7.5
>
> Location: `intradoc.server.archive.ArchiveImportStateInformation`

ArchiveService

The `Service` object for Archiver services. Contains several Archiver service methods.

> Added In: 3.0
>
> Location: `intradoc.server.ArchiveService`

ArchiveTableCallBack

Contains helper functions to process and filter tables during an archive.

> Added In: 7.5
>
> Location: `intradoc.server.archive.ArchiveTableCallBack`

BatchService

The `Service` object for Batch services, which are used to run multiple services at the same time. Typically used to check-in multiple content items based on a ZIP file and manifest.

> Added In: 4.0
>
> Location: `intradoc.server.BatchService`

BuildChanges
Used to scan the `Revisions` table for new items to index or expired content to delete.
> Added In: 3.0
> Location: `intradoc.indexer.IndexerBuildChanges`

ChunkedService
The `Service` object for Chunked services, used to upload large files with the check-in applet.
> Added In: 6.0
> Location: `intradoc.server.ChunkedService`

CollaborationService
The `Service` object for Collaboration services, used mainly by the Collaboration Server.
> Added In: 6.0
> Location: `intradoc.server.CollaborationService`

CommonSearchConfigCompanion
Contains code to parse a search query. It translates the query from the Universal Query Syntax into the syntax for the specific search engine.
> Added In: 7.0
> Location: `intradoc.search.DBSearchConfigCompanion`, `intradoc.search.`
`AvsSearchConfigCompanion`, or `intradoc.search.VeritySearchConfigCompanion`

ConverterHandler
The `ServiceHandler` for running Dynamic Conversions.
> Added In: 5.0
> Location: `intradoc.server.converter.ConverterHandler`

DataBinderProtocol
An object that controls how request data is parsed into a `DataBinder` object. The parsing is different for HTTP `GET`, HTTP `POST`, Multipart POST, WebDAV, and Simple Object Access Protocol (SOAP) requests. If you want to add support for another protocol, consider the `parseDataForServiceRequest` or `postParseDataForServiceRequest` Java filters instead.
> Added In: 7.5
> Location: `intradoc.server.DataBinderProtocolImplementor`

DBQueryService
The `Service` object for advanced database query management, such as canceling queries that are not responding.
> Added In: 8.0
> Location: `intradoc.server.DBQueryService`

DetermineSubscription

Used to determine how to scan the database for subscriptions and process the email messages. If the configuration flag `SubscriptionMethod` is set, it will use that flag. Otherwise, it performs a few tests to determine which method is likely to be faster.

> Added In: 3.0
>
> Location: `intradoc.indexer.DetermineSubscription`

DocCommonHandler

The `ServiceHandler` for commonly used Document service methods for check-in, update, and archiving.

> Added In: 3.0
>
> Location: `intradoc.server.DocCommonHandler`

DocIndexer

Creates bulk load files and processes documents into a full-text indexer engine.

> Added In: 4.6
>
> Location: `intradoc.indexer.DocIndexerAdaptor`

DocProfileService

The `Service` object for managing Content Profiles, such as adding new profiles and rules.

> Added In: 7.5
>
> Location: `intradoc.server.DocProfileService`

DocProfileStates

Contains low level code to execute Content Profile rules.

> Added In: 7.5
>
> Location: `intradoc.server.DocProfileStates`

DocService

The `Service` object for content contribution and management services. This contains a great deal of commonly used check-in and update methods.

> Added In: 3.0
>
> Location: `intradoc.server.DocService`

DocServiceHandler

The `ServiceHandler` for content contribution and management services. Contains more methods than any other handler for processing check-ins and updates.

> Added In: 3.0
>
> Location: `intradoc.server.DocServiceHandler`

DocumentAccessSecurity

Standard security object that determines whether a user should be able to run a service with the current document.

> Added In: 6.0
>
> Location: `intradoc.server.DocumentAccessSecurity`

DtmExtendedLoader

Initializes the `DtmServer` upon startup for use with Publisher.

    Added In: 4.0

    Location: `intradoc.server.IdcExtendedLoader`

ExpirationNotifier

The object that runs in the background, watching for documents about to expire. It also bundles a warning email message to users if they authored content that will expire soon.

    Added In: 7.0

    Location: `intradoc.server.ExpirationNotifier`

ExpiredContentHandler

The `ServiceHandler` used to run database queries for expired content.

    Added In: 7.0

    Location: `intradoc.server.ExpiredContentHandler`

FileService

The `Service` object for download services, including `GET_FILE` and Java Server Page (JSP) rendering.

    Added In: 3.0

    Location: `intradoc.server.FileService`

FormHandler

The `ServiceHandler` object to process HTML forms using `SUBMIT_HTML_FORM`.

    Added In: 4.0

    Location: `intradoc.server.FormHandler`

HttpImplementor

Standard HTTP interface for the `Service` object. Used to send data back to the user, including proper HTTP headers, cookies, and authentication challenges. It also has several utility functions to determine information about the user's session.

    Added In: 4.0

    Location: `intradoc.server.ServiceHttpImplementor`

IdcExtendedLoader

Performs extra initialization for when the server starts up, which generally alters the system database in the event of an upgrade.

    Added In: 3.0

    Location: `intradoc.server.IdcExtendedLoader`

IndexAdditions

Used to create bulk load files and process additions to the indexer. The root object is used for additions, deletions, and retries.

    Added In: 3.0

    Location: `intradoc.indexer.CommonIndexerBulkLoader`

IndexDeletions
Used to create bulk load files and process deletions from the indexer. The root object is used for additions, deletions, and retries.
Added In: 3.0
Location: `intradoc.indexer.CommonIndexerBulkLoader`

IndexRetries
Used to create bulk load files and process retries of additions to the indexer. The root object is used for additions, deletions, and retries.
Added In: 3.0
Location: `intradoc.indexer.CommonIndexerBulkLoader`

Indexer
The high level indexer object that controls indexer steps and execution.
Added In: 3.0
Location: `intradoc.indexer.Indexer`

IndexerDriver
Mostly deprecated indexer object.
Added In: 4.0
Location: `intradoc.indexer.IndexerDriverAdaptor`

IndexerExecution
Low-level indexer object that starts the indexer, typically by running a bulk load file through a command-line interface.
Added In: 7.0
Location: `intradoc.indexer.IndexerExecution`

IndexerExecutionHandler
Default handler for setting Verity flags before `IndexerExecution` runs the indexer.
Added In: 7.0
Location: `intradoc.indexer.VerityHandler`

(ALTAVISTA)IndexerExecutionHandler
The `IndexerExecutionHandler` specific to the AltaVista search engine.
Added In: 7.0
Location: `intradoc.indexer.AltavistaHandler`

(DATABASE)IndexerExecutionHandler
The `IndexerExecutionHandler` specific to the `DATABASE` search engine.
Added In: 7.0
Location: `intradoc.indexer.DatabaseHandler`

(DATABASEFULLTEXT)IndexerExecutionHandler

The `IndexerExecutionHandler` specific to the `DATABASEFULLTEXT` search engine.
> Added In: 7.0
> Location: `intradoc.indexer.DatabaseFullTextHandler`

IndexerService

The `Service` object for indexer methods, such as starting and canceling the indexer.
> Added In: 3.0
> Location: `intradoc.server.IndexerService`

IndexerTransition

Contains the table describing how to move from one state in the indexer to the next.
> Added In: 3.0
> Location: `intradoc.indexer.IndexerTransition`

JspServiceHandler

The `ServiceHandler` for starting and stopping web applications.
> Added In: 5.0
> Location: `intradoc.server.jsp.JspServiceHandler`

ListBoxService

The `Service` object supporting type-ahead option lists. Deprecated.
> Added In: 3.0
> Location: `intradoc.server.ListBoxService`

LocaleService

The `Service` object for localization services, which is used in applets and remote applications to initialize localized display strings, error messages, and date formats.
> Added In: 5.0
> Location: `intradoc.server.LocaleService`

LRUManager

Least Recently Used cache object, which is used to cache Schema database values locally in Java.
> Added In: 7.5
> Location: `intradoc.shared.LRUManager`

MetaService

The `Service` object for user metadata–based services, such as adding new fields.
> Added In: 3.0
> Location: `intradoc.server.MetaService`

OutgoingProviderManager

Used to maintain outgoing connections to other proxied Content Servers.
> Added In: 4.0
> Location: `intradoc.server.proxy.OutgoingProviderManager`

PageHandler

Used in the PageHandlerService to maintain the weblayout library and generate historical reports.

Added In: 3.0

Location: intradoc.server.PageHandler

PageHandlerService

The Service object for library page request services such as content queries and historical and active reports.

Added In: 3.0

Location: intradoc.server.PageHandlerService

PageRequestService

The Service for Page request services. Similar to PageHandlerService, but not restricted to the library.

Added In: 3.0

Location: intradoc.server.PageRequestService

ProblemReportHandler

The ServiceHandler for generating problem reports for Content Publisher.

Added In: 4.0

Location: intradoc.server.ProblemReportHandler

ProjectDocHandler

The ServiceHandler for Publisher project services.

Added In: 4.0

Location: intradoc.server.ProjectDocHandler

ProjectService

The Service object for Content Publisher project services.

Added In: 4.0

Location: intradoc.server.ProjectService

ProviderManagerService

The Service object used to update and test Providers.

Added In: 4.0

Location: intradoc.server.ProviderManagerService

ProxyImplementor

Used to proxy a request from one Content Server to another.

Added In: 4.0

Location: intradoc.server.proxy.ServiceProxyImplementor

Replication
Object used in the replication step of the indexer.
> Added In: 3.0
> Location: `intradoc.server.IndexerReplication`

RevisionImplementor
Object used to generate revision labels.
> Added In: 3.0
> Location: `intradoc.shared.RevisionImplementor`

ScheduledSystemEvents
The thread that runs scheduled system events, including compacting the database, running the update step in workflows, and checking for expired content. It runs at most once per hour.
> Added In: 7.0
> Location: `intradoc.server.ScheduledSystemEvents`

SchemaArchiveHandler
The `ServiceHandler` to process the archiving of schema tables from the database.
> Added In: 7.0
> Location: `intradoc.server.archive.SchemaArchiveHandler`

SchemaEditHelper
Used during schema editing to validate data and check for changes in the database.
> Added In: 7.5
> Location: `intradoc.shared.schema.SchemaEditHelper`

SchemaFieldConfig
A small class that contains information about the default schema fields in tables.
> Added In: 7.0
> Location: `intradoc.shared.schema.SchemaFieldConfig`

SchemaHandler
The `ServiceHandler` for schema services, such as generating static JavaScript files.
> Added In: 7.0
> Location: `intradoc.server.SchemaHandler`

SchemaHelper
Contains helper functions used throughout a schema.
> Added In: 7.0
> Location: `intradoc.shared.schema.SchemaHelper`

SchemaLoader
Loads up schema configuration data and initializes the `SchemaPubisherThread`.
> Added In: 7.5
> Location: `intradoc.server.schema.ServerSchemaLoader`

SchemaPublisher
Implements the publishing of all schema JavaScript files.
>   Added In: 7.0
>   Location: intradoc.server.schema.StandardSchemaPublisher

SchemaPublisherThread
Runs the SchemaPublisher when needed. This is a complex algorithm based on how much data has changed and how long the previous publishing step required.
>   Added In: 7.5
>   Location: intradoc.server.schema.StandardSchemaPublisherThread

SchemaRelationConfig
Configuration object for schema relation column names.
>   Added In: 7.0
>   Location: intradoc.shared.schema.SchemaRelationConfig

SchemaService
The Service object for schema methods.
>   Added In: 7.0
>   Location: intradoc.server.SchemaService

SchemaTableConfig
Configuration object for schema table column names.
>   Added In: 7.0
>   Location: intradoc.shared.schema.SchemaTableConfig

SchemaUtils
Object to help schema build its SQL queries and additional functions.
>   Added In: 7.0
>   Location: intradoc.server.schema.SchemaUtils

SchemaViewConfig
Configuration object for schema view column names.
>   Added In: 7.0
>   Location: intradoc.shared.schema.SchemaViewConfig

SearchCache
Object that maintains the search cache.
>   Added In: 4.0
>   Location: intradoc.search.SearchCache

SearchFieldInfo
Contains data about the fields in the search collection.
>   Added In: 6.0
>   Location: intradoc.shared.SearchFieldInfo

SearchImplementor

Implements a connection to the specific search engine for running queries. The class used depends on which search engine is running the search. The location depends on which search engine is used for the search.

    Added In: 7.0

    Location: `intradoc.search.VeritySearchImplementor`, `intradoc.search.`
`AltavistaSearchImplementor`, `intradoc.search.DatabaseFullTextSearchImplementor`,
`intradoc.search.DatabaseSearchImplementor`

SearchManager

Low-level object that creates connections to the search engine.

    Added In: 4.0

    Location: `intradoc.server.SearchManager`

SearchService

The `Service` object for running search engine queries.

    Added In: 3.0

    Location: `intradoc.server.SearchService`

SecurityImplementor

An extension to the `ServiceSecurityImplementor` that allows you to define the current user based on data besides HTTP authentication, such as temporary authentication strings.

    Added In: 3.0

    Location: `intradoc.upload.UploadSecurityImplementor`

ServerSchemaManager

High-level schema object to add, delete, and edit schema tables.

    Added In: 7.5

    Location: `intradoc.server.schema.StandardSchemaManager`

Service

The super class for all other `Service` objects. Contains the core methods that turn a service definition into a series of Java methods, SQL queries, and most authentication calls.

    Added In: 3.0

    Location: `intradoc.server.Service`

ServiceHandler

The super class for all other `ServiceHandler` objects. It contains very little.

    Added In: 3.0

    Location: `intradoc.server.ServiceHandler`

SmtpClient

The primary class that processes all sent email messages, which includes workflow notifications and subscriptions.

    Added In: 7.5.1

    Location: `intradoc.common.SmtpClient`

SubscriptionByDocument

The object that determines which subscriptions to process. This one scans for documents first and then subscriptions for each document.

> Added In: 3.0
> Location: intradoc.indexer.DocumentOrientedSubscription

SubscriptionBySubscription

The object that determines which subscriptions to process. This one scans for subscriptions and then documents for each subscription.

> Added In: 3.0
> Location: intradoc.indexer.SubscriptionOrientedSubscription

SubscriptionHandler

The ServiceHandler for running subscription services, such as displaying current subscriptions or subscribing to new items.

> Added In: 3.0
> Location: intradoc.server.SubscriptionHandler

SystemAuditHandler

The ServiceHandler for advanced auditing services on the System Audit Info page.

> Added In: 8.0
> Location: intradoc.server.SystemAuditHandler

tableArchiveValueMapData

This class is used by the Archiver to maintain and calculate value mappings during an import of content.

> Added In: 8.0
> Location: intradoc.server.ValueMapData

TargetedQuickSearchHandler

The ServiceHandler object for helping an administrator force personalization settings about quick searches to specific users.

> Added In: 8.0
> Location: intradoc.server. TargetedQuickSearchHandler

TransferHandler

An object to help transfer archives from one server to another.

> Added In: 4.0
> Location: intradoc.server.archive.TransferHandler

TransferServiceHandler

The ServiceHandler for archive transfers.

> Added In: 4.0
> Location: intradoc.server.archive.TransferServiceHandler

UserProfileHandler
The ServiceHandler for processing user profile data, such as decoding topic strings and saving changes to the personalization settings.
> Added In: 4.0
> Location: intradoc.server.UserProfileHandler

UserService
The Service object for user services, such as validating users through Lightweight Directory Access Protocol (LDAP), adding new users, and changing roles.
> Added In: 3.0
> Location: intradoc.server.UserService

UserServiceHandler
The ServiceHandler for user services.
> Added In: 3.0
> Location: intradoc.server.UserServiceHandler

WebFilterConfigHandler
The ServiceHandler for configuring the Web Filter file, such as turning on Web Filter debugging.
> Added In: 6.0
> Location: intradoc.server.filter.WebFilterConfigHandler

WebPublishingHandler
The ServiceHandler object for publishing JavaScript files into the weblayout directory.
> Added In: 8.0
> Location: intradoc.server. WebPublishingHandler

WebViewableConverterOutput
Object containing methods for processing content through the Refinery.
> Added In: 7.5
> Location: intradoc.server.WebViewableConverterOutput

WorkflowDocImplementor
Object containing the methods for processing a document through workflow.
> Added In: 3.0
> Location: intradoc.server.workflow.WorkflowDocImplementor

WorkflowHandler
The ServiceHandler for workflow services, such as creating and modifying workflows or approving and rejecting items in workflow.
> Added In: 3.0
> Location: intradoc.server.workflow.WorkflowHandler

WorkflowScriptHandler

The `ServiceHandler` for creating and testing workflow scripts.

Added In: 5.0

Location: `intradoc.server.workflow.WorkflowScriptHandler`

WorkflowService

The `Service` object for workflow services. Contains little more than security enhancements to prevent users from seeing documents in workflow that they shouldn't.

Added In: 3.0

Location: `intradoc.server.WorkflowService`

WorkflowStates

Class for computing the current workflow state and updating the database with the new states.

Added In: 4.0

Location: `intradoc.server.workflow.WorkflowStates`

WorkflowTemplateService

The `Service` object for adding and modifying workflow templates.

Added In: 3.0

Location: `intradoc.server.WorkflowTemplateService`

intradoc.server.UserStorageImplementor

This object implements how user data is retrieved from remote user providers and stored in local caches.

Added In: 6.2

Location: `intradoc.server.UserStorageImplementor`

intradoc.server.UserTempCache

Contains cached user credentials from remote user providers.

Added In: 6.2

Location: `intradoc.server.UserTempCache`

intradoc.soap.custom.SoapCustomSerializer

The custom serializer for SOAP requests and responses.

Added In: 7.5

Location: `intradoc.soap.custom.SoapCustomSerializer`

intradoc.soap.generic.SoapGenericSerializer

The generic serializer for SOAP requests and responses. It supports most SOAP requests, but if you use proprietary extensions to SOAP, you might need a different serializer.

Added In: 7.5

Location: `intradoc.soap.generic.SoapGenericSerializer`

APPENDIX J

■■■

HyperData Format

The HyperData format, also known as HDA, is used to store tabular and unstructured data. Most Content Server configuration files are in HDA format. This appendix describes the structure of HDA, and how it is used in the server.

HDA File Format

The purpose behind the HDA format is to quickly serialize tabular data while still retaining the flexibility of name-value pairs. It is similar in flexibility to XML. Unlike XML, however, the HDA format is more compact and focused on table-based data, so it is more quickly parsed by a computer.

The HDA format contains four main sections. In order, these sections are the following:

1. A header describing the encoding used in the HDA

2. The LocalData section containing key-value pairs

3. All ResultSets containing tabular data

4. All OptionLists containing simple lists

The following is a sample HDA file containing sample data in all four sections:

```
<?hda version="7.5.1 (050317)" jcharset=Cp1252 encoding=iso-8859-1?>
@Properties LocalData
key1=value1
key2=value2
@end
@ResultSet MyResultSet
3
field1 6 30
field2 6 30
field3 6 30
A1
A2
A3
B1
```

```
B2
B3
C1
C2
C3
@end
@OptionList MyOptionList
row1
row2
row3
row4
@end
```

The first part of an HDA file is the localization header:

```
<?hda version="7.5.1 (050317)" jcharset=Cp1252 encoding=iso-8859-1?>
```

This header contains information about the version of the Content Server that generated this file, along with character encoding data. The version information is used rarely because the HDA format has not changed much since it was created. It is sometimes used for backward compatibility when importing tabular data from older systems. The Archiver and Installer make use of the version when needed.

The jcharset and encoding headers contain standard file encoding information, which is used in multiple language environments to determine how to convert the bytes in the file into characters. For example, if Japanese characters are present in the file, the encoding might be shift_jis or utf-8. In the first case, a Japanese character is represented in two bytes. In the second, it is represented in three bytes.

The next part of the HDA file is the LocalData section, which begins with the token @Properties LocalData and ends with the token @end:

```
@Properties LocalData
key1=value1
key2=value2
@end
```

Between the beginning and end tokens are key-value pairs, which are formatted in the same way as a standard Java Properties file. Each line contains one key-value pair, separated with the equals sign.

The backslash is used to escape white space characters, which enables the key to contain multiple lines of text. It is also needed to escape the @ character because it is used to denote the end of the section:

```
emailAddress=user\@company.com
message=Reminder!\nThere is a company meeting on Friday.\nPlease attend.
```

The next section contains ResultSet objects, which contain table-based data that is typically extracted from a database.

Similar to the LocalData section, the data in the table is encapsulated with special tokens. At the beginning is the @ResultSet token, along with the name of the ResultSet. The next line is the number of columns in the ResultSet. The next few lines are the names of all the columns. After this is the data in the table. Finally, the last line is the @end token:

```
@ResultSet MyResultSet
3
field1 6 30
field2 6 30
field3 6 30
A1
A2
A3
B1
B2
B3
C1
C2
C3
@end
```

This defines a ResultSet named MyResultSet. The first number 3 denotes a three-column table. The next three lines contain the names and data types of these columns. The first parameter is the column name. The second and third parameters are optional, but are typically present when the data originates from a database. The second parameter is a flag representing the data type, and the third parameter is the maximum length of the data in the column. The following data types are supported:

Table J-1. *Supported Data Type Flags*

Flag	Data Type
1	Boolean
2	Character
3	Integer
4	Float
5	Date
6	String
7	Binary

In this case, we have a table with three columns: field1, field2, and field3. All three are strings with a maximum length of 30. The next three lines are the column values for the first row, corresponding to the columns in order. The next three are the values for the second row, and so on.

This `ResultSet` in tabular format looks like this:

Table J-2. *MyResultSet in Tabular Format*

field1	field2	field3
A1	A2	A3
B1	B2	B3
C1	C2	C3

The rules for encoding a line of data are the same as for the `LocalData`.

The last section is for `OptionList` objects, which are similar to `ResultSet` objects, but they contain only one column. They are simple lists of data, usually used on web pages to display `SELECT` based option lists.

These begin with the token `@OptionList` and the name of the `OptionList`. The next few lines contain all the items in the list. The `OptionList` ends with the `@end` token.

```
@OptionList MyOptionList
row1
row2
row3
row4
@end
```

Internal Usage

HDA files are used throughout the Content Server for table-based configuration data. A developer uses them for the Component Definition File, which contains references for all resources in a custom component. Another commonly used HDA file is the Workflow Companion File, which contains state and history information about an item currently in workflow.

The HDA format is the default serialization of the primary data structure in the Content Server. It is the Java object called a `DataBinder` and is located here:

```
intradoc.data.DataBinder
```

This object is used for all service requests. All parameters in the request are stored in the `LocalData` for the `DataBinder`. The response data is attached as `ResultSets`, `OptionLists`, and new `LocalData`. This `DataBinder` is then used to render the response.

This response is typically an HTML page. In addition, the full `DataBinder` can be serialized back to the user in HDA format. This is an HDA-based web service that occurs whenever the parameter `IsJava=1` is sent in the request.

This same `DataBinder` is used for data structures for various Content Server features: user personalization, items in workflow, archives, and components. The data for these items is serialized out to HDA files on the file system.

In addition, some of the data for these features is stored in the database, but it is not a good idea to place all the data for them in the database. An HDA file is highly extensible, whereas a database table should remain rigid. Adding a new column to a database table is a significant modification. However, adding a new column to an HDA table is frequently done to extend the data structure.

The idea is to place some data in the database and some in an HDA file. The database fields are needed for high-performance queries, structured data, and reporting. The HDA files allow for additional flexibility when needed, without requiring a modification to the database. For example, an item in workflow has its state stored in the database. It also contains information about tokens, jumps, and extended state flags in an HDA file. Doing so achieves a good balance between performance, portability, and extensibility.

Index

J

9 781590 596845